Communications
in Computer and Information Science 1897

Rationale

The CCIS series is devoted to the publication of proceedings of computer science conferences. Its aim is to efficiently disseminate original research results in informatics in printed and electronic form. While the focus is on publication of peer-reviewed full papers presenting mature work, inclusion of reviewed short papers reporting on work in progress is welcome, too. Besides globally relevant meetings with internationally representative program committees guaranteeing a strict peer-reviewing and paper selection process, conferences run by societies or of high regional or national relevance are also considered for publication.

Topics

The topical scope of CCIS spans the entire spectrum of informatics ranging from foundational topics in the theory of computing to information and communications science and technology and a broad variety of interdisciplinary application fields.

Information for Volume Editors and Authors

Publication in CCIS is free of charge. No royalties are paid, however, we offer registered conference participants temporary free access to the online version of the conference proceedings on SpringerLink (http://link.springer.com) by means of an http referrer from the conference website and/or a number of complimentary printed copies, as specified in the official acceptance email of the event.

CCIS proceedings can be published in time for distribution at conferences or as postproceedings, and delivered in the form of printed books and/or electronically as USBs and/or e-content licenses for accessing proceedings at SpringerLink. Furthermore, CCIS proceedings are included in the CCIS electronic book series hosted in the SpringerLink digital library at http://link.springer.com/bookseries/7899. Conferences publishing in CCIS are allowed to use Online Conference Service (OCS) for managing the whole proceedings lifecycle (from submission and reviewing to preparing for publication) free of charge.

Publication process

The language of publication is exclusively English. Authors publishing in CCIS have to sign the Springer CCIS copyright transfer form, however, they are free to use their material published in CCIS for substantially changed, more elaborate subsequent publications elsewhere. For the preparation of the camera-ready papers/files, authors have to strictly adhere to the Springer CCIS Authors' Instructions and are strongly encouraged to use the CCIS LaTeX style files or templates.

Abstracting/Indexing

CCIS is abstracted/indexed in DBLP, Google Scholar, EI-Compendex, Mathematical Reviews, SCImago, Scopus. CCIS volumes are also submitted for the inclusion in ISI Proceedings.

How to start

To start the evaluation of your proposal for inclusion in the CCIS series, please send an e-mail to ccis@springer.com.

Jiachi Chen · Bin Wen · Ting Chen

Editors

Blockchain and Trustworthy Systems

5th International Conference, BlockSys 2023
Haikou, China, August 8–10, 2023
Proceedings, Part II

 Springer

Editors
Jiachi Chen ⓘ
Sun Yat-Sen University
Zhuhai, China

Bin Wen ⓘ
Hainan Normal University
Haikou, China

Ting Chen ⓘ
University of Electronic Science
and Technology of China
Chengdu, China

ISSN 1865-0929   ISSN 1865-0937 (electronic)
Communications in Computer and Information Science
ISBN 978-981-99-8103-8   ISBN 978-981-99-8104-5 (eBook)
https://doi.org/10.1007/978-981-99-8104-5

This Springer imprint is published by the registered company Springer Nature Singapore Pte Ltd.
The registered company address is: 152 Beach Road, #21-01/04 Gateway East, Singapore 189721, Singapore

Paper in this product is recyclable.

Preface

Blockchain has become a hot research area in academia and industry. The blockchain technology is transforming industries by enabling anonymous and trustful transactions in decentralized and trustless environments. As a result, blockchain technology and other technologies for developing trustworthy systems can be used to reduce system risks, mitigate financial fraud, and cut down operational cost. Blockchain and trustworthy systems can be applied to many fields, such as financial services, social management, and supply chain management.

This proceedings volume contains the papers from the 2023 International Conference on Blockchain and Trustworthy Systems (BlockSys 2023). This conference was held as the fifth in its series with an emphasis on state-of-the-art advances in blockchain and trustworthy systems. The main conference received 93 paper submissions, out of which 45 papers were accepted as regular papers. All papers underwent a rigorous peer review process – each paper was reviewed by 2-4 experts. The accepted papers together with our outstanding keynote and invited speeches led to a vibrant technical program. We are looking forward to future events in this conference series.

The conference would not have been successful without help from so many people. We would like to thank the Organizing Committee for their hard work in putting together the conference. First, we would like to express our sincere thanks to the guidance from the Honorary Chair: Dusit (Tao) Niyato. We would like to express our deep gratitude to the General Chairs: David Lo, Weizhe Zhang, and Xiuzhen Cheng for their support and promotion of this event. We would also like to thank the program chairs: Bin Wen, Jiachi Chen, and Ting Chen supervised the review process of the technical papers and compiled a high-quality technical program. We also extend our deep gratitude to the program committee members, whose diligent work in reviewing the papers led to the high quality of the accepted papers. We greatly appreciate the excellent support and hard work of the Publicity Chairs: Changlin Yang, Taotao Li, and Tao Zhang; Publication Chairs: Jiangshan Yu, Jieren Cheng, and Peilin Zheng; Organizing Chairs: Chun Shan, Rao Zeng, Yuxin Su, and Ziqiang Luo; Industrial Chairs: Jiashui Wang and Huizhong Li; Special Track Chairs: Lulu Wang, Pengcheng Zhang, Shunhui Ji, Xiaobin Sun, xiaoxue, Zhangbing Zhou, Huaiguang Wu, Siqi Lu, Xueming Si, and Yongjuan Wang; Advisory Board: Huaimin Wang, Jiannong Cao, Kuan-Ching Li, and Michael R. Lyu; and Steering Committee: Hong-Ning Dai, Xiapu Luo, Yan Zhang, and Zibin Zheng. Most importantly, we would like to thank the authors for submitting their papers to BlockSys 2023.

We believe that the BlockSys conference provides a good forum for both academic researchers and industrial practitioners to discuss all technical advances in blockchain and trustworthy systems. We also expect that future BlockSys conferences will be as successful, as indicated by the contributions presented in this volume.

August 2023

David Lo
Weizhe Zhang
Xiuzhen Cheng
Bin Wen
Jiachi Chen
Ting Chen

Organization

Honorary Chair

Dusit (Tao) Niyato   Nanyang Technological University, Singapore

General Chairs

David Lo   Singapore Management University, Singapore
Weizhe Zhang   Harbin Institute of Technology, China
Xiuzhen Cheng   Shandong University, China

Program Chairs

Bin Wen   Hainan Normal University, China
Jiachi Chen   Sun Yat-sen University, China
Ting Chen   University of Electronic Science and Technology
          of China, China

Organizing Chairs

Chun Shan   Guangdong Polytechnic Normal University, China
Rao Zeng   Hainan Normal University, China
Yuxin Su   Sun Yat-sen University, China
Ziqiang Luo   Hainan Normal University, China

Publicity Chairs

Changlin Yang   Sun Yat-sen University, China
Taotao Li   Sun Yat-sen University, China
Tao Zhang   Macau University of Science and Technology,
          China

Publication Chairs

Jiangshan Yu   Monash University, Australia
Jieren Cheng   Hainan University, China
Peilin Zheng   Sun Yat-sen University, China

Industrial Chairs

Jiashui Wang   Ant Group, China
Huizhong Li   WeBank, China

Special Track Chairs: Anomaly detection on blockchain

Lulu Wang   Southeast University, China
Pengcheng Zhang   Hohai University, China
Shunhui Ji   Hohai University, China
Xiaobin Sun   Yangzhou University, China

Special Track Chairs: Edge Intelligence and Metaverse Services

xiaoxue   Tianjin University, China
Zhangbing Zhou   China University of Geosciences, China

Special Track Chairs: Blockchain System Security

Huaiguang Wu   Zhengzhou University of Light Industry, China
Siqi Lu   Henan Key Laboratory of Information Security,
                                China
Xueming Si   Fudan University, China
Yongjuan Wang   Henan Key Laboratory of Information Security,
                                China

Advisory Board

Huaimin Wang   National University of Defense Technology,
                                China
Jiannong Cao   Hong Kong Polytechnic University, China

Kuan-Ching Li   Providence University, China
Michael R. Lyu   Chinese University of Hong Kong, China

Steering Committee

Hong-Ning Dai   Hong Kong Baptist University, China
Xiapu Luo   Hong Kong Polytechnic University, China
Yan Zhang   University of Oslo, Norway
Zibin Zheng   Sun Yat-sen University, China

Web Chair

Renke Huang   Sun Yat-sen University, China

Program Committee

Alexander Chepurnoy   IOHK Research, China
Ali Vatankhah   Kennesaw State University, USA
Andreas Veneris   University of Toronto, Canada
Ao Zhou   Beijing University of Posts and
                                 Telecommunications, China
Bahman Javadi   Western Sydney University, Australia
Bo Jiang   Beihang University, China
Bu-Qing Cao   Hunan University of Science and Technology,
                                 China
Bijun Li   Hainan Normal University, China
Bin Wen   Hainan Normal University, China
Bing Lin   Fujian Normal University, China
Chang-Ai Sun   University of Science and Technology Beijing,
                                 China
ChangLin Yang   Sun Yat-sen University, China
Claudio Schifanella   University of Turin, Italy
Chunhua Su   Osaka University, Japan
Chunpeng Ge   Nanjing University of Aeronautics and
                                 Astronautics, China
Chuan Chen   Sun Yat-sen University, China
Daojing He   Harbin Institute of Technology (Shenzhen), China
Debiao He   Wuhan University, China
Fangguo Zhang   Sun Yat-sen University, China

Fenfang Xie	Sun Yat-sen University, China
Gerhard Hancke	City University of Hong Kong, China
Guobing Zou	Shanghai University, China
Haibo Tian	Sun Yat-sen Univeristy, China
Han Liu	Tsinghua University, China
Huawei Huang	Sun Yat-sen Univeristy, China
Jan Henrik Ziegeldorf	RWTH Aachen University, Germany
Jiakun Liu	Singapore Management University, Singapore
Jieren Cheng	Hainan University, China
Jiwei Huang	China University of Petroleum, China
Jiang Xiao	Huazhong University of Science and Technology, China
Jiajing Wu	Sun Yat-sen University, China
Kai Lei	Peking University, China
Kenneth Fletcher	University of Massachusetts Boston, USA
Kouichi Sakurai	Kyushu University, Japan
Laizhong Cui	Shenzhen University, China
Liehuang Zhu	Beijing Institute of Technology, China
Linfeng Bao	Zhejiang University, China
Liang Chen	Sun Yat-sen University, China
Lingjun Zhao	University of Aizu, Japan
Mario Larangeira	IOHK/Tokyo Institute of Technology, Japan
Meng Yan	Chongqing University, China
Muhammad Imran	King Saud University, China
Mingdong Tang	Guangdong University of Foreign Studies, China
Nan Jia	Hebei GEO University, China
Omer Rana	Cardiff University, UK
Pengcheng Zhang	Hohai University, China
Pengfei Chen	Sun Yat-sen University, China
Qianhong Wu	Beihang University, China
Qinghua Lu	CSIRO, Australia
Qian He	Guilin University of Electronic Technology, China
Raja Jurdak	Commonwealth Scientific Industrial and Research Organization, Australia
Shangguang Wang	Beijing University of Posts and Telecommunications, China
Shijun Liu	Shandong University, China
Shiping Chen	CSIRO, Australia
Shizhan Chen	Tianjin University, China
Shuiguang Deng	Zhejiang University, China
Sude Qing	China Academy of Information and Communications Technology, China

Tao Xiang	Chongqing University, China
Taotao Li	Sun Yat-sen University, China
Ting Chen	University of Electronic Science and Technology of China, China
Tingting Bi	CSIRO, Australia
Tsuyoshi Ide	IBM, China
Tianhui Meng	Shenzhen Institute of Advanced Technology, Chinese Academy of Sciences, China
Walter Li	Beijing University of Technology, China
Wei Luo	Zhejiang University, China
Wei Song	Nanjing University of Science and Technology, China
Weifeng Pan	Zhejiang Gongshang University, China
Wuhui Chen	Sun Yat-sen University, China
Weibin Wu	Sun Yat-sen University, China
Weili Chen	Sun Yat-sen University, China
Xiaodong Fu	Kunming University of Science and Technology, China
Xiaoliang Fan	Xiamen University, China
Xiangping Chen	Sun Yat-sen University, China
Xiaohong Shi	Guangzhou University, China
Xiapu Luo	Hong Kong Polytechnic University, China
Yu Jiang	Tsinghua University, China
Yuan Huang	Sun Yat-sen University, China
Yucong Duan	Hainan University, China
Yutao Ma	Wuhan University, China
Yuhong Nan	Sun Yat-sen University, China
Yiming Zhang	National University of Defense Technology, China
Yu Li	Hangzhou Dianzi University, China
Zekeriya Erkin	Delft University of Technology, The Netherlands
Zhe Liu	Nanjing University of Aeronautics and Astronautics, China
Zhihui Lu	Fudan University, China
Zhiying Tu	Harbin Institute of Technology, China
Zhiyuan Wan	Zhejiang University, China
Zihao Chen	Meta, China
Zihao Li	Hongkong Polytechnic University, China
Zoe L. Jiang	Harbin Institute of Technology, Shenzhen, China
Zibin Zheng	Sun Yat-sen University, China

Contents – Part II

Blockchain Architecture and Optimization

Protocols and Consensus

Contents – Part I

Empirical Study and Surveys

Federated Learning for Blockchain

AI for Blockchain

A General Smart Contract Vulnerability Detection Framework with Self-attention Graph Pooling

Lihan Zou[1], Changhao Gong[1], Zhen Wu[1], Jie Tan[2], Junnan Tang[2], Zigui Jiang[2], and Dan Li[2(✉)]

[1] School of Computer Science and Engineering, Sun Yat-Sen University, Guangzhou 510006, China
[2] School of Software Engineering, Sun Yat-Sen University, Zhuhai 519080, China
lidan263@mail.sysu.edu.cn

Abstract. In recent years, the increasing development of Web 3.0 has generated growing attention toward blockchain and smart contracts. However, due to their immutability, smart contracts still exhibit various vulnerabilities that hackers can exploit, resulting in significant losses. Numerous smart contracts on various blockchains, including Ethereum, have been attacked due to various vulnerabilities. The inefficiency of detecting these vulnerabilities has become a major bottleneck in advancing blockchain and smart contracts. Although detecting smart contract vulnerabilities has attracted much attention, most existing machine learning-based methods rely on adequate expert knowledge and target only specific known vulnerabilities via binary classification models. To address this limitation, our proposed approach introduced a general vulnerability detection method that can be applied to identify various common vulnerabilities via a uniform framework. We leveraged the Abstract Syntax Trees (AST) and self-attention-based graph pooling models to generate topological graphs from smart contract code analysis. We adopted Graph Neural Networks for vulnerability detection. Experimental results demonstrated that the proposed approach exhibited satisfactory performance in detecting multiple and unseen vulnerabilities compared to traditional methods.

Keywords: Blockchain · Smart Contract · Vulnerability Detection · Deep Learning · Self-Attention

1 Introduction

Blockchain is a transaction ledger distributed and shared among all miners within the blockchain network, adhering to a consensus protocol [1], which is revolutionizing the world. As an emerging technology, blockchain is characterized by its decentralization, tamper-proofing, irreversibility, and traceability. These features have revolutionized traditional industry models and have resulted in significant breakthroughs in various fields, including healthcare [2], copyright protection [3], and supply chain management [4]. As a core technology of Web 3.0, blockchain has enormous development prospects and has already shown its potential.

Smart contracts are one of the most successful applications of blockchain technology and have become a hot research topic in academia and industry. A smart contract is a computer program that runs on a blockchain, is written in a Turing complete language, and can automatically execute within the blockchain network. Due to the blockchain's special immutability mechanism, smart contracts cannot be changed once deployed on the blockchain. Therefore, once hackers exploit the vulnerability of smart contracts, it can easily cause serious losses.

According to Slowmist's statistics, the economic losses caused by smart contract security vulnerabilities have reached billions of dollars [6]. To date, numerous large-scale cases have been triggered by smart contracts, and serious security vulnerability incidents occur regularly. Due to the inception of smart contracts, one of the most impactful hacker attacks was exploiting the reentrancy vulnerability in DAO contracts in 2016 [7], which resulted in the theft of millions of dollars worth of Ether and shocked the entire blockchain research community. Subsequently, in 2017, there was the Delegatecall vulnerability, followed by the integer overflow vulnerability in 2018, and more recently, since 2020, new types of smart contract applications such as FarmEOS and LuckBet, among others, have also experienced varying degrees of hacking attacks, resulting in millions of dollars in losses. It can be said that effective vulnerability detection has become an urgent and critical issue and a significant challenge.

Due to the manual nature of code writing, it is impossible to eliminate vulnerabilities in smart contracts during the development stage, making vulnerability detection for smart contracts highly essential.

Traditional methods for detecting smart contract vulnerabilities typically rely on static analysis or dynamic execution techniques to identify vulnerabilities [8]. However, this approach often results in an over-reliance on existing expert knowledge and can only identify several known vulnerabilities. Moreover, manually defining detection patterns carries a high risk of error, especially for complex contracts.

In recent years, some scholars have attempted to use deep neural networks for vulnerability detection to improve accuracy and generalizability [9–11]. Deep learning-based approaches to smart contract vulnerability detection include training LSTM (Long Short-Term Memory) models to process the source code text of smart contracts [9], abstracting the source code into control flow graphs for vulnerability detection [10], and coupling expert knowledge with neural network structures to create hybrid models for detection [11].

The aforementioned approaches have three main limitations.

Firstly, most vulnerability detection models used in existing research are binary classification models with low detection efficiency and questionable accuracy. With the increasing number and complexity of smart contracts in the current environment, conventional binary classification models are struggling to adapt to the current environment.

Secondly, current vulnerability detection methods heavily rely on expert knowledge. This indicates that vulnerability detection is only based on summarizing completed expert knowledge. However, in reality, only well-known vulnerabilities have sufficient expert knowledge, which means these vulnerability detection methods can only be used for known and famous vulnerabilities and are unsuitable for environments with various vulnerabilities.

Lastly, both binary classification models and current neural network models lack generalization. Models without self-updating capabilities can only be trained and detected based on existing vulnerability detection data, making it difficult to perform vulnerability detection tasks in different environments. With the rapid development of smart contracts and the fast-changing working environment, the ability to adapt to different environments should be an important criterion for evaluating a vulnerability detection model.

In this paper, we proposed a general smart contract vulnerability detection method with self-attention graph pooling, and SAGP-detector to address the aforementioned limitations. Key contributions are:

1. We eliminated the reliance on traditional expert knowledge, freeing vulnerability detection from its constraints. The proposed model can detect vulnerabilities that may not be identifiable by expert knowledge, reducing the potential errors introduced by manually defined detection patterns.
2. The proposed SAGP-detector adopted a self-attention graph neural network that can internally update itself, aligning well with the rapidly evolving landscape of smart contracts. By continuously learning new vulnerabilities, vulnerability detection accuracy can be continuously improved.
3. Just like a pure data mining task, the proposed SAGP-detector is highly generalized and capable of learning and identifying various types of errors in different environments, making it highly applicable to wide-ranging potential applications.

The remainder of this paper is organized as follows. Section 2 introduces the related works. Section 3 presents our algorithm to implement the SAGP-detector and Sect. 4 conducts experiments on smart contracts to evaluate our proposed model. Finally, the paper is concluded in Sect. 5.

2   Related Work

2.1   Smart Contract Vulnerability Detection

Smart contract vulnerability detection is one of the core issues in determining blockchain development. Early efforts involved using formal verification methods to verify smart contract code [12–14]. [12] introduced a framework that converts Solidity code (the programming language of smart contract on Ethereum) and EVM (Ethereum Virtual Machine) into bytecode as input for the detection system; [13,14] defined the formal semantics of EVM using F* and K frameworks.

These frameworks can ensure the correctness of smart contracts to some extent, but they require manually defined models and cannot be automatically executed.

In recent years, with the continuous development of artificial intelligence technology, many scholars have turned their attention to using deep neural networks for vulnerability detection in smart contracts. These methods include using the BLSTM-ALL model for detecting reentrancy vulnerabilities [9], abstracting contract code into graphs and using graph neural networks [10], and constructing coupling models between expert knowledge and neural networks [11]. However, despite numerous related papers, deep learning-based methods for smart contract vulnerability detection is still in their early stages, leaving room for improvement in accuracy and other evaluation metrics.

2.2   Graph Neural Network

With the advancement of neural networks, graph neural networks have gained widespread recognition in various fields such as graph classification [15,16] and program analysis [17,18]. The graph neural network used in this study can be divided into two main components: convolution and pooling. In graph convolution, attention mechanisms for learning weights between neighboring nodes have recently been a hot topic. Graph pooling, on the other hand, is used to reduce the size of data and the number of parameters in convolutional models, thereby avoiding over-fitting, which is proven to be necessary for GNN models.

3   SAGP-Detector Framework

The overall architecture of the proposed framework is depicted in Fig. 1, including three phases: converting Solidity code into graphs (Sect. 3.1), which involves first translating the source code into an Abstract Syntax Tree (AST) and then transforming the syntax tree into the graph representation required; dealing with "raw graphs" with self-attention graph pooling (Sect. 3.2); detection vulnerabilities (Sect. 3.3).

3.1   Graph Construction

Parse Source Code into an Abstract Syntax Tree. Solidity has a context-free syntax. This programming language can be parsed into an AST. The AST is an abstract representation of the syntax structure of the source code. It represents the syntax structure of a programming language in the form of a tree. Each non-leaf node in the tree has information about a non-terminal structure in context-free syntax, and each leaf node is regarded as a terminal structure.

Parsing code into AST can fully extract and utilize ample syntax and semantic information and reduce the loss of parsing needless comments and blank lines. We use an open source tool Solidity-parser-antlr[1] to turn source code into AST.

---

[1] https://github.com/solidity-parser/parser

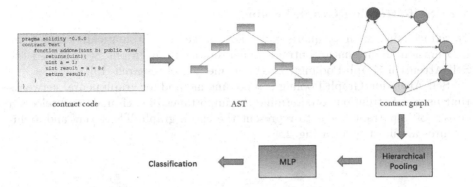

contract code   AST   contract graph

Classification ⟸ MLP ⟸ Hierarchical Pooling

Fig. 1. The overview of SAGP-detector. We first generate graphs from Solidity code, then utilize a hierarchical Pooling architecture with self-attention pooling to learn the graph. At last, we use a multilayer perceptron for vulnerability detection.

Generate Graph from AST. Extracting the syntax and semantic information from the source code is insufficient. To represent the complex relationship between nodes better, research [5] propose a method that can abstract the control flow and data flow between nodes as the edges between:

1. *NextNode*: A NEXTNODE edge will be added between two nodes if the two nodes are adjacent in the depth-first traversal output of the abstract syntax tree.
2. *NextToken*: A NEXTTOKEN edge will be added between two nodes if the two nodes are adjacent in the depth-first traversal output of the abstract syntax tree after removing nodes with empty node values.
3. *ConditionTrue*: There is a CONDITIONTRUE edge between the conditional subtree root node and the true branching subtree root node of the conditional branching structure.
4. *ConditionFalse*: There is a CONDITIONFALSE edge between the conditional subtree root node and the false branching root node.
5. *WhileExec*: A WHILEEXEC edge connects the root node of the loop condition subtree of the while loop structure and the root node of the loop body subtree.
6. *ForExec*: A FOREXEC edge connects the loop condition subtree of the for loop structure and the root of the loop body subtree.
7. *ForNext*: A FORNEXT edge connects the loop body subtree's root node and the update statement's root node.
8. *LastRead*: There is a LASTREAD edge between the current variable node and the variable node that was last seen and was read.
9. *LastWrite*: A LASTWRITE edge exists between the current variable node and the variable node that last appeared and was written.
10. *NextUsed*: A NEXTUSED edge exists between the current variable node and its next occurrence.

3.2   Self-attention Graph Pooling

To reduce reliance on adequate expert knowledge and automatically extract key information about smart contract vulnerabilities from graphs, we adopted the Self-Attention Graph Pooling (SAGPool) method of research [19].

Self-Attention Graph Pooling is a pooling method for graph neural networks that uses self-attention to determine the importance of each node and selects a subset of important nodes to represent the entire graph. The layers and architectures are illustrated in Fig. 2.

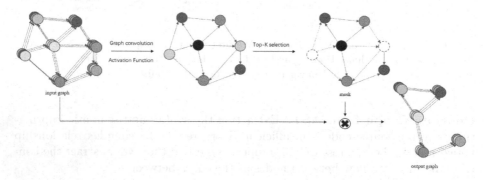

Fig. 2. An illustration of the SAGPool layer. We first use graph convolution and activation functions to obtain scores, perform top-k selection to obtain a mask, and apply pooling operations on the input graph with the mask.

Self-attention Scores. The attention mechanism is a widely used approach in recent deep learning studies, which can focus more on important features rather than unimportant features. The key point of SAGPool is that it uses a GNN to provide self-attention scores. We utilize graph convolutional networks to obtain self-attention scores due to their ability to capture the graph's structural and feature information jointly. By performing convolutions on the graph data, the network can aggregate information from each node's local neighborhood, which can capture its topological relations to other nodes in the graph. This approach allows the network to learn a rich representation of the graph, which can then be used to calculate the self-attention scores for each node.

Suppose we use the widely used graph convolution proposed by Kipf and Welling [20]. The self-attention score $Z \in \mathbb{R}^{N \times 1}$ is calculated as follows.

$$Z = \sigma\left(\tilde{D}^{-\frac{1}{2}}\tilde{A}\tilde{D}^{-\frac{1}{2}}X\Theta_{att}\right) \tag{1}$$

where σ is the activation function (e.g. $tanh$), $\tilde{A} \in \mathbb{R}^{N \times N}$ is the adjacency matrix, which $\tilde{A} = (A + I_N)$, $\tilde{D} \in \mathbb{R}^{N \times N}$ is the degree matrix of $\tilde{A}$, $X \in \mathbb{R}^{N \times F}$ is the input features of the graph with N nodes and F dimensional features, and $\Theta_{att} \in \mathbb{R}^{F \times 1}$ is the only parameter of the SAGPool layer.

Top-Rank Selection. We employed the node selection technique proposed by [21] to achieve a unified approach for processing input graphs of various sizes. The pooling ratio $k \in (0, 1]$ is a hyper-parameter determining the number of nodes to keep.

Based on the self-attention scores Z, we retain the top $\lceil kN \rceil$ nodes.

$$idx = \text{top-rank}(Z, \lceil kN \rceil), Z_{mask} = Z_{idx} \qquad (2)$$

where top-rank is the function that returns the indices of the top $\lceil kN \rceil$ values, idx is an indexing operation and Z_{mask} is the feature attention mask.

Graph Pooling. After we obtain Z_{mask}, We perform pooling operations on the input graph.

$$X' = X_{\text{idx},:}, X_{out} = X' \odot Z_{mask}, A_{out} = A_{\text{idx,idx}} \qquad (3)$$

where $X_{\text{idx},:}$ is the node-wise indexed feature matrix, $\odot$ is the broadcasted element-wise product, and $A_{\text{idx,idx}}$ is the row-wise and col-wise indexed adjacency matrix, X_out and A_out are the new feature matrix and the corresponding adjacency matrix.

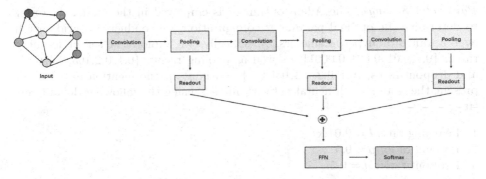

Fig. 3. The hierarchical pooling structure we use for vulnerability detection. The input graph is fed into the first block, and its output is passed to the next block and connected to a readout layer. The same process is repeated for the second block, and the output of the final block is connected to a final readout layer. The three readout layers are combined using an additive operation and passed to a feedforward neural network for classification.

3.3 Vulnerability Detection

Inspired by the hierarchical pooling study of [22], We implemented a hierarchical pooling structure shown in Fig. 3. This approach involves recursively applying a pooling operation to the graph data, with each successive layer capturing increasingly coarse-grained representations of the input graph. The key insight behind this method is that by aggregating information across multiple levels of abstraction, we can capture a more comprehensive view of the graph structure and its features.

The architecture primarily consists of three blocks and a feedforward neural network, which is designed specifically for the task of graph classification. Each block comprises three essential components: a GraphSAGE [33] layer for extracting features from the graph data, a SAGPool layer we mentioned before, and a readout layer for extracting useful information from the final graph representation to support the execution of follow-up classification. Combining these components allows the proposed model to handle complex graph structures effectively and provide satisfactory classification results.

4   Experiments

4.1   Experimental Settings

Datasets. We conducted experiments on two datasets, one of which consisted of real-world smart contract code collected on Ethereum and VNT Chain platforms, as previously collected by Research [11]. The other dataset is SmartBugs [23].

Parameter Settings. The Adam optimizer is employed in the model. In order to determine the optimal parameter configuration, we conducted a grid search over a range of hyperparameters. Specifically, we explored a set of learning rates, $\{0.1, 0.01, 0.001, 0.0001\}$, as well as pooling ratios, $\{0.1, 0.2, 0.3, 0.4, 0.5\}$, and dropout rates, $\{0.1, 0.2, 0.3, 0.4, 0.5\}$. Without special mention in texts, we present the results of all neural network models using the following default settings:

1. Learning rate: $l = 0.01.x$
2. Pooling ratio: $p = 0.5$.
3. Dropout ratio: $d = 0.5$.

For each dataset, we split it into 70% for training and the remaining 30% for testing.

4.2   Results

We compared the proposed model with existing vulnerability detection tools and neural network models. It was found that the SAGP-Framework is generally comparable or even superior to existing methods while avoiding the dependence on expert knowledge and exhibiting certain generalization capabilities.

Compared with Existing Vulnerability Detection Tools. We benchmarked our proposed method against the following existing vulnerability detection tools:

1. Oyente [24]: Oyente is one of the first symbolic verification tools for smart contract vulnerability detection. It constructs the control flow graph of a contract to detect vulnerabilities by exploring as many execution parts as possible.
2. Mythril [25]: Like Oyente, Mythril is a vulnerability detection tool based on symbolic execution. It combines concolic analysis, taint analysis, and control flow checking to obtain more accurate detection.
3. Smartcheck [26]: An extensible static analysis tool for discovering smart contract vulnerabilities.
4. Securify [27]: It is a vulnerability detection tool based on formal verification. The tool performs symbolic analysis on the contract's dependency graph and verifies compliance or violation patterns that represent the necessary conditions for proving the validity of a property.
5. Slither [28]: It is a static analysis framework to find vulnerabilities in Ethereum smart contracts transforming them into an intermediate *SlithIR* representation.

The aforementioned five existing methods and the proposed method were applied to detect the reentrancy and timestamp dependence vulnerabilities commonly seen in smart contracts. The performance of different methods is presented in Table 1.

Table 1. Performance comparison of different vulnerability detection methods regarding the accuracy, recall, precision, and F1 score.'-' denotes not applicable. SAGP-detector exhibits performance second only to the current state-of-the-art vulnerability detection methods.

Method	Reetrancy				Timestamp dependence			
	Acc(%)	Recall(%)	Precision(%)	F1(%)	Acc(%)	Recall(%)	Precision(%)	F1(%)
Smartcheck	52.97	32.08	25.00	28.10	44.32	37.25	39.16	38.18
Oyente	61.62	54.71	38.16	44.96	59.45	38.44	45.16	41.53
Mythril	60.54	71.69	39.58	51.02	61.08	41.72	50.00	45.49
Securify	71.89	56.60	50.85	53.57	-	-	-	-
Slither	77.12	74.28	68.42	71.23	74.20	**72.38**	**67.25**	**69.72**
SAGP-detector	**81.82**	**75.99**	**78.99**	71.59	**81.08**	60.18	58.04	57.54

For detecting the reentrancy vulnerability, as shown in Table 1, SAGP-detector delivered the best performance, which achieved 81.82% accuracy, 75.99% recall, 78.99% precision, and 71.59% F1 score. This is because conventional methods rely on simple and fixed patterns to detect vulnerabilities but underestimate the significance of rich information in data flow and control flow.

For detecting the timestamp dependence vulnerability detection, as shown in the right part of Table 1, The ASGP-detector also presented the best accuracy.

This indicates that most traditional methods detect timestamp dependence vulnerability by checking the existence of *block. Timestamp* statement in the function. The proposed method outperforms most traditional vulnerability detection methods but falls slightly behind Slither regarding precision and recall. Though Slither achieved a better outcome, it should be noted that its implementation complexity is significantly higher compared to our approach.

Compared with Neural Network-Based Methods. We also aimed to compare the proposed SAGP-detector with other neural network-based models to investigate their ability to extract feature information and topological structures while detecting vulnerability. The models used for comparison are:

1. Vanilla-RNN [29]: It is a two-layer recurrent neural network that accepts the code sequence as input and utilizes its hidden states to capture the sequential patterns present in the code by evolving recurrently.
2. LSTM [30]: LSTM, short for long-short-term memory, is the most commonly used recurrent neural network for handling sequential data. It updates the cell state recursively by reading the code sequence successively.
3. GRU [31]: The gated recurrent unit utilizes gating mechanisms to manage the code sequence.
4. GCN [20]: GCN is short for graph convolutional network. It performs layer-wise convolution on the graph by using graph Laplacian.
5. TMP [32]: The network known as the temporal message propagation network learns the features of the contracted graph by propagating information along edges in their temporal order. The resulting graph feature is then used to predict vulnerabilities.

The result is shown in Table 2. SAGP-detector outperformed other neural network-based models, and we found that GCN performs significantly better than RNN, LSTM, and GRU, which achieved similar performance to ours. This indicates that the detection performance can be improved by digging topological structures of smart contracts. Since GCN is also applied in the proposed model, comparing the performance of GCN and SGAP-detector suggests that SAG-Pooling improved the performance of GCN models by abstracting the "raw graphs" generated by AST.

Multiple Classification Result. SAGP-detector eliminates the reliance on expert knowledge for detecting smart contract vulnerabilities and defines it as a more general data mining approach. Testing whether the model can identify different types of vulnerabilities is necessary. In this section, we aim to test whether the proposed method can detect vulnerabilities in smart contracts and distinguish between different types of vulnerabilities. We mixed Solidity code with no vulnerabilities, code containing reentrancy vulnerabilities, code containing timestamp dependence vulnerabilities, code containing access control vulnerabilities, and code containing unchecked low-level calls vulnerabilities, labeled them differently, and trained the proposed model. We want to investigate whether

Table 2. Performance comparison of neural network-based methods regarding the accuracy, recall, precision, and F1 score. SAGP-detector achieved state-of-the-art accuracy but is comparable to other neural network-based methods for other metrics.

Method	Reetrancy				Timestamp dependence			
	Acc(%)	Recall(%)	Precision(%)	F1(%)	Acc(%)	Recall(%)	Precision(%)	F1(%)
Vanilla-RNN	49.64	58.78	49.82	50.71	49.77	44.59	51.91	45.62
LSTM	53.68	67.82	51.65	58.64	50.79	59.23	50.32	54.41
GRU	54.54	71.30	53.10	60.87	52.06	59.91	49.41	54.15
GCN	70.27	51.02	35.14	41.27	77.03	49.51	38.51	43.51
SAGP-detector	**81.82**	**75.99**	**78.99**	**71.59**	**81.08**	**60.18**	**58.04**	**57.54**

using a multi-class dataset results in lower model performance than a binary dataset. Moreover, the aforementioned five-class dataset was also tested by two classic classification methods, the decision trees and random forests, to generate baseline results.

Table 3. Performance comparison of decision tree, random forest, and the proposed model on multiple-class datasets regarding the accuracy, recall, precision, and F1 score.

Method	Accuracy(%)	Recall(%)	Precision(%)	F1(%)
Decision Tree	57.25	21.34	11.45	14.56
Random Forest	61.07	20.00	12.21	15.17
SAGP-detector	**65.65**	**38.72**	**35.28**	**32.01**

As shown in Table 3, the SAGP-detector has demonstrated its robustness and superiority when it comes to multi-class datasets, as its performance remains unaffected even with the increased complexity of the data. Notably, the detector has consistently outperformed the decision tree and random forest algorithms, which are well-established methods in the field of machine learning. This indicates that the SAGP-detector has the potential to become a highly effective tool for detecting vulnerabilities in smart contracts, offering improved accuracy and efficiency compared to traditional methods. In addition, the SAGP-detector helps improve the efficiency of vulnerability detection and demonstrates that SAGP-detector has a certain generalization ability and can be effective for different types of vulnerabilities.

4.3 Ablation Study

An important aspect of the proposed model is the application of self-attention graph pooling, which can adaptively select important nodes based on the structure and features of the input graph. This approach can better adapt to different graph structures and feature distributions, thereby improving the performance of graph neural networks. It is useful to investigate its significance for the model's performance. Therefore, we removed three blocks from the model to generate a simple classifier, leaving only the readout layer and the feedforward neural network used for classification to explore the impact of self-attention graph pooling on the model.

Quantitative results are in Table 4. We can observe that with self-attention graph pooling, the performance of the proposed model is better. It achieves a 20.24% and 15.64% improvement in recall and F1 scores, respectively.

The results show that using Self-Attention Pooling can help the network automatically learn and extract useful information from the graph without requiring data preprocessing, significantly improving subsequent classification tasks.

Table 4. Performance comparison of simple classifier and the proposed model regarding the accuracy, recall, precision, and F1 score.

Method	Acc(%)	Recall(%)	Precision(%)	F1(%)
Classifier	72.97	55.75	59.06	55.95
SAGP-detector	**81.82**	**75.99**	**78.99**	**71.59**

5   Conclusion and Future Work

In this paper, we proposed a self-attention graph pooling-based vulnerability detection method for smart contracts that departs from the reliance on traditional expert knowledge. Instead, we design a highly generalized vulnerability detection scheme. Furthermore, we conducted extensive experiments on the proposed model, and the results indicated that the proposed model outperforms existing vulnerability detection baseline methods in terms of accuracy. Deep learning for smart contract vulnerability detection is still a relatively new research direction with limited studies. Future improvements can be made by considering more vulnerabilities. The approach proposed in this study can also be extended to other areas, such as general coding performance testing.

Acknowledgments. This research was supported by the Guangdong Basic and Applied Basic Research Foundation (2022A1515011713), Guangdong Basic and Applied Basic Research Foundation (2023A1515011336), and National Natural Science Foundation of China (62002393).

References

1. Sankar, L.S., Sindhu, M., Sethumadhavan, M.: Survey of consensus protocols on blockchain applications. In: Proceedings of the ICACCS, pp. 1–5 (2017)
2. Zhang, P., Schmidt, D.C., White, J., et al.: Blockchain technology use cases in healthcare. In: Advances in Computers, vol. 111, pp. 1–41. Elsevier (2018)

3. Qian, P., Liu, Z., Wang, X., et al.: Digital resource rights confirmation and infringement tracking based on smart contracts. In: 2019 IEEE 6th International Conference on Cloud Computing and Intelligence Systems (CCIS), pp. 62–67. IEEE (2019)
4. Saberi, S., Kouhizadeh, M., Sarkis, J., et al.: Blockchain technology and its relationships to sustainable supply chain management. Int. J. Prod. Res. **57**(7), 2117–2135 (2019)
5. Tang, X., Gan, J., Jiang, Z.: A graph neural network-based code recommendation method for smart contract development. In: 2022 International Conference on Service Science (ICSS), Zhuhai, China, pp. 248–254 (2022). https://doi.org/10.1109/ICSS55994.2022.00046
6. Slowmist (2023). https://hacked.slowmist.io/
7. Sayeed, S., Marco-Gisbert, H., Caira, T.: Smart contract: attacks and protections. IEEE Access **8**, 24416–24427 (2020)
8. Luu, L., Chu, D.H., Olickel, H., et al.: Making smart contracts smarter. In: Proceedings of the ACM SIGSAC Conference on Computer and Communications Security, vol. 2016, pp. 254–269 (2016)
9. Qian, P., Liu, Z., He, Q., et al.: Towards automated reentrancy detection for smart contracts based on sequential models. IEEE Access **8**, 19685–19695 (2020)
10. Zhuang, Y., Liu, Z., Qian, P., et al.: Smart contract vulnerability detection using graph neural network. In: IJCAI, pp. 3283–3290 (2020)
11. Liu, Z., Qian, P., Wang, X., et al.: Combining graph neural networks with expert knowledge for smart contract vulnerability detection. IEEE Trans. Knowl. Data Eng. **35**, 1296–1310 (2021)
12. Bhargavan, K., Delignat-Lavaud, A., Fournet, C., et al.: Formal verification of smart contracts: short paper. In: Proceedings of the. ACM Workshop on Programming Languages and Analysis for Security, vol. 2016, pp. 91–96 (2016)
13. Grishchenko, I., Maffei, M., Schneidewind, C.: A semantic framework for the security analysis of ethereum smart contracts. In: Bauer, L., Küsters, R. (eds.) POST 2018. LNCS, vol. 10804, pp. 243–269. Springer, Cham (2018). https://doi.org/10.1007/978-3-319-89722-6_10
14. Hildenbrandt, E., Saxena, M., Rodrigues, N., et al.: Kevm: a complete formal semantics of the ethereum virtual machine. In: 2018 IEEE 31st Computer Security Foundations Symposium (CSF), pp. 204–217. IEEE(2018)
15. Zhang, M., Cui, Z., Neumann, M., et al.: An end-to-end deep learning architecture for graph classification. In: Proceedings of the AAAI Conference on Artificial Intelligence, vol. 32, no.1 (2018)
16. Errica, F., Podda, M., Bacciu, D., et al.: A fair comparison of graph neural networks for graph classification. arXiv preprint arXiv:1912.09893 (2019)
17. Zhou, Y., Liu, S., Siow, J., et al.: Devign: effective vulnerability identification by learning comprehensive program semantics via graph neural networks. Adv. Neural Inf. Process. Syst. 32 (2019)
18. Allamanis, M., Brockschmidt, M., Khademi, M.: Learning to represent programs with graphs. arXiv preprint arXiv:1711.00740 (2017)
19. Lee, J., Lee, I., Kang, J.: Self-attention graph pooling. In: International Conference on Machine Learning, pp. 3734–3743. PMLR (2019)
20. Kipf, T.N., Welling, M.: Semi-supervised classification with graph convolutional networks. arXiv preprint arXiv:1609.02907 (2016)
21. Gao, H., Ji, S.: Graph u-net. In: Proceedings of the 36th International Conference on Machine Learning (ICML) (2019)

22. Cangea, C., Velickovič, P., Jovanović, N., Kipf, T., Lió, 'P.: Towards sparse hierarchical graph classifiers. arXiv preprint arXiv:1811.01287 (2018)
23. Durieux, T., Ferreira, J.F., Abreu, R., et al.: Empirical review of automated analysis tools on 47,587 ethereum smart contracts. In: Proceedings of the ACM/IEEE 42nd International Conference on Software Engineering, pp. 530–541 (2020)
24. Luu, L., Chu, D.-H., Olickel, H., Saxena, P., Hobor, A.: Making smart contracts smarter. In: Proceedings of the 2016 ACM SIGSAC Conference on Computer and Communications Security, pp. 254–269 (2016)
25. Mueller, B.: Smashing ethereum smart contracts for fun and real profit. In: 9th Annual HITB Security Conference (HITBSecConf), vol. 54 (2018)
26. Tikhomirov, S., Voskresenskaya, E., Ivanitskiy, I., Takhaviev, R., Marchenko, E., Alexandrov, Y.: Smartcheck: static analysis of ethereum smart contracts. In: WETSEB, pp. 9–16 (2018)
27. Tsankov, P., Dan, A., Drachsler-Cohen, D., Gervais, A., Buenzli, F., Vechev, M.: Securify: practical security analysis of smart contracts. In: Proceedings of the 2018 ACM SIGSAC Conference on Computer and Communications Security, ser. CCS 2018. New York, NY, USA, pp. 67–82 Association for Computing Machinery (2018). https://doi.org/10.1145/3243734.3243780
28. Feist, J., Grieco, G., Groce, A.: Slither: a static analysis framework for smart contracts. In: WETSEB, pp. 8–15 (2019)
29. Goller, C., Kuchler, A.: Learning task-dependent distributed representations by backpropagation through structure. In: Proceedings of ICNN, vol. 1, pp. 347–352 (1996)
30. Sak, H., Senior, A., Beaufays, F.: Long short-term memory recurrent neural network architectures for large scale acoustic modeling. In: Fifteenth Annual Conference of the International Speech Communication Association (2014)
31. Chung, J., Gulcehre, C ., Cho, K., Bengio, Y.: Empirical evaluation of gated recurrent neural networks on sequence modeling, arXiv preprint arXiv:1412.3555 (2014)
32. Zhuang, Y., Liu, Z., Qian, P., Liu, Q., Wang, X., He, Q.: Smart contract vulnerability detection using graph neural network. In: Proceedings of the IJCAI-20, vol. 7, pp. 3283–3290 (2020)
33. Hamilton, W., Ying, Z., Leskovec, J.: Inductive representation learning on large graphs. Adv. Neural Inf. Process. Syst. 30 (2017)

The Best of Both Worlds: Integrating Semantic Features with Expert Features for Smart Contract Vulnerability Detection

Xingwei Lin[1], Mingxuan Zhou[2], Sicong Cao[2(✉)], Jiashui Wang[1,3], and Xiaobing Sun[2]

[1] Ant Group, Hangzhou 310000, China
xwlin.roy@gmail.com, jiashui.wjs@antgroup.com
[2] College of Information Engineering, Yangzhou University, Yangzhou 225009, China
MZ120220958@stu.yzu.edu.cn, {DX120210088,xbsun}@yzu.edu.cn
[3] Polytechnic Institute, Zhejiang University, Hangzhou 310015, China

Abstract. Over the past few years, smart contract suffers from serious security threats of vulnerabilities, resulting in enormous economic losses. What's worse, due to the immutable and irreversible features, vulnerable smart contracts which have been deployed in the the blockchain can only be detected rather than fixed. Conventional approaches heavily rely on hand-crafted vulnerability rules, which is time-consuming and difficult to cover all the cases. Recent deep learning approaches alleviate this issue but fail to explore the integration of them together to boost the smart contract vulnerability detection yet. Therefore, we propose to build a novel model, SMARTFUSE, for the smart contract vulnerability detection by leveraging the best of semantic features and expert features. SMARTFUSE performs static analysis to respectively extract vulnerability-specific expert patterns and joint graph structures at the function-level to frame the rich program semantics of vulnerable code, and leverages a novel graph neural network with the hybrid attention pooling layer to focus on critical vulnerability features. To evaluate the effectiveness of our proposed SMARTFUSE, we conducted extensive experiments on 40k contracts in two benchmarks. The experimental results demonstrate that SMARTFUSE can significantly outperform state-of-the-art analysis-based and DL-based detectors.

Keywords: Smart contract · Vulnerability detection · Code representation Learning · Graph neural network · Expert features

1 Introduction

Smart contracts are programs or transaction protocols which automatically execute on the blockchain [21]. The decentralization and trustworthy properties of smart contract have attracted considerable attention from different industries,

J. Chen et al. (Eds.): BlockSys 2023, CCIS 1897, pp. 17–31, 2024.
https://doi.org/10.1007/978-981-99-8104-5_2

and are used to support many tasks such as access control, task management or data management [9,22,35]. Taking the most famous blockchain platform Ethereum [31] as an example, there are more than 1.5 million smart contracts have been deployed [23].

However, due to several properties [29], smart contract is more vulnerable to attacks than traditional software programs [5,36]. On the one hand, the transparency of smart contracts expose a large attack surface to hackers, allowing them to call a smart contract with no limitations. On the other hand, as the blockchain is immutable and irreversible, once a vulnerable smart contract is deployed on the blockchain, it neither can be repaired nor interrupted. Considering the serious impact of smart contract vulnerabilities [6], timely detection of smart contract vulnerabilities is necessary and urgent.

Conventional smart contract vulnerability detection approaches often adopt static or dynamic analysis techniques. Unfortunately, these approaches fundamentally rely on several fixed expert rules, while the manually defined patterns bear the inherent risk of being error-prone and some complex patterns are nontrivial to be covered. Recently, benefiting from the powerful performance of Deep Learning (DL), a number of approaches [3,24,25,37] have been proposed to leverage DL models to learn program semantics to identify potential vulnerabilities. However, existing DL-based detection approaches fail to precisely model and extract critical features related to vulnerabilities, leading to unsatisfactory results, i.e., either missing vulnerabilities or giving overwhelmingly false positives.

To cope with the aforementioned challenges, in this paper, we propose a novel approach, called SMARTFUSE, which captures the distinguishing features of Smart contract vulnerabilities by Fusing Semantic features with Expert features. In particular, SMARTFUSE firstly performs static analysis to respectively extract vulnerability-specific expert patterns and joint graph structures at the function-level to frame the rich program semantics of vulnerable code. Considering that even a single function could have hundreds lines of code, which may introduce much noise, SMARTFUSE performs forward and backward slicing from the program point of interest based on control- and data-dependence to extract vulnerability-related code snippets. Second, we leverage Gated Graph Neural Network (GGNN) with hybrid attention pooling layer to focus on critical vulnerability features and suppress unimportant ones via the attention mechanism. Finally, the local expert features and global semantic features are fused to produce the final vulnerability detection results. To evaluate the effectiveness of our proposed SMARTFUSE, we conducted extensive experiments on 40k contracts in two benchmarks. The experimental results demonstrate that SMARTFUSE can significantly outperform state-of-the-art analysis-based and DL-based detectors.

The main contributions can be summarized as follows:

- We propose to characterize the contract function source code as graph representations. To focus on vulnerability-related features, we employ several expert patterns and program slicing to capture local and global vulnerability semantics.

- We propose a novel DL-based smart contract vulnerability detection technique, SMARTFUSE, with a fusion model to extract the distinguishing features from global semantic features and local expert features of source code.
- We comprehensively investigate the value of integrating the semantic features and expert features for smart contract vulnerability detection. The results indicate that SMARTFUSE outperforms the state-of-the-art approaches.

2   Background

2.1   Smart Contract Vulnerabilities

In this work, we concentrate on the following three common types of vulnerabilities in smart contract.

Reentrancy vulnerability occurs when the caller contract is simultaneously entered twice. In traditional programs, the execution is atomic when called a non-recursive function and there will be no new function execution before the current function execution ends. However, in smart contract, the malicious callee external contract may reenter the caller before the caller contract finishes when conducting an external function call.

Timestamp dependence vulnerability happens when *block.timestamp* is leveraged to trigger certain critical operations, e.g., generating specific numbers. Since the miners in the blockchain has the freedom to adjust the timestamp of the block as long as it is within a short time interval, they may manipulate the block timestamps to gain illegal benefits.

Infinite loop vulnerability, which unintentionally iterates forever, occurs when a smart contract contains a loop statement with no (or unreachable) exit condition. Such vulnerability will consume a lot of gas but all the gas is consumed in vain since the execution is unable to change any state.

2.2   Graph Neural Networks

Due to the outstanding ability in learning program semantics, Graph Neural Networks (GNNs) have been applied to a variety of security-related tasks achieved great breakthroughs. Modern GNNs follow a neighborhood aggregation scheme, where the representation of a node is updated by iteratively aggregating representations of its k-hop neighbors, to capture the structural information of graphs. This procedure can be formulated by:

$$h_v^{(t)} = \sigma \left(h_v^{(t-1)}, AGG^{(t)} \left(\left\{ h_u^{(t-1)} : u \in \mathcal{N}(v) \right\} \right) \right) \tag{1}$$

where $h_v^{(t)}$ is the feature representation of node v at the t-th iteration, $u \in \mathcal{N}(v)$ is the neighbors of v, and $AGG(\cdot)$ and $\sigma(\cdot)$ denote aggregation (e.g., $MEAN$) and activation (e.g., $ReLU$) functions for node feature computation.

According to different goals, the final node representation $h_v^{(T)}$ can be used for graph classification, node classification, and link prediction [33].

Graph Classification. Given a graph $G_i = (V, E, X) \in \mathcal{G}$ and a set of graph labels $\mathcal{L} = \{l_1, \cdots, l_m\}$, where each node $v \in V$ is represented by a real-valued feature vector $\boldsymbol{x}_v \in X$ and m denotes the number of graph labels, graph classification aims to learn a mapping function $f : \mathcal{G} \to \mathcal{L}$ to predict the label of the i-th graph G_i.

Node Classification. Given a graph $G_j = (V, E, X) \in \mathcal{G}$ and its node label set $\mathcal{L} = \{l_1, \cdots, l_n\}$, node classification aims to learn a mapping function $g : \mathcal{V} \to \mathcal{L}$ to predict the label of node v.

Link Prediction. Given node u and node v, link prediction aims to predict the probability of connection between node u and node v by $y_{u,v} = \phi\left(\boldsymbol{h}_u^{(k)}, \boldsymbol{h}_v^{(k)}\right)$, where $\boldsymbol{h}_u^{(k)}$ and $\boldsymbol{h}_v^{(k)}$ are the node representations after k iterations of aggregation and $\phi(\cdot)$ refers to the composition operator such as *Inner Production*.

Considering that existing GNNs suffer from the long-term dependency issue, which prevents nodes from effectively transferring messages, our work builds on Gated Graph Neural Network (GGNN) [15]. GGNN uses a gated recurrent unit to remember the key features. This allows GGNN to go deeper than other GNNs. So this deeper model has a powerful ability to learn more semantics features from graph data.

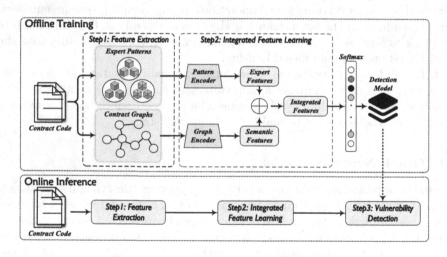

Fig. 1. The overall workflow of our approach.

3   Our Approach

The overview of our proposed approach is illustrated in Fig. 1, which consists of three components: 1) feature extraction, where vulnerability-specific expert patterns are obtained by adopting a fully automatic tool proposed by Liu et al.

[17] and semantic features are extracted with GGNN with a hybrid attention pooling layer; 2) integrated feature learning is proceeded with a fully connected layer, and 3) vulnerability detection is to predict the vulnerable smart contracts at the function-level with previously learned features. Details of SMARTFuSE are presented in the following subsections.

3.1 Feature Extraction

Feature extraction aims at converting the statistical data (i.e., expert features) and code representations (i.e., semantic features) into numeric representation that can be adapted to the deep neural network models to capture the distinguishing characteristics for the later vulnerability detection tasks.

Expert Feature Extraction. Expert features are a set of descriptive rules defined by experts according to their understanding of security-critical programming patterns with their professional knowledge and experience. In the literature, dozens of expert features have been defined from various dimensions (e. g., vulnerability types, security operations). The nine features (presented in Table 1) defined by Liu et al. [17] specific to three common smart contract vulnerabilities have been demonstrated for their effectiveness. Therefore, we follow the state-of-the-art work to adopt the nine expert features as an important part to mine the integrated features of source code for smart contract vulnerability detection.

Table 1. Studied nine common vulnerability-specific expert features.

Vulnerability Type	Expert pattern	Security-Critical Operations
Reentrancy	enoughBalance	call.value invocation
	callValueInvocation	a function that contains call.value
	balanceDeduction	the variable: correspond to user balance
Timestamp dependence	timestampInvocation	block.timestamp invocation
	timestampAssign	block.number invocation
	timestampContaminate	a variable: affect critical operation
Infinite loop	loopStatement	for
	loopCondition	while
	selfInvocation	self-call function

Semantic Feature Extraction. Semantic features represent the theoretical units of meaning-holding components which are used for representing word meaning, and capture the meaning of tokens in code as well as their contexts(e.g., semantic and syntactic structural information of code), that have been widely used to represent the intrinsic characteristics of code mined with DL models. In this work, we adopt a widely-used abstract representation Code Property Graph (CPG) [34], which merges Abstract Syntax Tree (AST), Control Flow Graph (CFG), and Program Dependence Graph (PDG) into a joint data structure, to reserve sufficient syntax and semantic features of source code. In addition, considering that a single function usually contains dozens of code lines while the vulnerability exists only in one or several lines of code, we further perform backward and forward program slicing [30] based on CPG from a program point of interest to filter noise induced by irrelevant statements. Our slice criteria can be divided into two categories: sensitive operations and sensitive data. For example, sensitive operations such as *.delegatecall* or *.call* will call an external contract may which may be malicious, while sensitive data are the insecure data which hackers can manipulate (e.g., *block.number*, *block.timestamp*). The details of our slice criteria are listed in Table 2.

Table 2. Studied eight common vulnerability-specific expert features.

Slice Criteria	Example
block info	*block.number, block.gaslimit*
delegatecall	*address.delegatecall*
arithmetic operations	$*, +, -$
external function call	*address.call*
selfdestruct operation	*selfdestruct*
input address parameters	*address input_ address*
block timestamp	*block.timestamp*
low level call operation	*address.call*

3.2 Integrated Feature Learning

With the expert and semantic features extracted in different ways, SMARTFUSE further needs to encode them into feature vectors and learn their integrated features. For local expert features, we adopt a feed-forward neural network (FNN) as feature encoders. For global semantic features, we utilize GGNN with a hybrid attention pooling layer to transform sliced contract graphs into deeper graph features. Then, the expert features and semantic features are merged by using a fusion network for vulnerability detection.

Local Expert Feature Learning. Each expert pattern formulates an elementary factor closely related to a specific vulnerability. We utilize One-Hot Encoding to represent each pattern, i.e., "0"/"1" indicates whether the function under test has this pattern or not, respectively. The vectors for all patterns related to a specific vulnerability are concatenated into a final vector x. The final vector x and the ground truth of whether the function has the specific vulnerability as the target label will be fed into a feed-forward neural network $\psi(\cdot)$ with a convolution layer and a max pooling layer to extract its corresponding d-dimensional expert feature E_r. The convolutional layer learns to assign different weights to different elements of the semantic vector, while the max pooling layer highlights the significant elements and avoids overfitting [16].

Global Semantic Feature Learning. To learn the global semantic feature from the sliced code graph, we firstly use *Word2Vec* [19] as the embedding model to convert each token v into an initial d-dimensional vector representation $x_v \in \mathbb{R}^d$. Then we use GGNN as the graph-level feature encoder to learn semantic features across the graph structure.

As GGNN is a recurrent neural network, the feature learning at time t aggregate features for node v from its neighbors along graph edges to get the aggregated features $a_v^{(t)}$:

$$a_v^{(t)} = A_v^T [h_1^{(t-1)T}, ..., h_m^{(t-1)T}] + b \tag{2}$$

where b is a bias and A_v is the adjacent matrix of node v with learnable weights.

In addition, limited by the one-way message propagation mechanism of GNNs, rich contextual information that essential for vulnerability detection in smart contract may be ignored. Following existing works [1,4], we also propose to conduct the adjacency matrix for a graph with both incoming and outgoing edges for each node. The aggregated feature $a_v^{(t)}$ of node v at time t will be put into the gated recurrent unit (GRU) with the node's previous feature vector at time $t-1$ to get its current feature vector $h_v^{(t)}$:

$$h_v^{(t)} = GRU(a_v^{(t)}, h_v^{(t-1)}) \tag{3}$$

This computation iterate by T times. Then, we use the state vectors computed by the last time step as the final node representations. The generated node features from the gated graph recurrent layers can be used as input to any prediction layer, e.g., for graph-level prediction in this work, and then the whole model can be trained in an end-to-end fashion. Considering that the importance of each node is different, we propose to use the hybrid attention graph pooling that combines self-attention pooling and global attention pooling to generate the final graph-level semantic feature S_r.

We first use a hierarchical self-attention graph pooling layer [14] to generate graph-level features from the most task-related nodes in a graph by self-attention mechanism. The self-attention pooling layer is consists of three blocks. In each block, it first calculates the attention score by a graph convention layer for each node. Then it picks up the top-k nodes based on the value of the attention score to construct a more task-related subgraph, which will be put into an average pooling to generate a subgraph-level feature. Finally, combining all these three blocks' subgraph-level features, it can get a graph-level feature h_{top-K}. Such hierarchical self-attention graph pooling can extract the most task-related features from all nodes, but just selecting top-K nodes from the graph may lose some global information. Thus, we add a global attention pooling layer to complement the whole graph feature. In this layer, we propose to conduct the global graph feature by the weighted sum of all nodes features. As shown in Eq. (4), we use a Multi-Layer Perceptron (MLP) to compute the attention score for each node's feature and use and a *Softmax* to get the weight for each node. By weighted sum all nodes' features, we get the global graph feature h_{global} for each function.

$$h_{global} = \sum_{i=0}^{N} Softmax\left(MLP\left(h_i^{(T)}\right)\right) * h_i^{(T)} \tag{4}$$

Combining the most task-related graph feature and global graph feature, we get the final graph-level semantic feature S_r by $S_r = h_{top-K} + h_{global}$.

Feature Fusion. After obtaining the local expert feature P_r and the global semantic feature S_r of the contract, we fuse them into the final feature X_r by using a convolution layer and a max pooling layer:

$$X_r = P_r \oplus S_r \tag{5}$$

where $\oplus$ denotes concatenation operation.

3.3   Vulnerability Detection

With the learned integrated features X_r, the last step of SMARTFUSE is to train a vulnerability detection model that will be applied to smart contracts under test. To this end, the learned integrated features are first fed into a network consisting of three fully connected layers and a sigmoid layer for the binary classification task:

$$\widetilde{y} = sigmoid(FC(X_r)) \tag{6}$$

where the fully connected layer $FC(\cdot)$ and the non-linear *sigmoid* layer produce the final estimated label $\widetilde{y}$. If the function is vulnerable, the value of $\widetilde{y}$ will be labeled as "1", otherwise labeled as "0".

4   Experiments

4.1   Research Questions

To evaluate the performance of SMARTFUSE, we design the following research questions:

RQ1: To what extent smart contract vulnerability detection performance can SMARTFUSE achieve?

RQ2: How do the integrated expert and semantic features affect the performance of smart contract vulnerability detection models?

RQ3: Can our proposed GGNN with hybrid attention pooling capture vulnerability-related program semantics?

4.2   Dataset

Following existing works [17,37], we built our evaluation benchmark by merging two real-world smart contract datasets, ESC and VSC.

4.3 Baselines

We selected five conventional analysis-based detectors and two state-of-the-art DL-based vulnerability detection approaches.

- **Oyente** [18] applies symbolic execution on the CFG of smart contract to check pre-defined vulnerable patterns.
- **Mythril** [20] combines multiple analysis techniques, such as concolic analysis and taint analysis, for smart contract vulnerability detection.
- **Smartcheck** [26] converts AST to a XML parse tree as an intermediate representation, and then check pre-defined vulnerability patterns on this intermediate representation.
- **Securify** [27] statically analyzes EVM bytecode to infer contract by Souffle Datalog solver to prove some pre-defined safety properties are satisfied.
- **Slither** [7] converts a contract to a specific intermediate representation named SlithIR, then doing the pre-defined vulnerability patterns match on this SlithIR representation.
- **Peculiar** [32] is a DL-based vulnerability detection tool which converts a contract to a crucial data flow graph and puts it into the GraphCodeBERT model for vulnerability detection.
- **TMP** [37] converts a contract to a normalized graph and then utilizes a deep learning model named temporal message propagation network for vulnerability detection.

4.4 Experimental Setup

Implementation. All the experiments are conducted on a server with an NVIDIA Tesla V100 GPU and an Intel(R) Core(TM) i9-12900k @3.90 GHz with 64 GB of RAM. The AST generate tool is implemented with typescript based on solc-typed-ast package, while CFG and PDG is conducted by Slither [7]. We use the pre-trained embedding model provided by SmartEmbed [8] to do the token embedding, and the GGNN model is implemented with python based on the dgl library [28]. The dimension of the vector representation of each node is set to 128 and the dropout is set to 0.2. ADAM [13] optimization algorithm is used to train the model with the learning rate of 0.001. The pool rate for self attention pooling layer is 0.5.

Evaluation Metrics. We apply the following four widely used evaluation metrics to measure the effectiveness of our approach and the other competitors.

- *Accuracy* (**Acc**) evaluates the performance that how many instances can be correctly labeled. It is calculated as: $Acc = \frac{TP+TN}{TP+FP+TN+FN}$.
- *Precision* (**Pre**) is the fraction of true vulnerabilities among the detected ones. It is defined as: $Pre = \frac{TP}{TP+FP}$.
- *Recall* (**Rec**) measures how many vulnerabilities can be correctly detected. It is calculated as: $Rec = \frac{TP}{TP+FN}$.
- *F1-score* (**F1**) is the harmonic mean of *Recall* and *Precision*, and can be calculated as: $F1 = 2 * \frac{Rec*Pre}{Rec+Pre}$.

5   Experimental Results

5.1   Experiments for Answering RQ1

Table 3 shows the overall results (the best performances are also highlighted in bold.) of each baseline and SMARTFUSE on smart contract vulnerability detection in terms of the aforementioned evaluation metrics. Overall, SMARTFUSE outperforms all of the five referred analysis-based detectors and two DL-based approaches.

Table 3. Evaluation results in percentage compared with state-of-the-art detectors.

Method	Accuracy	Precision	Recall	F1-score
Oyente	57.3	41.1	42.8	41.9
Mythril	53.9	64.7	36.4	46.6
Securify	50.5	53.2	55.2	54.2
Smartcheck	37.8	59.4	43.5	50.2
Slither	61.9	63.1	58.4	50.7
Peculiar	82.7	55.2	41.6	47.4
TMP	85.0	83.9	66.5	74.2
SMARTFUSE	**91.4**	**88.6**	**94.3**	**91.4**

We can find that the performance of bytecode-level approaches (Oyente, Mythril, and Securify) is poor. The reason is that most semantic and syntax features are lost during the compilation of bytecode. Compared to pattern-based detection tools (i.e., slither, smartcheck), SMARTFUSE still performs better because these pre-defined patterns are too simple or fixed to cover all situations. By contrast, our feature fusion model can automatically learn expert and semantic features from the representation of source code to detect different types of vulnerabilities.

In addition, we can also find that SMARTFUSE outperforms two DL-based detection approaches (Peculiar [32] and TMP [37]) in terms of all evaluation metrics. The reason is that although both Peculiar and TMP utilize the graph to represent the smart contract code like SMARTFUSE, neither of them can comprehensively and precisely capture the vulnerability-related syntax and semantic features inside the code. In particular, Peculiar [32] only uses the data flow alone to represent the smart contract code, which may lose several critical features such as control flow between statements. Thus, such a one-sided code representation approach makes the DL model hard to capture all potential vulnerability patterns from such insufficient vulnerability-related features.

5.2   Experiments for Answering RQ2

Table 4. Comparing results on vulnerability detection with different features.

Setting	Accuracy	Precision	Recall	F1-score
Expert Features	86.9	84.3	90.2	87.1
Semantic Features	83.2	81.5	88.6	84.9
SMARTFUSE	**91.4**	**88.6**	**94.3**	**91.4**

We set three training scenarios (i.e., expert features, semantic features, and their Fusion) to train SMARTFUSE for assessing the effectiveness of integrated features on boosting vulnerability detection. The experimental dataset is set the same as the experiment of RQ1 (i.e., 80%-10%-10% for training, validation, and testing). The comparison results are reported in Table 4 and the best performances are highlighted in bold for each approach on three different settings.

Obviously, we can observe that both expert features and semantic features have their own advantages in building an accurate prediction model, and expert features seem to have a better understanding of code characteristics than semantic features in the domain of smart contract vulnerability detection, revealing that incorporating security patterns is necessary and important to improve the performance. Furthermore, we can observe that combining semantic features with expert patterns indeed achieves better results compared to their pure semantic features counterparts. For example, SMARTFUSE respectively gains a 9.86% accuracy and 7.66% F1 improvements over its variant with the pure neural network model, demonstrating the effectiveness of combining semantic features with expert patterns.

5.3   Experiments for Answering RQ3

Table 5. Comparing results on vulnerability detection with different pooling layers.

Setting	Accuracy	Precision	Recall	F1-score
Sum Pooling	75.7	74.7	83.6	87.1
Avg Pooling	80.1	78.4	87.4	84.9
Global Attention Pooling	83.8	81.6	89.5	87.1
Self Attention Pooling	87.6	84.2	92.6	84.9
SMARTFUSE	**91.4**	**88.6**	**94.3**	**91.4**

We further investigate the impact of our graph feature learning module with a hybrid attention pooling layer by comparing it with its variant. Towards this, we use the pooling without attention, such as sum pooling and average pooling as the baseline, then conduct ablation experiments targeting the hybrid attention mechanism (i.e., respectively removing self-attention and global attention).

The comparison of our model with different pooling layers are shown in Table 5. We can see that our hybrid attention graph pooling layer get significant improvements in smart contract vulnerability detection task. The experimental results show that using pooling with attention mechanism can be more effective than other no-attention pooling layers. In addition, we can observe that compared to global and self attention pooling, the hybrid attention pooling is more effective than using them alone. The reason is that these two attention mechanisms are complementary, and combining them can improve the effectiveness.

6 Related Work

Traditional approaches employ static analysis or formal approaches to detect vulnerabilities [2,7,10,26]. For example, Slizer [7] and SmartCheck [26] are detectors of vulnerability patterns, which can perform static analysis on many types of source code. Bhargavan et al. [2] proposes a language-based formal approach to verify the safety and the functional correctness of smart contracts. Hirai et al. [10] proposed an interactive theorem prover to verify some safety properties of Ethereum smart contracts.

Another aspect of the work depends on symbol analysis and dynamic execution. Oyente [18] is the first symbol execution tool, which directly works with EVM byte code without access to corresponding source code. Zeus [12] employs both abstract interpretation and symbolic model checking to verify the correctness and fairness of smart contracts. ContractFuzzer [11] randomly generates test cases to identify vulnerabilities through fuzzing and runtime behavior monitoring during execution. Osiris [25] combined symbol execution and stain analysis to detect smart contract vulnerabilities related to integers.

Recently, several studies have demonstrated the effectiveness of Deep Learning (DL) in automated smart contract vulnerability detection. Qian et al. [24] proposed a novel attention-based BLSTM model to precisely detect reentrancy bugs. Zhuang et al. [37] combines contract graph and graph neural networks to detect three common smart contract vulnerabilities.

7 Conclusion

In this paper, we propose a novel approach SMARTFUSE, which fully utilizes both expert features and semantic features of source code to build a performance-better model for smart contract vulnerability detection. We also explore the possibility of using graph neural networks with hybrid attention mechanism to learn precise graph features from code graphs, which contains rich vulnerability-specific program semantics. Extensive experimental results show that our proposed approach can significantly outperform existing detection approaches.

References

1. Allamanis, M., Brockschmidt, M., Khademi, M.: Learning to represent programs with graphs. In: Proceedings of the 6th International Conference on Learning Representations (ICLR) (2018)
2. Bhargavan, K., et al.: Formal verification of smart contracts: short paper. In: Proceedings of the 2016 ACM Workshop on Programming Languages and Analysis for Security, PLAS@CCS 2016, Vienna, Austria, October 24, 2016, pp. 91–96. ACM (2016)
3. Cai, J., Li, B., Zhang, J., Sun, X., Chen, B.: Combine sliced joint graph with graph neural networks for smart contract vulnerability detection. J. Syst. Softw. **195**, 111550 (2023)
4. Cao, S., Sun, X., Bo, L., Wei, Y., Li, B.: BGNN4VD: constructing bidirectional graph neural-network for vulnerability detection. Inf. Softw. Technol. **136**, 106576 (2021)
5. Cao, S., Sun, X., Bo, L., Wu, R., Li, B., Tao, C.: MVD: memory-related vulnerability detection based on flow-sensitive graph neural networks. In: Proceedings of the 44th IEEE/ACM International Conference on Software Engineering (ICSE), pp. 1456–1468. ACM (2022)
6. Falkon, S.: The story of the DAO - its history and consequences (2017)
7. Feist, J., Grieco, G., Groce, A.: Slither: a static analysis framework for smart contracts. In: Proceedings of the 2nd International Workshop on Emerging Trends in Software Engineering for Blockchain (WETSEB@ICSE), pp. 8–15. IEEE / ACM (2019)
8. Gao, Z., Jiang, L., Xia, X., Lo, D., Grundy, J.: Checking smart contracts with structural code embedding. IEEE Trans. Software Eng. **47**(12), 2874–2891 (2021)
9. Hang, L., Kim, D.: Reliable task management based on a smart contract for runtime verification of sensing and actuating tasks in IoT environments. Sensors **20**(4), 1207 (2020)
10. Hirai, Y.: Defining the ethereum virtual machine for interactive theorem provers. In: Brenner, M., et al. (eds.) FC 2017. LNCS, vol. 10323, pp. 520–535. Springer, Cham (2017). https://doi.org/10.1007/978-3-319-70278-0_33
11. Jiang, B., Liu, Y., Chan, W.K.: Contractfuzzer: fuzzing smart contracts for vulnerability detection. In: Proceedings of the 33rd ACM/IEEE International Conference on Automated Software Engineering (ASE), pp. 259–269. ACM (2018)
12. Kalra, S., Goel, S., Dhawan, M., Sharma, S.: ZEUS: analyzing safety of smart contracts. In: Proceedings of the 25th Annual Network and Distributed System Security Symposium (NDSS). The Internet Society (2018)
13. Kingma, D.P., Ba, J.: Adam: a method for stochastic optimization. In: Proceedings of the 3rd International Conference on Learning Representations (ICLR) (2015)
14. Lee, J., Lee, I., Kang, J.: Self-attention graph pooling. In: Proceedings of the 36th International Conference on Machine Learning (ICML), vol. 97, pp. 3734–3743 (2019)
15. Li, Y., Tarlow, D., Brockschmidt, M., Zemel, R.S.: Gated graph sequence neural networks. In: Proceedings of the 4th International Conference on Learning Representations (ICLR) (2016)
16. Liu, Z., Qian, P., Wang, X., Zhuang, Y., Qiu, L., Wang, X.: Combining graph neural networks with expert knowledge for smart contract vulnerability detection. arXiv preprint arXiv:2107.11598 (2021)

17. Liu, Z., Qian, P., Wang, X., Zhuang, Y., Qiu, L., Wang, X.: Combining graph neural networks with expert knowledge for smart contract vulnerability detection. IEEE Trans. Knowl. Data Eng. **35**(2), 1296–1310 (2023)
18. Luu, L., Chu, D., Olickel, H., Saxena, P., Hobor, A.: Making smart contracts smarter. In: Proceedings of the 23rd ACM SIGSAC Conference on Computer and Communications Security (CCS), pp. 254–269. ACM (2016)
19. Mikolov, T., Sutskever, I., Chen, K., Corrado, G.S., Dean, J.: Distributed representations of words and phrases and their compositionality. In: Proceedings of the 27th Annual Conference on Neural Information Processing Systems (NeurIPS), pp. 3111–3119 (2013)
20. Mueller, B.: A framework for bug hunting on the ethereum blockchain (2017)
21. Nakamoto, S.: Bitcoin: a peer-to-peer electronic cash system (2008)
22. Park, J., Youn, T., Kim, H., Rhee, K., Shin, S.: Smart contract-based review system for an IoT data marketplace. Sensors **18**(10), 3577 (2018)
23. Pierro, G.A., Tonelli, R., Marchesi, M.: An organized repository of ethereum smart contracts' source codes and metrics. Future Internet **12**(11), 197 (2020)
24. Qian, P., Liu, Z., He, Q., Zimmermann, R., Wang, X.: Towards automated reentrancy detection for smart contracts based on sequential models. IEEE Access **8**, 19685–19695 (2020)
25. Tann, W.J., Han, X.J., Gupta, S.S., Ong, Y.: Towards safer smart contracts: a sequence learning approach to detecting vulnerabilities. arXiv preprint arXiv:1811.06632 (2018)
26. Tikhomirov, S., Voskresenskaya, E., Ivanitskiy, I., Takhaviev, R., Marchenko, E., Alexandrov, Y.: Smartcheck: static analysis of ethereum smart contracts. In: Proceedings of the 1st IEEE/ACM International Workshop on Emerging Trends in Software Engineering for Blockchain (WETSEB@ICSE), pp. 9–16. ACM (2018)
27. Tsankov, P., Dan, A.M., Drachsler-Cohen, D., Gervais, A., Bünzli, F., Vechev, M.T.: Securify: practical security analysis of smart contracts. In: Proceedings of the 25th ACM SIGSAC Conference on Computer and Communications Security (CCS), pp. 67–82. ACM (2018)
28. Wang, M., et al.: Deep graph library: a graph-centric, highly-performant package for graph neural networks. arXiv preprint arXiv:1909.01315 (2019)
29. Wei, Y., Sun, X., Bo, L., Cao, S., Xia, X., Li, B.: A comprehensive study on security bug characteristics. J. Softw. Evol. Process. **33**(10), e2376 (2021)
30. Weiser, M.: Program slicing. IEEE Trans. Softw. Eng. **10**(4), 352–357 (1984)
31. Wood, G.: Ethereum: a secure decentralised generalised transaction ledger (2014)
32. Wu, H., et al.: Peculiar: smart contract vulnerability detection based on crucial data flow graph and pre-training techniques. In: Proceedings of the 32nd IEEE International Symposium on Software Reliability Engineering (ISSRE), pp. 378–389. IEEE (2021)
33. Wu, Z., Pan, S., Chen, F., Long, G., Zhang, C., Yu, P.S.: A comprehensive survey on graph neural networks. IEEE Trans. Neural Netw. Learn. Syst. **32**(1), 4–24 (2021)
34. Yamaguchi, F., Golde, N., Arp, D., Rieck, K.: Modeling and discovering vulnerabilities with code property graphs. In: Proceedings of the 35th IEEE Symposium on Security and Privacy (SP), pp. 590–604. IEEE Computer Society (2014)
35. Zhang, Y., Kasahara, S., Shen, Y., Jiang, X., Wan, J.: Smart contract-based access control for the internet of things. IEEE Internet Things J. **6**(2), 1594–1605 (2019)

36. Zhou, Y., Liu, S., Siow, J.K., Du, X., Liu, Y.: Devign: effective vulnerability identification by learning comprehensive program semantics via graph neural networks. In: Proceedings of the 33rd Annual Conference on Neural Information Processing Systems (NeurIPS), pp. 10197–10207 (2019)
37. Zhuang, Y., Liu, Z., Qian, P., Liu, Q., Wang, X., He, Q.: Smart contract vulnerability detection using graph neural network. In: Proceedings of the Twenty-Ninth International Joint Conference on Artificial Intelligence (IJCAI), pp. 3283–3290 (2020)

A LSTM and GRU-Based Hybrid Model in the Cryptocurrency Price Prediction

Yue Liu[1], Guijiao Xiao[2(✉)], Weili Chen[3], and Zibin Zheng[4]

[1] School of Computer Science and Engineering, Sun Yat-sen University,
Guangzhou 510000, China
liuy636@mail2.sysu.edu.cn
[2] South China Business College, Guangdong University of Foreign Studies,
Guangzhou 510000, China
250761680@qq.com
[3] School of Information Science and Technology,
Guangdong University of Foreign Studies, Guangzhou 510000, China
[4] School of Software Engineering, Sun Yat-sen University, Guangzhou 510000, China
zhzibin@mail.sysu.edu.cn

Abstract. Cryptocurrency is a new type of digital currency that utilizes blockchain technology and cryptography to achieve transparency, decentralization, and immutability. Bitcoin became the world's first decentralized cryptocurrency in 2009. With increasing attention given to cryptocurrency, predicting its price has become a popular research topic. Many machine learning and deep learning algorithms, such as Gated Recurrent Unit (GRU), Neural Network (NN), and Long Short-Term Memory (LSTM), have been studied for cryptocurrency price prediction. In this paper, we propose a hybrid cryptocurrency price prediction model based on LSTM and GRU. The model achieves better results than the LSTM model in cryptocurrency price prediction and performs the best among existing hybrid models based on LSTM and GRU.

Keywords: cryptocurrency · price prediction · hybrid model · lstm · gru

1 Introduction

The traditional economic system relies on third-party financial institutions such as banks to process payments, which lack trust, security, transparency, and flexibility. To address these issues, a system that eliminates intermediaries is needed to enable direct transfer of funds and change the way the economy operates.

In 2008, Satoshi Nakamoto wrote a paper titled "Bitcoin: A Peer-to-Peer Electronic Cash System" [1], which introduced a solution for conducting electronic transactions without the need for a central authority. The system uses blockchain technology to store all transaction records in blocks on the transaction network, and validates the transactions' authenticity through a proof-of-work mechanism. This mechanism involves having network members collectively

J. Chen et al. (Eds.): BlockSys 2023, CCIS 1897, pp. 32–43, 2024.
https://doi.org/10.1007/978-981-99-8104-5_3

solve complex arithmetic problems to verify the transactions, ensuring their security and reducing the possibility of malicious behavior. The Bitcoin system also eliminates intermediaries like traditional financial institutions, with all network participants maintaining and managing the legality and credibility of transactions. This is particularly important because this decentralized design makes the Bitcoin system more open and transparent, with lower transaction costs. As a result, the emergence of Bitcoin has had significant impacts on the payment and financial industries, leading to the development of the concept of cryptocurrency.

Cryptocurrency is a decentralized digital asset that aims to provide a secure means of digital currency trading through encryption technology. Based on blockchain technology, cryptocurrency records all transaction records in a public ledger, eliminating the need for central control authorities. Unlike traditional currencies, the number of cryptocurrencies is determined through computer algorithms and the process of mining new currency. Cryptocurrency transactions are anonymous and not subject to national regulation and control, saving time and cost compared to traditional financial transactions. Although cryptocurrency was only a niche market a few years ago, its market capitalization has grown significantly as its characteristics have become more visible and practical. While the use of cryptocurrency is still subject to restrictions by many national regulatory agencies, they have achieved much commercial success, with more and more companies and organizations accepting cryptocurrency as a means of payment.

There are thousands of different cryptocurrencies in the cryptocurrency market. Bitcoin, Ethereum, and Ripple are among the most famous cryptocurrencies. These cryptocurrencies can be classified based on their protocol type and application area, such as blockchain protocol, privacy coins, asset-backed tokens, and stablecoins. According to CoinMarketCap's statistics, as of April 2021, the total market capitalization of cryptocurrencies worldwide had reached $ 2.2 trillion.

In recent years, although cryptocurrency prices have been volatile, the usage of cryptocurrencies has shown a rapid growth trend. Many countries have implemented strict regulations on the cryptocurrency market. Although the market value has fluctuated in the short term, the overall market value has continued to increase. Data shows that the number of cryptocurrency users was about 41 million in 2019, while it had increased to over 70 million by early 2021. Industry observers believe that cryptocurrencies still have huge potential for development in the future.

The rapid growth of the cryptocurrency market has made people highly concerned about its price prediction. In fact, the price fluctuations of most cryptocurrencies are significant, and their price predictions are often challenging due to instability caused by many factors. However, with the development of technology and algorithms, researchers and market analysts have begun to use machine learning and artificial intelligence methods to analyze and predict the prices of cryptocurrencies.

In this article, we present a hybrid model based on LSTM and GRU to predict cryptocurrency prices. We trained the model using cryptocurrency prices from the past few years and compared its predictive performance with existing models.

By analyzing the experimental data, we have drawn some interesting conclusions about the hybrid model.

The rest of this paper is organized as follows. In Sect. 2, we present the research status of cryptocurrency price prediction. In Sect. 3, we describe our experimental framework and introduce the LSTM and GRU models we used. In Sect. 4, we provide more specific experimental designs. In Sect. 5, we present the experimental results and analyze them to draw conclusions. Finally, in Sect. 6, we summarize the entire article and discuss future directions.

2 Related Work

Between 2010 and 2020, statistical and machine learning (ML) methods were two commonly used techniques for predicting cryptocurrency prices [2]. The integrated moving average line (ARIMA) model is a traditional time series method, which has been used by Garg et al. [3], Roy et al. [4], and Wirawan et al. [5] to forecast bitcoin prices.

However, machine learning has achieved better performance in time series prediction compared to these models. Among machine learning methods, recurrent neural networks (RNNs), especially long short-term memory (LSTM) networks, have been the focus of past research [6]. S. McNally et al. compared the predictive performance of RNNs, LSTMs, and ARIMA models and found that the LSTM model achieved the best results [7]. A. Demir et al. used a series of machine learning algorithms, including LSTM networks, support vector machines, artificial neural networks, naive Bayes, decision trees, and k-nearest neighbors, to estimate bitcoin prices and found that the LSTM model had the highest accuracy [8]. S. M. Raju et al. proposed an LSTM price prediction model that takes into account the impact of public sentiment on bitcoin prices by using bitcoin closing prices and current market sentiment as inputs [9]. Livieris et al. proposed a multi-input deep neural network model, CNN-LSTM, for predicting cryptocurrency prices and trends [10]. Compared to traditional fully connected deep neural networks, the proposed model can effectively utilize mixed cryptocurrency data, reduce overfitting, and lower computational costs. Many studies have also proposed more LSTM-related hybrid models, such as MRC-LSTM [11], LSTM-RNN [12], CNN-GRU [13] and SAM-LSTM [14].

In recent years, some studies have used a hybrid model of GRU and LSTM for prediction, involving areas such as carbon price trading [15], traffic speed prediction [16], electricity load and price model prediction [17], flood Prediction [18]and stock price prediction [19]. In the field of cryptocurrency price prediction, there have also been some studies on the hybrid model of LSTM and GRU [20,21], but the amount of research is relatively small, and it is aimed at a specific type of hybridization.

3   Experimental Architecture

We collected the daily closing prices over the past few years for several of the highest market-cap cryptocurrencies. Then, we normalized the data to keep it within the range of 0–1. We further processed the data by using the prices of the previous 30 days to predict the price of the 31st day. Therefore, we processed the data into multiple input-output pairs. After processing the data, we divided it into training and validation sets. We trained the price prediction model using the data in the training set. Once the training was complete, we used the data in the validation set to predict prices and evaluated the prediction results using evaluation metrics. We chose a mixed model of GRU and LSTM for our price prediction model. The specific experimental process is shown in Fig. 1:

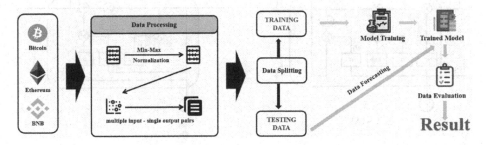

Fig. 1. Experimental Architecture

3.1   Long Short-Term Memory

Long short-term memory (LSTM) is a special type of recurrent neural network (RNN) that precisely passes on memory. LSTM utilizes a specific learning mechanism where the forget gate determines whether the previously learned information should be partially or completely forgotten, the input gate decides which values should be updated, and the output gate determines the final output of the model. Compared to a standard RNN, LSTM can track information over a longer period of time.

$$f_t = \sigma \left(W_f \cdot [h_{t-1}, x_t] + b_f \right) \qquad (1)$$

$$i_t = \sigma \left(W_i \cdot [h_{t-1}, x_t] + b_i \right) \qquad (2)$$

$$\tilde{C}_t = \tanh \left(W_C \cdot [h_{t-1}, x_t] + b_C \right) \qquad (3)$$

$$C_t = f_t * C_{t-1} + i_t * \tilde{C}_t \qquad (4)$$

$$o_t = \sigma \left(W_o \left[h_{t-1}, x_t \right] + b_o \right) \tag{5}$$

$$h_t = o_t * \tanh \left(C_t \right) \tag{6}$$

where h_{t-1} is the output of the previous time period, x_t is the current input, C_{t-1} is the information learned from the previous time period, f_t is the forget gate, which decides whether C_{t-1} is fully or partially passed through, i_t is the input gate, which determines the values to update, and o_t is the output gate, which decides the model's output (Fig. 2).

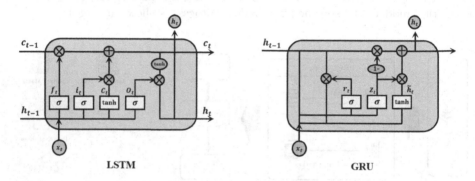

Fig. 2. Structure of LSTM and GRU

3.2   Gated Recurrent Unit

The Gate Recurrent Unit (GRU) is a type of recurrent neural network (RNN). GRU combines the forget gate and the input gate of LSTM into a single update gate and merges the data unit state and hidden state, making it simpler in structure than LSTM.

$$r_t = \sigma \left(W_r \cdot \left[h_{t-1}, x_t \right] \right) \tag{7}$$

$$z_t = \sigma \left(W_z \cdot \left[h_{t-1} x_t \right] \right) \tag{8}$$

$$\hat{h}_t = \tanh \left(W \cdot \left[r_t * h_{t-1}, x_t \right] \right) \tag{9}$$

$$h_t = (1 - z_t) * h_{t-1} + z_t * \hat{h}_t \tag{10}$$

where h_{t-1} is the previous output, x_t is the current input, r_t is the reset gate which determines how to combine new input information with previous memory, and z_t is the update gate which defines the amount of previous memory that is retained up to the current time step.

4 Experimental Design

LSTM and GRU have been widely used in time series prediction. Some studies suggest that a hybrid model of LSTM and GRU can achieve better results in prediction. We want to investigate whether this conclusion holds true for cryptocurrency price prediction. We compare the prediction performance of three different hybrid models based on LSTM and GRU and select the one with the best performance for comparison with existing hybrid models. Our experiment

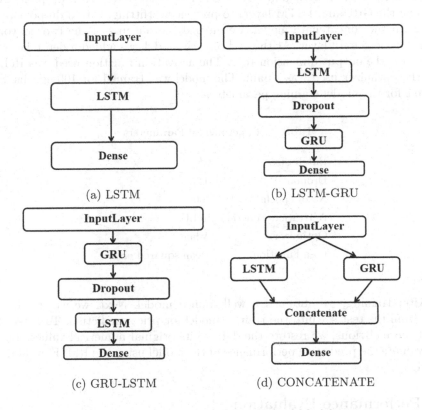

Fig. 3. LSTM and GRU-based Hybrid Models

selected the top three currencies in market capitalization - Bitcoin, Ethereum, and BNB. In the price prediction model, we combined LSTM and GRU models in different ways, referred to as LSTM-GRU, GRU-LSTM, and concatenate. By adjusting the number of neurons, we conducted multiple comparative experiments on these models. The frameworks of LSTM models and various hybrid models are shown in Fig. 3.

The first step in our research is to preprocess the collected price data by scaling it between 0 and 1. Next, we process the data into multiple input-output pairs. Specifically, we take $[x_0, x_1, \cdots, x_{n-1}]$ as an input and x_n as the output for that input. For the next input, we take $[x_1, x_2, \cdots, x_n]$ and output x_{n+1}. Here, we choose n to be 30, meaning that we use the prices of the past 30 days to predict the price of the 31st day. Finally, we split the data into training and testing sets with an 8:2 ratio.

The second step involves feeding the preprocessed training dataset into the model for training. We conducted multiple comparative experiments on each model by adjusting the number of neurons in the GRU and LSTM layers. Specifically, we sequentially adjusted the number of neurons to 10, 20, 30, 40, and 50. For both the LSTM-GRU and GRU-LSTM models, we added a dropout layer between the GRU and LSTM layers to prevent overfitting, with a dropout ratio of 0.2. In the concatenate model, we merged the outputs of the two networks using a concatenate layer. At the end of each model, we added a dense layer to transform the output dimension to 1. The activation function used was ReLU, and the optimizer used was Adam. The model was trained for 100 epochs. See Table 1 for the model training parameters.

Table 1. Experimental Parameters

Batch Size	64
Dropout Ratio	0.2
No of epochs	100
Activation Function	ReLU
Optimizer	Adam
Loss Function	Mean squared error

After training, we obtained a well-trained model. Next, we can input the data from the test set into the trained model for price prediction. To make the effect more obvious, we restore the data to its original numerical values. Then, we evaluate the predictive performance of the model using the RMSE evaluation metric.

5   Performance Evaluation

5.1   Dataset Description

The research utilizes data from Investing.com, collecting data on three types of cryptocurrencies: Bitcoin, Ethereum, and Binance Coin. We have collected daily closing prices for each currency, with detailed information on each dataset provided below.

- Bitcoin: June 21, 2019 - March 18, 2023 (1367 data points)
- Ethereum: June 21, 2019 - March 18, 2023 (1367 data points)
- June 21, 2019 - March 18, 2023 (1367 data points)

The relationship between price (in US dollars) and time is shown in Fig. 4.

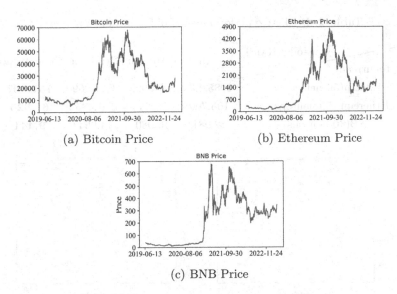

(a) Bitcoin Price   (b) Ethereum Price

(c) BNB Price

Fig. 4. Cryptocurrency prices

5.2   Data Preprocessing

We scale the data to the range of 0 to 1 using the min-max normalization. The specific operation is as follows:

$$x_{normalized} = \frac{x_{\text{original}} - x_{\min}}{x_{\max} - x_{\min}} \tag{11}$$

5.3   Evaluation Metrics

We use the root mean square error (RMSE) to evaluate the prediction performance in the academic paper on the topic of cryptocurrency price prediction.

$$RMSE = \sqrt{\frac{1}{N} \sum_{i=1}^{N} (\hat{p}_i - p_i)^2} \tag{12}$$

where $\hat{p}_i$ represents the predicted price generated by the model, p_i represents the actual price and N is the total number of data points used for testing.

5.4   Results

To evaluate the practical performance of our model, we made predictions using an untrained test set consisting of 268 data points. For clarity, we will use some abbreviations, such as LSTM(50) referring to the LSTM model with 50 neurons in the LSTM layer, and Concatenate(30) referring to the concatenate model with 30 neurons in both the GRU and LSTM layers.

Table 2. Predictive performance of different mixed models

Model_RMSE Cryptocurrency	Lstm	Lstm-gru	Gru-lstm	Concatenate
Bitcoin(50 neurons)	1085.495	2974.922	2667.969	**751.807**
Ethereum(50 neurons)	105.700	102.343	101.485	**67.326**
BNB(40 neurons)	12.981	16.080	14.664	**9.441**

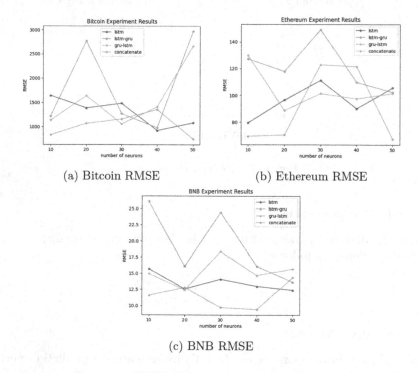

(a) Bitcoin RMSE   (b) Ethereum RMSE

(c) BNB RMSE

Fig. 5. Experimental results

For Bitcoin, the worst prediction performance was achieved with the LSTM-GRU(50) model, with an RMSE of 2974.922. The best prediction performance was achieved with the Concatenate(50) model, with an RMSE of 751.807. For Ethereum, the worst prediction performance was achieved with the LSTM-GRU(30) model, with an RMSE of 149.199. The best prediction performance was achieved with the Concatenate(50) model, with an RMSE of 67.326. For BNB, the worst prediction performance was achieved with the LSTM-GRU(10) model, with an RMSE of 26.102. The best prediction performance was achieved with the Concatenate(40) model, with an RMSE of 9.440. We found that the best prediction performance for these three cryptocurrencies was achieved with the Concatenate model, while the worst prediction performance was achieved with the LSTM-GRU model. Some specific experimental data can be found in the Table 2.

We further visualize the experimental results, and from Fig. 5, we can see that the concatenate model performs well in predicting the prices of all three currencies, and the prediction performance remains stable with changes in the number of neurons. Although the original LSTM model does not perform as well as the concatenate model in overall prediction, it shows stronger stability. However, the prediction performance of the LSTM-GRU and GRU-LSTM models is not satisfactory, and the prediction performance fluctuates greatly with changes in the number of neurons. I have seen some studies using the LSTM-GRU model for prediction, but experiments have shown that this is not a good choice for predicting cryptocurrency prices. In cryptocurrency price prediction, using the concatenate mixed model and selecting an appropriate number of neurons will result in better prediction performance than using LSTM alone (Fig. 6).

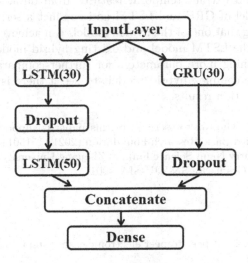

Fig. 6. Compare model

Empirical evidence shows that the concatenate model performs better than the classical LSTM model in cryptocurrency price prediction. In this paper, we conducted further comparative experiments by comparing the prediction performance of the concatenate model with a hybrid model from another related work [21]. The results demonstrate that our model achieves better prediction accuracy and is more concise, which can save computational resources (Table 3).

Table 3. Comparison of the prediction effect of the two models

	Concatenate_RMSE	Compare model_RMSE
Bitcoin	751.807	768.543
Ethereum	67.326	70.549
BNB	9.441	16.272

6   Conclusion

Cryptocurrency price prediction is a highly challenging task. LSTM and GRU have shown excellent performance in cryptocurrency prediction due to their ability to remember and extract temporal features from data. In this paper, we build a hybrid model of GRU and LSTM and conduct a series of comparative experiments, finding that one of the hybrid models can achieve better prediction performance than the LSTM model and existing hybrid models. In the future, we will consider tuning more parameters for further comparative experiments and exploring more complex hybrid models to see if there is room for further improving the prediction results.

Acknowledgments. The work described in this paper is supported by the Guang-dong Basic and Applied Basic Research Foundation (2021A1515011939), the Key-Area Research, and the Starry Night Science Fund of Zhejiang University Shanghai Institute for Advanced Study, Grant No. SN-ZJU-SIAS-001

References

1. Nakamoto S. Bitcoin: A peer-to-peer electronic cash system. In Decentralized business review, 2008
2. Khedr, A.M., Arif, I., El-Bannany, M., Alhashmi, S.M., Sreedharan, M.: Cryptocurrency price prediction using traditional statistical and machine-learning techniques: a survey. Intell. Syst. Account. Finan. Manage. **28**(1), 3–34 (2021)
3. Garg, S.: Autoregressive integrated moving average model based prediction of bitcoin close price. In: 2018 International Conference on Smart Systems and Inventive Technology (ICSSIT), pp. 473–478 (2018)
4. Roy, S., Nanjiba, S., Chakrabarty, A.: Bitcoin price forecasting using time series analysis. In: 2018 21st International Conference of Computer and Information Technology (ICCIT), pp. 1–5 (2018)
5. Wirawan, I.M., Widiyaningtyas, T., Hasan, M.M.: Short term prediction on bitcoin price using arima method. In: 2019 International Seminar on Application for Technology of Information and Communication (iSemantic), pp. 260–265 (2019)
6. Awotunde, J.B., Ogundokun, R.O., Jimoh, R.G., Misra, S., Aro, T.O.: Machine learning algorithm for cryptocurrencies price prediction. In: Misra, S., Kumar Tyagi, A. (eds.) Artificial Intelligence for Cyber Security: Methods, Issues and Possible Horizons or Opportunities. SCI, vol. 972, pp. 421–447. Springer, Cham (2021). https://doi.org/10.1007/978-3-030-72236-4_17

7. McNally, S., Roche, J., Caton, S.: Predicting the price of bitcoin using machine learning. In: 2018 26th Euromicro International Conference on Parallel, Distributed and Network-based Processing (PDP), pp. 339–343 (2018)
8. Demir, A., Nur Akılotu, B., Kadiroğlu, Z., Şengür, A.: Bitcoin price prediction using machine learning methods. In: 2019 1st International Informatics and Software Engineering Conference (UBMYK), pp. 1–4 (2019)
9. Raju, S.M., Tarif, A.M.: Real-time prediction of bitcoin price using machine learning techniques and public sentiment analysis (2020)
10. Livieris, I.E., Kiriakidou, N., Stavroyiannis, S., Pintelas, P.: An advanced CNN-LSTM model for cryptocurrency forecasting. Electronics 10(3), 287 (2021)
11. Guo, Q., Lei, S., Ye, Q., Fang, Z.: MRC-LSTM: a hybrid approach of multi-scale residual CNN and LSTM to predict bitcoin price. In: 2021 International Joint Conference on Neural Networks (IJCNN), pp. 1–8 (2021)
12. Ramadhan, N.G., Tanjung, N.A.F., Tanjung, N.A.F.: Indonesia J. Comput. (Indo-JC) 6(3), 17–24 (2021)
13. Jaiswal, R., Singh, B.: A hybrid convolutional recurrent (CNN-GRU) model for stock price prediction. In: 2022 IEEE 11th International Conference on Communication Systems and Network Technologies (CSNT), pp. 299–304 (2022)
14. Kim, G., Shin, D.H., Choi, J.G., Lim, S.: A deep learning-based cryptocurrency price prediction model that uses on-chain data. IEEE Access 10, 56232–56248 (2022)
15. Zhou, F., Huang, Z., Zhang, C.: Carbon price forecasting based on CEEMDAN and LSTM. Appl. Energy 311, 118601 (2022)
16. Zafar, N., Haq, I.U., Chughtai, J.U.R., Shafiq, O.: Applying hybrid LSTM-GRU model based on heterogeneous data sources for traffic speed prediction in urban areas. Sensors 22(9), 3348 (2022)
17. Khalid, A., Iqbal, S., Abbas, S.: Deep LSTM-BiGRU model for electricity load and price forecasting in smart grids. EasyChair (2022)
18. Cho, M., Kim, C., Jung, K., Jung, H.: Water level prediction model applying a long short-term memory (LSTM) gated recurrent unit (GRU) method for flood prediction. Water 14(14), 2221 (2022)
19. Kumar, R., Sharma, C.M., Chariar, V.M., Hooda, S., Beri, R.: Emotion analysis of news and social media text for stock price prediction using SVM-LSTM-GRU composite model. In: 2022 International Conference on Computational Intelligence and Sustainable Engineering Solutions (CISES), pp. 329–333 (2022)
20. Aslam, N., Rustam, F., Lee, E., Washington, P.B., Ashraf, I.: Sentiment analysis and emotion detection on cryptocurrency related tweets using ensemble LSTM-GRU model. IEEE Access 10, 39313–39324 (2022)
21. Patel, M.M., Tanwar, S., Gupta, R., Kumar, N.: A deep learning-based cryptocurrency price prediction scheme for financial institutions. J. Inf. Secur. Appl. 55, 102583 (2020)

Smart Contract Code Clone Detection Based on Pre-training Techniques

Chengfeng Zhang[1], Wei Shen[1], Yepeng Liu[1], Fan Zhang[2], Ya Li[3],
Zhuo Zhang[4(✉)], Jifu Cui[5], and Xiaoguang Mao[1(✉)]

[1] National University of Defense Technology, Changsha 410073, China
xgmao@nudt.edu.cn
[2] Army Logistics Academy, Chongqing 401331, China
[3] Shanghai Jiaotong University, Shanghai 200240, China
[4] Guangzhou College of Commerce, Guangzhou 511363, China
zz8477@126.com
[5] Qingdao Penghai Software Co., Ltd., Qingdao 266000, China

Abstract. Smart contract has been utilized to realize cryptocurrencies and crowdfunding initiatives. Due to its characteristics of immutable once deployed, the security issues have been widely studied and paid much attention. In practise, reusing pieces of smart contract code from reputable sources has taken risks. Thus, in this paper, we study the code cloning in Ethereum with pre-training techniques. Specifically, we analyze the similarity of two smart contract codes by comparing the similarity of the word vectors. We use the cosine similarity comparison method to analyze and compare a collection of 3814 smart contracts containing timestamp vulnerabilities, then perform code quality analysis on these contracts to study the relationships between code reuse and vulnerabilities. Finally, we analyze the characteristics of these existential code cloning contracts. The results show that the performance of our experimental method is 1%–4% better than the current best detection method.

Keywords: Ethereum · Smart Contract · Pre-training model · Code Clone · Vulnerability Detection

1 Introduction

Over the past 10 years, with the wide application of blockchain technology and digital cryptocurrency, new-generation of platforms represented by Bitcoin [1] and Ethereum [2] have been increasingly recognized and developed. Smart contracts [3] are one of the most important recent technological innovations: these are a consensus mechanism that uses all user confirmations on the blockchain to provide guarantees. This bold attempt has been recognized by the market, and many smart contracts have been released on Ethereum. Smart contracts are usually written in a higher-level language named Solidity [4] before being compiled into bytes of EVM(a smart contract virtual machine). As one of the most

© The Author(s), under exclusive license to Springer Nature Singapore Pte Ltd. 2024
J. Chen et al. (Eds.): BlockSys 2023, CCIS 1897, pp. 44–57, 2024.
https://doi.org/10.1007/978-981-99-8104-5_4

important rules of Ethereum, all purchases and sales are final and unchanging. However, for the convenience of deployment, most contracts are modified on the basis of the original code, which offers hackers the opportunity to attack. For example, Fomo3D [5] is a type of game that simply copies someone else's code;unfortunately,hackers found a vulnerability in the game that allowed them to cause very serious economic losses. Therefore, it is important to effectively detect code clones in smart contracts before they are deployed.

Clone detection is an important issue in software maintenance and development. Detecting similarities between two pieces of code also has a range of very important applications: for example, detecting candidate libraries [6,7], helping program comprehension [8], detecting malware [9], detecting plagiarism or copyright infringement [10,11], detecting context-based inconsistencies [12–14], and finding refactoring opportunities [15–17]. Roy and Cordy classify clone detection techniques through their "internal source code representation" [18]. So far, researchers have developed several code clone detection techniques. Johnson et al. proposed that the similarity could be gauged by comparing text sequences [19,20]. B. Baker et al. proposed a method of comparison at a higher level using annotation [21,22]. Jone et al. proposed a method of constructing syntactic correlations in grammar trees through comparison [23]. However, none of these methods can perform universal cloning detection, and we are building a universal code cloning detection method. To address the aforementioned limitations and help developers detect code clone more precisely, in this paper, we propose an approach to detect the code clone of the smart contract by state-of-the-art pre-trained model(i.e., CodeBERT).

The goal is to perform an efficient inspection of smart contracts and to identify the presence of code clones and vulnerabilities. Our approach is based on one main concept: Cosine similarity comparison using word vectors generated from two smart contract codes. Different types of code clone types in smart contracts can be identified through the above methods. Based on the above ideas, together with suitable similarity checking, and analysis techniques, the appeal method can be universally applied to various code clone checking and maintenance tasks. These tasks may include reuse (code clone) detection, detection of specific types of errors in certain corpora, or code verification against a set of known vulnerabilities. Based on the above ideas, we collected 3814 contracts with over 40,000 functions in Solidity source code that contain timestamp vulnerabilities, then manually annotated which contracts have timestamp vulnerabilities and which do not. We next generated Embed vectors using CodeBERT, after which we performed similarity detection based on these Embed vectors. Our evaluation results of 3814 contracts with a total of over 40,000 functions show that our method performs well on clone detection, error detection, and contract validation tasks. Compared with the most advanced smart contract checking tools/solidity-nica,/SmartEmb, our accuracy has improved by about 4%. Our active contribution to code clone can provide a reference for developers.

In summary, the main contributions of this paper are as follows:

- We use the pre-training technique to conduct detection of smart contract code cloning;
- To improve the accuracy of similar code detection, we detect the reuse of codes at the function level, which enables us to accurately identify the code reuse region;
- We apply the above approach to the timestamps vulnerability dataset manually labeled by ourself in real smart contracts. The results show that the proposed method can effectively identify timestamp vulnerabilities.

This paper is structured as follows. Section 2 presents the background on smart contract code clone and bug detection. Section 3 outlines our approach to smart contract code detection. Section 4 shows the evaluation results of our approach on actual contracts collected from the Ethereum blockchain. Section 5 discusses the limitations of our approach and its evaluation. Section 6 is related work and Sect. 7 is conclusion.

2   Background

2.1   Security Issues with Smart Contracts

An Ether account typically consists of two components, an External Ownership Account (EOA) and a Contract Account(CA). The EOA is controlled by a private key that is owned by an external user. There is no code associated with an EOA. Messages can be sent from the EOA by creating and signing transactions. The CA is controlled by its associated contract code, which may be activated when a message is received.

2.2   Code Cloning and Code Vulnerability

A large number of approaches have been proposed to Resolve code cloning issues, such as code clone detection, error detection, code verification, and program verification. We list some types of code cloning:

Typical Code Clone Types: Type I: Syntactically identical code snippets, except for spaces and differences in comments. Type II: Syntactically identical code fragments, but with different identifier names and literal values, except for cloning differences of Type I. Type III: Syntactically similar fragments that differ at the statement level. The fragments have statements added, modified, or removed concerning each other, in addition to Type I and Type II differences. Type IV: Syntactically different code fragments that achieve the same function.

Typical Code Vulnerability:

This paper focuses primarily on timestamp vulnerabilities. Specifically, timestamp dependency means that the execution of a smart contract depends on the timestamp of the current block; if the timestamp is different, then the execution of the contract has different results. Figure 1 shows an example of timestamp vulnerability.

```
/**
 * @dev UpgradeRig
 * @Exist timestamp vulnerabilities
 */
function UpgradeRig(uint8 rigIdx, uint256 count) external
{
    require(rigIdx < numberOfRigs);
    require(count > 0);
    require(count <= 512);
    require(rigFinalizeTime[rigIdx] < block.timestamp);
    require(miners[msg.sender].lastUpdateTime != 0);
}
```

Fig. 1. Timestamp vulnerability at cursor positioning.

2.3 Pre-trained Models

CodeBERT is a bimodal pre-trained model for programming language and natural language based on the Transformer architecture. The hybrid objective function used for training includes a replaced token detection (RTD) pre-training task. The input is then trained with a discriminator to predict whether each token in the corrupted input is replaced by a generator sample. This allows the CodeBERT model to utilize both bimodal data NL-PL pairs, which could provide input tokens for model training, and unimodal data, which helps to learn better generators. Figure 2 shows the code vector output after the CodeBERT model.

```
Example code  "c = a - b require(c <= a)"  Convert to word vectors
tensor([[[-0.1417,  0.2747, -0.0842,  ..., -0.2521, -0.3869,  0.3503],
         [-1.0454,  0.0970,  0.4211,  ..., -0.6557, -0.0948,  0.6433],
         [-0.9851,  0.3386,  0.0773,  ..., -0.5343, -0.5312,  0.6955],
         ...,
         [-0.0186,  0.0814,  0.0997,  ...,  0.1843, -0.8614,  0.7895],
         [ 0.2115, -0.2151,  0.3099,  ..., -0.0825, -0.6649,  0.5335],
         [-0.1423,  0.2753, -0.0836,  ..., -0.2527, -0.3883,  0.3516]]])
```

Fig. 2. Code vector output by CodeBERT.

CodeBERT can handle both natural and programming languages(such as Python, Java, JavaScript, etc.). It captures the semantic connections between natural languages and programming languages and outputs generic representations that can broadly support both NL-PL understanding tasks (e.g., natural language code search) and generative tasks (e.g., code document generation). CodeBERT models are built on a multilayer Transformer, which is widely used in large pre-trained models. To take advantage of bimodal data instances, NL-PL pairs, and a large number of available unimodal codes, researchers train Code-BERT using a hybrid objective function that includes standard masking language modeling (MLM) and replacement token detection (RTD). Here, where the replacement token detection leverages unimodal codes to learn better generators and thus output better replacement tokens.

Input-Output Representation. In the pre-training phase, the researcher sets the input as a combination of two fragments and a special separator, namely [CLS], w1, w2, . . wn, [SEP], c1, c2, . , cm, [EOS]. One of the fragments is a natural language text, and the other is a code written in some programming language. The output of CodeBERT consists of (1) a context vector representation of each token (for both natural language and code), and (2) a representation of [CLS] as an aggregated sequence representation.

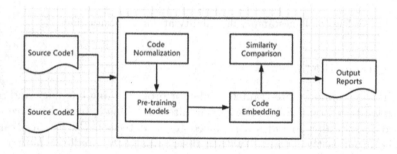

Fig. 3. Overview Of our Approach.

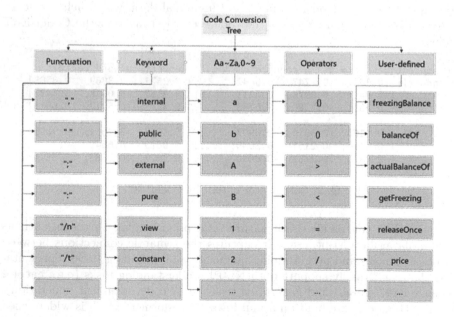

Fig. 4. Code conversion tree.

3 Approach

3.1 Overview

Figure 3 illustrates the overall framework of our model. Based on the comparison of word vector embedding similarity, the goal of the model is to perform two tasks: what's the detection of two code clones?; what's the detection of two code clones? Be more clear. The processing can be roughly divided into three steps. First, the two input source codes are normalized so that they can be used as input to the pre-training model; second the input source codes are transformed into word embedding vectors by the pre-training model; finally the similarity of the two codes is output following similarity comparison. To enable better similarity comparisons and reduce interference, the source code needs to be normalized; for this purpose, we build a code conversion tree, which is constructed to convert the input source code into a standard code that can be better used for feature extraction. An example of code conversion tree is shown in Fig. 4.

Figure 5 shows the output of the smart contract source code after standardising the code transformation tree. It can be seen that the standardized code has become more concise, in addition to retaining the logical semantic information of the source code.

```
function rollBlockNumber(address addr) public view returns (uint)
if rolls[addr].length > 0 return rolls[addr][0].blocknum
else return 0
```

Fig. 5. The converted contract code.

3.2 Embedding Similarity Comparison

In this stage, we compare the similarity of the word embedding vectors generated by the two smart contract source codes in order to determine the level of cloning present in the two code sets. Since we have more than 3800 smart contracts and more than 66000 functions extracted from these contracts, it would be computationally expensive (billions of comparisons) to compare them one by one. Thus, we here propose the small-batch random comparison method, which is able to perform cyclic comparisons with custom batch sizes and finally output similarity comparison results. Formally, the Cosine similarity formula is:

$$\textbf{Similarity} = \frac{\sum_{i=0}^{n}(a_i \times b_i)}{\sqrt{\sum_{i=0}^{n}(a_i)^2} \times \sqrt{\sum_{i=0}^{n}(a_i)^2}}$$

3.3   Model Algorithm

To compare the similarity of two matrices effectively, we propose an algorithm as shown in Algorithm 1. The purpose of this algorithm is to perform a straightening operation on the obtained two-dimensional word vectors,

$\mathbb{C}^{m \times n} \to \mathbb{C}^m$, which can reduce one layer of loops during the operation and thus increase the computational speed. The idea of using this algorithm is that we want to transform the calculation of similarity by comparing two matrix vectors and then summing them. The computational efficiency is improved by 1.3% compared with the original method by directly calling the cosine similarity library function through experimental calculations.

Algorithm 1: algorithm1

    Data: intputvector1   intputvector2
    Result: value
1 $m \leftarrow intputvector1.row$;
2 $n \leftarrow intputvector2.row$;
3 $V1$ $V2 \leftarrow empty$;
4 **while** $i \leq n$ *and* $j \leq m$ **do**
5   **if** $intputvector1[i][\;] \neq \emptyset$ **then**
6 | $V1$ *append* $intputvector1[i][\;]$;
7   **end**
8   **if** $intputvector2[j][\;] \neq \emptyset$ **then**
9 | $V2$ *append* $intputvector1[i][\;]$;
10   **end**
11     $i \leftarrow i + 1$;
12     $j \leftarrow j + 1$;
13 **end**
14 $value \leftarrow Compare(V1\;\;V2)$;
15 **return** value

---

4   Experiments

In this section, we will analyze the constructed model, then use this model to perform a code cloning analysis on our collection of 3814 smart contracts. Throughout this section, we will answer three research questions:

RQ1:What are the characteristics of the dataset after pre-processing?

RQ2:How can code cloning analysis of timestamp vulnerabilities be performed?

RQ3:What is the relation between code cloning and code vulnerability?

4.1 Data Collection and Pre-processing

We collected 3814 smart contracts containing the timestamp keyword from real Ethereum contracts. To facilitate better validation of our approach, we extract totally 1,201,365 functions from 3,814 contracts; after data cleaning (such as remove duplicate functions), 66,000 functions remained, As shown in Table 1, we can observe that data cleaning has produced a reduction in the number of functions of 94.5%. At the same time, the remaining 66,000 functions contain 62,136 functions with timestamp vulnerabilities, accounting for 94.1% (compared to 5.3% without data cleaning). This will be more conducive to our analysis of timestamp vulnerabilities in smart contracts.

Table 1. Timestamp vulnerability statistics table

Functions	Numbers	
	Contains timestamp vulnerability	*Percentage*
1,201,365	63598	5.3%
66,000	62136	94.1%

Furthermore, we cluster remaining 66,000 functions extracted from the smart contracts by code length and perform a clustering analysis on these functions. Figure 6 shows the clustering statistics by function character length for all 66,000 functions. Similarly, Fig. 7 shows the clustering statistics by function character length for the same contract. The top ten groups and their sizes are marked in red in both graphs. This provides reference dependent data for our subsequent analysis.

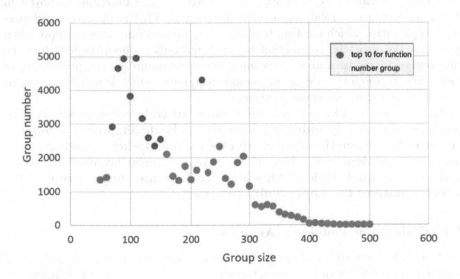

Fig. 6. The clustering effect after collecting all functions.

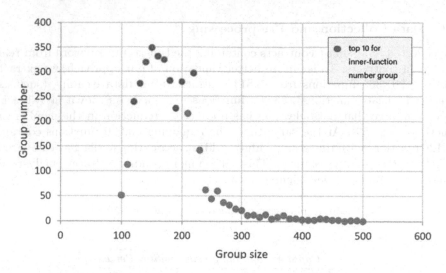

Fig. 7. The clustering effect after collecting the same functions.

From Fig. 6 and Fig. 7 we can draw three conclusions:

First, the graph shows that there are few functions longer than 400 charac-ters(accounting for only 4.3% of the total). This is because smart contracts are a kind of enforced code, and their execution requires a certain amount of gas (equivalent to the transaction tax rate in Ethernet, which is generally small); thus, the functions deployed on top of smart contracts are usually relatively short for the purpose of achieving basic functionality. This reduces not only the chance of code errors, but also the overall costs.

Second, as can be seen in Fig. 7, the length of the functions deployed in the same contract is relatively evenly distributed. This is because developers tend to prioritize which existing templates and formed functions to apply when using functions to achieve functionality; this not only reduces the length of the development cycle to improve efficiency, but also minimizes the probability of code errors through the use of ready-made templates, which is why there is a lot of code reuse in current smart contracts.

Conclusion 1: There is a large amount of code reuse in smart con-tracts, which greatly reduces the length of the development. However, because the transactions are conducted on the blockchain, when smart contracts are deployed, they often involve a large amount of money and account information. This gives hackers and other people with ulterior motives the opportunity to attack.

4.2   Code Clone Detection Analysis

First of all, in order to speed up the code comparison and make the experimental results more reflective of the characteristics of smart contracts, we compare the results from the same contract and from different contracts, respectively. In order to be able to show the difference between the code similarity among all functions and the code similarity of functions in the same contract, we conducted experiments on each of the 66,000 functions using Algorithm 1. The experimental results are shown in Figs. 8 and Fig. 9. Specifically, Fig. 8 shows the results of similarity comparison for functions from different contracts, while Fig. 9 shows the results of similarity comparison for functions in the same contract.

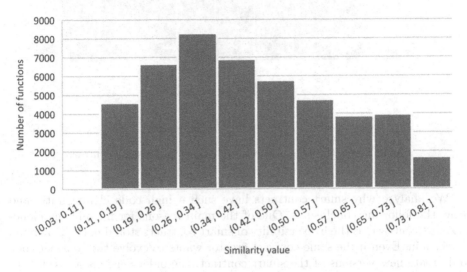

Fig. 8. Similarity comparison for functions from different contracts.

From Fig. 8 and Fig. 9, we can easily draw the following three conclusions:

First, in Fig. 8, 99.2% of the code similarity exceeds 0.11, while in Fig. 9, 98.8% of the code similarity is more than 0.16. From this, we can determine that most of the code in Ethernet is very similar, with many functions directly using ready-made templates and altering relatively small parts to achieve the desired result. This also confirms why the irrelevant code is streamlined so much when we perform code cleaning.

Second, as can be seen from the two graphs, most of the results are concentrated in the middle: this is true for 62.3% of results in Fig. 8, compared to 59.1% in Fig. 9. This shows that the code similarity between different contracts tends to be higher, because many contracts tend to reuse function templates with a single function to achieve their goals from a security perspective.

We further performed a comprehensive investigation of the contract pairs at different similarity ranges. Specifically, we randomly sampled 100 pairs at different ranges and manually examined their source code. We concluded that 0.7 is the best threshold, i.e., a contract pair with a similarity score higher than 0.7 will be regarded as a similar pair, which is in line with other fuzzy hashing-based code clone detection studies [26].

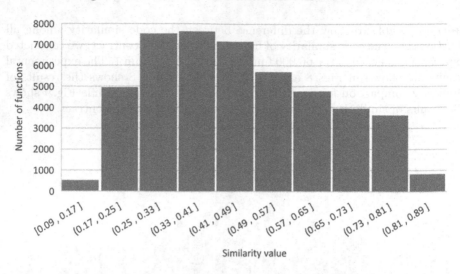

Fig. 9. Similarity comparison for functions in the same contract.

We analyze why smart contracts have such a high code cloning ratio and draw the following conclusions. One of the main reasons for introducing clones in smart contracts is the irreversibility of smart contracts stored in the Ethereum blockchain. Even if the same contract creator wants to evolve the contract code and create new versions of the smart contract, the older versions are still kept visible in the block-chain. We consider such a scenario, and recount all the clones by creator addresses (i.e., if the detected clones are code belonging to the same creator, we do not report them). Notably, these clone results still exhibit a considerable high clone ratio 51 % for similarity threshold 0.95 on contract level, reflecting the fact that cloning contracts across different creators is more common in this context that for other types of software. ERC20 is the main technical metrics for the imple-mentation of tokens. The standardization allows con- tracts to operate on different tokens seamlessly, thus boosting interoperability between smart contracts. From the implementation perspective, ERC20 are interfaces defining a set of functions and events, such as totalSupply(), balanceOf(address owner), transfer(address to, uint value).

Finally, in order to better verify the practicality of our approach, we compare it with solidity-nicad and SmartEmbed Tool. The configuration of the experimental machine used for our comparison experiments is as follows: processor: AMD Ryzen 7 5800H with Radeon Graphics 3.20 GHz, memory: 16.0 GB RAM, graphics card: NVIDIA GeForce RTX 3060 Laptop GPU. In order to simplify the experiment, we compare 66,000 pairs of code, and selected experimental results greater than 0.7 as indicating the existence of code clones. The results of the statistics are shown in Table 2.

Table 2. Comparison experiments

Methods	Standard		
	experiment codes	*code clones*	*Percentage*
solidity-nicad	66000	2769	4.19%
SmartEmbed Tool	66000	3241	4.91%
pre-train	**66000**	**3424**	**5.18%**

Conclusion 2: The analysis of the experimental results yields the conclusion that if the similarity of the two codes exceeds 0.7, they can be considered code clones.

4.3 Vulnerability Detection Analysis

To further discuss the properties of code cloning in depth, we first assume that two segments with high code similarity tend to inherit their vulnerabilities from each other. Drawing from the Conclusion 2, we manually collected 120 functions (100 of which contained timestamp vulnerabilities) selected from the functions with code similarity above 0.7, because this approach is more targeted. We cloned each of the above 120 functions with a standard timestamp vulnerability code at different thresholds; for the code pairs that exceeded these thresholds, we considered that there was a code vulnerability. Finally, we used manual verification to determine whether the reported code pairs actually have timestamp vulnerabilities. The statistical results are presented in Table 3.

As can be seen from the table, when the threshold is set relatively high, there are fewer vulnerability reports, but the corresponding accuracy increases. Conversely, if the threshold is set low, more vulnerability will be reported, but with a corresponding decrease in accuracy.

Table 3. Accuracy of vulnerability detection under different thresholds

Threshold	TimeStamp vulnerability		
	bugs reported	*Real Vulnerability*	*precision*
0.9	87	81	93.3%
0.8	96	86	89.5%
0.7	113	97	85.8%

Conclusion 3: The data in the table allows us to answer question 3 posed earlier. Code cloning often increases the risk of code vulnerabilities. In addition, code pairs with code similarity over 0.9 tend to inherit each other's vulnerabilities.

5   Conclusion

We propose a method for code similarity comparison based on pre-trained models, which is capable of code clone analysis and code vulnerability detection. In our experiments, we first verified the effectiveness of the method; second, we analyzed the similarity of 3814 contracts, finding that more than 90% of smart contracts have code cloning problems(some smart contracts simply change the judgment conditions, while the rest of the code is basically unchanged); third, we identified many smart contracts that are mostly manually marked data, which is not only time-consuming but also inefficient. Subsequently, we can use machine learning to automatically select contracts with timestamp vulnerabilities for marking. We hope that our work can provide a useful reference for peer research on smart contract code cloning, as well as enable the developers of smart contract to find smart contract loopholes in advance and thereby reduce economic losses.

Acknowledgments. This work is partially supported by the National Key Research and Development Project of China (No. 2020YFB1711900).

References

1. Bitcoin official website. https://bitcoin.org/en/
2. Ethereum official website. https://www.ethereum.org/
3. Wikipedia of ethereum. https://en.wikipedia.org/wiki/Ethereum/
4. Solidity. https://en.wikipedia.org/wiki/Solidity/
5. Official fomo3d website. https://exitscam.me/
6. Davey, N., Barson, P., Field, S., Frank, R., Tansley, D.: The development of a software clone detector. IJAST, 1(3/4) (1995)
7. Bailey, J., Burd, E.: Evaluating clone detection tools for use during preventative maintenance. In: SCAM 2002 (2002)
8. Rieger, M.: Effective clone Detection Without Language Barriers. PhD thesis (2005)
9. Walenstein, A., Lakhotia, A.: The software similarity problem in malware analysis. In: Dagstuhl Seminar Proceedings (2007)
10. Baker, B.: On finding duplication and near-duplication in large software systems. In: WCRE 1995
11. Brixtel, R., Fontaine, M., Lesner, B., Bazin, C., Robbes, R.: Language-independent clone detection applied to plagiarism detection. In: SCAM 2010 (2010)
12. Jiang, L., Su, Z., Chiu, E.: Context-based detection of clone-related bugs. In: ESEC/FSE 2007
13. Lo, D., Jiang, L., Budi, A.: Active refinement of clone anomaly reports. In: ICSE 2012 (2012)
14. Wang, X., Dang, Y., Zhang, L., Zhang, D., Lan, E., Mei, H.: Can i clone this piece of code here? In: ASE 2012 (2012)
15. Dang, Y., Zhang, D., Ge, S., Chu, C., Qiu, Y., Xie, T.: Xiao: tuning code clones at hands of engineers inpractice. In: ACSAC 2012
16. Milea, N., Jiang, L., Khoo, S.: Scalable detection of missed cross-function refactorings. In: ISSTA 2014 (2014)

17. Milea, N., Jiang, L., Khoo, S.: Vector abstraction and concretization for scalable detection of refactorings. In: FSE 2014 (2014)
18. Roy, C., Cordy, J.: A survey on software clone detection research. Queen's University, Technical report (2007)
19. Johnson, J.H.: Identifying redundancy in source code using fingerprints. In: CASCON 1993 (1993)
20. Johnson, J.H.: Visualizing textual redundancy in legacy source. In: CASCON 1994 (1994)
21. Baker, B.: A program for identifying duplicated code. In: Computer Science and Statistics (1992)
22. Baker, B." Parameterized pattern matching: algorithms and applications. JCSS, **52**(1) (1996)
23. Tai, K.S., Socher, R., Manning, C.D.: Improved semantic rep-resentations from tree-structured long short-term memory networks
24. Zhang, P., Xiao, F., Luo, X.: A framework and dataset for bugs in ethereum smart contracts. In: 2020 IEEE International Conference on Software Maintenance and Evolution (ICSME), pp. 139–150. IEEE (2020)
25. Mikolov, T., Sutskever, I., Chen, K., Corrado, G.S., Dean, J.: Distributed representations of words and phrases and their compositionality. In: Proceedings of 26th International Conference Neural Information Processing System, pp. 3111–3119 (2013)
26. Zhou, W., Zhou, Y., Jiang, X., Ning, P.: Detecting repackaged smartphone applications in third-party android marketplaces. In: Proceedings of the second ACM Conference on Data and Application Security and Privacy, pp. 317–326. ACM (2012)
27. Chen, T., et al.: Understanding ethereum via graph analysis. In: IEEE INFOCOM 2018-IEEE Conference on Computer Communications, pp. 1484–1492. IEEE (2018)

MF-Net: Encrypted Malicious Traffic Detection Based on Multi-flow Temporal Features

Guangchun Yue, Yanlong Zhai, Meng Shen$^{(\boxtimes)}$, Jizhe Jia, and Liehuang Zhu

School of Cyberspace Science and Technology, Beijing Institute of Technology,
Beijing 100081, China
{yueguangchun,ylzhai,shenmeng,jiajizhe,liehuangz}@bit.edu.cn

Abstract. Malicious attacks on the network continue to increase, seriously undermining cyberspace security. As the cost of Transport Layer Security(TLS) deployment decreases, attackers generally use encrypted traffic for camouflage to avoid network intrusion detection. Existing malicious traffic detection methods mainly focus on extracting traffic features at the single-flow level, but they have lost their effectiveness due to frequent malware updates and traffic obfuscation. In this paper, we propose MF-Net, an encrypted malicious traffic detection method based on multi-flow temporal features. We present a traffic representation named Multi-Flow Bytes Picture (MFBytesPic), which leverages the temporal features among multiple flows. Using MFBytesPic, we design a powerful Siamese Neural Network based classifier to effectively identify malicious traffic. In order to prove the effectiveness of MF-Net, we use a public dataset provided by Qi An Xin for experimental evaluation. Experimental results show that MF-Net outperforms Graph Neural Network based multi-flow method. MF-Net can achieve 98.13% accuracy and 98.10% F1 score using 5 flows, which enables effective encrypted malicious traffic detection.

Keywords: Encrypted Malicious Traffic Detection · Multi-Flow ·
Temporal Features · Siamese Neural Network · Traffic Analysis

1 Introduction

Network traffic encryption has become one of the development trends of the Internet. While encryption technology protects the privacy of user transmission data, it has also become an important means of hacker attacks. Attackers generally use encrypted traffic to transmit network data for evading detection, and they usually use malware to carry out remote attacks. In the field of blockchain, malicious attackers use encrypted traffic camouflage to mine illegal cryptocurrency [1]. Therefore, timely and effective detection of malicious traffic is crucial to protect user security and privacy.

Building an efficient and accurate method for detecting malicious traffic is very challenging. *Firstly*, due to the frequent version updates of malware [2], the features used by many detection methods are invalid, or classifiers need to be

J. Chen et al. (Eds.): BlockSys 2023, CCIS 1897, pp. 58–71, 2024.
https://doi.org/10.1007/978-981-99-8104-5_5

retrained, which incurs significant costs; *Secondly*, some attackers may interfere with traffic features, such as adding noise to malicious traffic using normal traffic packets [3], which further reduces the available information; The *third* challenge is acquiring robust features to deal with emerging malware attacks, such as zero-day attacks.

Traditional machine learning methods [4–7] often require manual feature design, which is not conducive to automatic deployment; further, although deep learning methods [8–12] can automatically extract features, they only focus on features at the packet-level or single-flow level. However, the associated features between flows are not taken into account. Recent studies [2, 11, 12] have noticed the association between traffic flows to improve the representation ability of features. They construct multiple flows into a traffic interaction graph and use a classifier to detect them. However, they ignored the multi-flow temporal features.

A recent work [13] notice that the flow-level sequence information of adjacent flows is conducive to traffic identification, but their consideration of multiple flows is too simplistic, only pre-arranging flows into sequences and ignoring information about packets. The design motivation of MF-Net is that when a normal service or malicious attack initiates a network request behavior, it will generate multiple flows temporally, which undertake different data transmission contents and return them to the requester. This inspires us that we can extract these association features and fully consider the association information of multiple flows temporally.

In this paper, we propose MF-Net, an encrypted malicious traffic detection method based on multi-flow temporal features, which provides a new idea for malicious traffic detection. Like the one-dimensional time series, we use a flow representation of MFBytesPic to map the multi-flow temporal information in three-dimensional space, and retain the rich packet association information contained in each flow in two-dimensional space. With MFBytesPic, we successfully construct a set of multiple flows into a unified sample, which can be trained and classified using our model. The main contributions are summarized as follows:

- We propose an encrypted malicious traffic detection framework MF-Net based on a siamese neural network, which can learn not only the association features between traffic packets, but also the association features between multiple flows.
- We propose a traffic representation named MFBytesPic, which provides efficient and reliable information. MFBytesPic maps the bytes sequence of each flow in the captured traffic package to a single picture, and reconstructs each picture of multiple flows in temporal order, taking full advantage of the temporal features between multiple flows.
- To verify the effectiveness of our method, we conduct extensive and comprehensive experiments using a public dataset provided by Qi An Xin. When using 5 flows, the accuracy of the model is more than 98%, which is significantly better than similar method, and is much lower than its time cost.

The rest of the paper is organized as follows. We summarise the related work in Sect. 2. Then, we present the traffic representation and methodology in

Sect. 3. In Sect. 4, we introduce the dataset and evaluate the performance of the proposed method, then compare it with a previous multi-flow approach. Finally, this paper is concluded in Sect. 5.

2   Related Work

Encrypted malicious traffic detection generally includes rule-based, packet-level, and flow-level methods. This section mainly summarizes the flow-level methods, which are divided into single-flow level and multi-flow level methods.

2.1   Single-Flow Level Methods

Some studies take one single flow as the input to the model and classify it using machine learning or deep learning methods. CUMUL [4] uses cumulative packet lengths to represent traffic traces, and then trains an SVM model to classify; k-FP [6] uses random forest to extract feature vectors from statistical features, and then performs the k-Nearest Neighbor(k-NN) algorithm to classify; FS-Net [8] uses a single flow sequence as input to the model and constructs an end-to-end model using a multi-layer encoder-decoder structure; DF [9] extracts fingerprint features from the directional sequence of a single flow and uses a well-designed CNN model to classify Tor traffic; GraphDApp [10] constructs a TIG for the upflow and downflow packets of a flow to transform the encrypted traffic classification problem into a graph classification problem; FC-Net [14] proposes a few-shot malicious traffic detection method based on meta-learning framework, and mainly uses the association information of adjacent packets in a flow. These methods mentioned above are based on the sequence or statistical features of a single flow for encrypted traffic recognition, but they ignore the association information between multiple flows and cannot provide robust features to face the challenge of traffic concepts drift, which refers to the change in the statistical distribution features of traffic over time.

2.2   Multi-flow Level Methods

Related studies have noticed that the adjacent flow information of multiple flows can provide more information to the classifier. FG-Net [11] notices the multiple flows information of flow-level bursts, constructs a multi-flow representation of FRG, and uses GNN classifier to classify; ST-Graph [2] constructs a host behavior interaction graph from the perspective of time and space, and finally uses RF algorithm to output suspicious malicious hosts; E-GraphSAGE [12] maps flow endpoints to graph nodes, network traffic to graph edges, and then uses a graph neural network method to classify graph edges to detect malicious network flows. Most of these methods build traffic interaction graphs for multiple flows and then use model to classify. This not only has a large model calculation overhead, but also ignores the temporal information of multiple flows.

3   Methodology

In this Sect. 3, we present an overview and specific details of our approach. First, in Sect. 3.1, we describe the data processing and traffic representation in detail. Then, we present an overview and steps of our approach in Sect. 3.2. Finally, in Sect. 3.3, we propose the construction of the model.

3.1   Traffic Representation

Traffic representation is extremely important for traffic analysis [15,16]. In studies related to encrypted traffic analysis, the object of study can be at packet-level, flow-level, or host-level, etc. In this paper, we take the flow-level traffic as the research object. A session flow [17] is composed of a set of packets with the same five-tuple, namely source IP, source port, destination IP, destination port and protocol (where the source and destination addresses are interchangeable).

Whether a normal service establishes a TCP connection or a malicious attack initiates a single attack, they use similar patterns to generate traffic:

1) Both generate multiple flows of encrypted traffic in temporal order;
2) Each flow contains multiple associated packets.

Previous studies [8] generally represent the original flow as a sequence of message types or packet lengths with the same flow length, or add timestamp information, but some important packet header information will be left out. In order to make full use of the information of the packet and the previous two related information, we sample the byte sequence of multiple flows as the input of the model [14]. The first M packets of a session flow can usually contain the process of establishing a connection as long as they are reasonably selected; the first N bytes of each packet can contain the packet header and a portion of the payload data if they are reasonably selected.

In order to take full advantage of the association features between packets and between multiple flows, we reconstruct the traffic representation of multiple flows and give the following two definitions.

Definition 1. *(FlowBytesPic).* A FlowBytesPic contains the first M packets of one flow $F_i = (P_1, P_2, ..., P_j, ..., P_M)$, in which P_j represents the jth packet in F_i, and each packet contains the first N bytes, so it is an $M * N$ bytes picture.

Definition 2. *(MFBytesPic).* A MFBytesPic refers to multiple flows in temporal generated when accessing a normal service or a malware, $MF = (F_1, F_2, ..., F_i, ..., F_N)$, where F_i is the ith flow. We construct a FlowBytesPic for each flow and then combine them in temporal order. Thus, this is a set of bytes pictures with dimension $(flows, packets, bytes)$ as shown in the Fig. 1.

Based on the above definitions, we structure the traffic input, using MFBytesPic as the input to the model below.

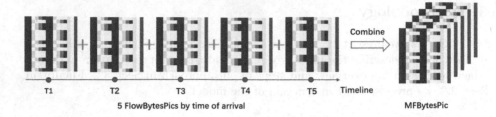

Fig. 1. Visualization of one MFBytesPic.

3.2 System Overview

To achieve accurate and efficient detection of malicious traffic, we use siamese neural network [18–20] as a classifier. The siamese neural network is composed of two neural networks that share weights. It uses two samples as input, and its two sub-networks each receive an input, and then output their feature representations embedded in high-dimensional spaces. Finally, the similarity of the two samples is compared by calculating the distance between the two feature representations.

We construct a binary classification model based on siamese neural network, aiming to distinguish malicious traffic from normal traffic. MF-Net consists of the following three main steps, as shown in the Fig. 2:

1) *Data Preprocess.* Collect the normal or malicious traffic of each request on the node of the target network and save it in a traffic package(e.g., a pcap file), and divide the traffic package of each request according to the five-tuple, construct the MFBytesPic mentioned in Sect. 3.1;
2) *Feature Extraction.* MF-Net takes a pair of MFBytesPic as input without manual feature selection and fine-tuning, as the feature extractor can automatically get a pair of feature vectors;
3) *Traffic Classification.* The unknown sample and a number of samples with known labels are formed into separate groups and input into MF-Net, and their distances are compared to derive the similarity. The label of the unknown sample is obtained according to the one with the smallest distance.

3.3 MF-Net Construction

We make full use of the temporal features of multiple flows and reconstruct them in the form of MFBytesPic. Therefore, we choose a three dimensional siamese neural network as the basic model. This section describes how MF-Net works in detail.

Problem Formulation. We use C as the number of classification targets. Since we construct a binary classification model, C is 2. Randomly sample k malicious samples and k normal samples to obtain a sample set, denoted as $S = \{(x_1, y_1), (x_i, y_i), ..., (x_{2k}, y_{2k})\}, y_i \in \mathbb{R}^C$.

Model Inputs. We take one MFBytesPic as the model input for a single CNN and a pair of MFBytesPic for MF-Net, denoted as (x_1, x_2, Y), where $Y = 1$

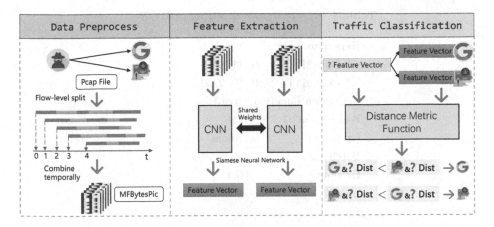

Fig. 2. The overview of MF-Net.

means samples from the same category, i.e., positive samples, and $Y = 0$ means samples from different categories, i.e., negative samples. The purpose of training the network is to make the distance of the positive samples small enough and the distance of the negative samples large enough.

Feature Extraction. We still select Convolutional Neural Network as the backbone of the siamese neural network because the input of the model we construct is a set of images, and CNN has better classification effect on images. A pair of MFBytesPic (x_1, x_2, Y) is input to two CNNs with the same structure sharing weights to obtain the corresponding feature vectors F_1 and F_2, respectively, as shown in Eq. 1.

$$F(i) = G(x_i; w), F(i) \in \mathbb{R}^{C*T} \tag{1}$$

where w is the parameter set in the model and w is exactly the same in both networks. C is the number of channels and is equal to the number of labels and T is the length of the feature map.

Model Architecture. The feature extraction network consists of 3–4 blocks. Each block contains a 3D Convolutional layer [14], a BatchNorm (BN) layer, an activation function, and a dropout layer. According to the number of flows, the Convolutional layer of each block is slightly different. Because the input with fewer flows has a smaller depth, and it cannot be convoluted in the depth dimension, so the association features of multiple flows cannot be extracted. The hyperparameters of the model are shown in the Table 1.

Classification. Calculate the Euclidean distance between two feature vectors to compare the similarity, as shown in Eq. 2, in the test phase, it is necessary to compare the similarity between the sample to be tested and all support set samples, and finally obtain the label with the smallest distance as the output.

$$E(x_1, x_2; w) = \|F_1, F_2)\|_2 \tag{2}$$

Table 1. Hyperparameters setting of MF-Net.

Hyperparameter	Final
4 * Conv3D ($F \leq 2$)	(1, 2, 2)
3 * Conv3D ($F > 2$)	(2, 2, 2)
Activation Function	RELU
BatchNorm3D	128
Optimizer	Adam
Batch Size	15
Dropout	0.4
Epoch	200
F	[1, 2, 3, 4, 5]
K	[5, 7, 9, 11, 13, 15]
N	[16, 32, 64, 128]

Loss Function. When training the model, it is necessary to use the loss function to update the parameters of the feature extraction network through the gradient backpropagation algorithm until the parameters of the network converge. Usually the siamese neural network uses contrastive loss [19] as the loss function. Thus, we also use this loss function, the specific definition is as shown in Eq. 3:

$$\mathcal{L} = \frac{1}{2\,\mathrm{N}} \sum_{n=1}^{N} Y {E_w}^2 + (1 - Y) \max(\mathrm{m} - \mathrm{E_w}, 0)^2 \tag{3}$$

where d represents the Euclidean distance between the feature vectors of two samples, Y is the label of whether the two samples match, $Y = 1$ represents that the two samples are similar or matched, $Y = 0$ represents that they are not similar or matched, and m is the set threshold.

4   Performance Evaluation

In this Sect. 4, we first introduce the dataset used in the experiment in Sect. 4.1, and analyze the content of this dataset. Then, in Sect. 4.2, we describe the setting of the experiment, including implementation details, evaluation metrics and comparison method. Finally, we introduce the evaluation results of the experiment in Sect. 4.3.

4.1   Evaluation Dataset

Although there are many publicly available malicious traffic datasets, the following two points must be met to verify the effectiveness of this method:

1) The traffic generated by accessing a normal service or a malicious attack is stored in a separate traffic package(e.g., a pcap file) and cannot be merged;
2) The number of temporal single flows in a traffic package is variable.

Based on the above two points, we select a public dataset of Encrypted Malicious Traffic (EMT) [21] from Qi An Xin Technology Research Institute. EMT is generated through Qi An Xin Technology Research Institute's sandbox and collects the traffic generated by it. EMT originates from malware and normal software collected from February to June 2020. Malicious traffic in EMT is encrypted traffic generated by malicious software (both exe type), and white traffic is encrypted traffic generated by normal software (both exe type). The content of the traffic is TLS/SSL packets generated on port 443. The size of EMT is shown in the Table 2. Unlike the division method of itself, we redivided the training set and test set in the experiment, see below for details.

Table 2. The number of black and white samples in the dataset EMT.

Numbers	Black Samples	White Samples
Train	3000	3000
Test	2000	2000
Total	5000	5000

As shown in the Fig. 3, in order to count *the number of flows for each sample* (denoted as F) in the dataset, we plot the cumulative histogram for all black samples'F in the EMT. It can be found that the number of black flows has exceeded 75% of the total number of samples when F is greater than 5. Therefore, in the next experiments, we choose the sample set with F in the range of 1 to 5 for evaluation, and divide this new dataset into a training set and a test set according to 8:2.

4.2 Experiment Setting

Implementation Details. All experiments are performed on a server equipped with Intel Core i7-13700K@3.40 GHz, 32.0 GB RAM, NVIDIA GeForce RTX 3080, and the neural network using a configuration of Pytorch 2.0.0, CUDA 11.8.

Evaluation Metrics. In order to verify the effectiveness of the proposed method, we use the evaluation metrics commonly adopted in the binary classification model. For binary classification, we can get a confusion matrix that contains four elements: true positive (TP), false positive (FP), true negative (TN) and false negative (FN) [14,15]:

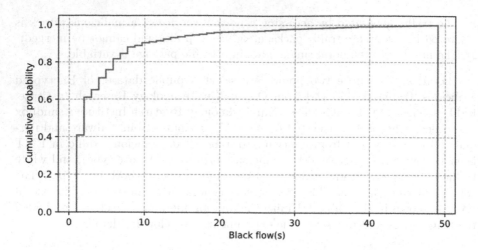

Fig. 3. The cumulative histogram for all black samples'F.

1) True Positive (TP): White samples are predicted as white ones;
2) False Positive (FP): White samples are misreported as black ones;
3) True Negative (TN): Black samples are classified as black ones;
4) False Negative (FN): Black samples are classified as white ones.

Based on above elements, we consider four metrics to measure the classifier. The calculation formulas are as follows:

Accuracy is calculated according to Eq. 4

$$Accuracy = \frac{TP + TN}{TP + TN + FP + FN} \tag{4}$$

FPR is calculated according to Eq. 5

$$FPR = \frac{FP}{TN + FP} \tag{5}$$

Precision is calculated according to Eq. 6

$$Prec = \frac{TP}{TP + FP} \tag{6}$$

F1 is calculated according to Eq. 7

$$F1 = \frac{2 \times Prec \times Recall}{Prec + Recall} \tag{7}$$

Comparison Method. Currently, relatively few works focus on multi-flow. To provide a comprehensive evaluation of this work, we compare our approach with a GNN based approach. *E-GraphSAGE* [12] is a network intrusion detection method for graph neural network that captures edge features and topological information of the graph for network intrusion detection in IoT networks.

4.3   Evaluation Results

A. Multi-flow Number Experiment (variable F, $K = 5$, $N = 16$)

We first verify the results of a sample containing different numbers of flows as model input. We conduct comprehensive experiments in the range of F from 1 to 5 and compatible with single flow scenario. As shown in the Table 3, when $F \geq 2$, the accuracy rate is above 80%, and as F decreases, the accuracy of the model gradually decreases. When the model degenerates into a traditional single-flow model, the accuracy drops significantly, by nearly 10%. Therefore, through comparative experiments with multiple flows, it can be verified that our model can effectively extract association features from the inputs of multiple flows. Our method fully utilizes the information of associated features and improves the accuracy of the model.

Table 3. Multi-flow number experiment result.

F	Accuracy	FPR	Prec	F1
1	0.7987	0.2103	0.7850	0.7964
2	0.8147	0.1884	0.8052	0.8115
3	0.8547	0.1590	0.8381	0.8533
4	0.8692	0.1272	0.8786	0.8721
5	0.8815	0.1303	0.8687	0.8810

B. Sample Number Experiment (variable K, $F = 5$, $N = 16$)

In the previous multi-flow comparison experiment, we verify that the model performs best when $F = 5$. Therefore, we use the case of $F = 5$ as input to verify the effect of different sample numbers K. We conduct extensive experiments in the range [5, 15], with an interval of 2. As shown in the Table 4, when $K < 10$, the model performs generally, and the accuracy, precision and F1 are all within 90%. Even if the K in the sample set is increased, the accuracy of the model does not improve substantially because K increases too small.

Table 4. Sample number experiment result.

K	Accuracy	FPR	Prec	F1
5	0.8802	0.1134	0.8847	0.8792
7	0.8805	0.1356	0.8511	0.8745
9	0.8923	0.1035	0.8941	0.8911
11	0.9048	0.0921	0.9069	0.9043
13	0.9145	0.0898	0.9124	0.9156
15	0.9222	0.0947	0.9067	0.9228

When $K > 10$, the accuracy of the model is slightly improved, and the accuracy of the model is already higher than 90%. Therefore, it can be concluded that increasing K can slightly improve the accuracy of the model, but it needs to be increased to more than 10.

C. Packet-Byte Number Experiment (variable N, $F = 5$, $K = 15$)

Since in the first two experiments, our model performed best when $F = 5$ and $K = 15$. Therefore, the experiment continues to use these two parameters to experiment with the number of Packet-Byte N. It can be seen from the Table 5 that the more the first N bytes of the intercepted packet, the higher the accuracy of the model. It works best when $N = 128$. This is because the larger N is, the more effective information the packet contains, which is more beneficial to the model. In terms of the composition of the Transmission Control Protocol(TCP) packet, it contains a 14-byte Media Access Control (MAC) layer header, a 20-byte Internet Protocol (IP) layer header, a 20-byte Transmission Control Protocol (TCP) layer header and a payload [14]. The headers alone already have more than 54 bytes, so when $N = 128$, it contains the most payload information and the model works best.

Table 5. Packet-Byte number experiment result.

N	Accuracy	FPR	Prec	F1
16	0.9277	0.0776	0.9187	0.9259
32	0.9390	0.0756	0.9222	0.9381
64	0.9685	0.0319	0.9679	0.9684
128	0.9813	0.0295	0.9695	0.9810

D. Comparison Experiment

In order to conduct a comprehensive evaluation of our method, we compare it with E-GraphSAGE, a graph neural network method.

As shown in the Fig. 4, our method converges faster in terms of accuracy. As shown in the Table 6, only 180 epochs can achieve 81.93% accuracy, while E-GraphSAGE can only reach 65.01%. On the other hand, in terms of time overhead, our method is more than 300 times faster than E-GraphSAGE, which shows that our method is faster and easier to converge in model training.

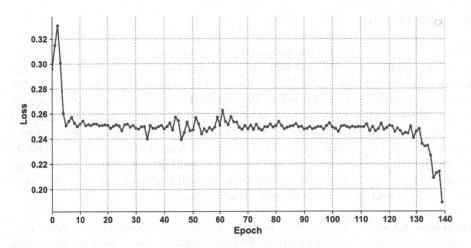

Fig. 4. The loss after per epoch during training.

Table 6. Comparison of accuracy and time between MF-Net and E-GraphSAGE.

Epoch	Accuracy		Training Time(s)	
	MF-Net	E-GraphSAGE	MF-Net	E-GraphSAGE
20	0.4895	0.4479	1.362	303.4669
40	0.5100	0.5449	1.361	372.2481
60	0.5152	0.4961	1.362	663.6882
80	0.5193	0.4535	1.347	413.0511
100	0.5420	0.4861	1.356	398.0021
120	0.5205	0.5634	1.122	404.8521
140	0.7730	0.5662	1.128	405.6571
160	0.7990	0.5920	1.133	682.3287
180	0.8193	0.6501	1.085	432.6441

E. Discussion

Through the extensive experiments presented above, we verify the effectiveness of MF-Net in multi-flow classification. We first conduct three sets of control variable experiments on F, K, and N. The experimental results show that the number of multiple flows, the number of samples, and the number of packet bytes all provide more valuable information to the model. We combine the information from the above three to effectively improve the accuracy of the malicious traffic detection model. Finally, we also verify that our method outperforms GNN based method in terms of efficiency and accuracy.

5   Conclusion

This paper proposes MF-Net, an encrypted malicious traffic detection method based on multi-flow temporal features. In order to take full advantage of the temporal features between multiple flows, we propose a multi-flow level traffic representation named MFBytesPic. We use MFBytesPic as input and carefully design a powerful Siamese Neural Network based classifier. To demonstrate the effectiveness of MF-Net, we conduct extensive experimental evaluations using a publicly available dataset provided by Qi An Xin. The experimental results show that MF-Net outperforms the multi-flow method based on GNN in terms of accuracy and efficiency. In future work, we will evaluate the effectiveness of MF-Net in detecting more malicious attack scenarios.

Acknowledgments. This work is partially supported by National Key R&D Program of China with No. 2020YFB1006100, China National Funds for Excellent Young Scientists with No. 62222201, Beijing Nova Program with Nos. Z201100006820006 and 20220484174, NSFC Project with No. 61972039, Beijing Natural Science Foundation with Nos. M23020, L222098 and 7232041.

References

1. Ye, K., Shen, M., Gao, Z., Zhu, L.: Real-time detection of cryptocurrency mining behavior. In: Svetinovic, D., Zhang, Y., Luo, X., Huang, X., Chen, X. (eds.) BlockSys 2022. CCIS, vol. 1679, pp. 278–291. Springer, Singapore (2022). https://doi.org/10.1007/978-981-19-8043-5_20
2. Fu, Z., et al.: Encrypted malware traffic detection via graph-based network analysis. In: Proceedings of the 25th International Symposium on Research in Attacks, Intrusions and Defenses, pp. 495–509 (2022)
3. Fu, C., Li, Q., Shen, M., Xu, K.: Realtime robust malicious traffic detection via frequency domain analysis. In: Proceedings of the 2021 ACM SIGSAC Conference on Computer and Communications Security, pp. 3431–3446 (2021)
4. Panchenko, A.: Website fingerprinting at internet scale. In: NDSS (2016)
5. Shen, M., Wei, M., Zhu, L., Wang, M.: Classification of encrypted traffic with second-order Markov chains and application attribute bigrams. IEEE Trans. Inf. Forensics Secur. **12**(8), 1830–1843 (2017)
6. Hayes, J., Danezis, G., et al.: K-fingerprinting: a robust scalable website fingerprinting technique. In: USENIX Security Symposium, pp. 1187–1203 (2016)
7. Shen, M., Liu, Y., Zhu, L., Du, X., Hu, J.: Fine-grained webpage fingerprinting using only packet length information of encrypted traffic. IEEE Trans. Inf. Forensics Secur. **16**, 2046–2059 (2020)
8. Liu, C., He, L., Xiong, G., Cao, Z., Li, Z.: FS-Net: a flow sequence network for encrypted traffic classification. In: IEEE Conference on Computer Communications, IEEE INFOCOM 2019, pp. 1171–1179. IEEE (2019)
9. Sirinam, P., Imani, M., Juarez, M., Wright, M.: Deep fingerprinting: undermining website fingerprinting defenses with deep learning. In: Proceedings of the 2018 ACM SIGSAC Conference on Computer and Communications Security, pp. 1928–1943 (2018)

10. Shen, M., Zhang, J., Zhu, L., Xu, K., Du, X.: Accurate decentralized application identification via encrypted traffic analysis using graph neural networks. IEEE Trans. Inf. Forensics Secur. **16**, 2367–2380 (2021)

11. Jiang, M., et al.: Accurate mobile-app fingerprinting using flow-level relationship with graph neural networks. Comput. Netw. **217**, 109309 (2022)

12. Lo, W.W., Layeghy, S., Sarhan, M., Gallagher, M., Portmann, M.: E-graphsage: a graph neural network based intrusion detection system for IoT. In: 2022 IEEE/IFIP Network Operations and Management Symposium, NOMS 2022, pp. 1–9. IEEE (2022)

13. Rezaei, S., Kroencke, B., Liu, X.: Large-scale mobile app identification using deep learning. IEEE Access **8**, 348–362 (2019)

14. Xu, C., Shen, J., Du, X.: A method of few-shot network intrusion detection based on meta-learning framework. IEEE Trans. Inf. Forensics Secur. **15**, 3540–3552 (2020)

15. Shen, M., et al.: Machine learning-powered encrypted network traffic analysis: a comprehensive survey. IEEE Commun. Surv. Tutor. **25**(1), 791–824 (2023)

16. Shen, M., Liu, Y., Zhu, L., Xu, K., Du, X., Guizani, N.: Optimizing feature selection for efficient encrypted traffic classification: a systematic approach. IEEE Netw. **34**(4), 20–27 (2020)

17. Shen, M., Gao, Z., Zhu, L., Xu, K.: Efficient fine-grained website fingerprinting via encrypted traffic analysis with deep learning. In: 2021 IEEE/ACM 29th International Symposium on Quality of Service (IWQOS), pp. 1–10. IEEE (2021)

18. Chopra, S., Hadsell, R., LeCun, Y.: Learning a similarity metric discriminatively, with application to face verification. In: 2005 IEEE Computer Society Conference on Computer Vision and Pattern Recognition (CVPR 2005), vol. 1, pp. 539–546. IEEE (2005)

19. Hadsell, R., Chopra, S., LeCun, Y.: Dimensionality reduction by learning an invariant mapping. In: 2006 IEEE Computer Society Conference on Computer Vision and Pattern Recognition (CVPR 2006), vol. 2, pp. 1735–1742. IEEE (2006)

20. Misra, I., van der Maaten, L.: Self-supervised learning of pretext-invariant representations. In: Proceedings of the IEEE/CVF Conference on Computer Vision and Pattern Recognition, pp. 6707–6717 (2020)

21. Dataset. https://datacon.qianxin.com/opendata/maliciousstream

Blockchain Applications

When Supply Chain Security Meets Blockchain: Applications and Challenges

Weijian Zhang[1], Li Di[1], Lijing Yan[2], Dingding Li[2], Wenjia Yu[3], and Jiajing Wu[3(✉)]

[1] State Grid Henan Electric Power Company, Zhengzhou 450018, China
{zhangweijian,dili}@ha.sgcc.com.cn
[2] State Grid Henan Information and Telecommunication Company (Data Center), Zhengzhou 450052, China
{yanlijing,lidingding1}@ha.sgcc.com.cn
[3] School of Computer Science and Engineering, Sun Yat-sen University, Guangzhou 510006, China
yuwj33@mail2.sysu.edu.cn, wujiajing@mail.sysu.edu.cn

Abstract. Supply chain security has always been an important issue concerned by enterprises and consumers. In the traditional supply chain system, security issues such as low transparency of transactions, low security of data storage, and difficulty in guaranteeing product safety have affected the healthy and orderly development of the supply chain. In recent years, as an emerging technology, blockchain has received more and more attention due to its characteristics, such as distributed storage and tamper-proof data. Several works have now started to study how blockchain technology can be applied to ensure supply chain security. In this paper, we first provide brief introductions to blockchain and the supply chain. We organize and summarize the existing literature on the application of blockchain in supply chain security management, which mainly includes logistics security, data security, and financial security. We also discuss the advantages and challenges of the application of blockchain technology in the supply chain.

Keywords: Blockchain · Supply chain · Security

1 Introduction

In recent years, the need for transparency, security, and efficiency in supply chains has grown significantly. Organizations have become increasingly aware of the risks associated with opaque supply chains, which include counterfeiting, fraud, and other types of criminal activity [9]. In response, there has been a growing interest in exploring new technologies that can help address these challenges. Blockchain technology has emerged as a promising solution, thanks to its potential to improve efficiency, security, and transparency across various industries.

One of the key advantages of blockchain technology is its ability to create a decentralized and immutable ledger of transactions. This means that the data

J. Chen et al. (Eds.): BlockSys 2023, CCIS 1897, pp. 75–88, 2024.
https://doi.org/10.1007/978-981-99-8104-5_6

recorded on the blockchain cannot be altered or deleted, and can be accessed and verified by all parties in the network. In supply chains, where there are numerous stakeholders involved in the movement of goods, this can significantly improve transparency and trust. The complexity of supply chain processes and the need for trust among different stakeholders make the blockchain technology an attractive solution for the industry.

Additionally, the use of blockchain technology in supply chains has the potential to reduce costs, improve efficiency, and enhance security. By leveraging the decentralized nature of the blockchain, organizations can streamline supply chain operations and reduce the time and resources required for data management. Moreover, the use of smart contracts, which are self-executing contracts with the terms of the agreement between buyer and seller directly written into lines of code, can automate various processes, including payments and dispute resolution. This can reduce the administrative burden and improve the speed and accuracy of transactions. Despite these advantages, the adoption of blockchain technology in supply chains is not without its challenges. One of the key challenges is scalability, as blockchain networks are currently limited in the number of transactions they can process per second. Interoperability is also a significant challenge, as different blockchains may have different technical specifications and may not be compatible with each other. Moreover, the regulatory environment around blockchain technology is still developing, and there is a need for greater clarity around issues such as data privacy and ownership.

In this paper, we will provide an overview of blockchain technology, including its basic concepts, characteristics, and applications. We will then focus on the demand for blockchain technology in the supply chain industry, including its benefits, such as improving efficiency, reducing costs, enhancing security and transparency, and ensuring product traceability and anti-counterfeiting. We will also analyze the challenges faced by blockchain technology in the supply chain industry, such as scalability, interoperability, and regulatory compliance. Furthermore, we will discuss in detail how blockchain technology can strengthen supply chain security, including logistics tracking and management, data security management, and supply chain finance. Finally, we will summarize the advantages and challenges of blockchain technology in the supply chain industry and emphasize its potential for future development.

Overall, this paper aims to contribute to the ongoing discussion of the role of blockchain technology in the supply chain industry. We will provide a comprehensive analysis of the benefits and challenges of adopting blockchain in the supply chain and emphasize the potential of blockchain technology to enhance supply chain security and transparency.

2 Blockchain Technology

2.1 Blockchain Technology Introduction

In 2008, a mysterious figure known as Satoshi Nakamoto published a white paper on blockchain titled "Bitcoin: A Peer-to-Peer Electronic Cash System"

[15]. This paper proposed a technology called "blockchain" for creating a decentralized electronic cash system based on cryptography. In this electronic cash system, all transaction records are stored in a decentralized database called blockchain, which is maintained by multiple nodes in the network, each having a complete database replica. When a transaction occurs, nodes in the network validate the transaction, package it into a new block, and record it on the blockchain. Each block contains the cryptographic hash value of the previous block, a timestamp, and the current transaction data. Figure 1 shows the basic structure of the blockchain. The core technologies of blockchain are decentralization and encryption algorithms. This means that blockchain does not rely on any central authority to manage and validate transactions, while all transaction records are encrypted to ensure data security and privacy. Although blockchain does not have a centralized management mechanism, all transaction records are encrypted and stored on multiple nodes in the network, and consensus mechanisms are adopted to make it difficult to tamper with transaction records once they are added to the blockchain. Overall, blockchain is a publicly transparent, decentralized digital ledger that enables secure and transparent transactions without the need for intermediaries.

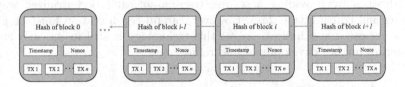

Fig. 1. The basic structure of the blockchain.

Originally designed as the foundational technology for the cryptocurrency Bitcoin, blockchain has gradually developed to support a wide range of applications beyond financial transactions, including supply chain management, gaming, and healthcare. These applications are all based on blockchain technology and provide secure, transparent, and efficient solutions for various business scenarios.

In general, the origin of blockchain technology can be traced back to the emergence of Bitcoin. Through decentralized and cryptographic technologies, blockchain provides a secure, transparent, and decentralized way of storing and exchanging data, becoming an important technology in today's internet field.

2.2 Classification

There are several types of blockchain technology, each with its own unique characteristics and use cases. The main types of blockchain technology include public Blockchain, private Blockchain, and consortium Blockchain.

Public Blockchain. The public blockchain is a decentralized blockchain technology that is open to anyone. It is a transparent distributed ledger that relies on a network of nodes to verify transactions and maintain the integrity of the network, without the need for a central authority. Data on a public blockchain is immutable, meaning that once data is recorded on the blockchain, it cannot be altered or deleted. Bitcoin is an example of a public blockchain.

In a public blockchain, transactions are verified and recorded through a consensus mechanism, such as PoW(proof-of-work) or PoS(proof-of-stake) [34]. This consensus mechanism ensures the integrity of the data on the blockchain and prevents any fraudulent or malicious activity from occurring. One of the key features of the public blockchain is its openness. Anyone can join the network, view the transactions and data stored on the blockchain, and participate in the verification process. This creates a level of transparency and trust that is difficult to achieve with traditional centralized systems. Another advantage of a public blockchain is its adaptability to attacks. Because the network is decentralized, there is no single point of failure that can be targeted by malicious actors. Furthermore, the use of cryptography and consensus mechanisms ensures that data on the blockchain is secure and tamper-proof.

Overall, public blockchain has the potential to fundamentally transform various industries by providing a secure, transparent, and decentralized way of recording and transmitting data. However, careful consideration must be given to their use cases and limitations, as this technology is still in its early stages and requires further development and refinement.

Private Blockchain. The private blockchain is a type of blockchain technology designed for exclusive use by a particular organization or group of organizations, licensed and controlled by a single entity or a group of entities [10]. They are typically used for enterprise applications that require higher levels of security and privacy and are commonly used in supply chain management applications. Unlike public blockchains, which are decentralized and open to anyone, private blockchains are permissioned, meaning only authorized participants have access. This allows private blockchains to maintain a high level of privacy and control over their network and data.

In private blockchains, participating nodes are typically pre-selected and trusted entities that collaborate to maintain the integrity of the network and verify transactions. The consensus mechanism used in private blockchains may vary depending on the network's requirements but typically involves fewer nodes than public blockchains [26]. Private blockchains typically use more energy-efficient consensus mechanisms, such as proof of authority, which enables faster transaction processing and reduces the required computing resources.

One of the key advantages of private blockchains is the level of control they provide to their owners. Private blockchains can be customized to meet the specific needs of the organizations using them, offering greater flexibility in data management, privacy, and security. Additionally, private blockchains can support smart contracts, automating the execution of contract terms and conditions, reducing the need for intermediaries and increasing efficiency.

However, private blockchains also face some challenges. Limiting access and centralizing control can raise concerns about transparency and auditability. Additionally, the scalability of private blockchains may be limited as the number of nodes is smaller and consensus needs to be reached among them.

Overall, private blockchains provide a promising solution for organizations seeking to leverage blockchain technology for specific use cases.

Consortium Blockchain. Consortium Blockchain, a hybrid of public and private blockchains, is a type of blockchain network that is managed by a group of organizations rather than a single entity [2]. Consortium blockchains are typically used by groups of companies or organizations that have a common interest in securely and efficiently sharing data and resources, especially in industries that require multi-party collaboration, such as the supply chain industry. One of the key features of a consortium blockchain is that it is permissioned, meaning that only authorized parties are allowed to access the network and participate in the consensus process. This is in contrast to public blockchains, such as Bitcoin and Ethereum, which are permissionless and allow anyone to join the network and participate in the consensus process. In a consortium blockchain, the participating nodes are typically pre-selected and trusted entities that collaborate to maintain the integrity of the network and validate transactions. Consensus mechanisms used in consortium blockchains can vary depending on the network's requirements, but they typically involve fewer nodes than public blockchains. Consortium blockchains offer several advantages over public blockchains, including greater control over network governance, increased privacy and security, and faster transaction processing times. They also allow for greater customization to meet the specific needs of the participating organizations, providing greater flexibility in data management, privacy, and security. In summary, consortium blockchains offer a promising solution for organizations looking to leverage blockchain technology for specific use cases, providing greater control, security, and efficiency than public blockchains while allowing for greater flexibility and customization to meet specific business needs.

2.3   Advantages and Disadvantages

Blockchain technology offers several advantages, including decentralization, immutability, transparency, and security. Decentralization enables a distributed network of nodes to validate transactions and maintain a secure ledger without the need for intermediaries, which reduces the risk of fraud, corruption, and censorship. Immutability ensures that once data is recorded on the blockchain, it cannot be altered or deleted, providing a high degree of trust and accountability. Transparency allows all parties to access and verify the data on the blockchain, promoting greater collaboration, accountability, and efficiency. Security is provided through cryptography, which ensures that data is encrypted and only accessible to authorized parties, making it difficult for hackers to compromise the system.

However, blockchain technology also has some limitations and challenges, including scalability, energy consumption, and regulatory challenges. Scalability is limited due to the computational power required to validate transactions and the size of the blockchain, which can lead to slow transaction processing times and high fees. Energy consumption is also a concern, as blockchain networks require significant amounts of electricity to operate, contributing to environmental concerns. Regulatory challenges arise due to the decentralized nature of blockchain networks, which can make it difficult for governments to enforce laws and regulations, and for companies to comply with them. Additionally, the complexity of blockchain technology and the lack of standardization can make it challenging for non-experts to understand and adopt the technology.

Overall, while blockchain technology offers many benefits, it also presents several challenges that must be addressed for it to realize its full potential as a transformative technology in various industries.

3   Requirement Analysis in the Supply Chain Field

The supply chain industry refers to the network of businesses and organizations involved in the creation and delivery of a product or service. This includes suppliers, manufacturers, distributors, retailers, and transportation companies that work together to move goods and services from production to consumption. The supply chain industry is a critical component of the global economy, with a significant impact on businesses, consumers, and society as a whole.

Supply chain management has become increasingly complex and challenging due to the globalization of trade, the rapid growth of e-commerce, and the need for greater transparency and traceability. The supply chain industry faces a range of issues, including inventory management, quality control, delivery delays, product counterfeiting, and supply chain disruptions caused by natural disasters, pandemics, and geopolitical tensions [16]. For example, the process of supply chain management involves multiple steps such as raw material procurement, production, sales, and logistics, and requires cooperation and information exchange among multiple parties. However, traditional supply chain management faces problems such as information asymmetry, poor traceability, and lack of trust, which leads to low efficiency, high risks, and increased costs. In order to address these problems, the supply chain industry has an urgent need for blockchain technology.

Firstly, the supply chain industry needs to ensure the security and transparency of information. In traditional supply chain management, there is a problem of information asymmetry, which makes it difficult to ensure the reliability and integrity of information. The distributed ledger mechanism of blockchain technology can achieve decentralized storage and management, with information recorded on each node. Each node has the right to verify data, ensuring the integrity and credibility of information, while also ensuring transparency and secure sharing of information.

Secondly, the supply chain industry needs to improve logistics efficiency and reduce costs. In traditional supply chain management, the logistics process requires coordination and communication among multiple parties, resulting in a waste of time and costs. Blockchain technology can achieve decentralized smart contracts, which can automatically execute contract terms, ensuring the transparency and efficiency of the logistics process, reducing communication costs, and improving logistics efficiency and cost-effectiveness.

In addition, the supply chain industry needs to achieve full traceability. In traditional supply chain management, the lack of transparency of information makes it impossible to trace the production, processing, and quality of goods, which increases the risk of food safety and other issues. Blockchain technology records information from every node, ensuring traceability at every stage, thereby improving supply chain traceability and reducing risk and management costs.

In summary, blockchain technology has a wide range of applications in the supply chain field, which can improve supply chain efficiency, reduce costs, enhance information security and transparency, and achieve traceability and anti-counterfeiting of goods, thereby improving enterprise competitiveness and market share.

4 Blockchain in the Field of Supply Chain Security

Logistics, information flow and capital flow are the basic elements of the supply chain [31], so their security is closely related to supply chain security. In this section, we summarize the works on applying blockchain in logistics security, data security and finance security. The overall framework is shown in Fig. 2.

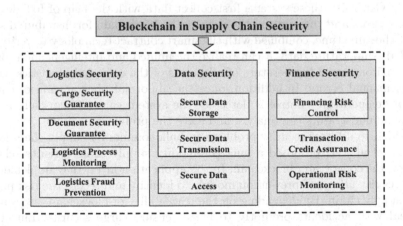

Fig. 2. The overall framework for blockchain in supply chain security management.

4.1   Logistics Security Management

Under the wave of global trade, the global supply chain network is becoming more and more huge and complex. As the most cost-effective mode of transport, maritime transport is an important carrier of cross-border trade. However, it also faces serious security problems, such as cargo theft, terrorist attacks, and other illegal activities. To cope with these problems and ensure the consistency between real information and on-chain information, Xu et al. [24] proposed a blockchain-based digital identity management scheme in which multiple government agencies work collaboratively. Zhang et al. [29] proposed a blockchain-based authentication mechanism to ensure the security and completeness of data during device access and information transmission. Moreover, there are a series of documents in the maritime transport process, which are usually processed inefficiently and are easily forged or lost during delivery, leading to fraudulent incidents [25]. To address such issues, in 2018, Maersk and IBM announced they would build a new blockchain-based global trade platform [22] that can help supply chain stakeholders use tamper-proof digital records and trade documents. By processing real-time information and trade documents from the maritime supply chain with smart contracts, the inefficiency of paper-based document processing is addressed and the risk of fraud is also greatly reduced.

Blockchain technology is also important to cold chain logistics security management. Cold chain logistics means that during the whole process from the production to the use of the products, refrigeration technology is used to make the environment at a suitable temperature to ensure that the product quality will not be damaged [8]. If the temperature at any logistics point is not within the required range, it will have a negative impact on product quality. There are already some works [14,23,28,30] proposing to combine blockchain technology and Internet of Things (IoT) technology to build cold chain logistics management systems. Generally, these systems first collect data with the help of IoT devices such as sensors and then upload the data to the blockchain for distributed storage. At the same time, combined with the smart contract technology to verify the uploaded temperature data, it can realize the unified and intelligent monitoring of the environmental temperature of all points of the cold chain logistics which reduces manual errors. In addition, once the abnormal phenomenon of equipment or temperature control is detected, the system can automatically alarm and the administrators can analyze and solve the problems in time.

Besides, to address security problems in bulk commodity supply chain logistics, Sun et al. [17] proposed a bulk commodity supply chain logistics scheme based on the consortium blockchain. In the application layer, they implemented a logistics risk alert and prevention module to identify and record the risk points in the supply chain. By depending on the traceability of blockchain, enterprises can deal with accidents promptly to better ensure cargo security. Liu et al. [12] proposed a blockchain-based logistics security enhancement method and designed smart contracts for logistics information security to solve the problems of logistics fraud and regulatory mechanism defects in e-commerce.

4.2 Data Security Management

The centralized data storage model used in traditional supply chain management systems suffers from issues such as data privacy leakage and opaque operations within the system. Blockchain has the characteristics of distributed storage, open and transparent data, and tamper-proof, which can provide a reliable underlying service for realizing distributed data security sharing systems. Many works start by proposing more secure consensus protocols to assure secure data sharing. Yin et al. [27] proposed a blockchain-based model for supply chain data security sharing. They improved the consistency protocol of the practical Byzantine fault tolerant consensus mechanism [1] and proposed a new consensus algorithm named CEBFT. And they employed the credit mechanism to improve the reliability of participants and incorporated a dynamic node management design. Dwivedi et al. [4] proposed a blockchain-based information sharing method for the pharmaceutical supply chain management system. Specifically, they proposed smart contracts based on the state machine model and a new consensus protocol for transaction and block authentication, and demonstrated the defense capability of the proposed protocol against possible attacks through security analysis. Besides improving the consensus protocols, some works try to improve smart contracts. Wen et al. [21] proposed a fine-grained supply chain data sharing scheme in which access policies are set on smart contracts to ensure that only nodes that satisfy the access requirements can execute these smart contracts.

In addition, the cryptographic foundation of blockchain technology can be integrated with many other cryptographic techniques to achieve data security management, such as multiple encryption algorithms and information hiding techniques. Zheng et al. [32] proposed a blockchain-based trusted data sharing scheme by using the tamper-proof property of blockchain to prevent the shared data from being tampered and the Paillier cryptosystem to achieve confidentiality of the shared data. To assure food supply chain data security, Wang et al. [20] proposed a novel framework based on consortium chain and smart contracts to track and trace the workflow in the agri-food supply chain. In this framework, after farmers upload data to the InterPlanetary File System (IPFS), the file IPFS hashes will be stored in the smart contracts to enhance data security. Meanwhile, the data stored in the blockchain and IPFS will be encrypted using digital signatures to further ensure data security. Wang et al. [18] constructed a blockchain-based rice supply chain information supervision system. They combined symmetric encryption and hash encryption algorithms to propose a data hierarchical encryption and storage mode to protect the sensitive data of companies in the supply chain, which ensures the security of the data during transmission and storage. For the medical supply chain, El Azzaoui et al. [5] proposed a blockchain-based information hiding technology architecture that uses information hiding technology to encrypt messages and smart contracts to automatically generate one-time keys. And the key is regenerated each time a new communication is started, solving the risk of the attackers having the key to decrypt the messages.

4.3   Finance Security Service

Supply chain finance is a new financing model for small and medium-sized enterprises, which effectively integrates capital flow into the process of supply chain management. This model not only provides trade capital services for enterprises in all points of the supply chain, but also provides new loan financing services for weaker enterprises in the supply chain, making it possible for enterprises in different scales to better develop together [6]. It is important to ensure the security of supply chain financial services for protecting the interests of all participants in the supply chain and supporting the good development of the supply chain. Compared with the third-party platforms and centralized designs used in traditional supply chain financial management solutions, the application of blockchain can better achieve the needs of financing risk control, transaction credit assurance and operational risk monitoring.

Wang and Wang [19] proposed an IoT data management model that uses blockchain technology to manage user access and data analysis related systems. Li et al. [11] proposed a consortium blockchain-based supply chain finance management system termed Fabric-SCF. This system utilized distributed consensus for data storage security and the attribute-based access control model for access control, and designed smart contracts from the perspective of user management, financing project management and access control. Du et al. [3] redesigned the business process of warehouse receipt pledge financing and accounts receivable factoring in supply chain finance and proposed a new supply chain finance platform, which employed blockchain technology to manage the whole process and solve the transaction credit problem. In addition, they improved the Paillier homomorphic encryption algorithm for the supply chain finance scenario, and combined this improved algorithm into the blockchain to meet the demand for sensitive data privacy protection. To address the problems such as fake credit information and low credit data security in the credit system of supply chain finance, Zheng et al. [33] proposed a blockchain-based enterprise credit information sharing model to improve the integrity of credit record storage. In this model, they designed a more suitable consensus mechanism for the credit system based on the credit information sharing environment. And a full life-cycle credit monitoring mechanism can be established based on blockchain technology, so as to reduce the possibility of supply chain finance-related subjects losing trust in transactions.

Besides the above mentioned works, there are also a small number of works considering designing hybrid chains to build supply chain financial management models. Liu et al. [13] proposed a hybrid chain model for trusted data, abbreviated as DFB, which can provide more reliable data storage and permission management. Specifically, they designed a consensus algorithm named PANDA for public blockchains and a consensus algorithm named X-Alliance for consortium blockchains, and combined these two algorithms to obtain the algorithm of the hybrid chain model, which can effectively prevent Witch attack and Distributed denial-of-service (DDoS) attack.

5   Advantages and Challenges

5.1   Advantage

The decentralized idea of blockchain and its smart contract and consensus mechanism technologies are highly coupled with the supply chain. Moreover, the consortium chain is more suitable for supply chain scenarios because it implements the access mechanism to manage visitors. Specifically, blockchain technology has the following main advantages when applied to the supply chain:

Firstly, the supply chain data can be stored in a distributed manner based on blockchain technology, which makes the data open and transparent among the transaction participants and forms a complete information flow. And the combination with digital signature and various encryption technologies can make data in the whole chain tamper-proof, standard uniformity and high-efficiency exchange, so as to enhance the authenticity and security of supply chain data and realize the orderly business among all participants in the supply chain with low trust cost. In addition, by constructing supply chain risk supervision schemes based on the blockchain system, participants can detect the problems in the supply chain in time and find solutions to them in a targeted manner.

Secondly, with the support of blockchain technology, goods can serve as traceable objects, allowing for the recording of information throughout the entire business process, including production, warehousing, testing, logistics, and circulation. Closed-loop management can be achieved as a result, ensuring information verification and traceability across the supply chain. This not only satisfies the tracking requirements of regulatory agencies, buyers, and related companies but also is crucial in ensuring logistics and product safety.

Finally, by converting paper contracts into smart contracts, the transaction information between the buyers and the sellers can be efficiently recorded and the verifiability and effectiveness of the information can be ensured. Smart contracts guarantee the normal execution of contracts or agreements among the participants in the supply chain, minimizing the occurrence of malicious transactions and unexpected situations. While ensuring the normal and efficient execution of key processes such as transaction payments, smart contracts also make the process of resolving supply chain issues more efficient, flexible, and objective.

5.2   Challenge

We further discuss the challenges of applying blockchain in the supply chain, which include technical challenges, cost challenges and regulatory challenges.

For technical challenges, firstly, the endogenous security problems of blockchain technology itself will affect supply chain security. Blockchain technology is exposed to security risks such as smart contract vulnerabilities, cyber attacks, private key security, and data leakage [7]. Next, the performance of blockchain is also a major challenge in the application process. A large number of transactions and data records are involved in the supply chain. If the blockchain performance cannot meet the transaction processing demand, it may lead to problems such as delayed transactions and slow processing, which affect the normal running of the supply chain. Moreover, blockchain technology cannot judge the authenticity of the data in the chain from the source. Especially in the field of supply chain finance, it is necessary to study how to further combine with other technologies to ensure the authenticity of the data in the chain. Lastly, it is also an important challenge to propose a more suitable solution by adopting blockchain technology to different supply chain scenarios. For example, although there are various consensus protocols in blockchain, none of them can be adapted to all application scenarios. And various technical problems may arise in practical applications.

For cost challenges, implementing blockchain technology into real use will face high equipment costs. For example, lots of servers and storage devices need to be purchased for data storage. And long-term maintenance and management of data will increase storage costs. And in the supply chain scenario, blockchain technology is often applied together with the IoT and other technologies, whose related equipment such as sensors will also increase the equipment costs. Meanwhile, blockchain needs to consume lots of computing resources and power resources to support algorithm operation during running. Therefore, the large-scale application of blockchain technology may result in higher energy costs and energy waste. Finally, it also faces human resource costs. For example, developing and maintaining blockchain-based systems require plenty of technical expertise.

For regulatory challenges, the expanding use of blockchain in the supply chain field has made it more difficult for regulatory agencies to supervise. And there are also some new legal risks arising from this technology integration process, such as data privacy, information security, intellectual property rights and other issues that need to be regulated and protected by laws and regulations. However, to our knowledge, there is no unified international regulatory standard in this area nowadays. Therefore, in order to guarantee the safe application of blockchain technology, it is also necessary to establish a sound system of laws, regulations and industry standards to clarify the scope and restrictions of the application of blockchain technology in the supply chain, so as to protect public interests.

6   Conclusion

Blockchain is an effective solution to supply chain security problems. In this paper, we briefly introduce blockchain technology and analyze the current requirements for it in the supply chain field. We further investigate the application of blockchain technology in supply chain security and summarize the existing research and landed applications from three perspectives: logistics security, data security and finance security. Finally, we analyze the advantages and challenges of applying blockchain in supply chain security. However, this paper mainly investigates the research situation in academia, and there is less content for industrial landing research in industry, which can be further studied in future work. Overall, this paper helps readers better understand the application and development of blockchain technology in supply chain security management and provides a reference for research and practice in related fields.

References

1. Castro, M., Liskov, B.: Practical Byzantine fault tolerance and proactive recovery. ACM Trans. Comput. Syst. (TOCS) **20**(4), 398–461 (2002)
2. Dib, O., Brousmiche, K.L., Durand, A., Thea, E., Hamida, E.B.: Consortium blockchains: overview, applications and challenges. Int. J. Adv. Telecommun. **11**(1), 51–64 (2018)
3. Du, M., Chen, Q., Xiao, J., Yang, H., Ma, X.: Supply chain finance innovation using blockchain. IEEE Trans. Eng. Manag. **67**(4), 1045–1058 (2020)
4. Dwivedi, S.K., Amin, R., Vollala, S.: Blockchain based secured information sharing protocol in supply chain management system with key distribution mechanism. J. Inf. Secur. Appl. **54**, 102554 (2020)
5. El Azzaoui, A., Chen, H., Kim, S.H., Pan, Y., Park, J.H.: Blockchain-based distributed information hiding framework for data privacy preserving in medical supply chain systems. Sensors **22**(4), 1371 (2022)
6. Gelsomino, L.M., Mangiaracina, R., Perego, A., Tumino, A.: Supply chain finance: a literature review. Int. J. Phys. Distrib. Logist. Manag. **46**(4) (2016)
7. Guo, H., Yu, X.: A survey on blockchain technology and its security. Blockchain: Res. Appl. **3**(2), 100067 (2022)
8. Han, J.W., Zuo, M., Zhu, W.Y., Zuo, J.H., Lü, E.L., Yang, X.T.: A comprehensive review of cold chain logistics for fresh agricultural products: current status, challenges, and future trends. Trends Food Sci. Technol. **109**, 536–551 (2021)
9. Houlihan, J.B.: International supply chain management. Int. J. Phys. Distrib. Mater. Manag. **15**(1), 22–38 (1985)
10. Lai, R., Chuen, D.L.K.: Blockchain-from public to private. In: Handbook of Blockchain, Digital Finance, and Inclusion, vol. 2, pp. 145–177. Academic Press (2018)
11. Li, D., Han, D., Crespi, N., Minerva, R., Li, K.C.: A blockchain-based secure storage and access control scheme for supply chain finance. J. Supercomput. **79**(1), 109–138 (2023)
12. Liu, H., Sun, R., Zhao, G.: A method of logistics information security based on blockchain technology. In: Proceedings of the 2018 3rd Joint International Information Technology, Mechanical and Electronic Engineering Conference (JIMEC 2018), Chongqing, China, pp. 200–204. Atlantis Press (2018)
13. Liu, J., Yan, L., Wang, D.: A hybrid blockchain model for trusted data of supply chain finance. Wirel. Pers. Commun. **127**, 919–943 (2022)
14. Menon, K.N., Thomas, K., Thomas, J., Titus, D.J., James, D.: ColdBlocks: quality assurance in cold chain networks using blockchain and IoT. In: Hassanien, A.E., Bhattacharyya, S., Chakrabati, S., Bhattacharya, A., Dutta, S. (eds.) Emerging Technologies in Data Mining and Information Security. AISC, vol. 1286, pp. 781–789. Springer, Singapore (2021). https://doi.org/10.1007/978-981-15-9927-9_76
15. Nakamoto, S.: Bitcoin: a peer-to-peer electronic cash system. Decentralized Bus. Rev. 21260 (2008)
16. Stadtler, H.: Supply chain management: an overview. In: Supply Chain Management and Advanced Planning: Concepts, Models, Software, and Case Studies, pp. 3–28 (2015)
17. Sun, Y., Niu, W., Liao, X., Huang, S., Huang, B., Zhang, X.: Research on the logistics scheme of bulk commodity supply chain based blockchain. J. Guangzhou Univ. (Nat. Sci. Ed.) **21**(2), 67–75 (2022). (in Chinese)

18. Wang, J., et al.: Blockchain-based information supervision model for rice supply chains. Comput. Intell. Neurosci. **2022** (2022)
19. Wang, L., Wang, Y.: Supply chain financial service management system based on block chain IoT data sharing and edge computing. Alex. Eng. J. **61**(1), 147–158 (2022)
20. Wang, L., et al.: Smart contract-based agricultural food supply chain traceability. IEEE Access **9**, 9296–9307 (2021)
21. Wen, Q., Gao, Y., Chen, Z., Wu, D.: A blockchain-based data sharing scheme in the supply chain by IIoT. In: 2019 IEEE International Conference on Industrial Cyber Physical Systems (ICPS), Taipei, Taiwan, pp. 695–700. IEEE (2019)
22. White, M.: Digitizing global trade with Maersk and IBM (2017). https://www.ibm.com/blogs/blockchain/2018/01/digitizing-global-trade-maersk-ibm/
23. Wisessing, K., Vichaidis, N.: IoT based cold chain logistics with blockchain for food monitoring application. In: 2022 7th International Conference on Business and Industrial Research (ICBIR), Bangkok, Thailand, pp. 359–363. IEEE (2022)
24. Xu, L., Chen, L., Gao, Z., Chang, Y., Iakovou, E., Shi, W.: Binding the physical and cyber worlds: a blockchain approach for cargo supply chain security enhancement. In: 2018 IEEE International Symposium on Technologies for Homeland Security (HST), Woburn, MA, USA, pp. 1–5. IEEE (2018)
25. Yang, C.S.: Maritime shipping digitalization: blockchain-based technology applications, future improvements, and intention to use. Transp. Res. Part E: Logist. Transp. Rev. **131**, 108–117 (2019)
26. Yang, R., et al.: Public and private blockchain in construction business process and information integration. Autom. Constr. **118**, 103276 (2020)
27. Yin, L., Kong, X., Liu, H., Zhang, Y., Liu, S.: Blockchain consensus algorithm design for supply chain data security sharing. J. Inf. Secur. Res. **8**(6), 605–612 (2022). (in Chinese)
28. Zhang, H.: Application of pharmaceutical cold chain logistics based on blockchain technology. Logist. Eng. Manag. **45**(1), 71–73 (2023). (in Chinese)
29. Zhang, P., Wang, Y., Aujla, G.S., Jindal, A., Al-Otaibi, Y.D.: A blockchain-based authentication scheme and secure architecture for IoT-enabled maritime transportation systems. IEEE Trans. Intell. Transp. Syst. **24**(2), 2322–2331 (2023)
30. Zhang, Y., Liu, Y., Jiong, Z., Zhang, X., Li, B., Chen, E.: Development and assessment of blockchain-IoT-based traceability system for frozen aquatic product. J. Food Process Eng. **44**(5), e13669 (2021)
31. Zhao, X., Feng, N., Xing, G.: Transformation and innovation of supply chain in the construction of modern circulation system: internal logic and realistic paths. Surg. Endosc. Other Interv. Tech. **2**(8), 69–79 (2021). (in Chinese)
32. Zheng, B.K., et al.: Scalable and privacy-preserving data sharing based on blockchain. J. Comput. Sci. Technol. **33**, 557–567 (2018)
33. Zheng, K., et al.: Blockchain technology for enterprise credit information sharing in supply chain finance. J. Innov. Knowl. **7**(4), 100256 (2022)
34. Zheng, Z., Xie, S., Dai, H.N., Chen, X., Wang, H.: Blockchain challenges and opportunities: a survey. Int. J. Web Grid Serv. **14**(4), 352–375 (2018)

ePoW Energy-Efficient Blockchain Consensus Algorithm for Decentralize Federated Learning System in Resource-Constrained UAV Swarm

Yuting Fan[1], Jianguo Chen[1(✉)], Longxin Zhang[2], and Peiqi Li[1]

[1] School of Software Engineering, Sun Yat-Sen University, Zhuhai 519000, China
chenjg33@mail.sysu.edu.cn
[2] College of Computer Science, Hunan University of Technology,
Zhuzhou 412007, China
longxinzhang@hnu.edu.cn

Abstract. With the proliferation of Unmanned Aerial Vehicles (UAV) and UAV swarms, there has been growing interest in using them for collaborative computing tasks. Blockchain-based Federated learning (BFL) is an excellent approach for training artificial intelligence models in UAV swarms, providing benefits such as privacy protection, trusted computing, node autonomy, and low communication overhead. However, due to limited battery life and processing power, UAVs require energy-efficient solutions that can handle blockchain consensuses in decentralized BFL manners. To address such challenges, we propose an energy-efficient Proof of Work (ePoW) consensus algorithm for the resource-constrained UAV swarms, which to achieve fault tolerance and data integrity while minimizing energy consumption. At the commencement of the ePoW protocol, the UAV nodes perform computation and dissemination of their engagement metrics to facilitate the selection of participating nodes in the ePoW competition. Following a successful BFL global generation event, the dynamic difficulty adjustment mechanism collaborates with the engagement metrics to identify the most reliable node and mitigate resource consumption during the consensus process. Our ePow algorithm is designed to work with BFL systems in a UAV swarm, where each UAV device acts as a node in the BFL system. We evaluate the algorithm's performance in various scenarios and found that it achieves high accuracy while consuming significantly less energy compared to existing consensus algorithms. Our proposed approach presents a promising solution for energy-efficient decentralized BFL systems in UAV swarms.

Keywords: Blockchain-based federated learning · UAV swarm · Consensus algorithm · Proof-of-work · Energy-efficiency

1 Introduction

Unmanned Aerial Vehicles swarms, which consist of multiple Unmanned Aerial Vehicles (UAVs) working together [10,14], have the ability to accomplish tasks

© The Author(s), under exclusive license to Springer Nature Singapore Pte Ltd. 2024
J. Chen et al. (Eds.): BlockSys 2023, CCIS 1897, pp. 89–101, 2024.
https://doi.org/10.1007/978-981-99-8104-5_7

rapidly and efficiently. By utilizing the collective intelligence of the swarm, UAV swarms can tackle complex tasks in hazardous environments, such as large-scale search and rescue missions, wide-area monitoring, and cargo transportation. Federated Learning (FL) [4,7] is a distributed machine learning approach that allows multiple devices to collaboratively train an artificial intelligence (AI) model while keeping their data locally. This technology offers several advantages when deployed in a resource-constrained UAV swarm, including privacy, low communication overhead, and robustness. Combining blockchain and federated learning [13] can create a powerful and secure system for data sharing and analysis, providing benefits for privacy, decentralization, transparency, incentives, and scalability. However, a crucial issue in this field is how to efficiently compute complex consensus algorithms in resource-limited UAV swarms, given the limited battery life and processing power of UAVs. Therefore, it is essential to develop energy-efficient solutions that can handle blockchain consensuses in decentralized BFL nodes.

The consensus algorithms play a critical role in the blockchain portion of the blockchain-based federated learning (BFL) system by enabling multiple nodes in a decentralized network to reach a consensus on the current state of the ledger or the validity of transactions. In a blockchain or BFL system, each node maintains a copy of the ledger or distributed database, and consensus algorithms provide a mechanism to implement this protocol in a trustless and decentralized manner [11]. However, the consensus algorithms used in blockchain can be computationally intensive and energy-consuming. Consensus algorithms present significant challenges to blockchain network security, including energy-intensive proof-of-work algorithms and centralization risks associated with proof-of-stake and proof-of-authority (PoA) algorithms. These challenges must be addressed to ensure the security and reliability of BFL systems on UAV swarms.

Some existing research has applied energy-efficient consensus algorithms directly to UAV networks, which are applied to blockchain-based federated learning and energy-efficient swarm coordination for UAV swarms. Focusing on For example, a "Proof of Randomnes" (PoR) is proposed to reduce the computational and energy requirements of the consensus process. A "Proof of Workload" (PoWL) is designed that uses the workload of the parties as a measure of their contribution to the consensus process. UAV swarms are groups of UAVs that can work together to accomplish complex tasks such as search and rescue, surveillance, and delivery. However, coordinating the actions of multiple UAVs can be computationally intensive and energy-consuming. On the other hand, researchers have proposed energy-efficient swarm coordination algorithms for UAV swarms. For example, a swarm coordination algorithm uses a decentralized approach to reduce the communication and computation requirements of the coordination process [6]. In [3], a machine learning model was used to predict the behavior of UAVs and optimize their trajectories to minimize energy consumption. Although existing research has made progress, there are several challenges associated with implementing blockchain consensus algorithms in resource-constrained

UAV swarms, such as limited processing power, limited energy resources, communication latency, fault tolerance, and scalability.

In this paper, we propose an energy-efficient improved Proof of Work (ePoW) algorithm for the blockchain federated learning architecture applied to UAV networks. Our algorithm considers the high dynamics and sensitivity to the overhead of UAV networks. Firstly, UAVs calculate their own engagement metrics based on their residual energy, computing resources, and network connections. These indicators are then broadcasted to the network and compute the overall average engagement metrics of the current round. UAVs decide whether to participate in the current round of block generation qualification competition based on the dynamic difficulty and average engagement metrics of this round. Experimental results demonstrate that compared to the PoW algorithm, our proposed algorithm saves up to 60% in energy consumption and can effectively continue to operate even when the UAV is hijacked or the UAV node fails.

The main contributions of this work are as follows:

- We propose an energy-efficient PoW algorithm called ePoW for the high dynamics and overhead sensitivity of UAV networks in the block-chain federated learning architecture applied to UAV networks, which allow 30% to 40% of nodes take part in the PoW process based on their engagement metrics and difficulty of this round.
- An engagement metrics is proposed to characterize the stability and resource abundance of nodes in order to provide references of ePoW participation. Nodes calculate engagement metrics in every round based on their residual energy, compute power and the number of nodes in the local routing table, and then compare to the global average to decide whether or not to participate in the ePoW.
- Dynamic difficulty adjustment method is based on the number of completion notifications received and the global average engagement metrics computed in the current round, which is used to adjust the difficulty of the next competition.

The rest of this paper is organized as follows: Work related to the energy-efficiency consensus algorithm is in Sect. 2. The ePoW consensus algorithm, within the system architecture of BFL and specific implementation of ePoW is placed in Sect. 3. A security analysis of ePoW at the BFL including the threat model is in Sect. 4. The experimental analysis of the ePoW is presented in Sect. 5. Section 6 concludes and looks at the possibility of our ePoW consensus algorithm of BFL system in UAV swarms.

2 Related Work

The research area of blockchain federated learning has gained increased attention in recent years. Federated learning is a machine learning technique that allows multiple parties to train a model without sharing data. The use of blockchain technology can enhance the security of the federated learning process and incentivize all parties to participate and contribute. Current research efforts are focused on optimizing the consensus mechanism of the blockchain federated learning system to reduce the accounting overhead of nodes while ensuring the selection of safe and stable nodes for accounting purposes. Jiang et al. [3] proposed approach, GaS-PBFT, suggests a two-layer IoT consensus network based on PBFT consensus and game-based node selection (GaS) consensus. This approach includes the design of an energy-efficient GaS consensus mechanism and performance evaluation through extensive simulation of consensus delay, transaction speed, node capacity, and security.

Golam et al. [1] proposed Another approach, Lightweight Blockchain, employs the PoA consensus algorithm to develop a UAV security transmission network based on blockchain. Sasikumar et al. [12] proposes an improved honorary commission-based real-time application delegated proof of stake (DPoS) consensus algorithm to expedite the creation of IoT blocks while reducing the burden of data transmission and energy consumption. Tang et al. [16] proposes the use of PoS to construct a blockchain network for secure UAV IoT data collection and models the UAV network as a multi-agent Markov game to study the maximum benefit strategy of UAVs.

Milutinovic et al. [8] presents a Proof-of-Luck consensus algorithm and design blockchain that utilizes the Intel SGX platform. Participants generate random values at the start of each round for mining new blocks to determine the winning block. The algorithm specifies that the luckier (larger) number has a shorter delay time, thereby selecting the winner and avoiding a large number of operations. Sun et al. [15] proposes a delegated proof-of-stake consensus algorithm with dynamic trust, DT-DPoS, with dynamic trust to reduce the risk of collusion attacks and ensure the security of blockchain systems. Kong et al. [5] proposes a lightweight asynchronous provable consensus Byzantine fault-tolerant consensus mechanism that runs in UAV networks. Each node monitors the data forwarding behavior of neighboring nodes in real time and evaluates the trusted discount of neighboring node forwarding. Delegated authorization nodes collect local state data for global reputation statistics and Byzantine fault-tolerant consensus. To reduce the energy consumption of PoW, Lasla et al. preposes Green-PoW [6] adjusts the election mechanism after the first round of mining to determine the champion. This allows the election of a small group of miners for exclusive mining in the second round, leading to significant energy savings of up to 50%.

3   Proposed Method

In this section, we present the proposed energy-efficient improved Proof of Work (ePoW) algorithm for the blockchain federated learning architecture applied to UAV networks.

3.1   BFL System on Resource-Constrained UAV Swarm

The blockchain federated learning architecture implemented on the UAV swarm with limited resources is depicted in Fig. 1.

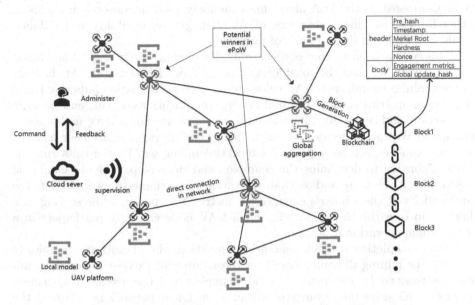

Fig. 1. Blockchain federated learning architecture on resource-constrained UAV swarm. The UAV in red represents the potential winners to block generation and global aggregation. (Color figure online)

The framework comprises an UAV network and a cloud server. The UAV network consists of UAVs that are responsible for collecting data and executing the federated learning framework to accomplish various tasks. On the other hand, the cloud server is responsible for issuing remote commands and monitoring the status of the UAV network. Notably, the cloud server does not engage in activities such as block generation and federated learning computing within the UAV network. Communication between UAVs is completed by node forwarding. The topology of the UAV network would be dynamically adjusted, with UAV swarms frequently changing formation during flight. Additionally, collisions or malfunctions during mission execution may cause UAVs to become incapacitated, necessitating the dynamic reorganization of the network topology.

Nodes that choose to participate in the competition count the current round of PoW, and the first node to complete broadcasts its qualifications. The other participating nodes continue to calculate until two completion notifications are received. The champion is responsible for generating the current round of blocks and global aggregation, while the runner-up verifies the champion's qualification and serves as the champion's backup.

3.2 ePoW Consensus Algorithm

The ePoW consensus algorithm is a highly efficient and energy-efficient alternative to the original PoW algorithm of Bitcoin [9]. Its computational load is reduced by up to 60%, while retaining all other important properties of the system. Compared to the PoA algorithm commonly used in consortium chains or other Internet of Things networks, ePoW offers greater flexibility and stability, while also avoiding single points of failure.

This consensus algorithm is specifically designed for use in a small and static UAV network, without the consideration of the link from new node. At the start of each mining round, each UAV calculates its own participation indicator based on various metrics such as residual energy, computing resources, and network connection, and sends this information to the network. Some UAV nodes would engage PoW process decided by the difficulty and average engagement metrics, which could be seen as a part of alternative miner set. Participants run the PoW algorithm to determine the champion and runner-up, with the champion performing block write and on-chain operations. The runner-up would verify the authenticity of the winner's engagement metrics and nonce, while serving as a backup in case the champion fails. Each UAV node can only participate in a single chain operation at a time.

After completing a block generation operation, the algorithm dynamically adjusts the mining difficulty based on the number of PoW completion notifications received by the current round champion and the average engagement metrics. This saves the resource overhead of the entire network by adapting the difficulty level to the current circumstances.

In contrast to the original PoW algorithm, where all network nodes stop mining a block once it is solved by a miner, ePoW works differently. Initially, each UAV node calculates its engagement metrics and sends them to the network to obtain the global average engagement metrics. Nodes with engagement metrics higher than the average are able to decide to participate in the PoW process by their strategy. When a node discovers the nonce and notifies the network, it becomes the winner of the competition. The runner-up is then determined by continuing the competition between the residual miners.

Once the winner of the competition is determined, the BFL process running on the champion node waits for other nodes to send their local parameter updates before starting the next round of BFL learning process. The runner-up verifies the authenticity of the champion's engagement metrics and global parameter updates and acts as a backup in case the champion fails, taking over the winner's work when the champion writes blocks and the global update times out.

After the previous round of champions completes the global update, the difficulty of the next round is dynamically adjusted, and the previous champions will not participate in the next round of block generation qualification competitions. When the model accuracy reaches the threshold or the UAV network resources are insufficient, the BFL process stops, and the UAV network performs further operations such as returning home according to the administrator's instructions.

3.3   Consensus Algorithm Steps

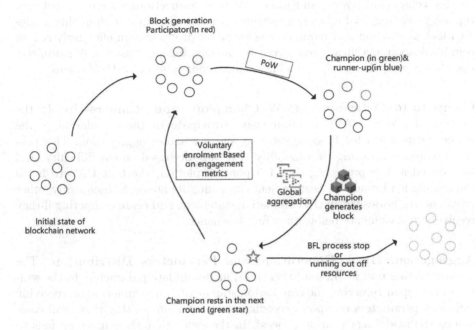

Fig. 2. the general process of ePoW consensus algorithm

Calculate Engagement Metrics. As illustrated in Fig. 2, the blockchain network employs a node stability model to calculate engagement metrics based on the Eq. (1). Prior to aggregating the federated learning model, nodes independently compute their unique global engagement metrics value for the current election cycle based on their computing resources and network connectivity.

$$Em = \sqrt{(En - Th_1)} * (CompPower - Th_2) * \frac{N_{rt}^{now}}{N_{total}} \qquad (1)$$

where Em refers to node engagement metrics, e represents the Euler number, En and $ComPower$ are the percentage of energy and compute power idle rate, Th_1 and Th_2 represent the safety threshold of energy and computing power usage rate that set by the administrator beforehand, N_{rt}^{now} means the number of nodes in the local routing list and N_{total} means the number of all the nodes in the UAV network.

From a empirical standpoint, it can be observed that the energy consumption of UAV nodes is primarily attributed to their flight time, while the energy consumption of their perception unit, computing unit, and execution unit remains relatively constant. Upon analyzing the formula, it can be inferred that the overall node engagement metrics decrease as the network run-time increases, which aligns with the energy consumption patterns of UAV nodes during task execution. High-quality nodes have characteristics such as higher residual energy, greater computing power, and more extensive connections within the network topology, leading to higher engagement metrics. Selecting high-quality nodes for block generation and parameter aggregation processes can effectively reduce communication overhead and decrease latency during the global parameter update process, ultimately reducing resource consumption of UAV nodes.

Compete to Determine ePoW Champions and Runners-Up. In the process of ePoW, UAVs autonomously participate in the calculation of the nonce competition for block generation and parameter aggregation. This process involves computing the eligibility of each node based on the difficulty level announced in the preceding round. Upon completion, the first UAV to finish the calculation broadcasts a statement containing its nonce. Subsequently, other participating nodes verify the completion statement and cease competing if they receive two statements before they find the nonce.

Aggregation, Block Generation, and Parameters Distribution. The non-competing nodes will send their local model update parameters to the winning node upon receiving the completion statement. The winner, upon receiving sufficient parameters or upon exceeding the maximum waiting time, will commence the model aggregation process. In the event that the runner-up fails to receive parameter update after exceeding the maximum waiting time, it will take over as the backup machine and instruct the remainder nodes to send gradients to restart the model aggregation process.

Dynamic Adjustment of Difficulty. In the ePoW consensus algorithm, the difficulty level is dynamically adjusted based on factors such as the number of statements received by the winner of the current round and the average engagement metrics base on Eq. (2). Additionally, the number of nodes participating in each round is regulated to ensure that it falls within a range from 30% to 40% of the total number of nodes in the network.

$$D_{new} = D_{old} * \left[1 + P * (node_{now}^{ePoW} - node_{last}^{ePoW}) + A * (E_{now}^{avg} - E_{last}^{avg})\right] \quad (2)$$

where D_{new} and D_{old} refer to the difficulty of the new round and the last round, $node_{now}^{ePoW}$ and $node_{last}^{ePoW}$ means the number of nodes that participate in the latest round and last round, E_{now}^{avg} and E_{last}^{avg} represent the average engagement metrics in UAV network in the latest round and last round, P and A are the factor that can be adjusted by the administrator based on the effect of Dynamic difficulty mechanism.

4   Security Analysis

4.1   Threat Model

We presents a blockchain-enabled federated learning system for the resource-constrained UAV swarm. The architecture consists of a network of UAVs and a cloud server, with the UAVs responsible for data collection and federated learning tasks, and the cloud server responsible for issuing instructions and monitoring the network. The network uses node forwarding to transmit communication between UAVs, with the topology dynamically adjusting as the UAV swarms change and reorganize in formation during flight.

We also considers potential security threats to the UAV network, such as hijacking UAVs for gradient attacks to manipulate global aggregation results, and physical attacks on the UAVs themselves. In this paper, we assumes that the cloud server is a completely reliable entity, while the UAVs are considered semi-trusted, with the possibility of up to one-fifth of the total being hijacked by adversaries.

To prevent adversaries from causing network nodes to go offline or winning block generation qualifications, the UAV network needs to have measures in place to be robust in dealing with single points of failure and prevent hijacked UAVs from writing blocks. Additionally, the UAV network needs to have the ability to prevent physical attacks on the UAVs themselves, as well as the ability to handle failures and adapt to changes in the network topology.

Cyber Attacks. To prevent network attacks, the focus should be on preventing hijacked UAVs from winning the ePoW competition. This can be achieved by allowing the runner-up to verify the winner of each round. During each round of aggregation, the participation metrics and global average participation metrics of each UAV node are recorded in blocks. Hijacked nodes can interfere with the decisions of other nodes by forging participation metrics, aiming to reduce the participation of potential competitors and increase their chances of winning the competition.

However, nodes that exaggerate computing resources are less likely to win in the PoW process if they have insufficient computing resources.

It is challenging to achieve careful and subtle fictitious fabrications about engagement metrics. The runner-up can query the participation indicator record of the champion in the blockchain for time series anomaly detection to detect whether the participation indicator submitted by the champion in this round of the competition is true. Once the champion is detected as faking the participation indicator, the whole network will broadcast the notification, and each node will further verify or directly block the malicious node.

However, if two or more high-quality nodes in the network are hijacked, there is a higher probability of a successful attack on the network because both the champion and the runner-up could be malicious nodes colluding to attack the network.

Node Failure. In general, UAV swarms can tolerate less than half of node failures and still maintain functionality and complete tasks [10]. If the UAV network goes offline due to human or accidental factors, a reorganization procedure can be implemented. Due to the limited resources of UAV nodes, it is difficult to back up the data of each UAV node. Thus, the data and local model of a failed node can only be treated as lost. In the event of the champion node failing in the current round of global aggregation, the runner-up can act as a backup and continue the work. If the champion and runner-up expire at the same time, and other nodes have not received the global aggregation parameter update for a certain period of time, they will check their network connectivity or spontaneously restart the global aggregation round through unanimous voting

5 Experiments

In this section, we conduct comparison experiments to evaluate the effectiveness of our proposed ePoW consensus algorithm along with a BFL system using the MNIST dataset.

5.1 Experiment Setup

We use an Intel Core i512400F processor to perform our experiments in a Windows 11 operating system environment. The PyTorch version employed is 1.13.1+cpu, while the programming language used is Python 3.7.12. For our BFL framework, we leverage the fedml [2], while the underlying blockchain is built in Python. The UAV network is set as a group of child processes that communicate with shared memory, which are assigned the same computing power. The global routing map would randomly change at the beginning of every round, which is used to calculate the simulated delay of the forwarding process in node communication. The threshold factor Th_1 and Th_2 are both set as 20%, while the factor P and A are respectively set to 0.2 and 0.5.

the first experiment shown in Fig. 3 is done in an ideal situation without the consideration of energy and computing power consumption, which means the engagement metrics would be only affected by the local routing list. It can tell that the FL process with a global server achieves the fastest speed on accuracy, while the BFL process with ePoW is slightly better than the one with PoW, which means the strategy to select the well-connected nodes play a role.

During the experiment, it was found that the number of communications significantly affects the speed of the process. This is because communication latency is much greater than the execution time of other program modules. Additionally, the communication process needs to account for waiting situations caused by asynchronous sub-threads. The duration of the PoW process is also related to the maximum network latency. As a result, FL-process would run faster, because it needs less communication round to complete parameter aggregation and it does not require the PoW process or completion of related communication processes. All of the processes achieve the basely same level of testing accuracy.

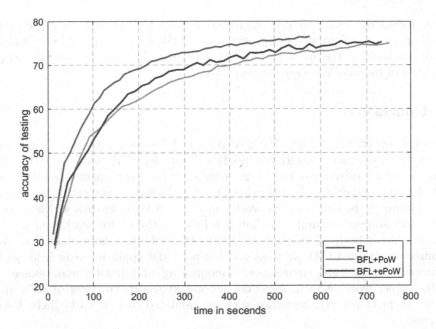

Fig. 3. The ideal testing accuracy of FL, BFL+ePoW, and BFL+Pow over time.

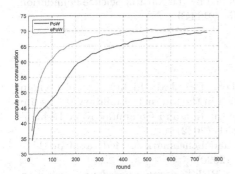

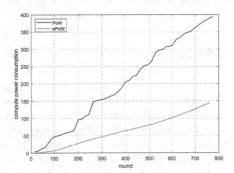

Fig. 4. Compete for power consumption metrics vs round

Fig. 5. The testing accuracy vs time in the simulated nodes network

$$Cp_{total} = \sum_n^i Cp_i * t_i \qquad (3)$$

Figure 4 shows the testing accuracy changed over time of the process with ePoW and PoW in the second experiment that takes into account the simulated energy and consumption, which lets to the result that the BFL process with ePoW Widening the gap between the one with PoW. Finally, Fig. 5 shows the compute power consumption metrics in rounds. The compute power consumption metrics are determined in the Eq. (3) where the Cp_i refer to the percentage of compute power avenge additional usage on nodes during the ePoW competition, the t_i means the usage time in microseconds and Cp_{total} represents the total consumption in each round. The process with ePoW saves nearly 60% of compute power compared to the one with PoW, which proves the advantage in the energy efficiency of the ePoW consensus algorithm.

6   Conclusion

The proposed energy-efficient Proof of Work (ePoW) algorithm solves the challenges of consistency algorithms and is suitable for UAV swarms with high dynamics and sensitivity to computing overhead. The experimental results show that the proposed ePoW algorithm is efficient and effective, indicating its potential to improve the collaborative work capability of UAV swarms which is 50% better in resource consumption than the PoW method. Our work contributes to the growing body of research on energy-efficient blockchain algorithms for resource-constrained UAV systems and has potential applications in fields such as precision agriculture, environmental monitoring, and disaster management.

In further work, we will focus on lightweight smart contracts of BFL and deploy them in realistic scenarios such as simulated or real-world flight UAV swarms.

Acknowledgments. This work is partially funded by the Natural Science Foundation of Guang Dong Province under Grant 2023A1515011179.

References

1. Golam, M., Akter, R., Tuli, E.A., Kim, D.S., Lee, J.M.: Lightweight blockchain assisted unauthorized UAV access prevention in the internet of military things. In: 2022 13th International Conference on Information and Communication Technology Convergence (ICTC), pp. 890–894. IEEE (2022)
2. He, C., et al.: Fedml: a research library and benchmark for federated machine learning. arXiv preprint arXiv:2007.13518 (2020)
3. Jiang, Y., Le, Y., Wang, J., You, X.: GaS-PBFT: a game-based node selection consensus mechanism for internet of things. In: 2022 14th International Conference on Wireless Communications and Signal Processing (WCSP), pp. 17–21. IEEE (2022)
4. Konečný, J., McMahan, B., Ramage, D.: Federated optimization: distributed optimization beyond the datacenter. arXiv preprint arXiv:1511.03575 (2015)
5. Kong, L., Chen, B., Hu, F.: LAP-BFT: lightweight asynchronous provable byzantine fault-tolerant consensus mechanism for UAV network. Drones **6**(8), 187 (2022)
6. Lasla, N., Al-Sahan, L., Abdallah, M., Younis, M.: Green-pow: an energy-efficient blockchain proof-of-work consensus algorithm. Comput. Netw. **214**, 109118 (2022)
7. McMahan, B., Moore, E., Ramage, D., Hampson, S., y Arcas, B.A.: Communication-efficient learning of deep networks from decentralized data. In: Artificial Intelligence and Statistics, pp. 1273–1282 (2017)
8. Milutinovic, M., He, W., Wu, H., Kanwal, M.: Proof of luck: an efficient blockchain consensus protocol, pp. 1–6 (2016)
9. Nakamoto, S.: Bitcoin: a peer-to-peer electronic cash system (2008)

10. Nasir, M.H., Khan, S.A., Khan, M.M., Fatima, M.: Swarm intelligence inspired intrusion detection systems-a systematic literature review. Comput. Netw. **205**, 108708 (2022)
11. ur Rehman, M.H., Salah, K., Damiani, E., Svetinovic, D.: Towards blockchain-based reputation-aware federated learning. In: IEEE INFOCOM 2020-IEEE Conference on Computer Communications Workshops (INFOCOM WKSHPS), pp. 183–188 (2020)
12. Sasikumar, A., Ravi, L., Kotecha, K., Saini, J.R., Varadarajan, V., Subramaniyaswamy, V.: Sustainable smart industry: a secure and energy efficient consensus mechanism for artificial intelligence enabled industrial internet of things. Comput. Intell. Neurosci. 2022 (2022)
13. Shayan, M., Fung, C., Yoon, C.J., Beschastnikh, I.: Biscotti: a blockchain system for private and secure federated learning. IEEE Trans. Parallel Distrib. Syst. **32**(7), 1513–1525 (2020)
14. Soria, E.: Swarms of flying robots in unknown environments. Sci. Rob. **7**(66), eabq2215 (2022)
15. Sun, Y., Yan, B., Yao, Y., Yu, J.: DT-DPoS: a delegated proof of stake consensus algorithm with dynamic trust. Procedia Comput. Sci. **187**, 371–376 (2021)
16. Tang, X., Lan, X., Li, L., Zhang, Y., Han, Z.: Incentivizing proof-of-stake blockchain for secured data collection in UAV-assisted IoT: a multi-agent reinforcement learning approach. IEEE J. Sel. Areas Commun. **40**(12), 3470–3484 (2022)

Applications of Consortium Blockchain in Power Grid Security: A Systematic Review

Li Di[1], Weijian Zhang[1], Lijing Yan[2], Han Liu[2], Qishuang Fu[3], and Jiajing Wu[3(✉)]

[1] State Grid Henan Electric Power Company, Zhengzhou 450018, China
{dili,zhangweijian}@ha.sgcc.com.cn
[2] State Grid Henan Information and Telecommunication Company (Data Center), Zhengzhou 450052, China
{yanlijing,liuhan3}@ha.sgcc.com.cn
[3] School of Computer Science and Engineering, Sun Yat-sen University, Guangzhou 510006, China
fuqsh6@mail2.sysu.edu.cn, wujiajing@mail.sysu.edu.cn

Abstract. With the development of the power industry, the security of the power grid has become a top priority. In recent years, blockchain technology has been proposed as a solution to the security problems of power grids. Specifically, the use of consortium blockchain technology can help solve issues in the power grid. In this paper, we first introduce consortium blockchain technology and then analyzes the security problems faced by power grids. Furthermore, we propose four possible applications of consortium blockchain technology in the power grid sector to address those security issues. Finally, we discuss the advantages and challenges of using consortium blockchain technology in the power grid sector.

Keywords: Power grid · Consortium blockchain · Security problems

1 Introduction

The power grid [7], also known as the electrical grid or power system, is a complex and interconnected network that delivers electricity from power plants to consumers. It is an essential infrastructure for modern society, powering homes, businesses, hospitals, and other critical facilities. The grid comprises a wide range of components, including generators, transformers, transmission lines, and distribution networks, and it relies on advanced control and monitoring systems to ensure its safe and reliable operation. With the increasing demand for energy and the development of smart grid technology, the power grid has become more complex and interconnected than ever before. While this has brought many benefits, it has also created new challenges for ensuring the security and reliability of the power grid [21]. The traditional centralized approach to power grid management has proven to be inadequate, as it lacks the flexibility and adaptability needed to

J. Chen et al. (Eds.): BlockSys 2023, CCIS 1897, pp. 102–115, 2024.
https://doi.org/10.1007/978-981-99-8104-5_8

respond to the dynamic changes in the grid. Moreover, it has also made the grid more vulnerable to cyber-attacks, natural disasters, and other security threats.

As the power grid sector faces security threats to the need for more efficient and transparent transaction management, there is a growing interest in exploring the potential of blockchain technology to address these challenges. Blockchain technology [8], as a decentralized and transparent ledger, offers a promising solution to these challenges. The use of consortium blockchain [5], in particular, has gained increasing attention as a potential solution in the power grid sector. Consortium blockchain technology enables multiple stakeholders in the power grid, including utilities, energy producers, regulators, and customers, to share data and manage transactions securely and transparently in real-time without the need for a central authority. This technology provides a more secure and efficient way to manage the power grid, as it facilitates the secure and transparent sharing of data and transaction management among the stakeholders. By leveraging this technology, stakeholders can collaborate more effectively, improving the overall efficiency and reliability of the power grid.

In this paper, we explore the potential of using consortium blockchain technology to enhance the security of the power grid. We first provide an overview of blockchain technology and its architecture, and discuss its potential applications in the power grid. We then analyze several security issues that the power grid faces, including data tampering and security, quality traceability, energy trading reliability, and process optimization. Furthermore, we propose four possible applications of consortium blockchain technology in the power grid sector to address those security issues. Finally, we discuss the advantages and challenges of using consortium blockchain technology in the power grid sector.

The remaining parts of the paper are organized as follows. Section X introduces the process of crawling downstream transactions of Upbit hacks and constructing a rough suspicious ML network. Section 2 describes the architecture of consortium blockchain and the application of consortium blockchain. In Sect. 3, we present 4 kinds of power grid security issues. Section 4 shows how consortium blockchain addresses these 4 kinds of security issues in the power grid. Section 5 introduces the advantages and challenges of consortium blockchain technology in power grid security. The conclusion is presented in Sect. 6.

2   Overview of Consortium Blockchain Technology

2.1   Consortium Blockchain

Consortium blockchain technology is a type of distributed ledger technology that enables a group of pre-authorized participants to share a tamper-proof and transparent record of transactions. Unlike public blockchains, consortium blockchains are private and only allow specific participants to access and validate transactions on the blockchain. Multiple designated nodes are selected as bookkeepers in the consortium chain, and the generation of each block is jointly determined by all designated nodes. Other access nodes can participate in transactions but do not intervene in the bookkeeping process. Other third parties can perform limited queries through the open API provided by the blockchain. Although the configuration of consensus or validation nodes and network environment has certain requirements for better performance, the access mechanism also makes improving transaction performance easier and avoids issues caused by participants' performance differences.

2.2   Consortium Blockchain Underlying Architecture

In general, consortium blockchain is composed of five parts [5]: data layer, network layer, consensus layer, contract layer, and application layer. The data layer mainly describes the physical form of blockchain technology, which is a chain-like structure starting from the genesis block, and each block contains random numbers, timestamps, and public-private key data, etc. It is the lowest-level data structure in the entire blockchain technology. As there are multiple nodes in the consortium blockchain, it is recommended to allocate different public and private keys to different nodes for encryption purposes in order to effectively manage node data and ensure data security. The network layer plays the role of information exchange between nodes in the blockchain network and is responsible for user-to-user information exchange. It mainly includes P2P (Peer-To-Peer network) network mechanism, data dissemination, and verification mechanism. The consensus layer ensures efficient consensus on the validity of block data among nodes in a decentralized system with a high degree of decision-making power distribution. The consensus layer adopts the PBFT (Practical Byzantine Fault Tolerance) consensus algorithm [4]. Unlike the mining mechanism in public chains, consortium chains focus more on the uniformity of node information, so mining can be eliminated and the goal of reaching consensus can be directly pursued. The contract layer mainly encapsulates various script codes, algorithms, and more complex smart contracts required for the operation of the blockchain system. The contract layer is the foundation for flexible programming and data manipulation in the blockchain system and also serves as a link between the application layer and the underlying architecture. The application layer provides various services and applications to users by developing decentralized applications (DApps) to enrich the entire blockchain ecosystem. Generally, the application layer of consortium chains is industry-oriented, solving problems within the industry.

2.3   Consortium Blockchain Applications

The consortium blockchain delegates power to various nodes to help various industries establish a decentralized trust system, achieve transparent sharing of information and efficient management, promote business flow and innovation, and improve data security and credibility. Currently, consortium blockchain technology has been widely used in multiple fields, including Supply chain, finance, logistics, healthcare, real estate registration, and more.

Eluubek *et al.* [6] applied consortium blockchain technology to agricultural supply chain systems, establishing a consortium with networked physical systems through the use of blockchain technology to enhance the system's high

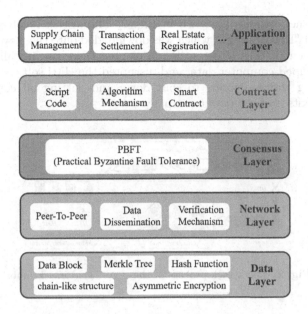

Fig. 1. The architecture of consortium blockchain.

trustworthiness. They also proposed a consensus algorithm suitable for a large number of farmers, solving the system's scalability issues (Fig. 1).

Hamed *et al.* [1] a consortium blockchain architecture for a fully decentralized stock market, which addressed the limitations of traditional stock trading platforms. The consortium network used organizations already involved in traditional stock exchanges as validating nodes and created smart contracts for trade exchanges. It addressed a single point of failure by replicating data and smart contracts across all participating nodes and resolved the complexity and inefficiency of data management by providing a shared ledger that was easy to update and maintain.

3   Power Grid Security Issues

3.1   Data Tampering Issue

In the field of power grids, the accuracy and integrity of data are crucial for the safe and stable operation of the power system [2]. However, traditional centralized data management methods are vulnerable to data tampering risks. For example, attackers can manipulate data by attacking the power grid management system or infiltrating sensors and measuring devices in the grid. These manipulated data can lead to erroneous decisions that may cause the grid to collapse or affect its normal operation.

In December 2015, the power grid in Ukraine was brought down by a hacker attack [31], resulting in a power outage for around 225,000 people for several hours. The attack process is shown in Fig. 2. The attack involved the use of malware called "BlackEnergy" which was downloaded onto the power company's computers via email. The hackers then implanted the virus, installed malicious components, wiped computer data, and disrupted the HMI software monitoring system, causing the computers to shut down and cutting off communication between residents and the power company.

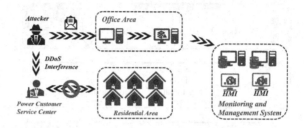

Fig. 2. The attack process of the power grid in Ukraine.

3.2   Quality Traceability Issue

Quality traceability [22] in the power grid domain usually refers to the full-process traceability of the production, transportation, installation, maintenance, and other aspects of power equipment and products to ensure their quality and safety. Quality issues with power grid equipment and products may lead to power grid failures and safety accidents, seriously threatening the safety and stable operation of the power system.

In the 2019 power outage event of the UK's National Grid [33], the cause of the failure was complex, including a fault in a high-voltage transmission line and automatic shutdown of some generators, but the investigation found that an important factor was the lack of correct recording and tracking of quality issues in the transmission line. This case highlights that the lack of quality traceability mechanisms in the power grid sector can have a significant impact on the safety and stability of the power system.

3.3   Trustworthiness Issue in Energy Trading

Energy trading [20] between parties in the field of the power grid involves complex transaction processes and a large amount of data exchange, including energy production, transmission, storage, and sales. The accuracy and credibility of these data are crucial to ensuring the fairness and legality of the transactions.

During extreme weather conditions in February 2021, Texas' power supply system was severely affected, resulting in millions of homes and businesses losing power. During this period, the price of electricity in the market sharply increased, and some energy suppliers took advantage of the increased demand by raising prices and selling electricity to those who could afford to pay the high prices.

This resulted in many users having to bear high electricity costs. However, these energy suppliers did not provide enough energy to meet market demand, which further exacerbated the severity of the power crisis.

3.4 Management Process Optimization Issue

Currently, many power companies still rely on traditional manual management processes, which result in low efficiency and potential threats to the security and stability of the power system due to errors and vulnerabilities. Additionally, with the widespread application of new energy and smart grid technologies, power system management and operation have become more complex and require more efficient and intelligent management processes [9] to ensure normal system operation.

The Porter Ranch natural gas leak in California in 2015 was caused by the failure of a wellhead at a natural gas storage facility, resulting in a significant amount of gas leakage. This incident exposed vulnerabilities in the management and monitoring system of the storage facility, including a lack of real-time monitoring and reporting system, as well as a lack of necessary safety audit procedures.

4 Application of Consortium Blockchain in the Field of Power Grid Security

4.1 Grid Data Security

Generally speaking, data security in the power grid field includes sharing, transmission, and tamper-proofing. In terms of power grid data sharing, Liu et al. uses IPFS as a secure channel for data transmission and sharing, and uses cross-chain technology to share data to another alliance chain, and applies secure multi-party computing to secure data sharing between two alliance chains [14]. Shen et al. uses smart contract technology to automatically complete the network-wide verification process of data encryption and zero-knowledge credentials to achieve data security interaction [23]. Si et al. proposed a federated learning based power data sharing mechanism [24].

In terms of data transmission, Ma et al. adopted Paillier homomorphic encryption algorithm and role-based access control strategy to ensure the privacy security in the process of multi-dimensional aggregation, data transmission and sharing of electric power data [18]. Liu et al. established a data transmission mechanism based on secure sovereign blockchain monitoring in the smart grid between users and power companies. The power company will process and negotiate the node's request according to the user's unique ID, and transmit the distribution operation record data to the data processing and monitoring layer [15]. Lu et al. proposed a power information collection model considering safe access and interaction. Based on this model, they proposed a strategy for secure access of power harvesting equipment and secure transmission of power measurement data.

In order to prevent the power data from being maliciously tampered with, Sun et al. completed the data block encryption through homomorphic encryption technology and used the data integrity verification method to verify the data [26]. Li et al. used smart contract technology to realize encrypted transmission, complete storage and trusted sharing of electronic data of power grid enterprises. Through high-performance keyword matching algorithms, they have realized rapid query and accurate evidence collection of electronic data, which not only promotes the development of power grid digitization, but also improves the legal quality and efficiency of electronic data storage [12]. Jiang et al. proposed a secure multi-party computing scheme for sharing energy storage indicators in a blockchain environment. Their solution also uses homomorphic encryption to protect the data encryption process and prevent data privacy leaks [11]. Liu et al. proposed an anti-forgery sharing model based on attribute encryption. In their model, data users entrust multiple nodes to participate in joint calculations and store part of the private key, while other data users cannot obtain the complete private key, thereby improving the efficiency of private key generation [17].

4.2 Quality Traceability

In terms of quality traceability, Tang et al. considered the application of a blockchain-based ring signature scheme in smart grids. In their scheme there exists an audit node that can distinguish the identity of the real signer without any secret information [27]. Zhao et al. designed a green power traceability mechanism covering the five links of "power generation-transmission-distribution-transaction-consumption" by sorting out and analyzing the green power transaction process of the Winter Olympics and relying on blockchain technology [36]. Key information about the whole process. Distributed storage of certification and core data effectively maintains data security and ensures the authenticity and credibility of key information throughout the entire Winter Olympics green power process. Similarly, Wang et al. proposed a green power traceability system based on blockchain technology to provide users with convenient green power charging services [28]. The system consists of main chain, transaction side chain and data side chain. Through the three dimensions of quantity, price and time, users can trace the type and area of energy. Oberko et al. provide a secure access regulatory design for smart grids that supports traceability and revocability [19]. They use the consortium chain for unified authentication, saving all public keys, user attribute sets, and revocation lists. Song et al. designed a data traceability mechanism based on blockchain to provide evidence for data authenticity, and adopted a proxy re-encryption method to ensure data sharing in view of the data isolation problem existing between suppliers and material companies in the material inspection and distribution links [25]. Shahzad et al. proposed a blockchain-based proof-of-concept solution to manage every transaction that occurs in an IoT-assisted smart grid system. Their IoT-assisted smart grid system can provide an immutable record of transactions. These records are always shared and transparent to every participant of the system [22].

4.3 Trusted Energy Trading

In terms of trusted transactions, Wang et al. proposed a supply chain credit evaluation mechanism that integrates federated learning and blockchain technology [30]. Xie et al. combined existing policies and market rules to conduct research on energy storage participating in ancillary services, and designed a market mechanism for energy storage participating in peak-shaving and frequency-regulating ancillary services [32]. Finally, they proposed a blockchain-based energy storage market-oriented transaction model and mechanism to improve the flexibility of the power system and promote clean energy consumption. Chi et al. conducted research on distributed new energy spot market technology through blockchain technology, and designed a weakly centralized trading system [3]. Through the operation and real-time supervision of power companies, the supply and demand sides interact directly, and the electricity price is used to guide the transaction, which realizes the incentive compatibility between member income and the overall interests of the system, and effectively promotes the real-time balance of supply and demand. Jiang et al. proposed a blockchain-based trusted adjustable load resource trading framework, using a two-layer consortium blockchain architecture to realize trusted grid load resource trading [10]. The main chain maintains all the data of the system, and the station nodes form the alliance chain. They also designed a distributed transaction processing mechanism based on hybrid consensus and sharding technology, which improves the speed of cross-site transaction consensus.

4.4 Management Process Optimization

In terms of management process, Liu et al. proposed a power system log partition collection and storage system based on consortium blockchain technology [13], which integrates blockchain technology into power system log management. Yuan et al. proposed a collaborative mechanism for supply chain management information systems from the perspective of alliance chains [35], including process and consensus collaborative management mechanisms. On this basis, they designed the supply chain management information system platform architecture under the collaborative mechanism, optimized the transaction process management and the consensus and accounting of the blockchain system. In terms of power dispatching, Liu et al. adopted a decentralized dispatching strategy and blockchain technology, proposed a practical Byzantine fault-tolerant algorithm consensus mechanism for integrated energy systems, and realized a two-stage robust optimal dispatching model [16]. Yang et al. proposed a decentralized dispatching and operation control mechanism for a multi-energy fusion system based on blockchain technology to realize energy supply and demand information sharing between different energy systems and different regions in multiple energy systems [34]. Wang et al. designed a cloud service platform for the integrated energy market [29]. Participants on the platform can be divided into integrated energy suppliers and integrated energy users. The two can use digital currency electronic payment for energy transactions in the blockchain smart contract provided by the cloud service platform, and use blockchain Internet of Things technology to realize decentralized intelligent scheduling.

5 Advantages and Challenges of Consortium Blockchain in the Field of Power Grid Security

5.1 Advantages

The advantages of consortium blockchain technology in the field of power grid security are mainly reflected in decentralization, controllability, data privacy and confidentiality, high efficiency and low cost.

- **Decentralization and Distribution.** The consortium blockchain technology adopts a decentralized design, connecting multiple nodes together to form a distributed network, each node has the same data copy, and does not need to rely on a single central node to manage and verify the data. This distributed structure can guarantee the stability and reliability of the system, and can avoid the risk of the entire system crashing due to the failure or attack of the central node.
- **Controllability and Transparency.** consortium blockchain technology allows the establishment of mutual trust mechanism among network members, and realizes automated business logic and rule execution through smart contracts. This mechanism can ensure the security and controllability of the system, and can ensure the transparency and fairness among network members, thereby avoiding the disadvantages of centralized management.
- **Data Privacy and Confidentiality.** Consortium blockchain technology can provide participants with a highly confidential data sharing environment. In the consortium chain network, participants can share data, but only authorized members can access specific data. This mechanism can ensure data privacy and confidentiality, and can prevent bad actors from obtaining sensitive information through illegal means.
- **High Efficiency and Low Cost.** Consortium blockchain technology adopts efficient consensus algorithm and distributed storage method, which can improve the processing speed and data throughput of the system, and can also reduce the maintenance cost and management cost of the system. This high-efficiency and low-cost feature can provide a more practical solution for the grid security field.

To sum up, compared with traditional technologies, consortium blockchain technology can provide more reliable and efficient solutions for grid security.

5.2 Challenges

Although the consortium chain has played a great role in solving power grid security issues, its continuous application still faces many challenges.

- **Network Scale Challenges.** As a huge system, the power grid involves many parties, and requires consortium blockchain technology to be able to expand to a large-scale network to ensure the stability and reliability of the system. However, with the increase of participants, consortium blockchain technology may face some technical challenges, such as:
  - Reasonable network topology design: In the consortium blockchain network, the connection relationship between nodes and the data transmission path are very important. It is necessary to reasonably design the network topology structure so that it can adapt to the complexity and variability of the power grid system.
  - Efficient consensus algorithm: The consensus algorithm is the core of the consortium blockchain technology, and it is necessary to ensure the scalability and reliability of the consortium blockchain network. However, in a large-scale consortium blockchain network, the efficiency and security of the consensus algorithm may face challenges.
- **Security Challenges.** The security of the consortium blockchain technology is one of the key factors to ensure the security of the power grid, but the consortium blockchain itself also has some security risks, for example, attackers may use the loopholes in the consortium blockchain to attack. Therefore, it is necessary to strengthen the security design of the consortium blockchain to ensure the security and stability of the system. Specifically, the following issues need to be addressed:
  - Data privacy protection: In the power grid system, data privacy is very important, and effective security protection measures need to be taken to prevent malicious attacks and data leakage.
  - Identity verification and authority control: Participants in the consortium blockchain network need to perform identity verification and authority control to ensure the security and compliance of the system.
  - Prevent 51% attack: 51% attack is a very dangerous attack method. Attackers can control more than 51% of the computing power of the consortium blockchain network, thereby tampering with transaction records and controlling the entire network. Therefore, it is necessary to take corresponding technical measures to prevent such attacks.
- **Reliability Challenges of Smart Contracts.** The smart contract is the core of consortium blockchain technology, which is responsible for realizing the business logic and rule execution of the system. However, there may also be loopholes in the smart contract itself, resulting in a threat to the security of the system. Therefore, it is necessary to strengthen the reliability and security design of smart contracts to prevent bad actors from attacking the system. Specifically, the following issues need to be addressed:
  - Smart contract loopholes: There are some security loopholes in smart contracts, such as re-entry attacks, overflow attacks, etc., which may lead to the system being hacked. Therefore, it is necessary to adopt corresponding technical means to strengthen the security and reliability of smart contracts.

- Contract execution efficiency: The execution efficiency of smart contracts has an important impact on the performance and scalability of the system. If the contract execution efficiency is low, it will lead to problems such as slow system response and increased transaction costs.
- Contract upgrade and maintenance: Due to the immutability of smart contracts, once there is a problem with the contract, it is difficult to repair and upgrade. Therefore, it is necessary to adopt corresponding technical means so that the contract can be upgraded and maintained to ensure the long-term reliability of the system.

– **Data Standardization Challenges.** In the power grid system, a large amount of data and information are involved. These data and information need to be standardized and classified before they can be utilized by consortium blockchain technology. However, data standardization and classification require a lot of time and effort. Specifically, the following issues need to be addressed

- Data quality and integrity: In the power grid system, data quality and integrity are very important for the application of consortium blockchain technology. Therefore, it is necessary to adopt corresponding technical means to ensure the quality and integrity of the data, so as to ensure the reliability and security of the system.
- Data sharing and exchange: There are many participants in the power grid system, and data sharing and exchange are required to better realize business processes. However, data sharing and exchange need to consider issues such as data privacy and security, and corresponding technical means need to be adopted to ensure data security and reliability.

6   Conclusions and Future Work

This paper summarizes the application status and development trend of consortium blockchain technology in the field of power grid security. First, we introduced the concept, characteristics, and architecture of consortium blockchain technology. Secondly, we analyzed data tamper-proof and security issues, quality traceability issues, energy transaction credibility issues, and management process optimization issues in the field of power grid security. We also investigate the existing technologies and applications of alliance chains in solving these problems. Further, we explore the advantages and challenges of consortium blockchain technology in the field of grid security. The advantages of consortium blockchain technology lie in its decentralization, high security, strong transparency, and high credibility, which make it have broad application prospects in the field of power grid security. However, there are still some challenges in the application of consortium blockchain technology in the field of grid security. First of all, the scale and complexity of the consortium blockchain network are getting larger and larger, and the challenges of network scale are becoming increasingly severe. Secondly, the security of consortium blockchain technology and the reliability of smart contracts need to be better guaranteed to ensure the security and credibility of grid data. Finally, in order to ensure interoperability between different consortium blockchain networks, we also need to solve the problem of data standardization.

In the future, with the continuous development and application of consortium blockchain technology, its application in the field of grid security will be further promoted and developed. In the face of network scale challenges, consortium blockchain technology can adopt hierarchical design and dynamic adjustment to improve the scalability and adaptability of the network. In terms of security challenges, measures such as encryption technology and multi-factor authentication can be used to ensure the security and credibility of grid data. The reliability of smart contracts can be solved by developing a more robust smart contract language and developing more complete testing tools. On the issue of data standardization, the interoperability between different consortium blockchain networks can be improved by formulating unified standards and specifications, and at the same time, the standardization and normalization process of consortium blockchain technology can be strengthened. In short, we need to continuously explore and apply consortium blockchain technology to solve the challenges in the field of grid security and promote the rapid development and application of consortium blockchain technology in the field of grid security.

References

1. Al-Shaibani, H., Lasla, N., Abdallah, M.: Consortium blockchain-based decentralized stock exchange platform. IEEE Access **8**, 123711–123725 (2020). https://doi.org/10.1109/ACCESS.2020.3005663
2. Bekara, C.: Security issues and challenges for the IoT-based smart grid. Procedia Comput. Sci. **34**, 532–537 (2014)
3. Chi, C., et al.: Research on distributed new energy spot trading method based on blockchain technology. In: Proceedings of the 2020 Chinese Automation Congress (CAC), pp. 275–278. IEEE (2020)
4. Choi, B., Sohn, J.Y., Han, D.J., Moon, J.: Scalable network-coded PBFT consensus algorithm. In: 2019 IEEE International Symposium on Information Theory (ISIT), pp. 857–861. IEEE (2019)
5. Dib, O., Brousmiche, K.L., Durand, A., Thea, E., Hamida, E.B.: Consortium blockchains: overview, applications and challenges. Int. J. Adv. Telecommun. **11**(1), 51–64 (2018)
6. Eluubek kyzy, I., Song, H., Vajdi, A., Wang, Y., Zhou, J.: Blockchain for consortium: a practical paradigm in agricultural supply chain system. Expert Syst. Appl. **184**, 115425 (2021)
7. Fang, X., Misra, S., Xue, G., Yang, D.: Smart grid-the new and improved power grid: a survey. IEEE Commun. Surv. Tutor. **14**(4), 944–980 (2011)
8. Hasankhani, A., Hakimi, S.M., Bisheh-Niasar, M., Shafie-khah, M., Asadolahi, H.: Blockchain technology in the future smart grids: a comprehensive review and frameworks. Int. J. Electr. Power Energy Syst. **129**, 106811 (2021)
9. Hussain, M.T., Sulaiman, N.B., Hussain, M.S., Jabir, M.: Optimal management strategies to solve issues of grid having electric vehicles (EV): a review. J. Energy Storage **33**, 102114 (2021)
10. Jiang, W., et al.: A credible and adjustable load resource trading system based on blockchain networks. Front. Phys. **11**, 123 (2023)

11. Jiang, X., Li, L., Qiu, W., Pei, Y., Tao, Y., Lin, Z.: Secure multi-party computation scheme of shared energy storage index based on blockchain environment. In: Proceedings of the 2021 IEEE/IAS Industrial and Commercial Power System Asia (I&CPS Asia), pp. 586–591. IEEE (2021)
12. Li, G., Xuanline, J., Xue, W., Jia, F.: Design and implementation of electronic data blockchain judicial deposit platform for power grid Gusiness. In: Proceedings of the 2022 International Academic Exchange Conference on Science and Technology Innovation (IAECST), pp. 876–881. IEEE (2022)
13. Liu, L., Luan, J., Yuan, L., Zhang, Y.: Power log partition collection and storage system based on alliance blockchain. In: Proceedings of the 2021 International Conference on Wireless Communications and Smart Grid (ICWCSG), pp. 390–394. IEEE (2021)
14. Liu, Q., Tang, W., Liu, X.: Power grid data sharing technology based on communication data fusion. In: Proceedings of the 2021 International Seminar on Artificial Intelligence, Networking and Information Technology, pp. 703–707. IEEE (2021)
15. Liu, S., Zhang, Q., Liu, H.: Privacy protection of the smart grid system based on blockchain. In: Journal of Physics: Conference Series, vol. 1744, p. 022129. IOP Publishing (2021)
16. Liu, X.: Research on decentralized operation scheduling strategy of integrated energy system based on energy blockchain. Int. J. Energy Res. **46**(15), 21558–21582 (2022)
17. Liu, Y., Wu, Z., Liu, Y., Fan, W., Wang, K., Lin, L.: Blockchain data anti-counterfeiting sharing model of power material alliance based on attribute-based encryption. In: Proceedings of the 2021 IEEE International Conference on Automation, Electronics and Electrical Engineering (AUTEEE), pp. 242–248. IEEE (2021)
18. Ma, Y., Su, H., Zhou, X., Tu, F.: Research on data security and privacy protection of smart grid based on alliance chain. In: Proceedings of the 2022 IEEE International Conference on Mechatronics and Automation (ICMA), pp. 157–162. IEEE (2022)
19. Oberko, P.S.K., Yao, T., Xiong, H., Kumari, S., Kumar, S.: Blockchain-oriented data exchange protocol with traceability and revocation for smart grid. J. Internet Technol. **24**(2), 497–506 (2023)
20. Otoum, S., Al Ridhawi, I., Mouftah, H.: A federated learning and blockchain-enabled sustainable energy-trade at the edge: a framework for industry 4.0. IEEE Internet Things J. **10**, 3018–3026 (2022)
21. Otuoze, A.O., Mustafa, M.W., Larik, R.M.: Smart grids security challenges: classification by sources of threats. J. Electr. Syst. Inf. Technol. **5**(3), 468–483 (2018)
22. Shahzad, A., Zhang, K., Gherbi, A.: Privacy-preserving smart grid traceability using blockchain over IoT connectivity. In: Proceedings of the 36th Annual ACM Symposium on Applied Computing, pp. 699–706 (2021)
23. Shen, S., Sun, C.: Research on framework of smart grid data secure storage from blockchain perspective. In: Proceedings of the 2021 International Conference on Advanced Electronic Materials, Computers and Software Engineering, pp. 270–273. IEEE (2021)
24. Si, Z., Xiao, D., Yang, C., Tian, X., Lei, Z., Ma, X.: Smart grid data security sharing mechanism based on alliance blockchain. In: Liu, Q., Liu, X., Chen, B., Zhang, Y., Peng, J. (eds.) Proceedings of the 11th International Conference on Computer Engineering and Networks. LNEE, vol. 808, pp. 784–792. Springer, Singapore (2022). https://doi.org/10.1007/978-981-16-6554-7_85
25. Song, J., et al.: Proxy re-encryption-based traceability and sharing mechanism of the power material data in blockchain environment. Energies **15**(7), 2570 (2022)

26. Sun, M., et al.: Data security storage method of power grid asset system based on blockchain. In: Proceedings of the 2022 International Conference on Information Science, Computer Technology and Transportation, pp. 1–6. VDE (2022)
27. Tang, F., Pang, J., Cheng, K., Gong, Q.: Multiauthority traceable ring signature scheme for smart grid based on blockchain. Wirel. Commun. Mob. Comput. **2021**, 1–9 (2021)
28. Wang, H., et al.: A green power traceability technology based on timestamp in a main-side chain system. In: Proceedings of the 2020 International Congress on Image and Signal Processing, BioMedical Engineering and Informatics (CISP-BMEI), pp. 1087–1092. IEEE (2020)
29. Wang, L., Ma, Y., Zhu, L., Wang, X., Cong, H., Shi, T.: Design of integrated energy market cloud service platform based on blockchain smart contract. Int. J. Electr. Power Energy Syst. **135**, 107515 (2022)
30. Wang, X., et al.: Research on trusted sharing and privacy computing technology of energy data in supply chain based on alliance chain. In: Proceedings of the 2022 IEEE International Conference on Civil Aviation Safety and Information Technology (ICCASIT), pp. 46–50. IEEE (2022)
31. Weerakkody, S., Sinopoli, B.: Challenges and opportunities: cyber-physical security in the smart grid. In: Stoustrup, J., Annaswamy, A., Chakrabortty, A., Qu, Z. (eds.) Smart Grid Control. PEPS, pp. 257–273. Springer, Cham (2019). https://doi.org/10.1007/978-3-319-98310-3_16
32. Xie, Y.S., Chang, X.Q., Yin, X., Zheng, H., et al.: Research on the transaction mode and mechanism of grid-side shared energy storage market based on blockchain. Energy Rep. **8**, 224–229 (2022)
33. Xu, S.: Electricity emergency management in the UK and Australia: exploring the enlightenments for china. In: IOP Conference Series: Earth and Environmental Science, vol. 295, p. 042029. IOP Publishing (2019)
34. Yang, T., Yang, F., Ji, X., Liang, Y., Wang, Y.: Research on operation and management of decentralized dispatching agency for multi-energy system based on block chain technology. In: Xue, Y., Zheng, Y., Bose, A. (eds.) PMF 2020. LNEE, vol. 718, pp. 314–326. Springer, Singapore (2021). https://doi.org/10.1007/978-981-15-9746-6_25
35. Yuan, H., Qiu, H., Bi, Y., Chang, S.H., Lam, A.: Analysis of coordination mechanism of supply chain management information system from the perspective of block chain. Inf. Syst. e-Bus. Manag. **18**, 681–703 (2020)
36. Zhao, L., Li, D., Yang, K., Guo, Q.: Design and implementation of green power traceability system based on blockchain technology in the 2022 Beijing winter olympics. In: Proceedings of the 2022 International Conference on Bigdata Blockchain and Economy Management (ICBBEM 2022), pp. 623–632. Atlantis Press (2022)

Blockchain and OR Based Data Sharing Solution for Internet of Things

Jiatao Li[1], Dezhi Han[1,2], Dun Li[1(✉)], and Hongzhi Li[2]

[1] College of Information Engineering, Shanghai Maritime University, Shanghai 200135, China
lidunshmtu@outlook.com
[2] School of Big Data and Artificial Intelligence, Chizhou University, Chizhou 247000, China

Abstract. Communication between nodes in the Internet of Things (IoT) is still in its infancy, and several contemporary security dangers and issues are impeding data transmission in this process. In this research, we initially use a communication control gateway on the edge server to distinguish malicious and non-malicious message requests from machines and forward them to the onion routing (OR) network to overcome the aforementioned security vulnerabilities. Next, by integrating the authentication token field in the initial message request, we connected the standard OR network with blockchain technology to improve its security and dependability. The suggested blockchain-based onion network beats the conventional network in terms of throughput and decryption speed, according to experimental results (with low computational cost).

Keywords: Blockchain · Internet of Things · Onion Routing · IPFS · Cryptography

1 Introduction

With the advent of the Internet of Things (IoT) technology, a plethora of devices are now connected to the internet, generating an enormous amount of data. This data can be utilized for a variety of purposes, ranging from enhancing user experience to improving business efficiency. However, with the increasing use of IoT devices, issues such as data security, privacy protection, and data reliability have become more complex and critical [1]. One of the most significant challenges in IoT data communication is ensuring the security and privacy of the data transmitted over the network [2,3]. Traditional data communication methods are no longer adequate for protecting the data transmitted through IoT devices due to the risk of data tampering, theft, and loss. Therefore, it is essential to have robust security measures to safeguard the privacy and integrity of the data being communicated. Another issue that arises in IoT data communication is the reliability of the data generated by these devices. The data collected by IoT devices can be sensitive, and its accuracy and reliability are of utmost importance. Inaccurate

© The Author(s), under exclusive license to Springer Nature Singapore Pte Ltd. 2024
J. Chen et al. (Eds.): BlockSys 2023, CCIS 1897, pp. 116–127, 2024.
https://doi.org/10.1007/978-981-99-8104-5_9

or unreliable data can lead to incorrect decisions, potentially causing significant losses to businesses or even endangering human lives.

As the security and privacy challenges of IoT data communication become increasingly complex, new solutions are being developed to address these issues. One solution that has garnered considerable attention is the blockchain-based OR component. This approach combines the tamper-evident nature of blockchain with the security of smart contracts to ensure the authenticity and privacy of data transmission. The blockchain-based OR component is designed to hide the transmission path of data, ensuring anonymity and privacy of data transmission. OR involves encrypting data in multiple layers, where each layer is stripped away as the data moves from one node to another, making it difficult to trace the source of the data [4]. This approach is particularly useful for transmitting sensitive data, such as personal information or financial transactions [5]. The use of blockchain technology further enhances the security of data transmission in the OR component. Blockchain provides a decentralized, tamper-evident ledger that records all transactions and data modifications [6,7]. Smart contracts, which are self-executing contracts with the terms of the agreement between buyer and seller being directly written into lines of code, are used to enforce the rules of data transmission, ensuring that only authorized parties have access to the data [8]. Blockchain and OR offers a powerful solution for secure and private data transmission in IoT networks. This approach can be used to protect sensitive data and prevent unauthorized access, while also ensuring the integrity and authenticity of the data transmitted. Moreover, the decentralized nature of blockchain makes it an ideal solution for IoT networks, which require a high level of scalability and resilience.

Therefore, this paper aims to introduce the application of blockchain-based OR components in IoT data communication to provide a reliable solution for the security and privacy of IoT data communication. Firstly, the paper will provide an overview of the challenges associated with IoT data communication and the limitations of traditional data communication methods in addressing these challenges. It will then discuss the concept of blockchain-based OR components and how they can be applied to IoT networks to ensure secure and private data transmission. The paper highlights the benefits of using blockchain technology for IoT data communication, including its decentralized and tamper-evident nature. It also explains how OR can be used to hide the transmission path of data, ensuring anonymity and privacy of data transmission. The paper then explores the use of smart contracts to enforce the rules of data transmission, ensuring that only authorized parties have access to the data. Finally, the paper will conclude by summarizing the advantages of using blockchain-based OR components for IoT data communication and highlighting the potential challenges and future directions of this technology.

The rest of the paper is organized as follows. Section 2 begins with a description of related work. Section 3 is a description of the detailed construction of the solution. Section 4 conducts simulation experiments on the proposed model. Section 5 concludes the paper.

2 Related Work

With the rapid development of Internet of Things (IoT) technology, IoT applications face challenges such as data security, trust establishment, and decentralization. Fortunately, blockchain, as a distributed and tamper-proof technology for data storage and transactions, provides new solutions for IoT applications. Han et al. [9] deployed an access control model to smart contracts on the blockchain and uploaded information and user operation records from the IoT to the blockchain network, achieving secure management and auditable access to data. Bataineh et al. [10] integrated blockchain into medical IoT devices to ensure data immutability in medical monitoring, ensuring the correct flow of business logic and securing the entire medical process. Ahmed et al. [11] proposed a blockchain-backed energy-saving data aggregation mechanism and integrated blockchain into cloud servers to provide validation for edge devices, thereby offering secure services to the IoT. The combination of blockchain technology and OR technology allows for more secure and reliable data sharing. The researchers implement the functions of intermediate node management and route path randomisation in OR through blockchain technology while using smart contracts to implement a trust mechanism between nodes to ensure data security and reliability. The method is significant in terms of privacy protection and data sharing. Gupta et al. [12] proposed an M2M communication scheme based on blockchain and OR, and combined edge intelligence and 5G network to realize secure message exchange between IIoT machines. Moreover, The zero-knowledge proof technique enables a method to prove certain facts without exposing private information, which has important privacy-preserving implications. Researchers use zero-knowledge proof technology to achieve anonymity and privacy protection for OR while using blockchain technology to ensure the security and reliability of the routing. The method has great potential for application in privacy preservation and data sharing. Voloch et al. [13] proposed a verification scheme based on zero-knowledge proof to solve the problem of outlet node vulnerability in onion routing. In addition, The encryption algorithm is the key technology to achieve encryption and decryption in OR. The researchers implement a trust mechanism between nodes by using blockchain technology to ensure the security and reliability of data while using modern encryption algorithms to ensure the privacy protection of data. The method has great potential for data sharing and privacy protection. Kelesidis [14] analyzed the current cryptographic methods for quantization resistance of the Onion router. Finally, The Distributed Hash Tables (DHTs) are a distributed technology for storing and finding data that enables distributed OR. By combining DHT and blockchain technology, researchers have achieved more efficient data sharing and privacy protection. The method has great application value in distributed scenarios. Jadav et al. [15] calculated the optimal path between the source node and target node in OR by using parallel computing DHTS.

3   Model Construction and Design

This section describes the functioning of the proposed IoT secure sharing mechanism.

3.1   Problem Definition

When IoT nodes issue data-sharing requests using traditional wireless network interfaces, they leave behind a large footprint of information port numbers, application version numbers, routing information, etc. This information can be a key element in an attacker's ability to exploit specific hardware or software vulnerabilities. Therefore, a key element of secure sharing is to maximise the number of concurrent message requests while maintaining the privacy of information requests and the security of OR nodes.

To protect the privacy of message requests and the security of OR nodes, this chapter first defines message requests as sets R, where each request includes the request data and associated parameters. Then, we introduce a secure data-sharing mechanism based on the OR network. Specifically, for each request, we send it through the OR network to three randomly selected relay nodes to protect the privacy of the request. We also introduce a batch processing technique that allows multiple requests to be processed simultaneously, thus maximising the number of concurrent message requests.

Thus, the proposed model consists of three layers: the IoT application node layer, the OR communication layer and the blockchain authentication layer as shown in Fig. 1. The IoT Secure Sharing System ensures the security and reliability of the data in the system through a layered design and multiple security measures. The various layers work together to achieve secure connectivity and data sharing between IoT devices and the blockchain network, providing strong support for the realisation of intelligent production and management. Each of these layers has different tasks and functions in the system, and the detailed work of each layer is described below.

3.2   IoT Application Node Layer Design

The IoT application node layer is the top layer of the whole system, which contains various IoT devices and applications that can communicate and exchange data with each other through the OR communication layer. In addition, before the IoT Node sends data to the network communication layer, it needs to evaluate the credibility of the message sent by the node. The communication gateway will divide all received messages into message group $(G_{N_i}^1, G_{N_i}^2, ..., G_{N_i}^f, ..., G_{N_i}^F)$, where $G_{N_i}^f$ represents node N_i of node function type f. Moreover, the credibility definition of a message is expressed as Eq. 1 and Eq. 2.

$$R_{t,i}^f = (R_{N_i} | G_{N_i}^f | T_{stamp}^i) \tag{1}$$

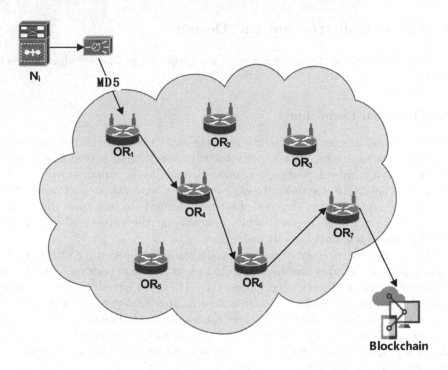

Fig. 1. Model design

$$c_{N_i}^f = R_{t,i}^{1-\rho g_i^f} + \theta \tag{2}$$

Here, $c_{N_i}^f$ is the credibility of message request R_{N_i} for N_i in group $G_{N_i}^f$, and g_i^f is the absolute value of the difference between N_i data sending frequency and normal or preset frequency. $R_{t,i}^f$ is the complete communication verification information after combining the time stamp T_{stamp} sent by the message and the node group; ρ is the criterion based on the effect of g_i^f on the rate of $c_{N_i}^f$; node θ is the lower limit constant of message rating.

After calculating $c_{N_i}^f$, the communication control gateway obtains the confidence set $(c_{N_1}^f, c_{N_2}^f ... c_{N_i}^f ... c_{N_i}^f)$. Therefore, Bayesian inference can be used to calculate the aggregate confidence of R_{N_i} according to the confidence set $c_{N_i}^f$. The calculation process can be defined as Eq. 3:

$$P[R_{N_i}|c_{N_i}^f] = \frac{P[R_{N_i}] \prod\limits_{P=1}^{N} P[c_{N_i}^f|R_{N_i}]}{\sum\limits_{m=1}^{I} (P[R_m] \prod\limits_{P=1}^{N} P[c_{N_i}^f|R_m])} \tag{3}$$

Where $P[R_{N_i}|c_{N_i}^f]$ is the prior probability of R_{N_i} and $P[c_N^f|R_{N_i}] = c_N^f$. Here, R_m is set to be the set of replenishment requests for R_{N_i} and $P[c_N^f|R_m] = 1 - c_N^f$. The decision value is $P[c_N^f|R_{N_i}] \in [0, 1], c_N^f = 0$, then the communication request is rejected immediately. Whether the request is made through communication is decided by the threshold set by the communication gateway. For example, the aggregated message confidence yields a decision value of 0.69, and if the threshold is defined as 0.51, the system will consider the communication request as trusted, pass it, and transmit it to the Tor communication layer.

3.3   OR Communication Layer Design

The OR Communication Layer is the core layer of the IoT Secure Sharing System, which uses an OR technology similar to the OR network to encrypt communication data and transmit it through multiple layers of tunnels, thus safeguarding the confidentiality and privacy of the communication data. At this layer, the system also supports a variety of security protocols and encryption algorithms, such as TLS/SSL, AES, RSA, etc.

3.4   Blockchain Layer Design

The blockchain authentication layer is the underlying layer of the IoT secure sharing system, which uses a distributed ledger technology to record all communication data and transaction information on the blockchain, thus safeguarding the integrity and authenticity of the data. At this layer, the system also supports the development and deployment of smart contracts and distributed applications, making the system more flexible and scalable.

Specifically, in this scheme, to improve the security of the Tor network, this chapter uses a blockchain-based data verification layer as a structural supplement. At the same time, the verification layer introduces the Verifying Token (VT) method. VT is a random hexadecimal number generated by the message R_{N_i} emitted by node N_i, which is used for encryption at the Tor layer. Every time R_{N_i} passes through the communication gateway and encrypts and encapsulates data at multiple layers in the Tor communication layer, a corresponding VT will be generated and stored in the blockchain, forming a SET of VT : $VT_{set} = \{VT_{R_{N_1}}, VT_{R_{N_2}}, ..., VT_{R_{N_t}}\}$. The number of VT is less than or equal to the number of sensor machines I, that is, $\{t = |VT|\} \leq I$. VT has the following three attribute characteristics: First, it is randomly generated by the sender N_i before initiating any communication with the target node N_j. Secondly, each IoT node is unique, and the private key of the node is unique. VT will expire after the first use by the receiver N_j. The sender then generates another random token, which is stored in the blockchain network through an encryption process. Algorithm 1 shows the generation, transformation, and stored procedures of VT with time complexity of $O(I)$. The validation process requires the validation of VT_{set} from the blockchain-based on N_i's message request R_{N_i}.

I indicates the number of IoT application nodes. $VT_t(HEX)$ is the value of the t th VT, expressed in hexadecimal. The $VT_tEncrypted$ is the t th VT

Algorithm 1. $VTGenerate(VT_{id}, Pk)$

Input: $VT_{id}, Pk//VT$ number and key used to encrypt VT
Output: $True\ or\ False$
   $InitVariable()-> (I, Seed)//$Initializes system related variables, including sensor
   number I, for $Seed$ set of random number algorithm.
   while $(I > 0)$ **do**
      $VT_t(Hex) = Random(Seed_t)$
      $VT_{R_{N_t}} = Int(VT_t(Hex))$
      $VT_tEncrypted = Pubk(VT_{R_{N_t}}, Pk)$
      $ERR = Store(VT_{id}, VT_tEncrypted)-> Blockchain$
      if ERR!=Null **then**
         return false
      end if
   end while
   return True

---

encrypted using the public key pk. After it is generated, it will be distributed to the t th node or Tor for the IoT node or Tor to decrypt the onion layer. The t-th encrypted token VT_t can only be decrypted with the private key of the t-th Tor. This ensures the privacy of the data from malicious nodes. Finally, the $VT_tEncrypted$ is stored in the blockchain in the form of a *Transaction*.

The one-time use of VT enhances data security and privacy, preventing malicious behaviour by malicious IoT nodes. The data decryption process on the target node is shown in Eq. 4. Where pri_{VT_t} is the private key of the t-th IoT node, which is used to decrypt the encrypted VT. Once the decryption process is complete, the corresponding node N_t attaches a shared key to decrypt the message or Tor layer. The modified shared key Sk_{VT_t} of any t-th IoT node N_t is shown in Eq. 5 :

In addition, to alleviate the storage burden of blockchain caused by the increase in the amount of data on the blockchain, this scheme uses IPFS as auxiliary storage. Specifically, the specific data of the device is uploaded to IPFS, while the blockchain only stores the index of the device information in IPFS. As shown in Eq. 6 and 7, IoT_{ID} indicates the number of the IoT device, $IoTData$ indicates the detailed data of the device, $IoTData_{hash}$ indicates the hash result of $IoTData$, and $IoTData_{hash}$ indicates the index of $IoTData$ in IPFS.

$$VT_tDecrypted = Pri(VT_tEncrypted, pri_{VT_t}) \tag{4}$$

$$\widehat{Sk_{VT_t}} = Sk_{VT_t} + VT_tDncrypted \tag{5}$$

$$IoTData_{hash} \xleftarrow{return} (IoTData \xrightarrow{Store} IPFS) \tag{6}$$

$$(IoT_{ID}, IoTData_{hash}) \to Blockchain \tag{7}$$

4   Simulation and Experimental Results

To verify the correctness of the scheme proposed above and to evaluate the performance of the scheme, we used Hyperledger Fabric as the blockchain development platform in the blockchain module. Among them, the hardware configuration, related software tools and version numbers used in this experiment are shown in Table 1, and the Hyperledger Fabric-related configuration deployed is shown in Table 2.

Table 1. Modules and tools

Hardware/software tools	Configuration/version number
CPU	Intel Core i5-7300
memory	8 GB
docker	v19.03.2
docker-compose	v1.24.1
node	v12.12.0
golang	v1.13.5
Hyperledger fabric	v1.4.3
IPFS	V0.10.0

Table 2. Node configuration for Hyperledger Fabric

name	number
CouchDB	4
CA	2
Peer	4
Order	1
Fabric-Tools	1
DC	4

4.1   Smart Contracts Test

We set up a set of experiments to test the throughput of the smart contract DC proposed in this scenario under different transaction concurrency conditions. We set the number of transaction concurrency to 50, 100, 200, 400, 500, 800 and 1000 to test the throughput of two operations in the DC, VTGenerate and VTSearch, respectively. The experimental results are shown in Fig. 2.

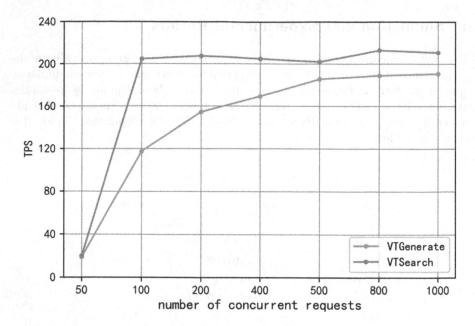

Fig. 2. Results of smart contract testing

According to the experimental results, as the number of concurrent transactions gradually rises, the throughput of the VTGenerate operation in the smart contract DC stabilizes above 200 and the throughput of the VTSearch operation stabilizes above 180. By analyzing the experimental results, we can make the following deductions. (1) In the smart contract DC, VTSearch read operations have higher throughput than VTGenerate write operations. (2) When the number of concurrent transactions rises, the throughput of the VTGenerate and VTSearch processes steadily rises and stabilizes. This stabilization takes place because the system's throughput stabilizes after the connection pool's maximum number of connections has been achieved on the blockchain network.

```
Suppose test the AirHumidityData is {IotId:D10000841 Temperature:10.2319 Humidity:52.32% Position
_X:1594.2 Position_Y:82.34 Manufacturer:PandaChuangxing AcquisitionTime:2023-02-15-09:59:58 Worki
ngGroup:Sensor_Group83}
The AirHumidityData byte size is 120
The AirHumidityData  Hashvalue returned from IPFS is QmU824S7FyRHWeso4BGcFqGDWobkx8tpYeRms4nGZhRk
zP
The AirHumidityData Hashvalue byte size returned from IPFS is 16
```

Fig. 3. Upload results of IPFS

4.2   IPFS Storage Analysis

Figure 3 displays the outcome of uploading the device information to IPFS, which returns the index of this data in IPFS, which is recorded on the blockchain.

Input Hashvalue is: QmU824S7FyRHWeso4BGcFqGDWobkx8tpYeRms4nGZhRkzP
The query data returned from IPFS is {IotId:D10000841 Temperature:10.2319 Humidity:52.32% Positio
n_X:1594.2 Position_Y:82.34 Manufacturer:PandaChuangxing AcquisitionTime:2023-02-15-09:59:58 Work
ingGroup:Sensor Group83}

Fig. 4. The retrieval results of IPFS

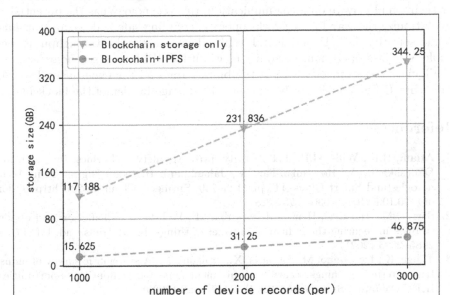

Fig. 5. Comparison between the proposed scheme and the size of data that needs to be uploaded into the blockchain without using secondary storage

According to the experimental results, detailed data of a device with a size of 120B is uploaded to IPFS, and an index with a size of 16B is returned. Storing this index in the blockchain saves (120–16) =104B of space for the blockchain. When more records of data are uploaded, IPFS will gradually lessen the blockchain's storage burden. The results of an IPFS lookup are displayed in Fig. 4. When a message receiver needs to find out device information, it must first get the device's IPFS index in the blockchain ledger and then visit IPFS to search for the information using this index. According to our proposed solution, we simulated the generation of 1000, 2000, and 3000 records using the designed data structure. We conducted simulation experiments using IPFS as the Cloud Service Provider in the proposed scheme. We compared the storage size required to store records in the blockchain between the proposed scheme and alternative solutions that directly upload records to the blockchain. As shown in Fig. 5, with an increasing number of records, the proposed scheme exhibits a relatively slower growth rate in the storage burden on the blockchain compared to the solution that solely relies on on-chain storage. This indicates that the design of the proposed scheme effectively reduces the storage requirements on the blockchain.

5   Conclusion

In conclusion, this paper aims to introduce the application of blockchain-based OR components in IoT data communication, providing a reliable solution for the security and privacy of IoT data transmission. With the growing demand for secure and private data communication, this technology has the potential to revolutionize the way IoT networks operate, enabling safe and secure transmission of sensitive data. Experimental results show a reasonable throughput for the whole VT pass operation. In addition, we utilise IPFS as a secondary storage to alleviate the storage burden of the blockchain, and the experimental results show that IPFS can effectively alleviate the storage burden of the blockchain.

References

1. Atlam, H.F., Wills, G.B.: IoT security, privacy, safety and ethics. In: Farsi, M., Daneshkhah, A., Hosseinian-Far, A., Jahankhani, H. (eds.) Digital Twin Technologies and Smart Cities. IT, pp. 123–149. Springer, Cham (2020). https://doi.org/10.1007/978-3-030-18732-3_8
2. Serror, M., Hack, S., Henze, M., Schuba, M., Wehrle, K.: Challenges and opportunities in securing the industrial internet of things. IEEE Trans. Ind. Inf. **17**(5), 2985–2996 (2021)
3. Tange, K., De Donno, M., Fafoutis, X., Dragoni, N.: A systematic survey of industrial internet of things security: requirements and fog computing opportunities. IEEE Commun. Surv. Tutor. **22**(4), 2489–2520 (2020)
4. Jadav, N.K., Gupta, R., Alshehri, M.D., Mankodiya, H., Tanwar, S., Kumar, N.: Deep learning and onion routing-based collaborative intelligence framework for smart homes underlying 6g networks. IEEE Trans. Netw. Serv. Manage. **19**(3), 3401–3412 (2022)
5. Zhang, Y., Weng, J., Weng, J., Li, M., Luo, W.: Onionchain : towards balancing privacy and traceability of blockchain-based applications (2019)
6. Li, D., Han, D., Liu, H.: Fabric-chain & chain: a blockchain-based electronic document system for supply chain finance. In: Zheng, Z., Dai, H.-N., Fu, X., Chen, B. (eds.) BlockSys 2020. CCIS, vol. 1267, pp. 601–608. Springer, Singapore (2020). https://doi.org/10.1007/978-981-15-9213-3_46
7. Li, J., Han, D., Zhongdai, W., Wang, J., Li, K.-C., Castiglione, A.: A novel system for medical equipment supply chain traceability based on alliance chain and attribute and role access control. Futur. Gener. Comput. Syst. **142**, 195–211 (2023)
8. Sengupta, J., Ruj, S., Bit, S.D.: A comprehensive survey on attacks, security issues and blockchain solutions for IoT and IIoT. J. Netw. Comput. Appl. **149**, 102481 (2020)
9. Han, D., Zhu, Y., Li, D., Liang, W., Souri, A., Li, K.-C.: A blockchain-based auditable access control system for private data in service-centric IoT environments. IEEE Trans. Industr. Inf. **18**(5), 3530–3540 (2022)
10. Bataineh, M.R., Mardini, W., Khamayseh, Y.M., Yassein, M.M.B.: Novel and secure blockchain framework for health applications in IoT. IEEE Access **10**, 14914–14926 (2022)
11. Ahmed, A., Abdullah, S., Bukhsh, M., Ahmad, I., Mushtaq, Z.: An energy-efficient data aggregation mechanism for IoT secured by blockchain. IEEE Access **10**, 11404–11419 (2022)

12. Gupta, R., Jadav, N.K., Mankodiya, H., Alshehri, M.D., Tanwar, S., Sharma, R.: Blockchain and onion-routing-based secure message exchange system for edge-enabled IIoT. IEEE Trans. Ind. Inf. **19**(2), 1965–1976 (2023)
13. Voloch, N., Hajaj, M.M.: Handling exit node vulnerability in onion routing with a zero-knowledge proof. In: Pardede, E., Delir Haghighi, P., Khalil, I., Kotsis, G. (eds.) iiWAS 2022. LNCS, vol. 13635, pp. 399–405. Springer, Cham (2022). https://doi.org/10.1007/978-3-031-21047-1_34
14. Evgnosia-Alexandra, K.: A note on post quantum onion routing. Cryptology ePrint Archive, Paper 2021/111 (2021). https://eprint.iacr.org/2021/111
15. Jadav, N.K., et al.: GRADE: deep learning and garlic routing-based secure data sharing framework for IIoT beyond 5G. Digit. Commun. Netw. **9**(2), 42–435 (2022)

Rearranging Inv Message in the Bitcoin to Construct Covert Channels

Qi Liu, Zhuo Chen, Feng Gao, and Liehuang Zhu[✉]

Beijing Institute of Technology, Beijing 100081, China
liehuangz@bit.edu.cn

Abstract. Covert channels aim to conceal the communication behaviors and are widely applied to transmit sensitive data. Blockchains are well-suited for building state-of-the-art covert channels due to their decentralization property. Most existing blockchain-based covert channels require the sender to create transactions. Creating transactions requires a fee, and transactions with covert information are permanently stored on the blockchain. Implementing such methods needs a high cost, and the on-chain covert information faces the risk of being exposed. In this paper, we first propose a Bitcoin-based covert channel that rearranges the transaction hashes in Bitcoin inv packets. To improve undetectability and transmission efficiency, we further propose a dynamic channel link scheme and a method for establishing channels with multiple receiving nodes. The dynamic channel link scheme provides the ability to change the connection between the sender and the receiver at any moment. The multiple receiving nodes method linearly increases the transmission efficiency according to the number of nodes. Theoretical and experimental analysis shows that our scheme is undetectable and has higher transmission efficiency than existing schemes.

Keywords: Bitcoin · Covert channel · Blockchain · Inv message

1 Introduction

The covert channel is an emerging technology to conceal the communication behavior. The core of the covert channel is to embed information in a public communication channel, while the embedded information can only be awared by the communication parites. The covert channel in the public communication channel should be undetectable.

Existing covert channel schemes mainly hide covert information in network protocols that is composed of protocol data units [8, 11, 15]. However, the network connection of the covert channel based on network protocols is static, making it easy for network protocol analyzers to monitor data packets. Statistical analysis methods can easily detect statistical anomalous features in network data packets and thus detect covert channels in the network. Furthermore, traditional covert channels rely on central servers to provide services. Once the central server is

J. Chen et al. (Eds.): BlockSys 2023, CCIS 1897, pp. 128–141, 2024.
https://doi.org/10.1007/978-981-99-8104-5_10

compromised, the covert channel is more likely to be exposed and destroyed. Besides, adversaries can also delay or tamper with packets to disrupt the covert channel.

As the core technology and infrastructure of Bitcoin [12], blockchain can be seen as a distributed shared ledger. Its characteristics such as decentralization, immutability, flood propagation, and anonymity can provide robustness and anti-tracing capabilities for covert channels. Blockchain is thus suitable for building reliable covert channels. Currently, studies focus on establishing blockchain-based covert channels. Fionov [5] summarizes the existing seven blockchain schemes, which are almost all embedded with covert information in blockchain transactions. These schemes have the following limitations. Firstly, creating a transaction requires a transaction fee. The average transaction fee for creating a transaction is approximately 1.5 USD [1], which is extremely expensive. Secondly, the transmission efficiency of existing schemes is low since the number of covert information created within a period of time is small. Finally, transactions carrying covert information will be permanently stored on the blockchain, leading to the risk of channel exposure.

To overcome the above limitas, we propose an embedding scheme in the Bitcoin system. We use the inv message in the network layer as the carrier and rearrange the transaction hashes (Txhashes) in the inv message to embed covert information. Bitcoin nodes broadcast inv message with covert information to other nodes. Furthermore, we propose a dynamic channel link method. It aims to further increase the undetectability of channels and ensures that the covert channel is always in a dynamically changing state. We also propose that establishing the channel with multiple receiving nodes method, which aims to increase the efficiency of channels. Main contributions are shown as below:

- We first propose a Bitcoin inv message Txhashes rearrangement scheme. This scheme has a low cost and does not require creating a transaction. The sender only needs to forward the transaction information in the network to transmit covert information. Moreover, the covert information transmitted by our scheme will not be permanently stored on the blockchain.
- We propose a dynamic channel link scheme and a method for establishing channels with multiple receiving nodes. The dynamic channel link scheme enables changing the connection of the sender and the receiver at any time to enhance undetectability. Utilizing the multiple receiving nodes method, the transmission efficiency is linearly increased according to the number of receiving nodes.
- We implemente the covert channel on the Bitcoin mainnet. We used the K-S and KLD tests to evaluate the undetectability of our scheme. Experiment results show that our scheme is undetectable. Meanwhile, we compare the transmission efficiency of our scheme with existing blockchain-based covert channels. The results show that our scheme has a higher transmission efficiency.

2   Related Work

Currently, several studies have focused on establishing covert channels in blockchain systems. The most direct storage carrier for blockchain-based covert channels is custom storage fields, such as the OP_RETURN field for Bitcoin and the INPUT field for Ethereum. The creators of transactions can fully control these fields. The Bitcoin system enables its users to input any data, up to 80 bytes in size, into the OP_RETURN field. Covert information can be embedded in the OP_RETURN field [2,3,6], which can either carry covert information or be used to mark special transactions for filtering. However, the OP_RETURN field has the obvious format and character features, so there is a significant difference between the normal OP_RETURN field and the OP_RETURN field carrying special information. Basuki [4] embedded covert information using the INPUT field. However, the INPUT field carrying covert information also has obvious differences from the normal INPUT field. Partala [13] proposed the blockchain covert channel (BLOCCE) and verified its feasibility and security. This scheme embeds covert information into the least significant bit (LSB) of the Bitcoin output address. However, the embedding rate of the scheme is too low, and the channel cost is high. Fionov [5] introduced various blockchain covert channels. One of which uses custom transaction output addresses to embed covert information, but this leads to unspendable outputs. Unspendable outputs lead to high costs and fill dead elements in the list of unused inputs, which hinders the circulation of Bitcoin and affects its benign development. The digital signature algorithm can ensure the integrity of transactions, and the algorithm needs to use random parameters to perform the signature process. The sender can use these random parameters to send covert messages [5,7,9], and the capacity can be as high as 255 bits. This scheme has high undetectability. Covert information can be also embedded in the transaction amount field of the blockchain network, such as Bitcoin Network [14] and Ethereum Network [10]. The sender simulates the transaction amount field, ensuring that special amounts are indistinguishable from normal amounts. The cost of this scheme restricts the channel capacity.

3   System Model and Design Goals

3.1   System Model

The covert channel model consists of the sender, the receiver, and the blockchain network. The covert channel system includes modules for information pre-negotiation, encoding modulation, and decoding demodulation. The information pre-negotiation module ensures that both communication parties receive the necessary information to establish the channel through a secure channel. During communication, the sender encodes and modulates the original information into carrier symbols. Then, the sender transmits the covert information through the blockchain network. The receiver demodulates and decodes the received information symbols to obtain the original information. This system model applies not only to the Bitcoin system but also to other public blockchain systems. Since the decoding demodulation module is the inverse of the encoding modulation module, we primarily focus on explaining the encoding modulation module.

We utilize the RSA asymmetric encryption algorithm for encrypting and decrypting the original data. After the receiver generates a key pair, the public key is sent to the sender, and the receiver retains the private key. Both parties must safely guard their keys to prevent leaks. Before modulating data into the carrier, the sender encrypts the covert information with the public key. Then, the sender divides the ciphertext into several ciphertext segments and sends them to different receiving nodes individually. Specifically, the sender modulates different ciphertext segments into the order of Txhashes of the inv messages. Then, the sender broadcasts the inv messages carrying the covert information to the Bitcoin network. According to the inv messages received by multiple receiving nodes, the receiver can quickly recover the original data from it. Furthermore, the sender can achieve the dynamic channel link through the backup sending node. Figure 1 describes the covert communication process based on the Bitcoin network.

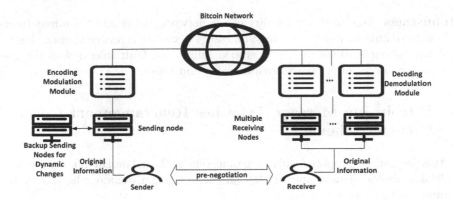

Fig. 1. System model.

3.2   Threat Model

We assume there is a powerful adversary in the Bitcoin network. The adversary can use powerful traffic monitoring and data analysis capabilities to detect the existence of covert channels in the network. The adversary can monitor and store communication traffic between the sender and the receiver. Both covert traffic carrying covert information and legitimate traffic not carrying covert information can be easily obtained by the adversary. Through data analysis capabilities, the adversary can easily obtain the characteristics of Bitcoin traffic, including the frequency of sending messages and the number of Txhashes in a message. However, if the adversary cannot detect traffic anomalies, it is difficult for them to identify the covert channel.

3.3 Design Goals

We design the covert channel according to the three goals of undetectability, efficiency, and robustness.

Undetectability. We define covert traffic as traffic carrying covert information, and legitimate traffic as traffic not carrying covert information. Undetectability means that the adversary cannot distinguish covert traffic from legitimate traffic, thus making it impossible to detect covert channels. The methods available to the adversary include data feature statistics and machine learning.

Efficiency. Efficiency refers to the ability of the sender to transmit as much information as possible to the receiver in a specific time. In this paper, transmission efficiency is used to evaluate efficiency. Transmission efficiency refers to the amount of covert information transmitted per second, in units of bit/s.

Robustness. Due to the instability of the network, delay and noise may interfere with communication, resulting in message decoding errors or message losses. Robustness refers to the anti-interference ability and fault tolerance of the system in the face of interference such as delay and noise.

4 Bitcoin Inv Message Txhashes Rearrangement Covert Channel Scheme

In this section, we propose a covert channel scheme based on Bitcoin inv message Txhashes rearrangement and display all the algorithm pseudocodes during the communication process.

4.1 Channel Establishment for Multiple Receiving Nodes

Algorithm 1 describes the pseudocode of the sender and receiver establishing a channel connection. All receiving nodes open the port required for the Bitcoin mainnet. According to the IP address of sending node, all receiver nodes listen to the port for Bitcoin traffic from the sending node. The sending node uses the "connect" property of the Bitcoin configuration code to establish connections with all IP addresses in the IP address list.

4.2 Information Embedding

Before embedding covert information, the sender encrypts the original message p into binary ciphertext b using asymmetric encryption public keys. Based on b and IP_List, the sender divides b into several ciphertext segments and each corresponding to an IP address in IP_List. Then, the sending node synchronously

---

Algorithm 1: Channel Establishment Process

Input: IP_List, Sende_IP
Output: True
All Receiving nodes in the IP_List open the port required for the Bitcoin mainnet;
All receiving nodes in the IP_List listen to the Bitcoin traffic from the Sender_IP;
The sending node connects to the receiving nodes in the IP_List using the connect property
of the Bitcoin configuration code;
if *The connection is successfully established* **then**
 | return True;
else
 | Continue to establish a connection;
end

Algorithm 2: Channel Establishment Process

Input: p, public_key, IP_List
Output: b_List
The sender encrypts the original information p into binary ciphertext b using the
public_key;
Based on the number of IP addresses in the IP_List, the sender divides the ciphertext b into
a ciphertext segments list b_List, each of which corresponds to each IP address in the
IP_List;
return b_List;

---

sends the corresponding ciphertext to each receiving node. Algorithm 2 describes
the pseudocode of the information segmentation process.

Algorithm 3 describes the pseudo-code for the sender to embed covert information in the inv messages. Based on the pre-negotiated embedding position m,
the sending node determines the information embedding location of the Txhash
and uses the m-th bit of each Txhash to transmit information. When the sending node sends a ciphertext segment to a receiving node, the node will rearrange
all Txhashes in the inv messages so that the m-th bit of each Txhash in the inv
messages matches the ciphertext segment. Specifically, for each bit of the ciphertext, the sender first retrieves a Txhash from the transaction pool whose m-th
bit matches the bit of the ciphertext and then continues to match the remaining
bits of the ciphertext until the ciphertext is sent out. Since there is an upper
limit on the number of Txhashes in the inv message, the sending node will send
inv messages to the receiving node according to the length of the ciphertext.

4.3 Information Extraction

Algorithm 4 describes the pseudo-code for the receiver to extract covert messages. After the channel is established, all receiving nodes continuously listen to
the Bitcoin port. When the communication start flag is detected, the receiver
starts storing the extracted information until the end flag appears. Each receiving node gets the inv message during communication and obtains the covert
information based on the m-th bit of each Txhash in the inv message. Each
receiving node concatenates the covert information carried in each inv message
in chronological order to obtain the ciphertext segment. Finally, the receiver concatenates the covert information again according to the order of the receiving

---

Algorithm 3: Information Embedding Process

Input: b_List, IP_List, m
Output: invs_List
foreach *IP address ipl in IP_List and corresponding ciphertext segment bl in b_List* **do**
    Init i = 0;
    while *i <length of bl* **do**
        init inv = {};
        while *the size of an inv message is less than the upper limit* **do**
            Fetch a Txhash tx from the transaction pool;
            if *the m-th bit of tx matches the i-th bit of ciphertext bl* **then**
                Add tx to inv;
                i++;
            else
                Put tx back into the transaction pool;
            end
        end
        Send the inv message to ipl;
    end
    The sending node will send multiple inv messages according to the length of b;
    Generate an inv message based on the current Txhashes
end
After the ciphertext is sent out, the sending node sends a list invs_List containing the set of inv messages to IP_List;
Return invs_List;

---

node list to obtain the ciphertext b. The receiver can obtain the original information c by decrypting the ciphertext b using asymmetric encryption private key. Since the number of Txhashes in the transaction pool of sending node is constant for each receiving node, this ensures that multiple receiving nodes will increase transmission efficiency exponentially.

Algorithm 4: Information Extraction Process

Input: m, IP_List, invs_List, private_key
Output: c
All receiving nodes of IP_List listen to the port, an ipl in IP_List receives a collection of the inv messages invl during communication, IP_List corresponds to invs_List;
foreach *inv ∈ invl* **do**
    Node ipl concatenates the mth bit of each Txhash in the inv message in chronological order;
end
Node ipl obtains a ciphertext segment bl
According to the IP_List order, the receiver concatenates all ciphertext segments to obtain ciphertext b;
The receiver decrypts the ciphertext b using private_key to extract the original information c;
Return c;

4.4 Dynamic Channel Link

Dynamic change means that the sender changes the IP address and uses the new IP address to establish a connection with the receiver again. This method implements a dynamic change between the communicating parties and aims to further increase undetectability. At any time after the channel is established, the sender can send an instruction for a dynamic change to the receiver through Algorithm 5. The instruction includes the dynamic change identifier and the new IP address.

Algorithm 5: Dynamic Channel Link Process for the Sender

Input: new_IP, flag, public_key, m
Output: True
The sender combines the dynamic change identifier and the new IP address new_IP as the original information p;
The sender encrypts p into binary ciphertext b using public_key;
Based on the length of IP_List, the sender divides the binary ciphertext into ciphertext segments list b_List, corresponding to IP addresses in IP_List;
The sending node transfers b_List to the receiving node based on Algorithm 3;
After sending the dynamic change instruction, the sender establishes connections with all receiving nodes in IP_List using new_IP;
if *the connection is successfully established* **then**
  | Return True ;
else
  | Continue to establish a connection;
end

Algorithm 6 describes the pseudo-code for the receiver to make dynamic changes. After receiving the dynamic change identifier, the receiver extracts the new IP address carried in the inv messages. The receiver modifies the listening IP address of all receiving nodes to ensure the connection is established smoothly.

Algorithm 6: Dynamic Channel Link Process for the Receiver

Input: m, IP_List, invs_List, private_key
Output: True
The receiver uses Algorithm 4 to extract original information c;
if *c includes a dynamic change identifier* **then**
  | The receiver obtains new_IP and modifies the listening address of all IP addresses in
  | IP_List to new_IP;
end
if *the connection is successfully established* **then**
  | Return True;
else
  | Continue to establish a connection;
end

Example: For ease of understanding, we give a communication example in Fig. 2. To simplify, we assume that the ciphertext to be sent is "100101010110". The sender divides the information into segments based on Algorithm 2 and sends the inv messages to each receiving node based on Algorithm 3. The receiving nodes use Algorithm 4 to extract the covert information carried in the inv messages during communication. Finally, the receiver gets the ciphertext "100101010110".

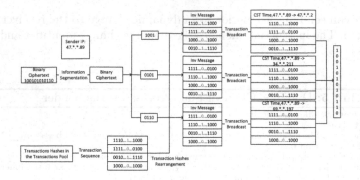

Fig. 2. An example of Bitcoin inv message Txhashes rearrangement scheme.

5   Experimental Results and Analysis

5.1   Experimental Setup

We chose Linux cloud servers, where the operating system of the sender is Centos 7 and the three operating systems of the receiver included Centos 7 and Ubuntu 20. The Bitcoin node version for each server was 0.20.0. Our scheme could be successfully deployed on different versions of operating systems as long as the devices and systems support running Bitcoin nodes.

Our scheme was deployed on the Bitcoin mainnet. To analyze the performance, we used the network protocol analyzer tshark to capture the traffic between the sender and the receiver. The duration of each traffic capture was 15 min. We mainly evaluated the undetectability and transmission efficiency of our scheme. We analyzed the characteristics of the traffic, such as the inter-packet delay (IPD) of the inv message and the number of Txhashes in an inv message. We evaluated undetectability using the Cumulative Distribution Function (CDF), the Kolmogorov-Smirnov (K-S), and Kullback-Leibler divergence (KLD) tests. We used transmission efficiency to measure channel capacity.

5.2   Undetectability

We calculated the CDF of the covert traffic and legitimate traffic. By comparison, we could intuitively judge whether covert traffic and legitimate traffic are strongly indistinguishable. We used both the ipd of the inv messages and the number of Txhashes in an inv message as CDF statistical features. Figure 3a describes the CDF comparison using the ipd of the inv messages as the feature, and Fig. 3b describes the CDF comparison using the number of Txhashes in an inv message as the feature. The results showed that our scheme traffic simulated legitimate traffic well.

We used two standard statistical tests to visualize and validate the undetectability. We used the p-value of the K-S test to determine if there is a difference between the distributions of the two samples. When the p-value is greater

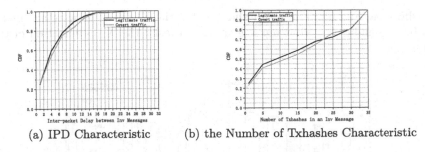

(a) IPD Characteristic   (b) the Number of Txhashes Characteristic

Fig. 3. CDF Diagrams for Legitimate Traffic and Covert Traffic.

than 0.05, it means that the two samples are considered to have the same distribution and that the covert channel can resist the K-S test. The KLD test is a method for describing the difference in distribution between two probability density functions. A larger value of KLD indicates a larger difference between the two distributions. In the experiment, we calculated the KLD threshold for the legitimate traffic and performed the KLD test for the covert traffic. If all KLD values of the covert traffic are less than the KLD threshold, it means that the two samples are considered to have no significant difference, indicating that the covert channel can resist the KLD test.

We selected the ipd of the inv message as the feature for K-S and KLD tests. In the K-S test, we selected a legitimate traffic as the baseline traffic. Then we performed K-S tests with this baseline traffic using the legitimate traffic and the covert traffic respectively. The K-S results for the legitimate traffic and the covert traffic were shown in Fig. 4a and Fig. 4b . The results showed that the p-values of the covert traffic were all greater than 0.05, indicating that our scheme can resist the K-S test for this feature.

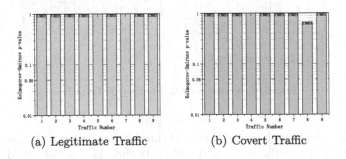

(a) Legitimate Traffic   (b) Covert Traffic

Fig. 4. K-S Test for IPD.

In the KLD test, we calculated the KLD threshold of legitimate traffic through legitimate traffic and baseline traffic. The result was shown in Fig. 5a, with a threshold of 0.1286. Then we calculated the KLD value of covert traffic and compared the results with the threshold. The experimental results were shown in Fig. 5b. The result showed that the KLD values were all smaller than 0.1286, indicating that our scheme could resist the KLD detection of this feature.

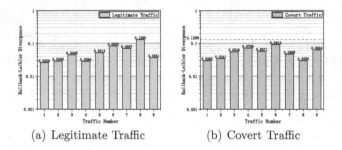

(a) Legitimate Traffic   (b) Covert Traffic

Fig. 5. KLD Test for IPD.

We then selected the number of Txhashes in an inv message as the feature for K-S and KLD tests. In the K-S test, we likewise selected a legitimate traffic as the baseline traffic. We calculate the p-value of K-S for both legitimate traffic and covert traffic. The results were shown in Fig. 6a and Fig. 6b. The results showed that the p-values of the covert traffic were all greater than 0.05, indicating that our scheme could resist the K-S test for this feature.

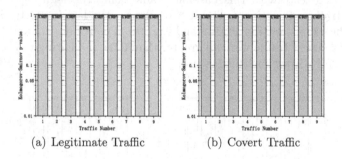

(a) Legitimate Traffic   (b) Covert Traffic

Fig. 6. K-S Test for the Number of Txhashes.

In KLD tests, we calculated the KLD threshold value of the legitimate traffic by the legitimate traffic and the baseline traffic. The result could be shown in Fig. 7a, with a threshold of 0.1122. Then we calculated the KLD values of the covert traffic and compare the results with the threshold. The experimental results were shown in Fig. 7b. The results showed that the KLD values were all less than 0.1122, indicating that our scheme can resist the KLD test.

There is no significant difference between the CDF of our scheme and the CDF of legitimate traffic. Our scheme is proven undetectable under the KLD and K-S tests. From theoretical and experimental results, it can be seen that the

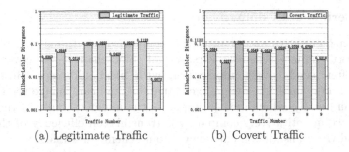

(a) Legitimate Traffic   (b) Covert Traffic

Fig. 7. K-S Test for the Number of Txhashes.

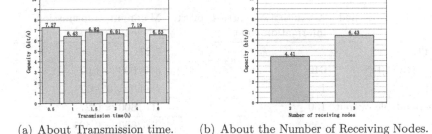

(a) About Transmission time.   (b) About the Number of Receiving Nodes.

Fig. 8. Transmission Efficiency.

Bitcoin inv message Txhashes rearrangement covert channel scheme has undetectability. This is because there is no statistical regularity in the characters within the inv message, and the Txhashes rearrangement will not affect the frequency of sending the inv messages and the number of Txhashes in inv messages.

5.3   Transmission Efficiency

Our scheme establishes channels using multiple receiving nodes. In the experiment, we established channels using three receiving nodes. We tested the transmission efficiency against transmission time and used the transmission time as the horizontal coordinate. The result is shown in Fig. 8a. It can be seen that the transmission efficiency of our scheme reaches a minimum of 6.43bit/s and a maximum of 7.27 bit/s. And the transmission efficiency of our scheme is relatively stable. The fluctuation is due to the different number of transactions generated by the Bitcoin network at different times.

Assume that the number of receiving nodes is N and the transmission efficiency of a single node is E. The theoretical transmission efficiency of our scheme is N*E. In the test, we tested the transmission efficiency with two receiving nodes and three receiving nodes as examples. We took the number of receiving nodes as the horizontal coordinate to test the channel transmission efficiency. The results were shown in Fig. 8b. Relatively speaking, the transmission efficiency of our scheme increases linearly with the number of receiving nodes.

5.4 Experimental Comparison

We conduct qualitative and quantitative comparisons with existing blockchain-based covert channel schemes. First of all, blockchain-based covert channel schemes often send covert information with fixed addresses. However, our scheme(BITR) realizes the dynamic channel link and can change the channel at any time and easily, which greatly improves the undetectability of the channel. Moreover, we quantitatively compare the transmission efficiency of the Bitcoin scheme and the transmission efficiency of our scheme in Table 1.

Table 1. Comparison of transmission efficiency and cost

Embedding method	A transaction carries covert information (bit)	Maximum transmission efficiency (bit/s)
BITR	/	7.27
OP_RETURN	640	$640/600 \approx 1.07$
LSB	1	$1/600 \approx 0.0017$
Unspendable output	160	$160/600 \approx 0.27$
DSA	255	$255/600 = 0.425$

The results show that the transmission efficiency of our scheme is much higher than that of the existing Bitcoin schemes. This is because existing schemes evaluate channel capacity with covert information carried by a single transaction. But the receiver needs to wait for the transaction to be uploaded to the chain to extract covert information. The current transaction on-chain time is 10 min. As a result, the great majority of existing Bitcoin schemes transmit less than 1 bit per second. This means that the transmission efficiency of existing Bitcoin schemes is much lower than the transmission efficiency of our scheme.

6 Conclusion

In this article, we introduce a Bitcoin inv message Txhashes rearrangement covert channel scheme. We also use the multiple receiving nodes method to increase transmission efficiency and use the dynamic channel link method to improve undetectability. Theoretical and experimental analyzes show that our scheme is undetectable and has high transmission efficiency.

Acknowledgments. This work is supported by the National Key Research and Development Program of China (Grant No. 2020YFB1006100) and the National Natural Science Foundation of China (Grant No. 62232002).

References

1. Transaction fees in bitcoin. https://bitinfocharts.com/zh/comparison/bitcoin-transactionfees.html/. Accessed 2 Feb 2023
2. Ali, S.T., McCorry, P., Lee, P.H.-J., Hao, F.: ZombieCoin: powering next-generation botnets with bitcoin. In: Brenner, M., Christin, N., Johnson, B., Rohloff, K. (eds.) FC 2015. LNCS, vol. 8976, pp. 34–48. Springer, Heidelberg (2015). https://doi.org/10.1007/978-3-662-48051-9_3
3. Bartoletti, M., Pompianu, L.: An analysis of bitcoin OP_RETURN metadata. In: Brenner, M., et al. (eds.) FC 2017. LNCS, vol. 10323, pp. 218–230. Springer, Cham (2017). https://doi.org/10.1007/978-3-319-70278-0_14
4. Basuki, A.I., Rosiyadi, D.: Joint transaction-image steganography for high capacity covert communication. In: 2019 International Conference on Computer, Control, Informatics and its Applications (IC3INA), pp. 41–46. IEEE (2019)
5. Fionov, A.: Exploring covert channels in bitcoin transactions. In: 2019 International Multi-Conference on Engineering, Computer and Information Sciences (SIBIR-CON), pp. 0059–0064. IEEE (2019)
6. Franzoni, F., Abellan, I., Daza, V.: Leveraging bitcoin testnet for bidirectional botnet command and control systems. In: Bonneau, J., Heninger, N. (eds.) FC 2020. LNCS, vol. 12059, pp. 3–19. Springer, Cham (2020). https://doi.org/10.1007/978-3-030-51280-4_1
7. Frkat, D., Annessi, R., Zseby, T.: ChainChannels: private botnet communication over public blockchains. In: 2018 IEEE International Conference on Internet of Things (iThings) and IEEE Green Computing and Communications (GreenCom) and IEEE Cyber, Physical and Social Computing (CPSCom) and IEEE Smart Data (SmartData), pp. 1244–1252. IEEE (2018)
8. Gianvecchio, S., Wang, H.: An entropy-based approach to detecting covert timing channels. IEEE Trans. Dependable Secure Comput. 8(6), 785–797 (2010)
9. Hartl, A., Annessi, R., Zseby, T.: A subliminal channel in EdDSA: information leakage with high-speed signatures. In: Proceedings of the 2017 International Workshop on Managing Insider Security Threats, pp. 67–78 (2017)
10. Liu, S., et al.: Whispers on ethereum: blockchain-based covert data embedding schemes. In: Proceedings of the 2nd ACM International Symposium on Blockchain and Secure Critical Infrastructure, pp. 171–179 (2020)
11. Llamas, D., Allison, C., Miller, A.: Covert channels in internet protocols: a survey. In: Proceedings of the 6th Annual Postgraduate Symposium about the Convergence of Telecommunications, Networking and Broadcasting, PGNET, vol. 2005 (2005)
12. Nakamoto, S., Bitcoin, A.: A peer-to-peer electronic cash system. Bitcoin, vol. 4, p. 2 (2008). https://bitcoin.org/bitcoin.pdf
13. Partala, J.: Provably secure covert communication on blockchain. Cryptography 2(3), 18 (2018)
14. Sleiman, M.D., Lauf, A.P., Yampolskiy, R.: Bitcoin message: data insertion on a proof-of-work cryptocurrency system. In: 2015 International Conference on Cyberworlds (CW), pp. 332–336. IEEE (2015)
15. Tian, J., Xiong, G., Li, Z., Gou, G.: A survey of key technologies for constructing network covert channel. Secur. Commun. Netw. 2020, 1–20 (2020)

Long-Term Blockchain Transactions Spanning Multiplicity of Smart Contract Methods

Chris G. Liu[1], Peter Bodorik[1(✉)], and Dawn Jutla[2]

[1] Faculty of Computer Science, Dalhousie University, Halifax, NS B3H 4R2, Canada
{Chris.Liu,Peter.Bodorik}@dal.ca
[2] Saint Mary's University, Halifax, NS B3H 3C3, Canada

Abstract. Research on blockchains addresses multiple issues, with one being writing smart contracts. In developing smart contracts, blockchains have complex constraints that complicate the design and development of smart contracts, software that controls the blockchain transactions. Blockchain applications that involve collaborations of multiplicity of actors, such as in trade of goods and services, give rise to additional complexity in that transaction activities tend to be long term, perhaps hours or days, and thus spanning multiplicity of methods of a smart contract. The problem is that a block-chain only supports the concept of a transaction within the scope of an execution of a single smart contract method. We compare the requirements and properties of long-term transactions and blockchain transactions and examine their mismatch. We then propose how to represent long-term blockchain transactions in smart contracts, and we describe a mechanism to support such transactions using patterns. Finally, we evaluate the proposed mechanism in terms of supporting transactional properties and its cost of execution.

Keywords: Blockchain · Long-term Blockchain Transaction · Smart Contract Transaction Spanning Multiplicity of Methods · Transaction Mechanism · Optimistic Commitment Methods

1 Introduction

Blockchain scalability, transaction throughput, and high cost are some of the main issues investigated by research on the blockchain infrastructure. Smart contract design and development also received much attention by the research and development communities as is evidence by numerous surveys, e.g., [1–3]. Khan et al. [1] survey and classify research on blockchain smart contracts into two broad categories. The usage category, which contains a large body of papers that explore usage of the blockchain technologies in many different and dissimilar fields, such as IoT, health, voting, supply chains, and the list goes on. The second category includes research on improvement of smart contracts by developing approaches and tools to improve smart contracts either when writing them or once they exist.

© The Author(s), under exclusive license to Springer Nature Singapore Pte Ltd. 2024
J. Chen et al. (Eds.): BlockSys 2023, CCIS 1897, pp. 142–155, 2024.
https://doi.org/10.1007/978-981-99-8104-5_11

A sub-category of smart-contract improvement includes approaches that define a programming language that facilitates creation of smart contracts with desirable properties. Although such approaches lead to smart contract programs with formally proven safety properties, they have not been adopted in practice by developers due to their perceived complexity. In another sub-category includes research that uses a well-known and used Business Process Management Notation (BPMN) to model the application requirements and transform a BPMN model automatically into the methods of a smart contract(s) [6–10]. In some instances, the BPMN model is augmented with additional information that is required for the transformation process from a BPMN model into methods of a smart contract. The additional information deals primarily with details on information/data as it flows through the PBMN model [9].

1.1 Motivation

Trade of goods and services, as opposed to securities, includes many types of collaborative activities that arise with a sale or trade of goods and/or services between two or more parties. Purchase of goods or services, particularly for higher priced items such as combines, may include many types of different activities, such as price negotiations, letter-of-credit financial instrument to guarantee payment, and transport of goods that may also include insurance and customs. Thus, trade transactions involve many parties that collaborate in activities that may be long term, e.g., spanning, minutes, hours, or days, as the collaborative activates may involve different software or human events that trigger invocation of the smart contract methods by a distributed application. Furthermore, activities may be dependent on each other in that an activity may have to wait until output is produced by another activity, output that affects how the activity is completed. We shall refer to such transactions simply as *long-term collaborative transactions*, or as *long-term transactions*.

Blockchains are not yet ready to support general transactions that appear in trade of goods and services. The difficulties arise due to the mismatch between the blockchain transaction definition and the long-term transactions requirements that are the results of collaborative activities. The overall result is that a transaction for trade of goods and services is naturally expressed as a collaboration of a multiplicity of methods, wherein a blockchain only supports a transaction that is a result of any one method of a smart contract that writes to the ledger. This results in a *mismatch between the long-term transaction requirements and transactions properties of current blockchains*. This mismatch is analogous to the *object relational impedance mismatch* [11]. And how to overcome this mismatch is the main goal of this paper.

1.2 Goal and Objectives

The *goal* of this paper is to propose an approach to overcoming the blockchain limitation and propose an approach to supporting a long-term transaction that is a result of execution of a multiplicity of methods of a smart contract – and, currently, a blockchain transaction is the result of an execution of an execution of any (one) smart contract method that writes to the ledger. *Objectives* of this paper are:

- Representation of a long-term transaction in a smart contract.
- Supporting mechanism that implements a long-term blockchain transaction that spans a multiplicity of executions of smart contract methods.
- Minimization of the developer's effort in declaring a long-term transaction and in implementing the long-term transaction mechanism.
- Evaluation of the proposed approach to supporting long-term transactions in terms of the transactional properties and overhead costs.

1.3 Contributions

Meeting the above objectives, we provide the following contributions to the problem of supporting long-term transactions, i.e., transactions that span a multiplicity of executions of smart contract methods:

- Long-term Blockchain (LtB) transaction representation: We present motivation for support of a long-term blockchain transaction and propose how to represent/define an LtB transaction in current blockchains.
- We analyze the source of the mismatch between the requirements of LtB transaction mechanisms and the properties of transactions of current blockchains and propose an approach for the LtB mechanism implementation using patterns.
- Our approach for the proposed LtB transaction mechanisms minimizes the developer's involvement in facilitating the LtB transaction mechanism: The developer simply creates the smart contract that contains the LtB transaction definition and then invokes a tool that amends the smart contract methods with appropriate patterns that implement the mechanism to support LtB transactions.
- We evaluate our transactional mechanism in terms of the transactional properties they support and overhead cost.

1.4 Outline

The second section describes how to represent a long-term blockchain transaction and provides an overview of our approach with an objective to minimize the software developer's effort in writing the long-term transactions and in supporting them, i.e., in implementing a mechanism to support the required transactional properties. The third section describes our approach to implementing the long-term transaction mechanism by augmenting the smart contract written by the developer with patterns that implement the long-term transaction mechanism. The fourth section evaluates the overhead cost of the mechanism. The penultimate section provides related work, while the last section provides a summary and concluding remarks, and our future research.

2 Long-Term Blockchain Transaction

Blockchain transactions and long-term transaction requirements are first discussed and compared to identify shortcomings of current blockchain transactions in supporting the requirements of a long-term transaction. We then propose how a long-term transaction may be represented and discuss properties that should be supported by a mechanism to support such transactions.

We then identify general approaches to supporting such transactions and select the approach we deem the most appropriate. We then propose a definition of a long-term blockchain transaction and discuss the long-term transaction properties.

2.1 Blockchain Transaction vs. Long-Term Transaction

As blockchains are frequently referred to as distributed DBs with additional features, and the concept of DB transactions is well established and understood, we first briefly review DB transactions and their properties and then review how such properties are supported by the blockchain transaction mechanism. We then compare the blockchain and long-term transactions to derive the transactional properties that need to be supported by mechanism to support the long-term blockchain transactions.

DB Transactions. A DB transaction is a collection of reads and writes issued against a DB, wherein the reads and writes are delineated explicitly by the application using the transaction begin and end operations/instructions. The DB system ensures that the DB operations within a transaction satisfy the properties of atomicity (all or nothing), consistency (correctness when executing transactions concurrently), isolation (no dirty reads), and durability. These properties are referred to briefly as transactional or ACID (Atomicity, Consistency, Isolation, Durability) properties. The operations issued against the DB may simply be referred to as Create, Read, Update, Delete (CRUD) operations.

Blockchain Transactions. Documentation on the various blockchains generally states that a transaction is any change to the state of the ledger. Thus, a blockchain transaction may be defined in the following way:

> *Definition: A blockchain transaction is a collection of reads and appends to the (immutable and append-only) ledger made by an execution of any of the smart contract methods that writes to the ledger.*

Thus, the scope of a transaction is a sequence of reads and appends, also referred to as writes, to the ledger as executed by operations of any one of the smart contract methods that updates the ledger.

In a blockchain, ledger writes made by an execution of a smart contract method are submitted for inclusion in a block that is appended to the blockchain. Block validation ensures that updates made by a smart contract method are consistent relative to the state of the ledger and relative to all transactions within that block. Consequently, writes of a smart contract method form an *atomic* transaction in that either all writes (appends) made by the method are performed on the ledger or none are. Furthermore, the consensus method also ensures consistency because all ledger updates included in a block are validated to be consistent relative to the ledger and relative to the other transactions within the same block. As smart contract methods may access the transaction's updates only after the block is appended to the blockchain, dirty reads are prevented and hence *isolation* is also achieved. Finally, as updates are written to the replicated ledger, the successfully completed/committed transactions are *durable* in that the results of their executions are not lost after the block is appended to the chain.

In short, the ACID transactional properties are supported by the current blockchain transaction and hence also need to be supported by any mechanism supporting the long-term transactions.

Long-Term Transactions and Their Properties. We already described the need for a long-term transaction, perhaps spanning days when representing transportation of a product. Such activities are not naturally represented by one blockchain method, but rather as a collection of methods of a smart contract. Thus, a *long-term transaction in a smart contract is a subset of the smart contract methods that read and write to the ledger such that ACID properties are supported*. In the following subsections we propose how to represent a long-term transaction in a smart contract.

2.2   Representing/Defining an LtB Transaction

LtB Transaction Scope. The scope of the transaction is determined by the developer by identifying which of the methods of the smart contract form the transaction, and it thus includes all ledger data accessed by those transaction methods. Thus, any ledger writes made by the transaction methods must be accessible to all the transaction methods before the transaction is committed. In other words, all ledger writes made by the transaction methods *must persist across executions of the transaction methods before the transaction is committed*.

Furthermore, as the state of a transaction should not be visible outside the scope of the transaction and should be accessible only by the transaction methods, the transaction methods must be *independent*, i.e., they may not access any of the non-transaction methods of the smart contract.

Another question that arises is how to identify the transaction begin and end and the scope of the transaction. We discuss how we approach these two issues and then present our proposal for defining a LtB transaction for smart contracts.

Identifying the LtB Transaction Start and End. Generally, identifying the start and an end of a transaction can be achieved in two ways:

1. As in a DB system, the application program signals explicitly the start and end of a transaction by invoking two special methods dedicated to such purposes.
2. There is no explicit signalling to begin or end a transaction. Instead, the mechanism itself determines when a transaction begins and ends by keeping track of the internal state of the transaction.

We choose the first method of explicit signalling using two methods of the long-term transaction mechanism, one method to begin the transaction and one to end it. The reasons for selecting this option are:

– This option is analogous to DB systems in which an application signals explicitly to the DB system the beginning and ending of a transaction.
– Perhaps the main reason is that an end of a transaction, whether successful or not, requires that certain activities be completed to terminate the transactions. Ensuring that the transaction termination activities are properly handled is easier if they are situated in one method, the method dedicated for ending the transaction.

Long-Term Blockchain (LtB) Transaction Definition.

Definition: *Long-term Blockchain (LtB) transaction* in a smart contract is a subset of the smart contract methods, such that the transaction methods are *independent* and include two special methods, *LtB-transaction-begin* and *LtB-transaction-end,* to start and end the transaction, respectively.

The semantics of the long-term transaction model are:

- The LtB transaction mechanism enforces the ACID transactional properties.
- Methods of an LtB transaction must be *independent* in that they may not access any objects or data that are external to the LtB transaction.
- *LtB-transaction-begin* method must be invoked by the application to begin the transaction.
- *LtB-transaction-end* method is invoked by the application to terminate the transaction, wherein:

  – The first input parameter indicates whether the transaction completion is commitment or abort of the transaction.
  – The method may return a value that is defined by the developer.

2.3 LtB Transaction Mechanism Implementation Using Patterns

The LtB transaction mechanism may be created using two general approaches:

1. Augment the blockchain infrastructure to support a blockchain transaction that spans execution of more than one method.
2. Prepare software patterns as an add-on mechanism that utilizes the current blockchain infrastructure but provides support for LtB transaction.

The first option would be a major undertaking that requires major changes to the blockchain infrastructure and thus requiring major redesign, resources, and time. The second option is viable in our context, provided that the proposed mechanism to support blockchain trade transactions is (relatively) easy to use by a developer when writing a blockchain smart contract. We adopt the second option as it is less disruptive.

Developer's Responsibilities in Implementing the LtB Transaction. There are two major issues that need to be addressed when considering using patterns for implementing the LtB transaction mechanism:

– The first one deals with how a *long-term transaction is defined/represented* while at the same time minimizing the developer's effort, which is addressed in a following subsection.
– The second one is on finding a mechanism to support LtB transactions and their properties, which is the topic of the next section.

From the implementation perspective, the developer can *apply patterns* on smart contracts, patterns such as those that facilitate access control [12] or patterns that implement the LtB transaction mechanism, which is our objective. Applying the patterns means that once the developer prepares the LtB transaction methods, appropriate patterns must be inserted in appropriate places in the smart contract methods for the patterns to implement the LtB transactions with their properties. However, instead of relying on the developer to insert such patterns in the LtB transaction code, to minimize the developer's effort and room for errors, the pattern augmentation should be automatically provided by a tool, such as a pre-compiler:

1. The developer writes the methods of the smart contract and methods of a long-term transaction as per usual but with additional requirements:
    (a) The transaction methods must be *independent* in that they do not make any reference to object or methods that are not defined withing the scope of the transaction.
    (b) The developer must provide the pre-compiler with information on which of the smart contract methods form the *LtB transaction methods.*
2. The developer uses a pre-compiler to augment the transaction methods with appropriate patterns at appropriate places in the smart contract methods.

The transaction must be started and ended by invocation of the *LtB-transaction-start* and *LtB-transaction-end* methods, respectively, that must be invoked by the application to signal the start and end of a transaction. However, the two methods are not provided by the developer, but rather automatically through pattern augmentation.

The developer must identify, using special codes, which of the smart-contract methods belong to the LtB transaction. This is required so that prior to the compilation, the smart contract methods can be augmented with patterns that implement an LtB transaction mechanism using a pre-compiler that recognizes the special codes identifying the LtB transaction methods. We could create a tool to perform the pattern augmentation and provide it with information on which of the methods form the LtB transaction; however, once the tool is invoked, its functionality would be equivalent to that of the pre-compiler.

The smart contract methods are augmented with appropriate patterns that implement a LtB transaction mechanism, while ensuring that the transaction state persists across the execution of an LtB transaction. Only after the LtB transaction patterns are augmented can the smart contract be compiled and deployed. Information provided to the pre-compiler is the *minimal information* needed by any mechanism used to provide an LtB transaction mechanism.

3   LtB Transaction Mechanisms

First, we review how the blockchain properties affect the design of an LtB transaction mechanism and then we present the LtB transaction mechanism architecture.

3.1   Impact of Blockchain's Immutability on the LtB Transaction Mechanism

Blockchain ledger is immutable by allowing only read and append operations, wherein appends are also referred to as writes. To ease the development of smart contracts, the developer views the ledger content as a key-value store, wherein the blockchain infrastructure looks after creating a new instance of the object written to the DB by issuing a *write (k, v)* operation in which k is the key and v is the value to be written.

Implications of the above are that, if an LtB transaction method issues a ledger append/write, when the method issuing such a write completes, a new instance is created and that new instance is also available and can be read by any smart contract methods if the method knows the value of the key, k. However, an LtB transaction contains executions of a multiplicity of the transaction methods and, consequently, any ledger writes by one of the transaction methods is immediately available for reading by any of the smart contract methods. More importantly, as the ledger is immutable, the LtB transaction mechanism cannot "undo" a transaction's write to the ledger by restoring the item's old image/value before the update, as may be performed in a DB. Thus, any mechanism supporting the ACID properties can use only *optimistic* concurrency control approaches, in which the transaction's writes to the ledger are made in some *private workspace*. Only when the transaction is committed are its ledger writes made to the ledger itself as a part of the commitment phase of the transaction.

The main issue to overcome is that the LtB transaction mechanism can only use the native blockchain transaction support that provides for a transaction as reads and writes made by an execution of only one smart-contract method. Thus, the LtB transaction mechanism must record ledger reads and writes in some *private workspace,* to which we shall refer as an *LtB transaction cache,* or simply as a *cache* for short. Only when the *LtB-transaction-end* method is called, that method needs to propagate all reads and writes, performed on the ledger data in the cache, from the cache to the ledger itself as a part of execution of that method.

3.2 Private Workspace

The pre-compiler augments the smart contract methods with the following patterns.

– The method *LtB-transaction-begin* is created as a part of an LtB transaction, wherein the method prepares the cache and seeds it with the ledger initial data.
– The cache must persist across executions of the LtB transaction methods and must be accessible by them.
– Each read or write to the ledger by any of the LtB transaction methods must be replaced with a pattern to make that read or write using the cache instead.
– The method *LtB-transaction-end* is created using patterns to propagate all transaction reads and writes, made using the cache, to the ledger itself.

It should be noted that the cache stores all ledger reads and writes made by the LtB transaction methods. Furthermore, the *LtB-transaction-end* method does not only propagate/replay all writes from cache to the ledger itself, but it also replays reads, i.e., it re-issues all reads that the LtB transactions made on the ledger. This is required, as some blockchains, such as Hyperledger fabric, need to know both the read and write sets of a blockchain transaction to ensure consistency/correctness of the transactions.

Also to be noted is that, due to the dynamic nature of the LtB transaction methods, they may perform reads on the cache that cause cache faults that need to be serviced from the ledger, i.e., the LtB transaction must be augmented by a method in the smart contract that reads the ledger and stores the read values in the cache and thus service the cache fault.

3.3 LtB Transaction Mechanism

The following subsection presents an architecture for cache implementation that exploits data structures, which are provided by some of the blockchains, that persist across execution of smart contract methods. Following this we describe the LtB transaction mechanism, while in the next section we perform its evaluation.

Cache Hosted by Persisting Blockchain Data Structure. Examples of blockchain persisting data structures include *memory variables* provided by the Ethereum blockchains and *private data* provided by the Hyperledger fabric. Both data structures persist across executions of the methods of a smart contract, although both data structures provide different features. We briefly review both before describing how they are used.

Memory Variables: Ethereum provides three types of storage that can be used by the methods of a smart contract. They include the *ledger, memory variables,* and *stack.* The most expensive is the ledger that the smart contract methods may access using the *Level DB,* which is the previously described key-value data store. Cheapest is the method's stack storage, but with a limit on the size of data that may be stored on the stack. *Memory variables* are also expensive, and they persist across and are accessible by all smart contract methods.

Private Data: Hyperledger fabric provides the option of declaring persisting private data that is accessible only to designated actors. In essence, the private data is a separate blockchain that enables reading and writing only to the designated actors.

LtB Transaction Mechanism Implementation. At the risk of redundancy, we review the process of creating an LtB transaction and its supporting mechanism:

1. The developer proceeds with the development of the smart contract, including writing the methods of the LtB transaction, while satisfying the constraints on the transaction methods: The transaction methods must be *independent.* Furthermore, the methods of the LtB transaction must be identified by the developer using special codes that are recognizable by a pre-compiler.
2. The pre-compiler is used to augment the smart contract methods with the patterns that implement the LtB transaction mechanism. The patterns ensure that instead of manipulating the ledger, the transaction methods use the cache. In addition, the prep-compiler insert the two methods that are used to start and end the transaction, i.e., the *LtB-transaction-begin* and *LtB-transaction-end* methods.

   We note that the *atomicity* and *consistency* of the LtB transaction are assured as all ledger writes are made on the cache and that the ledger is updated from the cache by the execution of the *LtB-transaction-end* method. As the ledger is updated by an execution of a single method, the native blockchain ensures the consistency and atomicity of the ledger updates by the *LtB-transaction-end* method. Durability is achieved through the ledger's replication.

However, although updates are made to the cache and not to the ledger itself, updates are written using keys that may be known outside the LtB transaction methods and hence are accessible by non-transaction methods – violating the *isolation* property. To prevent that, the cache needs to perform a translation of the keys, used to write to the ledger, into keys known only to the transaction methods – this translation is maintained by the LtB transaction mechanism.

Following the pre-compilation, the augmented smart contract is ready for compilation and deployment on a blockchain – actions that are automated. It should be noted that a custom pre-compiler is needed for each blockchain supporting LtB transactions.

4   LtB Transaction Mechanism Overhead Cost

In this subsection, we examine the overhead cost of an LtB transaction mechanism. As our assumed environment is that of long-term transactions, comparing the total delays of long-term transactions without and with an LtB transaction mechanism is not appropriate as the overhead delays due to the LtB transaction mechanism would be insignificant in comparison of the long-term delays of the transaction activities itself. Instead, we determine the cost of executing the patterns inserted into the smart contract methods to implement the LtB transaction mechanism. We first discuss our method used to determine the overhead costs and then we discuss evaluation results.

4.1   Cost Estimation Method

To determine the cost of executing patterns that are used to implement the LtB transaction mechanism, we utilize the Ethereum blockchain tools that enable estimation of the cost of execution of smart contract methods written in the Solidity language. Solidity is a Turing-complete, high-language used to write Ethereum smart contracts. We use Remix to compile smart-contract methods. In addition to producing the object code, the Remix compiler also estimates the gas cost to execute each method.

The cost of a unit of gas fluctuates and depends on the load on the system at any point in time: Increased demand for executing smart contracts by users, means increase in the dollar cost per unit of gas. Thus, the Remix compiler can be used to estimate the gas requirements for a method so that the user would able to estimate how much gas to allocate for executing a smart contract method. We use the Remix compiler to measure the gas cost of execution of each method of the smart contract with and without the patterns to implement the LtB transaction mechanism and thus estimate the relative overhead cost of providing an LtB transaction mechanism when compared to executing the LtB transaction without an LtB transaction mechanism.

We performed two measurements using a smart contract that contains the following three methods before the smart contract is augmented with patterns, wherein one method is not a part of the transaction and two methods that are a part of an LtB transaction:

- A simple method that is not a part of the transaction. The method writes a string "start" to a memory variable and returns.
- Two methods that are a part of an LtB transaction:

- Method m1(x1: objectSizeX) ... the method writes to the ledger an object of size X bytes.
- Method m2() ... the method reads the object written by the method m1 and then writes it back to the ledger again as a new object.

We used the Remix compiler to compile the smart contract and calculated the estimated gas cost for the three methods. Thus, the gas-cost is the sum of estimated execution costs of each of the methods for the case without the LtB transaction mechanism. However, the cost for the case when the LtB transaction is implemented, in addition to the cost of the three methods, the cost of the methods to start and end the transaction, the *LtB-transaction-begin* and *LtB-transaction-end* mehods, are also included. We used a strip-down version of a pre-compiler, which was simplified to work with the simple example, to replace each read/write to a ledger with a read/write from the cache, i.e., using the Ethereum memory variables. Furthermore, the smart contract was also augmented with the *LtB-transaction-begin* and *LtB-transaction-end* methods, wherein the *LtB-transaction-end* method also replays all the reads and writes stored in the cache to on the ledger itself.

For each of the two cases, the smart contract, written in the Solidity language, was compiled using the Remix compiler that, in addition to the compiled code, also provides the estimate of the gas cost to execute each method. The gas costs for the methods are added up to produce the total gas cost execution for each case, with the gas-cost expressed in gwei units.

4.2 Cost Estimates

Table 1 shows the gas-cost estimates. There are three rows, with the first containing the column headings. Each of the following two rows is for one of the two cases that is identified by the label in the first column: Label *No-LtB* is for the case when there is no LtB transaction mechanism, while the label *With-Ltb* is for the case when the smart contract is augmented with patterns implementing the LtB transactions mechanism. The second and subsequent columns are the gas-cost estimates for the size of the object X being X = 75, 512, 1024, and 1875 Kb. Note that the 1875Kb is the maximum data size that one transaction can store in one block of public Ethereum [13]. The table data is shown graphically in Fig. 1. We make several observations:

- The overhead cost of the LtB transaction mechanism is not cheap for the Ethereum blockchain.
- The cost is a direct function of the size of the object that is written to and read from the ledger.

Furthermore, the overhead cost of the LtB transaction mechanism is not cheap. Even if the transaction methods themselves were minimal in terms of the access to the ledger, the overhead cost includes setting up the cache. However, for permissioned blockchains that have fewer network nodes and for sidechains with a low cost, the cost of replication and the consensus algorithm may be significantly lower and hence the cost of the overhead LtB mechanism may also be lower.

Table 1. Gas-cost Estimates.

Label	75 kb	512 kb	1024 kb	1875 kb
No-LtB	4545000	31027200	62054400	113625000
With-LtB	9405000	64204800	124109382	227250582

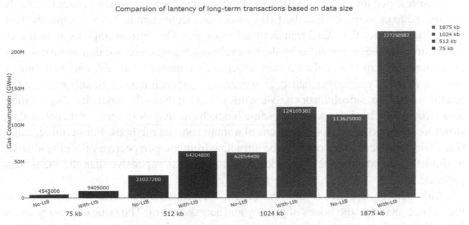

Fig. 1. Comparison of Gas-cost Estimates

5 Related Work

We showed that in trade of goods and services, there is a need for long-term transaction consisting of multiple methods as transaction activities may be long-term, with unpredictable delays and sequencing of inputs to the transaction by various collaborators. To the best of our knowledge, this problem has is yet to be addressed in the scientific literature. Instead, research and industry concentrated on supporting cross-chain transactions, particularly in support of **Non-f**ungible **T**okens (**NFT**s).

Closest is our previous work on supporting the long-term transactions in blockchains in the context of transforming a BPMN model into the methods of a smart contract [14]. A BPMN model goes through several transformations, eventually resulting in a smart contract(s) that is deployed on a blockchain – all automatically under the guidance of the developer [9]. The BPMN model is extended with a concept of a BPMN long-term transaction that represents the transaction's collaborative activities by the transaction participants. The BPMN model, with the long-term transaction as represented in an extended BPMN, is analyzed, and it proceeds through several transformations that eventually produce the methods of a smart contract(s) that support the long-term BPMN transaction. Here we addressed the issue of supporting long-term blockchain transactions consisting of multiple methods of a smart contract.

6   Summary, Concluding Remarks, and Future Research

This paper described our initial results on supporting long-term blockchain transactions that span executions of a multiplicity of the methods of a smart contract, wherein such transactions are not supported by blockchains. We provided motivation for supporting the LtB transaction and presented a model of our approach for an LtB transaction mechanism using a generalized roll-up techniques used for blockchains.

We presented an LtB transaction model that includes a set of independent methods and use patterns to implement the LtB transaction mechanism that ensures that the LtB transaction satisfies the ACID transactional properties. Our current implementation uses a data structure that is provided by the blockchain infrastructure and that persists across executions of the methods of a smart contract, such as *memory variables* in Ethereum, or *private data* in Hyperledger fabric. However, our approach may be readily extended to use the mainchain, sidechain or cross-chains, instead of using the blockchain's persisting data structures. This is important as some blockchains may not support data native data structures that persist across executions of a smart contract methods. Furthermore, using sidechains as layer-2 network may be attractive from the perspective of overhead costs of the LtB mechanism when the sidechain is much less expensive than the mainchain processing.

Although our approach assures that the LtB transaction satisfies the ACID properties, we did not yet tackle the issues of privacy and access control. The issue of privacy arises in blockchains because the ledger data is accessible to all smart contracts. Another issue that arises is access control to execute methods of an LtB transactions. We are currently working on how to resolve the above issues and nested transaction.

References

1. Khan, S.N., Loukil, F., Ghedira-Guegan, C., Benkhelifa, E., Bani-Hani, A.: Blockchain smart contracts: applications, challenges, and future trends. Peer-to-Peer Netw. Appl. **14**, 2901–2925 (2021). https://doi.org/10.1007/s12083-021-01127-0
2. Belchior, R., Vasconcelos, A., Guerreiro, S., Correia, M.: A survey on blockchain interoperability: past, present, and future trends (2021). http://arxiv.org/abs/2005.14282
3. Taylor, P.J., Dargahi, T., Dehghantanha, A., Parizi, R.M., Choo, K.-K.R.: A systematic literature review of blockchain cyber security. Digit. Commun. Netw. **6**, 147–156 (2020). https://doi.org/10.1016/j.dcan.2019.01.005
4. Vacca, A., Di Sorbo, A., Visaggio, C.A., Canfora, G.: A systematic literature review of blockchain and smart contract development: techniques, tools, and open challenges. J. Syst. Softw. **174**, 1 (2021). https://doi.org/10.1016/j.jss.2020.110891
5. Yang, D., Long, C., Xu, H., Peng, S.: A review on scalability of blockchain. In: Proceedings of the 2020 The 2nd International Conference on Blockchain Technology, pp. 1–6. ACM, New York (2020). https://doi.org/10.1145/3390566.3391665
6. Weber, I., Xu, X., Riveret, R., Governatori, G., Ponomarev, A., Mendling, J.: Untrusted business process monitoring and execution using blockchain. In: La Rosa, M., Loos, P., Pastor, O. (eds.) Business Process Management. Lecture Notes in Computer Science, vol. 9850, pp. 329–347. Springer, Cham (2016). https://doi.org/10.1007/978-3-319-45348-4_19
7. Tran, A.B., Lu, Q., Weber, I.: Lorikeet: a model-driven engineering tool for blockchain-based business process execution and asset management

8. López-Pintado, O., García-Bañuelos, L., Dumas, M., Weber, I., Ponomarev, A.: CATERPIL-LAR: a business process execution engine on the Ethereum blockchain (2019). https://doi.org/10.48550/arXiv.1808.03517

9. Bodorik, P., Liu, C.G., Jutla, D.: TABS: transforming automatically BPMN models into blockchain smart contracts. Elsevier J. Blockchain: Res. Appl. (2022). https://doi.org/10.1016/j.bcra.2022.100115

10. Liu, C., Bodorik, P., Jutla, D.: From BPMN to smart contracts on blockchains: transforming BPMN to DE-HSM multi-modal model. In: 2021 International Conference on Engineering and Emerging Technologies (ICEET), pp. 1–7 (2021). https://doi.org/10.1109/ICEET53442.2021.9659771

11. Object–relational impedance mismatch (2023). https://en.wikipedia.org/w/index.php?title=Object%E2%80%93relational_impedance_mismatch&oldid=1134321907

12. HeartBank®: Smart Contract Design Patterns. https://medium.com/heartbankstudio/smart-contract-design-patterns-8b7ca8b80dfb. Accessed 02 Jan 2023

13. Ethereum Average Block Size. https://ycharts.com/indicators/ethereum_average_block_size. Accessed 24 Jan 2023

14. Liu, C.G., Bodorik, P., Jutla, D.: Supporting long-term transactions in smart contracts. In: 2022 Fourth International Conference on Blockchain Computing and Applications (BCCA), pp. 11–19 (2022).https://doi.org/10.1109/BCCA55292.2022.9922193

Market Derivative Risks and Regulation of Cryptocurrency Trading Using "PaoFen" Platforms

Xiaolei Xu[1], Zhen Wu[1], Yunlong Wang[2], Xintong Du[3], Haifeng Guo[3(✉)], and Yuxi Zhang[3]

[1] National Internet Emergency Center, CNCERT/CC, Beijing 100044, China
[2] School of Finance, Southwestern University of Finance and Economics, Chengdu 610000, China
[3] Department of Finance, School of Management, Harbin Institute of Technology, Harbin 150001, China
haifengguo@hit.edu.cn

Abstract. With the accelerated pace of digital transformation and the popularity of third-party payments, the financial industry has been facing escalating threats of blackmail attacks. Currently, the use of the "Paofen" platform for money laundering is an emerging form of cryptocurrency laundering, providing payment and settlement assistance for fraud, gambling and other illegal crimes, contributing to the spread of cybercrime and greatly undermining the order and security of cyberspace. This paper analyzes the operation process of "Paofen" money laundering from the concept of "Paofen", proposes the characteristics of identifying "Paofen" money laundering, and proposes to strengthen cross-sectoral cooperation and guide third-party payment institutions to strengthen their control of "Paofen" money laundering. It also proposes to strengthen cross-sectoral cooperation, guide third-party payment institutions to strengthen monitoring and analysis of "Paofen" money laundering, and block the spread of the Internet. For the governance of network blackmail, we should achieve a chain-wide crackdown on related crimes, construct a modeled abnormal data monitoring model, and strengthen the publicity of data security governance related to network payment accounts.

Keywords: "Paofen" platform · fourth-party payment · risk prevention and control

1 Introduction

The basis of currency issuance is credit (Shaw, 1927). Compared with sovereign currencies, cybercurrency transcend the concepts of countries, governments and regions, eliminate differences in systems, ownership patterns and races, and the issuing entities are mostly specific communities, less reflecting the will of governments, and issuing with a certain degree of autonomy, which is a manifestation of strong group recognition of individual credit (Mabunda, 2018). The issuers of cybercurrency do not need

J. Chen et al. (Eds.): BlockSys 2023, CCIS 1897, pp. 156–161, 2024.
https://doi.org/10.1007/978-981-99-8104-5_12

special authorization from the government or licenses and qualifications issued by regulatory agencies, so the issuers can range from multinational startups, projects, online communities to merely just a group of natural persons in temporary combinations, and thus, investors have little knowledge of the issuers' credit status and related projects, which provides opportunities for deliberate fraudulent criminals, and some so-called cryptocurrency may be just an ordinary IOU or even a scam, which has nothing to do with blockchain technology applications or innovative projects. Such false propaganda, bookmaking, price manipulation, insider trading and other unlawful acts are subject to greater credit risks (Minehan, 1996).

Cryptocurrency fraud rose from the seventh highest risk in 2020 to the second highest risk in 2021, according to the BBB Scam Tracker. Speculative activities using cryptocurrency transactions are seriously disrupting the economic and financial order and breeding gambling, illegal fund raising, fraud, pyramid schemes, money laundering and other illegal and criminal acts. Cryptocurrency scams have the greatest impact on people between the ages of 25 and 64, the researchers said. Scammers typically use social media to lure victims with promises of low-risk, high-return investments. The main reason why cryptocurrency -related crimes are showing a proliferation is that cryptocurrencies have strong anonymity and hidden transactions, and payments can be made without the need to bind real-name information such as bank accounts, thus making the source and destination of funds difficult to trace, making it difficult for regulators to quickly form a complete chain of evidence and funds when investigating related cases, and making supervision correspondingly more difficult, making them highly favored by criminals. This makes it difficult for regulators to quickly form a complete chain of evidence and funds when investigating related cases.

2 Overview of the "Paofen" Platform

In terms of funding channels, the proportion of traditional money laundering operations through third-party payments and public accounts has been greatly reduced. Nowadays, it is more likely that a large number of money laundering is done by using generation payment platforms plus digital currencies (Yan, 2022), especially the most serious harm is done by using USDT (TEDA coin). Most commonly, for example, gambling platforms use the payment accounts of normal users to launder money in order to avoid regulation. They often pay such users to pay commissions through a collection agency platform and package the collection agency platform as a thousand dollar a day online income project.

This kind of collection agency platform is generally known as a "PaoFen" platform in China (Jiao, 2022). "PaoFen" refers to the act of using the collection codes held by normal users, such as bank cards or WeChat or Alipay collection codes, to collect money for others and earn commissions, this process is actually refers to the "collection type" mode. Another corresponding mode, which requires a payment code, is called the "payment on behalf of" mode. This means that in the money flow chain of the black and gray industry involved in payment settlement, the user may not only act as a recipient, but also as a payer. The "Paofen" platform is essentially a form of fourth-party payment platform, so it has similarities with most fourth-party payment platforms, both of which have not obtained payment licenses issued by the People's Bank of China, and are illegal platforms that rely on collecting a large number of QR codes from the public and using the collection codes provided by the public for the flow of illegal funds, from which a commission is extracted for profit.

One of the most important features of the "paofen" platform is that it is highly concealable. The platform will pack itself through various means, disguise itself as a normal part-time job platform, set other normal part-time job recruitment or related information on the platform, so as to cover up the ears, login to view the platform and ordinary part-time job website is not much different, and then through other ways to promote the real purpose, to easily earn high returns as bait to cheat others to join, users often do not know that they are engaged in illegal criminal activities.

3   Money Laundering Operations Using the "Paofen" Platform

As noted earlier, there are two methods of operation for "Paofen" money laundering. The process of "collection type" will involve four nodes: the gambler, the gambling website, the "Paofen" platform, and the user, and how it works is as follows (Fig. 1): a user and the gambler use their respective online platforms, and the user can provide the Alipay collection code he uses on the running platform and pay a deposit of 1000 yuan. The deposit means that he can take orders up to a total amount not greater than 1000 yuan. At this point, the gambler initiates a top-up request of 1000 yuan at an offshore gambling site to be used as gambling funds. The gambling site then presents the user's Alipay payment code to the gambler through an interface from the "Paofen" platform, and the gambler scans the code to complete the transfer. At this point the user's account receives $1000, and the "Paofen" platform deducts $1000 from the user's deposit as gambling money and gives $900 to the gambling site, while giving the user a commission of $50. This is the end of the "Paofen" process for the "collector type".

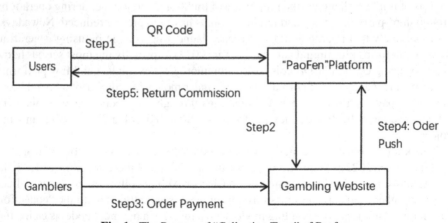

Fig. 1. The Process of "Collection Type" of Paofen.

Figure 2 shows the flow of funds involved in the "collection type" mode. The dotted line shows the flow of funds for collection, while the solid line shows the flow of funds for payment. This operation successfully hides the funds of the black industry chain in the normal payment behavior of users.

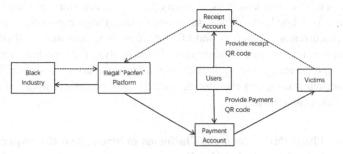

Fig. 2. Flow of fund

The "payment on behalf of type" of operation process is slightly more complex: first, the downstream black industry would go to the "Paofen" platform in the form of advance payments to recharge, usually paid once a month or once a day. When the downstream black industry has a demand for external payment, they will send a payment order to the "Paofen" platform, which usually contains the recipient's account and the amount of payment. The "Paofen" platform adopts a mechanism similar to Uber's order grabbing mode, in which the funds are released to the platform for payment orders, and the users who join the platform grab the order for payment and send the funds to the destination account. Under the traditional "collection type" mode, users are often required to pay a certain amount of deposit to the platform in advance. Under the "payment on behalf of" mode, the deposit mechanism also exists, but the role of guarantee is swapped, with the platform prepaying certain fees to the participating users, who use the platform's prepayment to make external payments after grabbing orders. The user can get a commission according to a certain percentage of the paid order amount after payment.

It can be seen that these two modes are similar in principle and approach, but the direction of the funds are completely opposite, one is the illegal income mixed in the normal user collection behavior, and the other is the black money hidden in the normal user payment behavior. These two models have the same principle and similar methods, but the funds go in the opposite direction, one is to mix the illegal income in the normal user collection behavior, and the other is to hide the black money in the normal user payment behavior.

4   Regulation and Prevention Countermeasures

The current problems of cryptocurrency trading have caused the state to be alerted. The relevant departments of the People's Bank have interviewed some banks and third-party payment institutions on the issue of banks and payment institutions providing services for cryptocurrency trading speculation. The relevant departments of the People's Bank pointed out that cryptocurrency trading speculation activities disrupt the normal economic and financial order, breed the risk of illegal cross-border transfer of assets, money laundering and other illegal and criminal activities, and seriously infringe on the safety of people's property. Therefore, banks and payment institutions shall not provide products or services such as account opening, registration, transaction, clearing and settlement for related activities. Institutions should comprehensively investigate and identify cryptocurrency exchanges and OTC dealers' fund accounts, and promptly cut off the transaction fund payment chain; they should analyze the fund transaction characteristics of cryptocurrency trading speculation activities, increase technical investment, improve abnormal transaction monitoring models, and effectively improve monitoring and identification capabilities.

4.1   Guiding Third-Party Payment Platforms to Strengthen the Supervision of Anti-money Laundering Work

In response to the increasingly complex status quo of cryptocurrency trading speculation, and also to further improve the market supervision of cryptocurrency, the People's Bank of China issued the Notice on Further Preventing and Disposing of the Risk of Cryptocurrency Trading Speculation, which comprehensively prohibits services related to the settlement of cryptocurrency and the provision of trader information, and engaging in illegal financial activities will be held criminally liable.

The Notice reiterates that business activities related to cryptocurrencies are illegal financial activities. These activities include, but are not limited to: conducting legal tender and cryptocurrency exchange business, exchange business between cryptocurrencies, providing information intermediary and pricing services for cryptocurrency transactions, token issuance financing, and cryptocurrency derivatives trading. These cryptocurrency-related business activities are suspected of illegal sale of tokens and coupons, unauthorized public offering of securities, illegal operation of futures business, illegal fund raising and other illegal financial activities, which are strictly prohibited by the relevant state departments and resolutely banned according to law.

At the same time, there are legal risks in participating in cryptocurrency investment and trading activities. For those who carry out related illegal financial activities that constitute crimes, they will be held criminally liable according to law. Any legal persons, unincorporated organizations and natural persons who invest in cryptocurrencies and related derivatives against public order and morality, the relevant civil legal acts are invalid and the resulting losses are borne by them; those suspected of damaging the financial order and endangering financial security will be investigated and dealt with by the relevant departments according to law.

4.2   Strengthen Multi-sectoral Collaboration to Jointly Combat the Crime of "Score-Running" Money Laundering

The "paofen" money laundering crime involves the People's Bank of China's anti-money laundering authorities, the public security system, third-party payments, the CBRC, and many other departments, and a single department cannot effectively deal with this new form of money laundering. Meanwhile, in response to the results of the last round of FATF evaluation, AML will need to be implemented in real estate, jewelry, precious metals, accountants and lawyers, which will involve more sectors and industries. A single department cannot achieve sound AML regulation, so it is necessary to strengthen multi-sectoral collaboration across departments. In dealing with cross-border online gambling "Paofen" money laundering, the public security system can be used as an entry point to combat cross-border gambling, and the third-party payment platform detection data can be used as a starting point, while the anti-money laundering department of the People's Bank and the financial supervision department can coordinate and analyze the clues to study the criminal activities involving money laundering. Multiple departments need to strengthen collaboration to form a synergy of anti-money laundering work to more effectively combat "Paofen" money laundering, a new type of money laundering criminal activity.

Therefore, in order to actively manage the network black and gray industry engaged in money laundering illegal acts, the relevant departments need to increase supervision and regulation, and collaborate with banks and third-party payment platforms for common governance (Xu, 2021). Internet platforms should take full advantage of their own mastery of a large number of user resources and account information, communication data, strengthen research and judgment, establish a sound risk prevention mechanism, once found in the movement, timely warning.

Acknowledgments. This work was supported by The National Key Research and Development Program of China (2020YFB1006104).

References

Jiao, W.D.: Research on "Paofen" Money Laundering Risks and Preventive Measures. Times Finance (1), 3 (2022)

Mabunda, S.: Cryptocurrency: the new face of cyber money laundering. In: 2018 International Conference on Advances in Big Data, Computing and Data Communication Systems (icABCD) (2018)

Minehan, C.E.: The net, cybermoney, and credit risks : new technologiy, and payment system risks. World Bank Other Operational Studies (1996)

Shaw, W.A.: Currency, credit and the exchanges during the great war and since (1914–26): more particularly with reference to the British empire. Harrap, G.G (1927)

Xu, P.: Financial risks and governance countermeasures of illegal fourth-party payment platforms. J. Beijing Police Acad. **2**, 89–94 (2021)

Yan, C.H.: The risk potential of "running score" platform and its prevention and control measures. J. Eco. Res. (23), 3 (2022)

Research on Regulation Oriented Decentralized Oracle Machine

Xinjian Ma[1,2], Haiou Jiang[1,2], Kun Liu[1,2], Yanchun Sun[3], Tiancheng Liu[1,2], and Xiang Jing[1,2,3(✉)]

[1] Advanced Institute of Big Data, Beijing 100195, China
maxinjian@pku.edu.cn,
{jiangho,liukun,liutc}@aibd.ac.cn
[2] National Key Laboratory of Data Space Technology and System, Beijing 100195, China
[3] Peking University, Beijing 100871, China
{sunyc,jingxiang}@pku.edu.cn

Abstract. As a new computing mode, blockchain has been applied in various fields and urgently needs effective regulation. However, due to the lack of an effective information-sharing mechanism, regulating blockchain faces some challenges. Current related research mainly focused on asset circulation between independent blockchains or transferring data from single trusted data source to blockchain, but they cannot solve the problem of trusted information sharing in the blockchain regulation process. Therefore, this paper proposed a regulation oriented decentralized oracle machine method. The method mainly focuses on collecting data from the target blockchain for regulatory authorities. It uses multi-party joint verification and verifiable random selection mechanism to ensure the authenticity of data captured from blockchain and improve the efficiency and the scalability. The security, scalability, and efficiency of the method was analyzed, and the results showed that the method has lower overhead and good scalability while maintaining security.

Keywords: Blockchain · Regulation · Decentralized Oracle Machine · Trusted Information Sharing · Random Selection

1 Introduction

Blockchain is a new computing mode that comprehensively utilizes computer technologies such as distributed storage, consensus mechanisms, and encryption algorithms, and has been applied in multiple fields. According to the application scenarios, node manage mechanism, and the decentralization degree of blockchain, it can be divided into three categories: public chain, private chain, and consortium chain [1]. The public chain is fully decentralized, nodes can freely join and exit, the represented projects are Bitcoin [2] and Ethereum [3]. The private chain is highly centralized, all system permissions are centrally controlled, the typical product is Morgan Chase's Quorum [4]. The consortium chain is

J. Chen et al. (Eds.): BlockSys 2023, CCIS 1897, pp. 162–175, 2024.
https://doi.org/10.1007/978-981-99-8104-5_13

managed jointly by multiple organizations, and requires admission to join the network, Hyperledger Fabric [5] and Corda [6] are the typical projects.

Effective regulation is the foundation for the healthy development of blockchain. As applications become more complex, one enterprise often needs to be regulated by multiple regulatory authorities. In this background, regulate blockchain (called target blockchain) by blockchain (called regulatory blockchain) has been proposed [7]. In this model, the regulatory object is multiple independent blockchains, and the regulatory party is composed of multiple regulatory departments based on blockchain. This regulatory approach is expected to achieve joint supervision of the same object by multiple departments, which can improve regulatory efficiency.

The main challenge in the above scenario is how to reliably transfer the data required by regulation from the target blockchain to the regulatory blockchain, while ensuring that the entire process is completed under the supervision of all regulators. Specifically, this requires addressing two issues: Firstly, ensure the authenticity of data collected from the target blockchain. Secondly, efficiently verify the correctness of data before writing it to regulatory blockchain.

Two kinds of related technologies are cross chain technology [8] and oracle machine technology [9]. The cross chain technology is mainly used to let individual user to transfer asset data from one blockchain to other blockchain. The oracle machine technology is mainly used to retrieve trusted data from offline data sources (such as the Internet or sensors) and write it to blockchain.

Since existing technologies cannot directly solve the problems faced in this paper, we proposed a regulation oriented decentralized oracle machine method, which focused on transferring data from target blockchain to regulatory blockchain in a reliable and scalable way. This method uses multi-party joint verification to ensure the authenticity of data captured from target blockchain and uses verifiable random selection mechanism to improve the efficiency and the scalability. Analyzed results showed that our method has lower overhead and good scalability while maintaining security.

Main contributions of this paper are as follows:

1. We proposed a regulation oriented decentralized oracle machine method, which uses multi-party joint verification and verifiable random selection mechanism to ensures the authenticity of data captured from blockchain while keep efficiency and scalability.
2. We analyzed the security, scalability and efficiency of the method, the results showed that our method can achieve high efficiency and good scalability without compromising security.
3. We compared our method with base line method, the results showed that our method has lower overhead and better scalability.

2   Related Work

The regulation process of blockchain can be abstracted as transferring data reliably from one blockchain to another. Related work is cross chain technology and oracle machine technology. Cross chain is a protocol that enables asset circulation and value transfer operations between two or more independent blockchains, which is not consistent with the application scenario in this paper. Therefore, we mainly focus on the research status of oracle machine technology.

According to the working mode, oracle machine can be divided into centralized oracle machine and decentralized oracle machine. The centralized oracle machine usually needs to have a trusted execution environment (TEE) which provided by trusted hardware. Decentralized oracle machine adopts a form like blockchain network, uses multiple oracle machine nodes to reach consensus on results, and then give the consensus results to blockchain nodes.

Provable [10] is a centralized oracle machine service that can obtain data from external data sources on the network and provide it to smart contracts. It uses the TEE trust model and a cryptographic based authenticity proof mechanism (TLS Notary). TownChier [11] is also a centralized oracle machine service. Its core technology is to use Intel SGX environment to execute the TLS Notary protocol to verify the transmitted data. ChainLink [12] is an oracle machine that uses a decentralized trust model. It supports the safe transmission of data between smart contracts and network APIs and maintains fairness between oracle machine nodes through incentive and punishment mechanisms. DOS Network [13] is a decentralized oracle machine that uses DOS tokens as an incentive mechanism to maintain the operation of nodes. It can support secure data transmission and data validation computing services for mainstream blockchain systems. Truora [14] is an oracle machine solution for WeBank's FISCO-BCOS blockchain platform. It has two deployment modes: centralized and decentralized. In centralized mode, the oracle machine will run the optimized TLS protocol in trusted hardware environment. While in decentralized mode, it supports aggregation of multiple data sources. Lian Yu. et al. [15] proposed a consortium blockchain oriented distributed oracle machine system. The system uses threshold signature based consensus method to ensure the credibility of the data while improving the scalability of the oracle machine system.

The main goal of existing oracle machine technology is to ensure that data can be reliably transferred from trusted data source to blockchain. But in the scenario of this paper, the data source is a blockchain system. Due to the possibility that there will be Byzantine nodes in blockchain system, one single node cannot be regarded as trusted data source, therefore we cannot directly use current oracle machine technology. We can simply obtain data from all data sources, and consensus between all regulators, but it will inevitably bring significant overhead. Therefore, it is necessary to research corresponding mechanisms to capture data reliably and efficiently from blockchain.

3   Application Scenario and Security Assumptions

This paper focus on reliably and efficiently transfer data from target blockchain to regulators. The scenarios in this paper are different from the existing oracle machine system. This section describes the application scenario and the security assumptions before introducing our proposed approach.

3.1 Application Scenario

As shown in Fig. 1, the application scenario of this paper is for regulatory agencies to regulate the target blockchains running specific applications. The regulatory blockchain composed of multiple regulatory agencies which needs to continuously obtain reliable application data from multiple blockchains running actual business. The regulation process needs to be done under the joint supervision and management of multiple regulatory parties, so that the entire process of data collection, data transmission, and data storage is controllable.

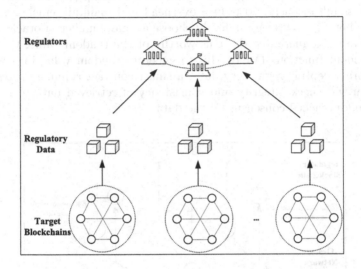

Fig. 1. The application scenario of this paper.

3.2 Security Assumptions

During the process of data collection, data transmission, and data storage, information systems and communication channels may be compromised by adversary. For the application scenario of this paper, the following security assumptions are made:

1. There are Byzantine nodes in blockchain network, and the Byzantine node may delete or modify local data, may modify the received data or denial of service. Multiple Byzantine nodes may collude, but the total number of Byzantine nodes will not exceed 1/3 of total blockchain nodes (as most consortium blockchain assumptions).
2. Byzantine nodes in the regulatory blockchain and the target blockchain would not collude.
3. Communication channels between blockchain nodes may be eavesdropped by adversary.

4   Regulation Oriented Decentralized Oracle Machine

4.1   Overall Approach

According to above security assumptions, this paper proposed a decentralized oracle machine method suitable for blockchain regulation. Since one single data source node cannot be trusted, this method uses oracle node to choose multiple blockchain nodes to retrieve application data. The oracle node verifies the integrity and consistency of captured data to ensure its authenticity. Considering that oracle node may be compromised, we choose multiple oracle nodes to capture data simultaneously. To reduce overhead and maintain efficiency, instead of using all oracle nodes we randomly choose a small number of oracle nodes to capture data. To guarantee the trustworthy of the random value, we use verifiable random functions (VRF) [16] to generate random value in a verifiable way. Before accepting regulatory data, a smart contract running on regulatory blockchain will check integrity and consistency of retrieved data to make sure related nodes reached consensus on the data.

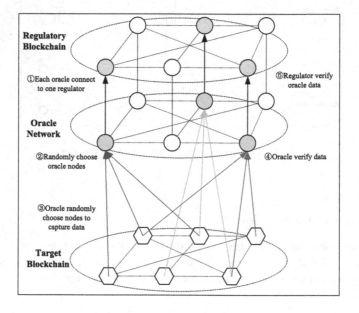

Fig. 2. The architecture of decentralized oracle machine.

As shown in Fig. 2, the oracle machine proposed in this paper works between regulatory blockchain and target blockchain. In the network topology, each oracle machine node connected to a corresponding regulatory blockchain node. Oracle machine nodes can communicate with each other through peer-to-peer networks, and each oracle machine node can communicate with target blockchain node. The oracle machine system collects data from target blockchains regularly, and we call each collection cycle as a round. During initialization, blockchain nodes and oracle machine nodes generate keypairs, and the oracle machine node establishes secure connections with the corresponding regulatory node. At the beginning of each round, regulators select a small number of oracle machine nodes to perform data collection tasks by running random algorithms. Subsequently, each selected oracle machine node will randomly select a few target blockchain nodes for data collection. After data collection, the oracle machine node verifies whether the data is correct by comparison of the data retrieved from different nodes. After each oracle machine node complete the data collection task, the oracle machine node sends the collected data to the regulatory node, and the regulatory node verifies the results by running the smart contract. The details of this method will be described in below sections.

4.2 Initialization

Before the oracle machine start working, an initialization process is needed. In this process, nodes in blockchain and oracle network will obtain unique number and bind to its identity. The binding result will be stored on the blockchain. The specific process is that each regulatory blockchain node generates its own public and private keys for message signing, as well as certificates and private keys for secure communication. Subsequently, each oracle machine generates its own VRF public and private key pair (its purpose will be explained later) and publishes $<PublicKey_{vrf}, NodeNumber>$ to the blockchain. At last, a data verification smart contract is deployed on regulatory blockchain. After initialization, the regulatory blockchain has the following information: blockchain node number and its message signature public key, oracle machine node number and its VRF public key.

4.3 Selection of Oracle Nodes

Considering that there may be Byzantine nodes in oracle machine nodes, if a single oracle machine node is selected for data collection, the collection results will be untrustworthy. If all oracle machine nodes are required to collect data, the overhead is unacceptable when it has a large scale of nodes. Therefore, the compromise method is to select an appropriate number of nodes to collect data while providing reliable guarantees, which can be achieved by randomly selecting nodes.

Due to the inability to directly execute the random number generation algorithm in smart contracts, this article implements node random selection through two steps. (1) Preparation stage. Select some nodes to execute the random number generation algorithm through the deterministic algorithm running in the smart contract. (2) Execute random algorithm stage. The selected nodes run a random number generation algorithm to generate random numbers and select the nodes to perform data collection. The specific process will be explained in detail below.

Preparation Stage. At the beginning of each round, the smart contract on the regulatory blockchain runs a node selection algorithm. The algorithm takes the current number of rounds and the number of needed nodes as input. It uses a deterministic computing logic to select the oracle machine node that executes the random algorithm in this round. Considering the possibility that the node may be attacked, multiple nodes will be selected in each round to execute the random number generation algorithm.

The specific algorithm is as Algorithm 1. Firstly, the list of all nodes in oracle network is retrieved from regulatory blockchain. Then the hash value is calculated according to current round and the total number of oracle nodes. After that, the hash value is converted to a big integer, and the node number is chosen as the reminder of the big integer against the total number of nodes. If multiple oracle nodes are needed, the above process will repeat until all oracle nodes are decided.

Algorithm 1: Select oracle node to execute random algorithm

Input: $CurrentRound, NumberOfNodes$
Output: $SelectedNodesList$
$TotalNumberOfNodes \leftarrow$ Read the List of Current Nodes;
$count \leftarrow 0$;
$HashResult \leftarrow$ null;
$SelectedNodesList \leftarrow$ null;
$TimeStamp \leftarrow$ null;
while $count \leq NumberOfNodes$ **do**
  if $HashResult$ is null **then**
  | $HashResult \leftarrow$ ComputeHash($CurrentRound \parallel$
  | $TotalNumberOfNodes$);
  else
  | $TimeStamp \leftarrow$ GetCurrentTime();
  | $HashResult \leftarrow$ ComputeHash($HashResult \parallel TimeStamp$);
  end
  $HashNumber \leftarrow$ ConvertToInteger($HashResult$);
  $NodeNumber \leftarrow HashNumber \% TotalNumberOfNodes$;
  Add $NodeNumber$ to $SelectedNodesList$;
  $count \leftarrow count + 1$;
end

Random Algorithm Execution Stage. Since the node executing the random number generation algorithm is selected by the deterministic algorithm, it may be a Byzantine node. To prevent it from forging random numbers, it is necessary to verify the generated random numbers to ensure that the results are generated through random methods. We use verifiable random functions to achieve this goal.

Verifiable random function was proposed by Micali, Rabin, and Vadhan, the random numbers generated using this method can be verified. When calculating VRF, the first step is to generate a pair of public and private keys. Then a random seed is calculated and is used combined with the private key to generate the random number and the proof. At this time, others can use the public key, random seed, random number, and proof to verify that the random number is indeed generated by the random algorithm with the private key and random seed as inputs.

Since random seed is publicly available, and it can affect the generation of random number, attackers may manipulate the results of random number by controlling random seed. Therefore the generation mechanism of random seed is very important. Requirements for random seed here is that each seed should be used only once, each round should use different seed, and the nodes running the random algorithm cannot predict the next round of random seed before executing the random algorithm. we use the hash value of the current block and the result of the previous round of random numbers to calculate the random seed.

In the proposed scheme, the calculation process of VRF is shown in Algorithm 2, which can be divided into three steps:

1. The node obtains block info and the random number of last round from the blockchain and calculates random seed.
2. The node executes VRF generation algorithm to calculate the random value according to the node's private key and random seed.
3. The node execution VRF prove algorithm to generate the corresponding proof according to the node's private key and random seed.

Algorithm 2: Generate verifiable random value

Input: $LatestBlock, LastRoundRandom, PrivateKey_{vrf}$
Output: $RandomValue, Proof$
$LatestBlockHash \leftarrow$ GetBlockHash($LatestBlock$);
$seed \leftarrow$ ComputeHash($LatestBlockHash \parallel LastRoundRandom$);
$RandomValue \leftarrow VRF_{value}(PrivateKey_{vrf}, seed)$;
$Proof \leftarrow VRF_{prove}(PrivateKey_{vrf}, seed)$;

Then the oracle machine put the round number $RandomValue$ and $Proof$ on the blockchain, the smart contract on the blockchain is triggered to verify the correctness of the random value. During verification, smart contract computes random $seed$ and reads VRF public key of oracle machine, random value, and the proof from the blockchain, then executes the VRF verification algorithm $VRF_{Verify}(PublicKey_{vrf}, seed, RandomValue, Proof)$.

4.4   Joint Data Capture

In each round of data capture, when oracle machine nodes are selected, each oracle machine randomly selects multiple target blockchain nodes, and then collects data from these nodes. The number of selected nodes is related to the size of the scale of the target blockchain network. As we described in assumptions, communication channel could be eavesdropped, so the oracle machine node should establish secure channel (bidirectional identity authentication is required during the connection establishment process) with the target blockchain node when retrieving data. Then the data is packaged into a specified format and send to the oracle machine node.

After the oracle machine node receives all the data (the same oracle machine node will receive multiple data retrieved from different target node), it would verify the integrity and consistency of the data. The integrity of data is mainly guaranteed by digital signature. While the consistency is checked by the comparison of multiple data. Assuming the number of selected targets blockchain nodes is M, and f is the consistency threshold. The process of consistency verification is as follows: when no less than f out of M data are consistent, the data is considered valid otherwise the data is considered invalid. The selection of parameter M is determined by the total number of blockchain nodes and the value of f is determined by equation: $f = \lfloor \frac{M+1}{2} \rfloor$. Detailed explanation of this equation will be described in Sect. 5.

4.5   Verification of Regulatory Data

In each round, when the regulatory blockchain collects enough regulatory data, it will run the verification smart contract for data validation. This smart contract will read the data collected by all oracle machine nodes in this round and perform integrity verification and consistency verification on the data. The process of consistency verification is like the process described in Sect. 4.4.

5   Security Analysis

Security is the prerequisite for the oracle to work properly, and the setting of parameters is very important. Due to the using of random selection mechanism in our method, inappropriate setting of parameters would bring security risks to our method. In this section, we analyze the security of our method and propose principles to determine appropriate parameters.

In our method, each oracle machine randomly requests data from several target blockchain nodes, and when the data is obtained, it needs to check the consistency of the data. In addition, when all oracle machine nodes responsible for collecting data have collected data, regulators need to verify the consistency of collected data. In the above data verification process, to ensure security and efficiency, a consistency threshold is set in this method. When the number of identical copies exceeds this threshold, the data is considered valid, otherwise the data is considered invalid. If the selected threshold is too small, it is easy to be attacked by collusion. If the threshold is too high, the cost is relatively high. The compromise is to select as few nodes as possible while ensuring a sufficiently low probability of collusion attacks. As we assumed that Byzantine node in regulatory blockchain and target blockchain would not collude, the process of Sect. 4.4 and Sect. 4.5 are independent. Therefore, we only need to analysis one of them. To determine the appropriate parameters, we conducted the following analysis.

Assuming that there is a total of N nodes in the network, in which there are B Byzantine nodes. As the assumptions we have described, the number of Byzantine nodes will not exceed $1/3$, then we have the constraint condition: $B \leq 1/3N$. The probability of randomly selecting M nodes, of which there are k Byzantine nodes is obey hypergeometric probability distribution:

$$P(k|M, B, N) = \frac{C_B^k \cdot C_{N-B}^{M-k}}{C_N^M} \tag{1}$$

Use f to represent the consistency threshold. To verify the validity of the data, it is required that at least f nodes are honest nodes. The situation where the data is valid is: $M - k \geq f$ and $k \leq f - 1$. That is: $k \leq M - f$ and $k \leq f - 1$. Then, the probability of success is:

$$P_{success} = \min\{P(k \leq M - f|M, B, N), P(k \leq f - 1|M, B, N)\} \tag{2}$$

To maximize the probability of success, the value of f needs to meet the following conditions: $M - f = f - 1$, that is: $M = 2f - 1$. Or expressed as: $f = \lfloor \frac{M+1}{2} \rfloor$.
Then the probability of success can be reduced to:

$$P_{success} = P(k \leq f - 1|M, B, N) = P(k \leq \left\lfloor \frac{M+1}{2} \right\rfloor - 1|M, B, N) \tag{3}$$

Then the probability of successful attack is: $P_{attack} = 1 - P_{success}$. To minimize overhead while ensuring security, we can choose a minimum M value while ensuring a sufficiently small attack probability. Referring to the parameter settings of Bitcoin, it can be considered that the system is sufficiently secure when the probability of being attacked does not exceed 0.001. For a blockchain network with a total number of 200 nodes, the selection of relevant parameters is shown in Table 1. In the worst-case scenario, when the number of Byzantine nodes reaches 33%, the randomly selected number of nodes is 55, and the consistency threshold is set to 28, the probability of being attacked is 9.6×10^{-4}, not exceeding 0.001. Therefore, as long as we set appropriate parameters, our method can achieve reasonable security.

6 Scalability Analysis

To analyze the scalability of our method, we investigate the changes in relevant parameters as the total number of nodes in the blockchain network increases from 200 to 1000. To obtain more intuitive results, we investigate the changes in the number of randomly selected nodes and consistency threshold in the worst-case scenario (33% of Byzantine nodes).

As showed in Fig. 3, it can be seen that the number of randomly selected nodes determined by this method will not significantly increase with the increasing of the total number of nodes. When the probability of being attacked is

Table 1. Parameter selection to ensure security.

Total Nodes (N)	Number of Byzantine Nodes (B)	Byzantine Proportion (*ratio*)	Number of Selected Nodes (M)	Consistency Threshold (f)	Probability of Attack (P_{attack})
200	10	5%	5	3	8.7×10^{-4}
200	20	10%	9	5	5.9×10^{-4}
200	30	15%	13	7	7.8×10^{-4}
200	40	20%	19	10	8.4×10^{-4}
200	50	25%	29	15	7.1×10^{-4}
200	60	30%	43	22	8.3×10^{-4}
200	66	33%	55	28	9.6×10^{-4}

sufficiently low (not exceeding 0.001), the number of randomly selected nodes increases from 55 to 73, and the growth trend is shown as sublinear throughout the increasing process. This way, it can effectively control the overall cost in the face of large-scale networks and therefore this method has good scalability.

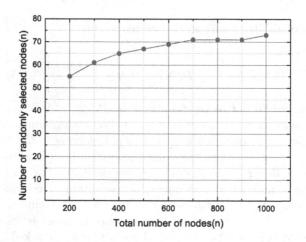

Fig. 3. Scalability analysis of decentralized oracle machine

7 Efficiency Analysis

Meanwhile, to evaluate the usability of the proposed method, this section will analyze its working efficiency and compare it with the base line method. The base line method selected here is the full copy reading method, which requires all regulatory nodes to collect data from all target blockchain nodes. We investigate the work efficiency of our method from time overhead aspect.

To analyze the time cost of our method, we focused on the time cost of each round. As we described in Sect. 4, the work in one round included three parts:

selection of oracle nodes, joint data capture and verification of regulatory data. The stage of joint data capture can be divided into two parts: data packaging and data transmission. Assuming the number of regulatory blockchain nodes is N_1, the number of target blockchain nodes is N_2, the number of nodes selected for generating a verifiable random function in each round is N_{vrf}, the number of oracle machine nodes selected in each round is N_o, and the number of blockchain nodes selected in each oracle machine node is N_c. Assuming the time required for generating a single verifiable random function is T_{vrf}, the data packaging time of a single node is T_p, the single data transmission time between two nodes is T_t, and the time spent to store data is T_s. When ignoring the parallelization, the total time cost in one round of two methods can be express in Table 2.

Table 2. Time cost in one round without considering parallelization.

Task Stage	Time Cost of this paper	Time Cost of base line
Selection of Oracle Nodes	$N_{vrf} \times T_{vrf}$	/
Joint Data Capture	$N_o \times N_c \times (T_p + T_t)$	$N_1 \times N_2 \times (T_p + T_t)$
Verification of Regulatory Data	$N_o \times T_s$	$N_1 \times T_s$

Considering that when performing verifiable random algorithms, data packaging, data transmission and data storage, multiple nodes can perform the operation simultaneously, the time cost needs to be divided by the number of nodes. We assume that the internal execution of computing tasks is serial within the node. According to the above description, the time cost comparison between this method and the base line method is shown in Table 3.

Table 3. Time cost in one round considering parallelization.

Task Stage	Time Cost of this paper	Time Cost of base line
Selection of Oracle Nodes	T_{vrf}	/
Joint Data Capture	$N_o \times (T_p + T_t)$	$N_1 \times (T_p + T_t)$
Verification of Regulatory Data	T_s	T_s

Then the total time cost in one round of this paper is: $T_r = T_{vrf} + N_o \times (T_p + T_t) + T_s$. While for base line the time cost is: $T_f = N_1 \times (T_p + T_t) + T_s$. Since both methods have the T_s item, we ignored this value when comparing the total time cost.

In an experimental environment showed in Table 4, the typical time for T_{vrf} is 0.02 s (using a secret key with a length of 2048 bits, and the random number length is 20 bits). The typical time to complete a single data packaging (reading one block, encapsulating, and signing) for T_p is 0.006 s and the typical time to

Table 4. Experimental environment

Category	Parameter
CPU	Intel Core i7-10700 2.90 GHz
Memory	32 GB
Disk	512 GB
Operating system	Windows 10 21H2

complete transmission of 1 KB data T_t is 0.063 s. We investigate the time cost of each round of data collection when the number of nodes in the regulatory blockchain increases from 200 to 1000. The comparison results between this paper and the base line method are shown in Fig. 4. It can be seen that, our method has lower time cost than base line method, and the time cost of our method only slightly increases as the number of nodes increases.

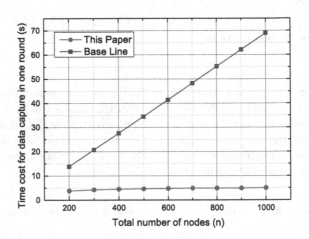

Fig. 4. Efficiency analysis of decentralized oracle machine.

8   Conclusion

Blockchain is a new type of computing, as blockchain technology continues to evolve and expand, effective regulation is crucial for its healthy development. This paper proposed a regulation oriented decentralized oracle machine method which provided a novel solution for the joint supervision of blockchain applications by multiple regulatory parties. The security, scalability, and efficiency of this method was analyzed, and the result showed that it not only ensures the authenticity of data but also improves the efficiency and scalability of the regulatory process while maintaining security.

Acknowledgments. The research is supported by the National Key R&D Program of China (No. 2020YFB1006001).

References

1. Types of Blockchains Explained- Public vs. Private vs. Consortium. https://www.blockchain-council.org/blockchain/types-of-blockchains-explained-public-vs-private-vs-consortium/. Accessed 13 Apr 2023
2. Bitcoin: a peer-to-peer electronic cash system. https://bitcoin.org/bitcoin.pdf. Accessed 13 Apr 2023
3. A next-generation smart contract and decentralized application platform. https://github.com/ethereum/wiki/wiki/White-Paper. Accessed 13 Apr 2023
4. Quorum whitepaper. https://github.com/jpmorganchase/quorum-docs/blob/master/Quorum%20Whitepaper%20v0.2.pdf. Accessed 13 Apr 2023
5. Cachin, C.: Architecture of the hyperledger blockchain fabric. In: Proceedings of the Workshop on Distributed Cryptocurrencies and Consensus Ledgers (2016)
6. Corda: An introduction. https://docs.corda.net/_static/corda-introductory-whitepaper.pdf. Accessed 13 Apr 2023
7. Lu, Y., Zhu, Y.: A cross-chain supervision mechanism for consortium blockchain based on relay-chain technology. Comput. Eng. Appl. https://kns.cnki.net/kcms/detail//11.2127.TP.20221212.1900.023.html
8. Blockchain Interoperability: Why Is Cross Chain Technology Important? https://101blockchains.com/blockchain-interoperability/. Accessed 13 Apr 2023
9. Al-Breiki, H., Rehman, M.H.U., Salah, K., et al.: Trustworthy blockchain oracles: review, comparison, and open research challenges. IEEE Access **8**, 85675–85685 (2020)
10. Provable documentation. https://docs.provable.xyz. Accessed 13 Apr 2023
11. Zhang, F., Cecchetti, E., Croman, K., et al.: Town crier: an authenticated data feed for smart contracts. In: Proceedings of the 2016 ACM SIGSAC Conference on Computer and Communications Security, pp. 270–282. ACM, New York (2016)
12. Blockchain Oracles for Connected Smart Contracts. https://docs.chain.link. Accessed 13 Apr 2023
13. A dencentralized oracle service boosting blockchain usability with off-chain data & verifiable computing power. https://s3.amazonaws.com/whitepaper.dos/DOS+Network+Technical+Whitepaper.pdf. Accessed 13 Apr 2023
14. Truora document. https://truora.readthedocs.io. Accessed 13 Apr 2023
15. Yu, L., Li, Z., Wang, S., et al.: Research on distributed oracle machine for consortium blockchain. J. Inf. Secur. Res. **8**(5), 418–428 (2022)
16. Micali, S., Rabin, M., Vadhan, S.: Verifiable random functions. In: 40th Annual Symposium on Foundations of Computer Science (Cat. No. 99CB37039), pp. 120–130. IEEE (1999)

Obric: Oblivious Keyword Search in Hyperledger Fabric Platform

Xin Zhao[1], Xu Yang[2], Jianfeng Wang[1(✉)], and Saiyu Qi[2(✉)]

[1] School of Cyber Engineering, Xidian University, Xi'an, China
jfwang@xidan.edu.cn
[2] School of Computer Science and Technology, Xi'an Jiaotong University, Xi'an,
China
saiyu-qi@mail.xjtu.edu.cn

Abstract. Access pattern disclosure can reveal sensitive information related to search queries, posing a threat to user privacy. Malicious attackers may infer users' search intentions, behavior, and interests from access patterns, which can be used for targeted attacks, phishing, or identity theft. Access pattern disclosure may also jeopardize the confidentiality of the searched data, as it may reveal sensitive information related to the queried data.

Traditional searchable encryption allows for searching encrypted data directly, but suffers from privacy leaks due to access pattern disclosure and cannot guarantee data integrity. Additionally, traditional searchable encryption only supports single-keyword search and leads to significant computational overhead when searching for a large number of ciphertexts. To address these issues, we propose a two-stage protected ciphertext retrieval scheme called Obric that supports oblivious multi-keyword search in hyperledger fabric platform. In specific, we store encrypted data using the distributed point function (DPFs) on the Order node set and the ORAM encryption algorithm on the Peer nodes. Finally, we implement a secret information storage system so that users' access pattern privacy is not compromised by malicious adversaries.

Keywords: Searchable encryption · Blockchain · Keyword search · Privacy protection

1 Introduction

Searchable encryption (SE) [1] is an encryption technique that is designed to protect user privacy. It allows for searching and matching operations on encrypted data while ensuring data confidentiality and integrity. Searchable encryption with keyword search (SEKS) [2] is a common type of searchable encryption scheme that allows users to search encrypted data using keywords and returns matching results. SE was developed to address the problem of protecting user

Supported by organization x.

privacy and confidentiality. Traditional data encryption techniques can protect data confidentiality, but they are unable to perform searching and matching operations on encrypted data, requiring the data to be decrypted before it can be processed. This creates potential risks such as data leaks and malicious attacks. SE enables matching results to be obtained through encrypted searching and matching operations without revealing the content of the data. This makes SE an effective method for protecting user privacy and confidentiality, and SE is widely used in a lot of scenarios such as cloud computing, Internet of Things (IoT), and mobile applications to ensure the protection of user data and privacy.

Searchable encryption protects data confidentiality by encrypting both data and search queries. However, traditional searchable encryption schemes may leak query patterns to third parties, which can be exploited to infer users' sensitive information. Searchable encryption only allows authorized users to retrieve search results, ensuring keyword privacy. Traditional searchable encryption schemes are computationally expensive and impractical for large-scale data searches. There are some issues with using searchable encryption in traditional cloud servers. Searchable encryption requires cryptographic techniques to support keyword searching, which increases storage overhead and leads to higher cloud data storage costs. The data stored on cloud servers may face external attacks and internal abuse, which may result in sensitive data and privacy leakage. In the case of large-scale data, searchable encryption needs to support efficient data partitioning and query parallelization. With the development of blockchain [3,4] technology, searchable encryption based on blockchain has many advantages.

Recent years, blockchain-based searchable encryption schemes have attracted a lot of attention [5,6]. The decentralization and distributed nature of blockchain technology ensures the security and immutability of data, while searchable encryption protects the confidentiality of data, making it more secure. Blockchain technology can provide data immutability and traceability, while searchable encryption can protect the integrity of data, ensuring that it is not tampered with during storage and transmission. On the blockchain, multiple nodes can share data, while searchable encryption can control data access permissions, thus achieving secure sharing of data. Searchable encryption can be used for data privacy protection in fields such as healthcare, finance, and security, while blockchain-based searchable encryption technology can further enhance data privacy and security and expand application scenarios. Currently, there are still some issues with searchable encryption based on blockchain. Most existing searchable encryption schemes are designed for single-keyword searches, and multi-keyword search remains a challenging problem. In addition, these schemes are typically used for internal use within an organization, with a limited number of read and write participants, and do not support multiple participants. Most importantly, existing searchable encryption schemes can only guarantee that the information in the search ciphertext is not leaked during the search process. However, they may reveal the access patterns, which can be analyzed by malicious attackers to obtain user privacy and even plaintext information. When access patterns are leaked, it can reveal sensitive information about the search query and potentially compromise the privacy of the user. Malicious attackers may be able to infer the user's search intent, behavior, and interests from access patterns, which could be used for targeted attacks, phishing, or identity theft. Access pattern leakage can also compromise the confidentiality of the data being searched, as it may reveal sensitive information about the data being queried.

To address the issue of access pattern leakage in traditional searchable encryption, in this paper, we propose a two-stage access pattern protection ciphertext retrieval scheme called Obric based on the Hyperledger Fabric consortium blockchain. Leveraging the Fabric platform, we construct a system that utilizes distributed point functions (DPFs) [11] secret sharing technology for file index storage on the Order node set, and employs Oblivious RAM (ORAM) [9] for secure file content storage on the Peer node set. The contributions of this research are summarized as follows:

- We have implemented protection for user access patterns based on distributed trust, anonymous access, and blockchain technology, which prevents malicious third parties from obtaining information about the user's access frequency, address, and time, thus safeguarding the user's privacy.
- Obric supports multiple participants to perform secret file writing and keyword queries, freeing them from the limitation of being members of the same organization. Additionally, Obric enables multi-keyword queries and ensures the correctness and integrity of query results.
- Based on the idea of bitmap, the features of blockchain smart contracts, and the application of trusted execution environment technology, we have improved the operational efficiency of Obric, reduced communication overhead, and enhanced system availability.

2   Preliminaries

2.1   Distributed Point Function

Distributed Point Functions (DPFs) [11–13] are a cryptographic primitive used for secret sharing, allowing multiple parties to share a message and compute a function on the shared data without revealing the data to any individual party.

One can define a point function $f_{a,b}(x)$ (a variant of the Kronecker delta function) given any two values a and b. $f_{a,b} : \{0,1\}^u \to \{0,1\}^v$:

$$f_{a,b}(x) = \begin{cases} b & for \quad x = a \\ 0 & for \quad x \neq a \end{cases}$$

It means, the function is zero everywhere except at a, where its value is b.

We abstract the *DPFs* encryption process into three algorithms:

The key generation algorithm:generate a key set based on the security parameter λ and the shared function f.

$$Gen\left(1^{\lambda}, f_{I,1}\right) \to (k_1, k_2, ..., k_t)$$

The response valuation algorithm: compute the feedback y_i based on i, k_i, and the file content X.

$$Eval\,(i, k_i, X) \to y_i$$

The decryption algorithm: decrypting y with y_i provided by multiple feeders.

$$Dec\left(\{y_i\}_{i\in[t]}\right) \to y$$

2.2 Path ORAM

Path ORAM [9,10] is a privacy-preserving technique for accessing external storage, used to hide data access patterns and prevent external attackers from inferring sensitive information from these patterns. It achieves this by dispersing data across external memory to hide access patterns. Path ORAM accesses data in external memory using a method called "path-based access." It maintains a binary tree where each node represents a storage area, and each leaf node stores a data block. To access a data block, Path ORAM needs to traverse the tree structure from the root node downwards, randomly selecting nodes to hide access pattern.

2.3 Enclave

Intel SGX [14] is a hardware-based TEE that uses memory encryption to isolate application code and data within an Enclave, providing confidentiality and integrity. It also includes security mechanisms like remote attestation to prevent tampering or counterfeiting of the code and data within the enclave.

3 Problem Formulation

3.1 System Model

As shown in Fig. 1, Obric mainly consists of three components: Data Owners, Data Requestors, and a blockchain network. In Obric, we use a two-stage process of indexing and retrieving files to obtain file information, therefore, we use a Hyperledger Fabric [7,8] network with Order nodes that have an independent channel.

Data Owners refer to entities that own the data. They need to use cryptographic techniques to upload normalized data to the blockchain network and define access rules and permissions through smart contracts. They are responsible for ensuring the authenticity and integrity of the uploaded data and the security and correctness of the smart contracts.

Data Requestors are entities that need to query data. They need to input keywords through the client, use cryptographic algorithms, and call smart contracts to request data, and obtain corresponding data according to cryptographic algorithms, access rules, and permissions. They need to comply with access rules and permission restrictions.

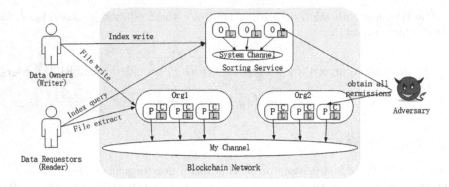

Fig. 1. System model

The Fabric network is a decentralized distributed database consisting of multiple nodes. Nodes need to jointly maintain the entire blockchain network, including data validation and storage, consensus algorithms, smart contract execution, and security guarantees.

3.2   Threat Assumptions

In Obric model, we assume that if an adversary breaches a node in the Fabric network, they could manipulate the node's operating system and privileged software to obtain all privileges on that node. The adversary could either be the system administrator or a malicious hacker. Once the adversary gains access to the node, they can access requests submitted by users and information stored on the node, and respond to users with error messages. However, we assume that the adversary cannot control the entire consortium blockchain network or all order nodes. Additionally, we assume that the cryptographic primitives used in Obric are safe and secure.

3.3   System Goals

- **Query confidentiality:** In Obric, adversaries cannot recover plaintext queries submitted by users through any means, and users' keys will not be disclosed, ensuring the security and reliability of user access.
- **User access pattern protection:** The user's access patterns are protected, preventing adversaries from obtaining the user's access address, access time, and access frequency. This mitigates the risk of malicious attackers inferring user privacy through access patterns.
- **Correct and available:** We perform message verification on the obtained results to ensure that the querying user receives the correct feedback. While ensuring the security of the system, we have optimized it to ensure its efficiency and availability.

4 System Design Overview

4.1 Design Thinking and System Architecture

Traditional searchable encryption allows for searching encrypted data directly, but it suffers from privacy leaks due to access pattern disclosure and cannot guarantee data integrity. Additionally, traditional searchable encryption only supports single-keyword search and leads to significant computational overhead when searching for a large number of ciphertexts. To address these issues, we propose a two-stage protected ciphertext retrieval scheme Obric which supports multi-keyword search.

Obric divides the retrieval operation into two stages: index retrieval and file extraction. Firstly, we obtain the index through encryption algorithms, then we retrieve the ciphertext storage address based on the index, and finally, we extract the file based on an algorithm that hides the real query address. To store file indexes and contents, we require different organizations. As a decentralized and distributed data storage platform, blockchain ensures that data is not tampered with. The consensus feature of smart contracts provides favorable technical support for verifying the integrity and correctness of data. We note that in the Hyperledger Fabric blockchain network, the ordering service organizations have their own System Channel, and Peer nodes have a My Channel. Furthermore, Fabric has plug-and-play and strong extensibility advantages, which is why we use Fabric as our server to store file information. Order nodes have higher trustworthiness, but they are not suitable for storing large amounts of files. Moreover, Order nodes perform multiple tasks in the blockchain network, and their workload is high. Therefore, the added computation module should not be too excessive. Based on the differences between the two, we store index content in the ledger of the Order node and use the world state database of the Peer node to store file content.

Distributed point function and Oblivious RAM (ORAM) are both technologies used to achieve incognito access. In terms of encryption performance, both have strong performance, and in terms of access delay, the access delay of Distributed point function is very low because it computes locally and generates keys in batches, requiring only one network transmission to complete. However, the access delay of ORAM is relatively high because it requires multiple accesses and data migration operations to protect access pattern privacy. In terms of throughput, the throughput of Distributed point function is relatively low and is suitable for small-scale data access, while the throughput of ORAM is relatively high and is suitable for large-scale data access. Considering the characteristics of Fabric nodes and the differences between index and file storage, we can see that Distributed point function has a lower throughput and is suitable for storing small-scale data. Additionally, Order nodes are suitable for storing small-scale data because they perform multiple functions in the blockchain network. Distributed point function requires multiple servers for secret sharing, while the Order node set consists of multiple Order nodes that jointly complete sorting services on the blockchain. Distributed point function supports batch updates, and since a single keyword may exist in multiple files, index updates are usually performed in batches.

Based on the above analysis, we have determined that the Distributed point function encryption scheme should be used to store indexes on the Order node set, while the ORAM encryption scheme should be used to store file encryption data on the Peer node. This is the basic system structure of our proposed scheme.

For the purpose of describing the details of the implementation of the system later on, we provide a normative definition of the concepts commonly used in the system. As shown in Table 1, we describe the user write file formally as $W_I = (I, K_I, D_I)$, where I denotes the *File id*, K_I denotes the set of keywords of the file, D_I denotes the content of the file, and the user search file input *key* represents the keyword and give a formula for some of the concepts used in the system.

Table 1. Notations

Notations	Definitions
K	Set of keywords
$W_I = (I, K_I, D_I)$	W:file, I:File id, K:keywords set, D:content
hash	Algorithm for processing keyword into a number
Hash	Set of hash functions
A_I	BitMap resulting from hashs set keywords set
MA	Matrix of BitMap collections
X	Index Array
$Gen\left(1^\lambda, f_i\right)$	Key generation algorithm
$Eval\left(i, k_i, X\right)$	Node response algorithm
$Dec\left(\{y_i\}_{i\in[t]}\right)$	Decryption algorithms
Position Map	Map storing the path where I is located
Stash	Stash stored in enclave
$Position\left(I\right)$	Algorithm to get leaf node x by *Position Map*
$P\left(x\right)$	The path from the root to node x
$P\left(x, l\right)$	The bucket in $P\left(x\right)$ at level l

As shown in Fig. 2, the data owner uses the Bloom Filter algorithm and Hash function to compute K_I as a BitMap M_I for the data to be shared, and applies for access permission and identity authentication from the Certificate Authority (CA) node. Then, the data owner sends I and M_I to a set O containing t sorting nodes. Each O_j $(0 < j < t+1)$ combines I, M_I, and an index matrix X to obtain a new index matrix. After completing the above steps, the data owner connects to a Peer node and writes the key-value pair (I, D_I) into the blockchain. At this point, the data state is written to the LevelDB database of the consortium chain, and then the Enclave retrieves the new block through P2P communication and

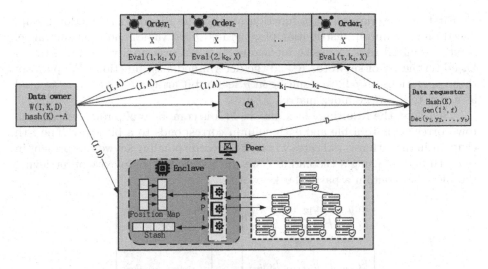

Fig. 2. System architecture

performs Merkle verification. The Enclave writes I into the Position Map and D_I into the Stash, and then synchronizes them to the Path ORAM tree structure of the Peer node.

When a data user queries a keyword set K, they obtain permission and identity authentication from the Certificate Authority (CA) node, and compute $Hash(K)$ using the Bloom Filter algorithm. Then, they generate a key group $(k_1, k_2, ..., k_t)$ using the algorithm $Gen(1^\lambda, f)$ and send k_j to sorting node O_j. O_j obtains the corresponding y_j using the algorithm $Eval(j, k_j, X)$ and returns it to the data user. The data user then obtains the necessary index array information using $Dec(y_1, y_2, ..., y_t)$ and retrieves the required file ID I from the BitMap. Finally, the data query requester obtains Enclave access permission, calls the $Position(I)$ function to obtain the specific location x of the file, and retrieves the file. The Path ORAM database and Position Map complete randomization after accessing the file.

The above content provides a general overview of Obric design's basic ideas and initial architecture. In the following sections, we will elaborate on the distributed storage of file indexes and the construction of a storage system for encrypted data with anonymous access.

4.2 Index Struct

According to the standardized input mentioned earlier, the owner of a file inputs it as $W_I = (I, K_I, D_I)$, where I represents the file ID and K_I represents the set of keywords associated with the file. After inputting p files, an index matrix can be generated. Since each file may have a different number of keywords and retrieving them could be too complex, we use a Bloom filter to optimize our index table.

First, we determine r *hash* functions, called the BloomHash function group, based on the uniform distribution of generated *hash* values and their relevance. Next, we initialize a fixed-size bit array, A. Then, we modify the bit array A based on the set of keywords K and the determined *hash* functions. We perform these operations on p files, resulting in p sets of bit arrays. Each array is treated as a row to form the index matrix, MA.

Therefore, the resulting index matrix MA is composed of p rows, where each row corresponds to a file and each column corresponds to a bit array. The i-th element in the j-th row indicates whether the corresponding keyword is present in the j-th file. By using a Bloom filter, we can reduce the complexity of retrieving the files that contain a particular keyword.

$$
\begin{bmatrix}
key_{11} & key_{12} & \ldots & key_{1q} \\
key_{21} & key_{22} & \ldots & key_{2q} \\
\vdots & \vdots & \ddots & \vdots \\
key_{p1} & key_{p2} & \ldots & key_{pq}
\end{bmatrix}
\rightarrow
\begin{bmatrix}
a_{11} & a_{12} & \ldots & a_{1n} \\
a_{21} & a_{22} & \ldots & a_{2n} \\
\vdots & \vdots & \ddots & \vdots \\
a_{p1} & a_{p2} & \ldots & a_{pn}
\end{bmatrix}
$$

To improve the efficiency of storage, querying, and authentication operations, we aggregate the index matrix MA by columns and generate an array of length n.

$$X = \{X_1, X_2, ..., X_n\}$$

The data query process involves processing the keyword set K using the Bloom filter algorithm to obtain a list of r' *hash* values, denoted as M. We then use a key generation function Gen to derive r' keys for each element in M. Specifically, for $\delta \in M$, we have $Gen(1^\lambda, P_{\delta,1}) \rightarrow (k_1, k_2, ..., k_t)$, where t is the number of keys derived for each element in M. These keys are distributed in order to the Order nodes. For each $Order_j$, $1 \le j \le t$, it obtains the corresponding r' keys k_j in sequence and applies the response algorithm $Eval(j, k_j, X) \rightarrow y_j$ to generate the response value y_j. The Order node then sends the response values back to the client, which uses the decryption algorithm Dec to reconstruct the r' index information needed. The client then performs bitwise and operation on the r' index information to obtain a binary string, where the 1-bits correspond to the files that contain the keyword set K. The ids of these files are stored in a final array slice R, which represents the encrypted data set that contains the keyword set K searched by the data query process.

By using this process, we ensure the privacy of the keyword set K while still allowing efficient querying of the encrypted data set. The use of Bloom filters allows for efficient filtering of irrelevant files, and the use of encryption and distributed computing techniques ensures the confidentiality and efficiency of the query process.

It is worth noting that when the query user interacts with the Order node set, there is no use of smart contracts, only simple communication. Therefore, at this time, we can only ensure the immutability of the index array X, but cannot confirm whether the Order nodes have correctly returned the correct y value to the user. Thus, we need to verify the integrity and correctness of the message.

Running smart contracts requires broadcasting to all nodes in the same channel, which contradicts the need for distributed secret sharing of the distributed point function. In other words, if the encryption and decryption of the distributed point function are done through smart contracts, all nodes on the channel can access all transactions and block data, including transactions and blocks containing the results of smart contract execution, through t accesses and broadcasts. Therefore, all Order nodes have obtained all secrets, and each Order node can restore the entire request according to the Dec algorithm.

To solve the above problems, we analyze the system characteristics and find that the index array X is stored in the world state database of the Order node set and has immutability, that is, the index array must be correct. At this point, we consider using smart contracts to perform $hash$ operations on each bit of the index array, generating a verification array $Y = \{hash(X_1), hash(X_2), ..., hash(X_n)\}$. Since this verification array is generated based on smart contracts and has consensus, we can ensure that the index array must be correct.

4.3 Encrypted Data Storage

To address the issue of privacy leakage caused by malicious adversaries observing the access patterns of encrypted data in the blockchain world state database, this paper proposes an optimization using Path ORAM technology while retaining the basic functionality of the world state. Path ORAM uses path compression and position hiding techniques to reduce access time complexity and ensure data privacy. The core idea of Path ORAM is to use a tree structure to store data blocks, and protect data privacy during access using path compression and position hiding techniques.

Path ORAM mainly consists of a tree structure for storing data, a Position Map, and a Stash. The Position Map is a dynamic data structure that is continuously modified as users read or write data, and all users need to maintain this data structure online. However, this approach introduces another problem: there are many data writers and data queryers in Obric, and too many participants can pose a significant risk to user data security by accessing this sensitive information. Therefore, we propose a solution that uses a secure execution environment to store the Position Map and Stash. We use Intel SGX technology to build an "Enclave" memory area to store the secret information in Stash and Position Map. In the Position Map, we store a set of correspondences between file id I and leaf node x, which store the position of the bucket path. Therefore, we can define Position(I) to obtain the leaf node x. In the algorithm, a small number of blocks may overflow in the tree bucket, or $P(x)$ needs to be extracted to the user during the access implementation process, so we set an area in the Enclave as Stash.

In the Enclave: we first obtain the leaf node x according to the Position(I) function. Then, we remap Position(I) to a new random location. Next, we obtain the buckets of the entire path based on $P(x)$ and write them to Stash. We perform read and write operations in Stash. If it is a write operation, we write the encrypted data that needs to be written to Stash. Finally, in the node pair: the buckets in Stash are written back to the binary tree from bottom to top. To ensure that the linked Enclave is secure and reliable, and that the code and data have not been maliciously tampered with, we need to authenticate the Enclave. When the Enclave is created, it generates a public key and a private key, and stores the public key in a secure area, which is made public by the application. When our public key is verified, we send the encrypted data and operation information using that public key. Only the private key of the Enclave can decrypt and read these messages, ensuring that the Enclave service is secure and reliable.

To optimize the Path ORAM database as a world state, it is necessary to synchronize the latest state of the data on the blockchain. We construct a block listener module and connect it to the Fabric network, where the module acts as a node in the blockchain network. The listener module mainly communicates with the Enclave by obtaining block and ledger information from MyChannel to complete data synchronization.

When a new block appears in the blockchain network, the listener module detects its presence and retrieves it. The current block's *hash* value is calculated based on the block number, the *hash* value of the previous block, and the *hash* value of the current block's data, as shown in the following equation:

$$BlockHash = Hash(Blocknumber, PreHash, DataHash)$$

This block *hash* value is then passed to the Enclave for block verification to ensure the integrity and correctness of the data. At the same time, the listener module unpacks the data block into individual transactions.

The listener module then sends the processed block *hash* value and transaction data in order to the Enclave. At this point, the Enclave begins Merkle verification. We obtain the root *hash* value of this set of transaction data and compare it with the block *hash* value sent from the listener module. If they are different, there is a problem with the transmission of this block, and it needs to be retransmitted.

As shown in Fig. 3, the file extraction model consists of several parts, including data owner, data requester, Fabric network, monitoring module, Enclave, ORAM storage, etc. It is worth noting that when the data owner completes the work of encrypting and uploading data to the chain, they first interact with the blockchain network and write the encrypted data into the world state database of Peer nodes. Then, the monitoring module obtains the latest block, completes verification, sends it to the Enclave trusted execution environment zone, and finally synchronizes data with the ORAM storage. When the data requester queries encrypted data, they directly access Enclave, complete authentication, and perform a query operation in Enclave to interact with ORAM storage, thereby obtaining encrypted data and information for data integrity and correctness verification.

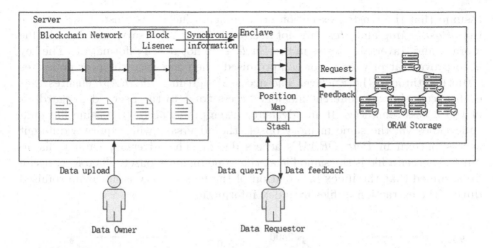

Fig. 3. File extraction

5 Security Guarantees

Security Definition: In Obirc design, users input the keyword set information K to retrieve all files containing the keyword set K. During the index extraction phase, after the Order node set, which cannot be breached by any malicious parties due to the blockchain consensus protocol, conspires, no information about the user's query for the keyword set can be obtained, and it is impossible to infer which elements in the index array X the user is interested in. At the same time, when extracting files, the blockchain network cannot obtain any information about the file ID I that the user requires for data queries, nor can it differentiate where the user reads the file in the real memory address. If some malicious nodes send false information to the client, the authenticity of the data can be verified through cryptographic algorithms when the user obtains the false information. If the above conditions are met, we believe that the system is secure.

Assumptions: 1) The *hash* algorithm is an irreversible one-way function. 2) The *Enclave* store cannot be breached by the adversary. 3) The random number generation in the system cannot be predicted by the adversary.

Proof: When a user enters a keyword set K in a query operation, a *Hash* operation is first performed locally, which is known to be irreversible, so there is no risk of an adversary deciphering the K through the inverse operation. Given the adversary's use of *Hash* collisions and the construction of a *Hash* correspondence table, we hide the transmitted location information h from the *Order* node. We use distributed trust for secret sharing and the security guarantees of the point function secret sharing technique demonstrated in Ref [11], so that no strict subset of the database server can get any information about the point function $f(h, 1)$, so the adversary cannot obtain any information about the retrieval of h. Thus, the location information h is hidden during the proof access. Since we assume that the trusted execution environment Enclave is trusted, we assume that *PositonMap* and *Stash* are not accessible by an adversary, and that our file storage and traversal accesses in the *Envlave* do not reveal information. The key is to prove that privacy is not compromised when accessing the peer node tree structure through the Enclave. The access design in *PathORAM* ensures that each access shows a different memory access trace to the peer side, regardless of the access semantics. If an adversary attempts to access the same file multiple times via the same memory offset, the adversary will acquire a different access pattern in *Path ORAM*'s access design. The adversary cannot distinguish whether a file is the same file at the same memory offset. Therefore, it can be assumed that the index information of the user's query is not compromised during the extraction of files by index information.

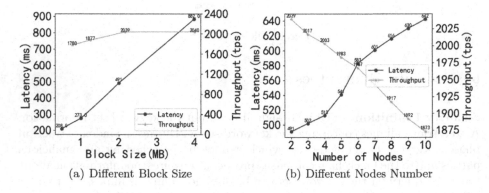

(a) Different Block Size   (b) Different Nodes Number

Fig. 4. Basic Fabric Evaluation

6   Evaluation

We will evaluate Obric through the areas of Latency, Throughput and Phased test.

Experimental setup: Both the server side and the client side of the experiment use Intel(R) Core(TM) i710700 processors with 16 GB of 3200 MHz memory.

Experimental dataset: The experimental dataset used in this paper consists of randomly generated strings. We randomly generated several sets of strings ranging from 1 KB to 10 KB in size for experimental testing. To obtain accurate experimental results, we assume that each set of data structures is similar, meaning that for each 1 KB string, an equal amount of keyword information can be extracted. We take the extraction of 30B of keyword information from each KB file as the experimental benchmark, assuming that the keyword size is fixed and using ASCII encoding. Each keyword size is 5B, which means that each KB of file information includes 6 keywords.

6.1 Basic Performance

As shown in Fig. 4 we conducts performance tests on transaction submission latency and throughput of data on-chain for the consortium blockchain Fabric. The evaluation mainly focuses on the basic performance impact of the consortium blockchain Fabric from two aspects: the size of the consortium blockchain block and the number of consortium blockchain nodes. As the block size increases, the number of transactions in each block increases, and the throughput gradually increases, but it tends to stabilize when it reaches a certain system processing threshold. On the other hand, as the number of nodes in a block increases, transactions go through multiple nodes for processing and verification, causing the throughput to gradually decrease.

As shown in Fig. 5, we conducts performance tests on the basic performance of Obric. It can be seen that the query efficiency is relatively high, while the write efficiency is relatively low. Parallel write has slightly higher efficiency than serial write. The throughput shows a similar pattern, with Obric having a high query throughput. Comparing the throughput data in Fig. 5(b) with that in Fig. 4, we can see that for a file size of 1KB, Obric's query throughput is about 9–10 times higher than that of the Fabric network. We believe that this is mainly due to our optimization of the query operation, including the use of Bloom filters for queries and trusted hardware to speed up file extraction. In addition, the query operation does not require calling smart contracts for implementation.

Based on the experimental analysis above, Obric can provide efficient and secure query functions, fully demonstrating the performance required for practical use.

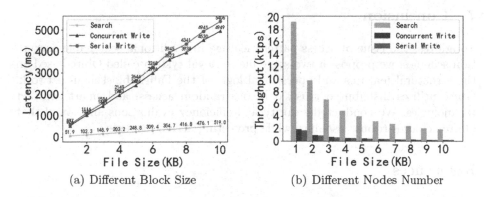

(a) Different Block Size   (b) Different Nodes Number

Fig. 5. Obric Evaluation

6.2 Stage-Wise Experimental Testing

As shown in Fig. 6, we conducted a phased test of the index query efficiency and file query efficiency of Obric, and compared it with other solutions. Firstly, in the horizontal comparison, we found that the time delay of index queries in

Obric is approximately one-tenth of that of file queries. In Fig. 6(a), it can be seen that using Obric to query the index is about 2 times faster than using the ORAM solution, and about 3 times faster than using the DPFs solution with bloomfilter. The advantage is quite significant. At the same time, in Fig. 6(b), it can be seen that using Obric to query files is more than 10 times faster than using DPFs solution or ORAM solution without Enclave, and has a great advantage. Based on the above analysis, it can be seen that the index compression methods and trusted execution environment used in this paper have a significant impact on the query performance of the system.

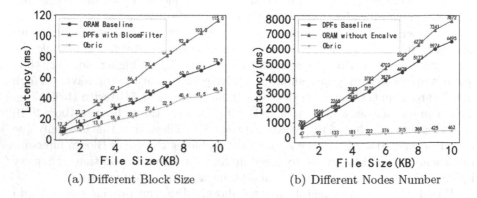

(a) Different Block Size   (b) Different Nodes Number

Fig. 6. Stage-wise Evaluation

7   Conclusion

To address the issue of access pattern leakage in traditional searchable encryption schemes, we propose a two-stage file retrieval system called Obirc based on the structural features and operational logic of the Fabric blockchain network. Obirc utilizes distributed trust, oblivious random access, and smart contract technologies. We conducted security and efficiency evaluations and found that Obirc achieves robust usability while protecting access patterns.

References

1. Song, D.X., et al.: Practical techniques for searches on encrypted data. In: IEEE Symposium on Security and Privacy (2000)
2. Jho, N.S., Hong, D.: Symmetric searchable encryption with efficient conjunctive keyword search. KSII Trans. Internet Inf. Syst. (TIIS) **7**(5), 1328–1342 (2013)
3. Zheng, Z., Xie, S., Dai, H.N., et al.: Blockchain challenges and opportunities: a survey. Int. J. Web Grid Serv. **14**(4), 352–375 (2018)
4. Monrat, A.A., Schelén, O., Andersson, K.: A survey of blockchain from the perspectives of applications, challenges, and opportunities. IEEE Access **7**, 117134–117151 (2019)

5. Cao, Y., Sun, Y., Min, J.: RETRACTED: hybrid blockchain-based privacy-preserving electronic medical records sharing scheme across medical information control system. Meas. Control **53**(7–8), 1286–1299 (2020)
6. Li, H., Wang, T., Qiao, Z., et al.: Blockchain-based searchable encryption with efficient result verification and fair payment. J. Inf. Secur. Appl. **58**, 102791 (2021)
7. Androulaki, E., et al.: Hyperledger fabric: a distributed operating system for permissioned blockchains. In: Proceedings of the Thirteenth EuroSys Conference (2018)
8. Shalaby, S., et al.: Performance evaluation of hyperledger fabric. In: 2020 IEEE International Conference on Informatics, IoT, and Enabling Technologies (ICIoT). IEEE (2020)
9. Goldreich, O., Ostrovsky, R.: Software protection and simulation on oblivious RAMs. J. ACM (JACM) **43**(3), 431–473 (1996)
10. Stefanov, E., et al.: Path ORAM: an extremely simple oblivious RAM protocol. J. ACM (JACM) **65**(4), 1–26 (2018)
11. Gilboa, N., Ishai, Y.: Distributed point functions and their applications. In: Nguyen, P.Q., Oswald, E. (eds.) EUROCRYPT 2014. LNCS, vol. 8441, pp. 640–658. Springer, Heidelberg (2014). https://doi.org/10.1007/978-3-642-55220-5_35
12. Boyle, E., Gilboa, N., Ishai, Y., Kolobov, V.I.: Programmable distributed point functions. In: Dodis, Y., Shrimpton, T. (eds.) CRYPTO 2022. LNCS, vol. 13510, pp. 121–151. Springer, Cham (2022). https://doi.org/10.1007/978-3-031-15985-5_5
13. Boyle, E., et al.: Information-theoretic distributed point functions. In: 3rd Conference on Information-Theoretic Cryptography (ITC 2022). Schloss Dagstuhl-Leibniz-Zentrum für Informatik (2022)
14. Costan, V., Devadas, S.: Intel SGX explained. IACR Cryptology ePrint Archive 2016, vol. 86 (2016)

Blockchain Architecture
and Optimization

A Distributed, Penetrative and All-Dimensional Supervision Architecture for Consortium Blockchain

Xiao Chen[1], Zibin Zheng[1(✉)], Weiqi Dai[2], Yanchun Sun[3], Xinjian Ma[3], and Jinkai Liu[2]

[1] Sun Yat-sen University, Guangzhou, China
`chenx553@mail2.sysu.edu.cn, zhzibin@mail.sysu.edu.cn`
[2] Huazhong University of Science and Technology, Wuhan, China
`{wqdai,liujink}@hust.edu.cn`
[3] Peking University, Beijing, China
`{sunyc,maxinjian}@pku.edu.cn`

Abstract. Consortium blockchain has been used widely in the field of bank, insurance, securities, commerce association and enterprise. However, the supervision for consortium blockchain faces serious challenges: Firstly, due to the sealed feature of consortium blockchain, it should build up the effective and robust computation mechanism for distributed supervision between various platforms; Secondly, due to the sensitivity of supervision data, data transmission between various platforms introduces the asset privacy disclosure and equity losses. In addition, due to the heterogeneity of supervision data, it should build up an effective data access and management mechanism.

To overcome these challenges, we propose a novel supervision architecture for consortium blockchain. Specifically, first, we build up a federal-learning-based distributed supervision computation system, which leverages the committee mechanism and sharding to enable the highly robust and efficient computation mechanism for supervision data. Second, we build up a zero-knowledge-proof- based penetrative cross-chain evidencing method, which leverages the attribute encryption, Merkle tree and authorization hiding method to enable the highly reliable data transmission mechanism for consortium blockchain. Third, we build up an all-dimensional data access and management method, to enable the highly effective supervision data extraction for consortium blockchain. In summary, we propose a consortium-blockchain-oriented distributed penetrating and all-dimensional architecture, which satisfies the cross-organization supervision demand in consortium blockchain supervision.

Keywords: Consortium blockchain supervision · Federated learning · Privacy protection · Zero-knowledge-proof · Data management

© The Author(s), under exclusive license to Springer Nature Singapore Pte Ltd. 2024
J. Chen et al. (Eds.): BlockSys 2023, CCIS 1897, pp. 195–208, 2024.
https://doi.org/10.1007/978-981-99-8104-5_15

1 Introduction

Blockchain is a novel application paradigm that integrates computer technologies such as distributed data storage, peer-to-peer transmission, consensus mechanism, and encryption algorithms. The consortium blockchain [9] is an open blockchain technology architecture for members within the consortium organization and is an important force in the development of blockchain industry. In fact, the consortium blockchain is a blockchain composed of multiple private blockchains and managed by multiple institutions. The various organizational entities form an interest-related consortium to jointly maintain the healthy operation of the blockchain. With its strong controllability, fast transaction speed, and strong transaction performance, the consortium blockchain has been widely used in banks, insurance, securities, business associations, group enterprises, and upstream and downstream enterprises.

However, due to the distributed storage and decentralized data of consortium blockchain, traditional centralized supervision technologies are difficult to satisfy the need of consortium blockchain supervision. Therefore, distributed, penetrative, and all-dimensional supervision has become a rigid demand for supervision. At present, there are still challenges in distributed supervision of consortium blockchain: first of all, distributed supervision actually requires the establishment of an effective supervision computing mechanism between different platforms. Federated learning [17] is an effective way for establishing distributed and privacy computing. However, how to apply federated learning to consortium blockchain supervision scenarios is still a challenge. Secondly, the distributed supervision of consortium blockchain requires penetrative access to the data information of distributed applications. However, current penetrative data access can easily cause problems such as asset privacy leakage and equity losses. In addition, the sharing and circulation of data is an urgent need for all-dimensional supervision in consortium blockchain supervision. However, due to the arbitrary data replication, the supervision may encounter the risks of data abuse and data loss. Therefore, effective management over consortium blockchain data is required during the data sharing process.

To overcome these challenges, this paper proposes a distributed, penetrative and all-dimensional supervision architecture for consortium blockchain. Specifically, the architecture is composed of a distributed supervision computation system based on federal learning, a penetrative cross-chain evidencing method based on zero-knowledge proof [11], and an all-dimensional data access and management method. The supervision computation system is designed to meet the distributed supervision computation demands of the consortium blockchain, which integrates key technologies including committee mechanism, federal tensor decomposition, and consortium blockchain sharding to effectively achieve systematic, robust, and efficient distributed supervision computation for consortium blockchain. The cross-chain evidencing method focuses on the demand of secure and private data transmission in the evidencing process, which leverages key technologies including the attribute encryption, Merkle tree [20] and authorization hiding to effectively realize cross-chain data transmission in the consortium blockchain supervision process and ensure that the data transmission does not disclose important information such as its assets and holdings. The data access and management method is aimed at the data access, query, and verification in the all-dimensional data supervision process of consortium blockchain, which integrates key technologies including non network consensus ledger, remote-proof-based data integrity verification, and multi-node data collection to effectively achieve all-dimensional supervision over data extraction.

In summary, this paper makes the following contributions:

- We propose a distributed, penetrative and all-dimensional supervision architecture for consortium blockchain. To the best of our knowledge, such supervision architecture is the first of its kind for the supervision of consortium blockchain in a generic manner.
- We design a set of novel mechanisms to ensure the effectiveness of such supervision architecture. Particularly, the architecture utilizes a federal-learning-based computation system to meet the demand of distributed supervision, leverages a zero-knowledge proof method to meet the demand of penetrative cross-chain evidencing and uses a non-network-consensus-based method to meet the demand of all-dimensional data access and management.

2 Background and Motivation

2.1 Consortium Blockchain and its Supervision Demands

Consortium blockchain is a typical type of blockchain network that is maintained and managed by a group of trusted organizations or entities. Unlike public blockchains, consortium blockchains require permission to join the network and only authorized participants can participate in the blockchain's transactions and consensus processes. Consortium blockchains are commonly used for data exchange and processing within enterprises and organizations. They can help organizations share data and information more securely and efficiently because only authorized participants can access and update information.

The current status of consortium blockchain supervision mainly has two aspects. On the one hand, effective information sharing mechanisms have not been established between different platforms, and there are problems of sealed feature, sensitivity, and heterogeneity due to the lack of interoperability and coordination. On the other hand, traditional supervision technologies are difficult to cover the continuously changing supervision demands and adapt to various heterogeneous underlying blockchain technologies. Incremental and dynamically adjustable deployment has become a rigid demand for supervision.

2.2 Motivation and Challenges

We consider the supervision background of consortium blockchains as shown in Fig. 1. From bottom to top, consortium blockchain supervision actually needs to extract supervision data from the supervised consortium blockchain to complete

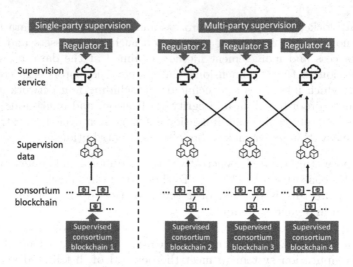

Fig. 1. Supervision background of consortium blockchain.

the corresponding supervision services for the regulator. There are two main supervision scenarios in consortium blockchain supervision: single-party supervision and multi-party supervision. In single-party supervision, similar to traditional centralized supervision technologies, supervision mainly needs to overcome the correctness verification and completeness verification during the data extraction process. In multi-party supervision, the supervision demands are much more complex and differ from traditional centralized supervision technologies. Multi-party supervision needs to solve the problems of sealed feature, sensitivity, and heterogeneity. Specifically, in terms of data extraction, the data between different platform applications is highly heterogeneous and lacks an effective data access and management method. In terms of data transmission, penetrative cross-chain evidencing usually brings about problems of privacy leakage and equity losses. Finally, in terms of data computation, there is still a lack of a robust and efficient distributed computing system to complete reliable computation for supervision services.

To satisfy the above supervision demands of consortium blockchain, we aim to propose a distributed, penetrative and all-dimensional supervision architecture for consortium blockchain. However, establishing such supervision architecture is by no means trivial, it faces the following challenges.

- **Sealed feature.** The content of the consortium blockchain is only open to members within the organization. Therefore, how to build a secure, robust and efficient distributed supervision computing system to meet the computation demands of the consortium blockchain supervision services.
- **Sensitivity.** Cross-chain data transmission between consortium blockchains often brings serious risks of privacy leakage and equity losses. Therefore, how to build a penetrating cross-chain evidencing method that hides attributes, identity association relationships and authorization relationships.

- **Heterogeneity.** The application data on different platforms of the consortium blockchain is highly heterogeneous. Therefore, how to build a full-dimensional data access and management method for data integrity verification and correctness verification.

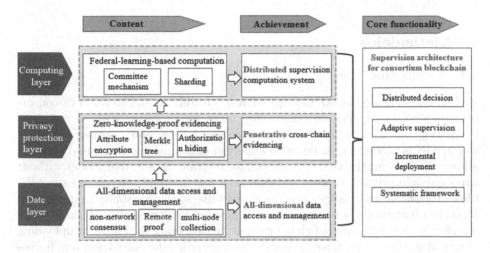

Fig. 2. The framework of our proposed distributed, penetrative and all-dimensional supervision architecture for consortium blockchain.

3   Overview

To overcome the above challenges, we propose a distributed, penetrative and all-dimensional supervision architecture for consortium blockchain. Figure 2 shows the framework of our proposed distributed, penetrative and all-dimensional supervision architecture for consortium blockchain. The supervision framework is divided into three layers: the computing layer, the privacy protection layer, and the data layer. These are used to implement data calculation, data transmission, and data extraction in the consortium blockchain supervision process. Among three layers, supervision demand penetrates from top to bottom, while supervision data is transmitted from bottom to top. Specifically, on the computing layer, oriented to the challenge of sealed feature, we utilize the key technologies including committee mechanism and consortium blockchain sharding, to establish a federal-learning-based distributed supervision computation system. On the privacy protection layer, oriented to the challenge of sensitivity, we use the key technologies including attribute encryption, Merkle tree and authorization hiding, to establish a zero-knowledge-proof-based penetrative cross-chain evidencing method. On the data layer, oriented to the challenge of Heterogeneity, we leverage the key technologies including non network consensus, remote proof, and multi-node data collection, to establish an all-dimensional data access and management method.

Based on the contents and achievements on the above layers, we build up an effective supervision architecture with the core functionalities that include distributed decision, adaptive supervision, incremental deployment and systematization.

4 Methodology

4.1 Computing Layer

Federal-Learning-Based Computation Model. In the scenario of consortium blockchain supervision computing, there are problems such as malicious tampering and missing of consortium blockchain data, and a secure and effective model is needed for distributed supervision computing. Federated learning allows multiple participants to collaborate to train an effective model without exposing data privacy. However, classic federated learning systems are susceptible to Byzantine and malicious server attacks due to their inability to implement serverless frameworks and authenticate uploaded local gradients. Attackers can interfere with the training of global models by modifying the model or uploading incorrect gradients. We have designed a new serverless federated learning framework - federated learning based on a committee mechanism. Our key insight is to utilize committee mechanisms to achieve a decentralized framework. We have set up a committee system to filter and monitor the gradient aggregation process and prevent malicious clients and servers from interfering with the training of the global model. Based on different considerations of model performance and defense, two opposite selection strategies were designed to ensure accuracy and robustness.

Robustness of Computation Model. Each supervised node in the alliance chain is responsible for collecting data from specific nodes within the alliance chain. The data distribution of different supervised nodes in the alliance chain depends on the usage of their ordinary nodes, which may be heterogeneous, resulting in a significant decrease in the performance of some client models that are heterogeneous to the global data distribution and affecting their willingness to participate in federated learning. We have designed a federated learning fairness algorithm based on Gini coefficient, which evaluates the fairness of the federated learning process by testing the accuracy of the client's Gini coefficient. Divide federated learning into label fitting and data fitting training stages to intervene in the fairness of federated learning at appropriate times. At the same time, we designed a federal fairness optimization algorithm to balance fairness and model effectiveness.

In the computing layer, regulatory data from various institutions often has missing data during the generation process, resulting in sparse data and poor global model performance for federated learning. We propose a two-layer federated tensor decomposition algorithm for data heterogeneity, establish a relationship model between data sparsity and data heterogeneity, and transform the sparsity problem into a heterogeneous completion problem. Propose a two-layer federated tensor decomposition framework that preserves the value brought by heterogeneous client data while reducing the negative impact of heterogeneity on the global model.

Efficiency of Computation Model. The current performance of the consortium blockchain can no longer meet the requirements of distributed sharing of supervision information. One of the key methods to improve the performance of the consortium blockchain is sharding. However, most blockchain sharding research focuses on public blockchains. For the federated blockchain, previous research cannot support high cross sharding efficiency, flexible multi sharding contract invocation, strict transaction atomicity and sharding availability, which are challenges to the basic requirements of the federated blockchain system. Faced with these challenges, we have designed a cross shard communication protocol for the blockchain of custody, with the main idea of maintaining multiple blockchain transaction execution environments in a single consortium. We have designed a cross shard message consolidation strategy, implemented flexible invocation of cross shard contracts, designed an exception playback mechanism to ensure strict transaction atomicity within the block, and proposed a backup and recovery algorithm based on shadow sharding to improve the availability of shards.

4.2   Privacy Protection Layer

Attribute Hiding Identity Authentication Method. Blockchain regulators sometimes share data with other blockchain regulators. This data may contain very sensitive information, and there is a need to ensure that no one can access this data without authorization. Depending on the requirements it is usually attribute-based encryption (ABE) that is used to achieve fine-grained access control of the data. However, the attributes and access policies in ABE are sensitive in some cases, e.g., attributes set to certain types of regulators can alert some users, exposing access policies with "or" can allow attackers to choose attributes that are more easily accessible, etc. The process of access control also needs to be able to resist replay attacks and man-in-the-middle attacks. Traditional ABE has a central authorization authority, and this single-node model can make the ABE solution create certain security risks and availability risks. We use Distributed Attribute Encryption (DABE) to encrypt private data instead of traditional ABE. The use of DABE can avoid the decryption operation that is not authorized by the user as expected if a single attribute authorization authority is attacked. Multiple authorization authorities are independent of each other and any individual authorization authority cannot complete the decryption process alone. The encrypted data is stored properly and the storage address is placed on the blockchain. Next, we construct attribute-based Merkle trees to store and protect the user-set attributes. Two commitments are generated using the roots of the completed Merkle tree constructed with random numbers and visitor addresses, respectively, and the corresponding zero-knowledge proofs are constructed. The zero-knowledge proof proves that the visitor knows that accessing the encrypted data requires some property and that he or she possesses and satisfies that property. Finally, the visitor can get the address where the data is stored after passing the verification. The above process achieves data privacy protection sharing among regulators without identity attributes being discovered by anyone.

Identity Association Relationship Hiding Data Acquisition Method. When one or more users of the blockchain report a suspicious user on the blockchain to the blockchain regulator and provide information about that suspicious user, no one can obtain the relationship between the suspicious user and the reported user from the information on the blockchain. From the information on the blockchain, one can only observe that someone has made a report about a user, but the specific identities of the reported user and the reported user are not exposed. The concealment of the relationship also prevents the attacker from directly launching an attack on the whistleblower. This shows the necessity of hiding the relationship. In order to facilitate the regulators to manage the accounts of the participating blockchain users, blockchain users need to decentralize and pass key information to multiple other users when they join the blockchain. At the same time, the information of these users is hidden through a Merkle tree. The users included in the Merkle tree have a better understanding of the behavior and information of the shared users, are less likely to report maliciously. Commitment to the root of the Merkle tree and uploading the commitment to the blockchain completes the initialization process of the user. In the subsequent blockchain supervision process, if several auxiliary users want to report certain behaviors of sharing users and provide evidential materials to the regulator, the participating users first use their private information to generate zero-knowledge proofs to prove that they are recorded in the auxiliary users' Merkle trees, and the proofs posted by multiple auxiliary users are constructed into a new Merkle tree for on-blockchain publishing. Eventually, through a new zero-knowledge proof, everyone can verify that the whistleblower does belong to the blockchain user, but cannot identify the identity of the whistleblower or the relationship with the reported user. All these process information is recorded in the blockchain, which is equally convenient for regulators to verify the rationality of the reporting behavior.

Authorization Relationship Hiding Authorization Authentication Method. In the scenario of multi-blockchain supervision, the regulator may need multiple supervised consortium blockchains to cooperate in providing data support in the process of supervision of a supervised consortium blockchain. In order to prevent the leakage of supervision behavior and protect the identity of the cooperating blockchain nodes, it is expected to provide data support for the regulator without leaking the privacy of the cooperating blockchain nodes, i.e., the authorization relationship is hidden when authorizing data, and the authorization content and the authorization object are not exposed. We propose an authorization authentication mechanism that hides the authorization relationship to ensure that the privacy of the cooperating nodes is not exposed during the authorization process. Therefore, we incorporate zero-knowledge proof technology into the blockchain to hide the authorization relationship in the authorization process. Next, the design idea of this authorization and authentication mechanism is described in detail. First, the cooperating node needs to initiate an authorization transaction on the blockchain, which contains a commitment protocol that hides the authorization data. Then, the cooperating node generates a zero-knowledge proof of authorization locally to provide to the regulator to prove that the data is authorized. The regulator can then use the proof provided by the node on the matching blockchain to pass the validation of the authorization verification contract. Only if the proof passes the validation, the regulator can obtain the authorized data, otherwise it cannot obtain it.

4.3 Data Layer

Efficient Query of Data. For consortium blockchains that adopt network wide consensus, it is easy to achieve efficient data reading because all transaction data is stored on a single node. For consortium blockchains that adopt non network wide consensus, since there no longer exists a single node that stores all transaction data, transaction data may be scattered throughout the entire network, making it difficult to query the data on chain. Although traditional distributed database systems also have distributed query issues, its methods cannot be directly applied in this scenario since they did not consider the Byzantine attacks. To adapt to the characteristics of decentralized storage of non network consensus ledger data, we propose a data governance ledger oriented data query system. This work adopts an Int-BFS based ledger query method and designs and implements a non network consensus ledger query system. Compared with traditional methods, this method can reduce response time, improve query performance, and provide support for efficient data reading.

Guarantee Authenticity of Data Interface. On the basis of efficient data query capability, data can be captured through interface. Considering that the integrity of the data may be compromised during the data collection process, the data needs to be ensured to be authentic and not tampered with without authorization. Existing data integrity assurance technologies mainly focus on the transmission and storage process of data, and cannot guarantee the integrity of the data provided by the data source externally. To solve this problem, a remote proof based data access integrity verification method is proposed. In this method, the static code, execution process, and execution results of related interface will be reliably measured while data source provided data to achieve multidimensional measurement of data access integrity. Then, the measurement results are verified before data is consumed to ensure the integrity of the data. This work provides support for authenticity of data interface.

Data Correctness Verification. In the supervision process of the consortium blockchain, the regulators need to collect the application data they care about. There are multiple nodes in the consortium blockchain, and there may be Byzantine nodes within these nodes. Therefore, regulators cannot only collect data from a single node during supervision. Because it cannot determine whether the data it collects is real application data. One solution is for regulators to collect data from multiple nodes and compare the collected data. If all or most of the data is consistent, the collected data is considered valid. (Because the current blockchain assumes that most nodes are honest, and only a few nodes are Byzantine nodes). One of the tasks we are working on is to propose a multi node data collection scheme that ensures data authenticity while balancing efficiency and security.

5   Related Work

5.1   Federal Learning

The appeal of federated learning relies on a centralized model that can be trained on user devices without the need to upload user data. However, due to the lack of local gradient authentication, such frameworks are easily vulnerable to Byzantine attackers. Many works have designed a series of Byzantine tolerance algorithms to further ensure the robustness of the training process. For example, Blanchard et al. [4] proposed Krum, which aims to select global model updates based on the Euclidean distance between local models. Yin et al. [29] proposed median and pruned mean values, aiming to remove extreme local gradients to ensure the robustness of the algorithm. [21] propose a hidden Markov model to learn the quality of local gradients and design a robust aggregation rule that discards bad local gradients during the aggregation process. The above algorithms all attempt to ensure the robustness of federated learning by designing more suitable aggregation mechanisms. However, these tasks cannot provide effective defense in the presence of malicious servers.

In practical applications, server errors or malicious servers can also cause irreparable damage to federated learning systems. Therefore, researchers have proposed many serverless federated learning frameworks to address these issues. For example, Abhijit et al. [24] proposed a P2P serverless federated learning framework where any two clients exchange information end-to-end and update their local model at each epoch. Hu et al. [15] used the Gossip protocol to complete the model aggregation process, which assumed the role of a central server. In addition, other works have constructed a serverless federated learning framework based on blockchain systems. For example, Kim et al. [16] proposed a blockchain federated learning architecture that divides blockchain nodes into devices and miners. The device node provides data, trains the model locally, and uploads the local gradient to its associated miners in the blockchain network. Miner nodes exchange and verify all local gradients. Although these works have achieved corresponding performance to some extent, there is a lack of theoretical analysis of model convergence under serverless federated learning frameworks and consideration of client side Byzantine attacks.

5.2 Zero-Knowledge-Proof

Currently, the mainstream non interactive zero-knowledge proof suitable for application in blockchain includes zk-SNARKs [14], zk-STARKs [3], AZTEC [27] and Bulletproof [5]. The zk-SNARKs technology originated from the emergence of Zcash electronic currency. zk-SNARKs technology is also one of the most effective zero-knowledge-proof technologies to solve the blockchain privacy problem. The zk-STARKs was proposed by BEN et al., and its predecessor was the SCI (Scalable Computational Integrity) proof system. Its development goal was to rely on anti-collision hash functions to replace trust settings, thereby solving the trust crisis problem of traditional zk-SNARKs. AZTEC was proposed in December 2018 as a new privacy protection scheme based on zero-knowledge proof at the smart contract end. AZTEC has abandoned zero knowledge chain computing and deployed zk-SNARKs in smart contracts, with the aim of encrypting blockchain data in a lower computational cost and more effective way, aiming to implement privacy transaction protection on the blockchain platform. Bulletproof is a range proof designed using the inner product method, proposed by Stanford University cryptographer BenediKT et al. The drawbacks of this scheme are long validation time and high cost.

5.3 All-Dimensional Data Access and Management

EtherQL [18] implements an efficient query layer for public chain systems and can be used for various analytical queries, such as time range queries and top K queries. VQL [23] rearrange blockchain data into a database through an additional data middleware layer, providing users with reliable results while reducing query latency. StarChain [28] proposed verifiable AC tree and GCA tree structures, providing verifiable range, connection, and aggregation query functions for light weight nodes.

To ensure the integrity of the data access process, the key is to ensure the integrity of the information system that provides the data and avoid attacks. Remote Attestation is a technique used to verify the integrity of software running on remote devices. Researchers have proposed Control Flow Attestation (CFA) [1], which supplements static remote proof by capturing the execution path of the target program and verifying it to resist control flow attacks. In addition, for pure data stream attacks that cannot be detected by CFA, the idea of Data Flow Attestation (DFA) was proposed [22], which detects pure data stream attacks by recording data input and combining control flow information for abstract execution to reconstruct the complete data stream of program execution.

The related existing research work includes cross chain technology [25] and oracle machine technology [2]. Cross chain is a protocol that enables asset circulation and value transfer between two or more independent blockchains. Typical cross chain mechanisms include notary scheme [8], hash locking [7], side chain [13], relay [12], distributed private key control [26], and so on. Oracle machine is a technology that enables blockchain to access data outside the chain. Typical examples are Probable [6], TownChier [30], etc. Decentralized oracle machine adopts a form similar to blockchain network. It uses multiple oracle machine nodes to consensus results and then inputs the consensus results to blockchain nodes. Typical examples are ChainLink [10], DOS Network [19], etc.

6 Conclusion

In this paper, we propose a distributed, penetrative and all-dimensional supervision architecture for consortium blockchain. The supervision architecture can be mainly divided into three layers. Firstly, we implement an all-dimensional data access and management method, for meeting the demand of supervision data extraction. Secondly, we propose a zero-knowledge-proof-based penetrative cross-chain evidencing method, to meet the demand of supervision data transmission. Thirdly, we establish a federal-learning-based distributed supervision computation system, for satisfying the demands of supervision data computation. With the above three layers, we build an effective supervision architect with the core functionalities that include distributed decision, adaptive supervision, incremental deployment and systematic framework.

Acknowledgments. This work is partially supported by fundings from the National Key R&D Program of China (2020YFB1006001), National Natural Science Foundation of China (62072202), and Technology Program of Guangzhou, China (No. 202103050004).

References

1. Abera, T., et al.: C-FLAT: control-flow attestation for embedded systems software. In: Proceedings of the 2016 ACM SIGSAC Conference on Computer and Communications Security, pp. 743–754 (2016)
2. Al-Breiki, H., Rehman, M.H.U., Salah, K., Svetinovic, D.: Trustworthy blockchain oracles: review, comparison, and open research challenges. IEEE Access **8**, 85675–85685 (2020)
3. Ben-Sasson, E., Bentov, I., Horesh, Y., Riabzev, M.: Scalable, transparent, and post-quantum secure computational integrity. Cryptology ePrint Archive (2018)
4. Blanchard, P., El Mhamdi, E.M., Guerraoui, R., Stainer, J.: Machine learning with adversaries: byzantine tolerant gradient descent. In: Advances in Neural Information Processing Systems, vol. 30 (2017)
5. Bünz, B., Bootle, J., Boneh, D., Poelstra, A., Wuille, P., Maxwell, G.: Bulletproofs: short proofs for confidential transactions and more. In: 2018 IEEE Symposium on Security and Privacy (SP),D pp. 315–334. IEEE (2018)

6. Community, P.: Provable documentation. https://docs.provable.xyz
7. Dai, B., Jiang, S., Zhu, M., Lu, M., Li, D., Li, C.: Research and implementation of cross-chain transaction model based on improved hash-locking. In: Zheng, Z., Dai, H.-N., Fu, X., Chen, B. (eds.) BlockSys 2020. CCIS, vol. 1267, pp. 218–230. Springer, Singapore (2020). https://doi.org/10.1007/978-981-15-9213-3_17
8. Dai, B., Jiang, S., Li, D., Li, C.: Evaluation model of cross-chain notary mechanism based on improved page rank algorithm. Comput. Eng. **47**(2), 26–31 (2021)
9. Dib, O., Brousmiche, K.L., Durand, A., Thea, E., Hamida, E.B.: Consortium blockchains: overview, applications and challenges. Int. J. Adv. Telecommun. **11**(1), 51–64 (2018)
10. Ellis, S., Juels, A., Nazarov, S.: Chainlink: a decentralized oracle network. Retrieved March **11**(2018), 1 (2017)
11. Fiege, U., Fiat, A., Shamir, A.: Zero knowledge proofs of identity. In: Proceedings of the Nineteenth Annual ACM Symposium on Theory of Computing, pp. 210–217 (1987)
12. Frauenthaler, P., Sigwart, M., Spanring, C., Schulte, S.: Testimonium: a cost-efficient blockchain relay. arXiv preprint arXiv:2002.12837 (2020)
13. Gaži, P., Kiayias, A., Zindros, D.: Proof-of-stake sidechains. In: 2019 IEEE Symposium on Security and Privacy (SP), pp. 139–156. IEEE (2019)
14. Gennaro, R., Gentry, C., Parno, B., Raykova, M.: Quadratic span programs and succinct NIZKs without PCPs. In: Johansson, T., Nguyen, P.Q. (eds.) EUROCRYPT 2013. LNCS, vol. 7881, pp. 626–645. Springer, Heidelberg (2013). https://doi.org/10.1007/978-3-642-38348-9_37
15. Hu, C., Jiang, J., Wang, Z.: Decentralized federated learning: a segmented gossip approach. arXiv preprint arXiv:1908.07782 (2019)
16. Kim, H., Park, J., Bennis, M., Kim, S.L.: Blockchained on-device federated learning. IEEE Commun. Lett. **24**(6), 1279–1283 (2019)
17. Li, T., Sahu, A.K., Talwalkar, A., Smith, V.: Federated learning: challenges, methods, and future directions. IEEE Signal Process. Mag. **37**(3), 50–60 (2020)
18. Li, Y., Zheng, K., Yan, Y., Liu, Q., Zhou, X.: EtherQL: a query layer for blockchain system. In: Candan, S., Chen, L., Pedersen, T.B., Chang, L., Hua, W. (eds.) DASFAA 2017, Part II. LNCS, vol. 10178, pp. 556–567. Springer, Cham (2017). https://doi.org/10.1007/978-3-319-55699-4_34
19. Ltd, D.F.: A dencentralized oracle service boosting blockchain usability with off-chain data & verifiable computing power (2019)
20. Mohan, A.P., Gladston, A., et al.: Merkle tree and blockchain-based cloud data auditing. Int. J. Cloud Appl. Comput. (IJCAC) **10**(3), 54–66 (2020)
21. Muñoz-González, L. Co, K.T., Lupu, E.C.: Byzantine-robust federated machine learning through adaptive model averaging. arXiv preprint arXiv:1909.05125 (2019)
22. Nunes, I.D.O., Jakkamsetti, S., Tsudik, G.: Dialed: data integrity attestation for low-end embedded devices. In: 2021 58th ACM/IEEE Design Automation Conference (DAC), pp. 313–318. IEEE (2021)
23. Peng, Z., Wu, H., Xiao, B., Guo, S.: VQL: providing query efficiency and data authenticity in blockchain systems. In: 2019 IEEE 35th International Conference on Data Engineering Workshops (ICDEW), pp. 1–6. IEEE (2019)
24. Roy, A.G., Siddiqui, S., Pölsterl, S., Navab, N., Wachinger, C.: BrainTorrent: a peer-to-peer environment for decentralized federated learning. arXiv preprint arXiv:1905.06731 (2019)

25. SHEN, C.: Review on cross-chain technology research of blockchains. Chin. J. Internet Things **6**(4), 183 (2022). https://doi.org/10.11959/j.issn.2096-3750.2022. 00301

26. Shi, L., Guo, Z.: Baguena: a practical proof of stake protocol with a robust delegation mechanism. Chin. J. Electron. **29**(5), 887–898 (2020)

27. Williamson, Z.J.: The Aztec protocol (2018). https://github.com/AztecProtocol/ AZTEC

28. Yanchao, Z.: Research on query processing for blockchain system. Ph.D. thesis, Shanghai: East China Normal University (2020). (in Chinese)

29. Yin, D., Chen, Y., Kannan, R., Bartlett, P.: Byzantine-robust distributed learning: towards optimal statistical rates. In: International Conference on Machine Learning, pp. 5650–5659. PMLR (2018)

30. Zhang, F., Cecchetti, E., Croman, K., Juels, A., Shi, E.: Town crier: an authenticated data feed for smart contracts. In: Proceedings of the 2016 ACM SIGSAC Conference on Computer and Communications Security, pp. 270–282 (2016)

SC-Chain: A Multi-modal Collaborative Storage System for Medical Resources

Yuchen Zhang, Xiao Zhang$^{(\boxtimes)}$, Yulong Shi, Linxuan Su, Jinyang Yu, Yonghao Chen, and Zhaohui Pan

School of Computing, Northwestern Polytechnic University, Xi'an 710000, China
2596139269@qq.com

Abstract. At present, collaborative healthcare faces a series of problems such as inconsistent standards, prominent information silos, and inadequate information security management. Because of this, the application of a blockchain-based collaborative healthcare system has been born, and blockchain has become the main driving force for the development of collaborative healthcare. However, the existing blockchain HIS (Hospital Management Information System) has the disadvantages of low node access requirements, weak storage capacity, and no support for SQL query indexing that cannot meet the demand for collaborative sharing of massive multi-modal medical resources. To this end, based on Ceph and Tendermint, this paper constructs a low-cost, high-performance, and highly reliable on-chain and off-chain collaborative storage system SC-Chain for secure storage and efficient sharing of massive multimodal medical resources and reducing system storage pressure. In addition, we designed a relational state database, a high and low time data update policy, and an authorized access control policy based on electronic health codes to guarantee further the secure storage and reliable query of medical resources. Finally, the multi-modal medical data read and write performance analysis experiments found that the storage performance of SC-Chain is significantly better than that of traditional blockchain, especially the latency of Tendermint reaches 4 orders of magnitude of SC-Chain when reading and writing CT (Computed Tomography) data.

Keywords: blockchain · collaborative storage · multi-modal data · Ceph

1 Introduction

To comprehensively promote the construction of a healthy China and achieve the goals of the 14th Five-Year Plan and the 2035 Vision with high quality, the State Council has intensively released the Opinions of the General Office of the State Council on Promoting the Development of "Internet + Medical Health" (Guo Ban Fa [2018] No. 26 It aims to promote the in-depth integration of new-generation information technology with medical services through cloud computing, big data, Internet of Things, blockchain, fifth-generation mobile communication (5G) and other information technology, and promote the application of health information for all people. At present, blockchain technology

© The Author(s), under exclusive license to Springer Nature Singapore Pte Ltd. 2024
J. Chen et al. (Eds.): BlockSys 2023, CCIS 1897, pp. 209–222, 2024.
https://doi.org/10.1007/978-981-99-8104-5_16

is developing at a rapid pace, and related industries are developing comprehensively. The integration of blockchain technology and medical information has promoted the construction of the "trinity" of electronic cases, smart services and smart management, and gradually built a new information-based medical system based on blockchain to support the sharing of massive multimodal medical data [1, 2], which can better meet the needs of patient referral and simplify consultation procedures, and truly achieve the "patient-centered"[3] smart medical treatment.

With the increasing medical information technology, multi-modal medical data has emerged. The existing medical data management methods have gradually revealed weak storage capacity, poor reliability and poor sharing, which cannot meet the demand for multi-modal data management sharing and collaboration. Therefore, this paper proposes a multi-modal data on-chain and off-chain collaborative storage method to achieve more efficient multi-modal data sharing and secure storage.

1.1 Problems with Existing Methods and Solutions

As the level of medical informatization continues to improve, medical data gradually presents massive, heterogeneous, highly sensitive and multi-modal characteristics [7]. The data stored in medical systems range from a few kilobytes of electronic medical records to up to terabytes of CT, MRI and other pictures and images [8,9]. Therefore, the primary optimization goal of medical data management is to support the collaborative sharing of massive multi-modal medical data among heterogeneous medical databases, and on this basis to achieve the secure sharing of susceptible patient data. Although cloud-based HIS and blockchain-based HIS can, to a certain extent, solve the problems of information silos and inadequate information security management faced by healthcare data sharing, they still have shortcomings in the face of multi-modal data sharing.

Cloud-based HIS relies on third-party organizations that provide cloud computing and cloud storage, but it is centralized and the reliability of user data depends entirely on the third party providing the cloud service, so this is unacceptable for highly sensitive medical data storage. In addition, the high costs incurred in the day-to-day maintenance of cloud services and the single point of failure of cloud storage are also significant drawbacks of this solution.

While blockchain-based HIS avoids the disadvantages of centralization in its structure, it poses several problems: (1) Low access requirements for public chain nodes. The data on the chain can be accessed by all legitimate users, potentially risking the leakage of user privacy; (2) weak storage capacity. Due to the blockchain's all-node, all-copy storage model, it does not support massive multi-modal medical data storage. Blindly uploading massive multi-modal data onto the chain will seriously affect the blockchain network's consensus speed and communication rate, ultimately reducing the transaction throughput of the entire medical system; (3) Single type of query support and low efficiency. The default storage backend of blockchain is a key-value database, which does not support SQL queries and indexes, making it difficult to meet the needs of complex queries; the slow traceability queries of blockchain can hardly meet the needs of doctors to retrieve patients' consultation records under high time-efficient application scenarios.

This paper proposes SC-Chain, a multi-modal medical resources collaborative storage system based on distributed file system and blockchain, which stores multi-modal original medical data in the off-chain system and only keeps the storage metadata, data description information and data characteristics of the off-chain system on the chain, solving the problems of poor data storage security, single query function, low efficiency and difficulty in supporting the sharing of massive multi-modal medical resources in the existing medical system. It solves the problems of poor data storage security, single query function, low efficiency and difficulty in supporting the sharing of massive multi-modal medical resources.

The main work of this paper consists of three aspects.

(1) A collaborative multi-modal data storage system is designed and implemented. Ceph is used as the off-chain system to support the reliable storage of massive multi-modal raw medical data. Tendermint is the on-chain system to support tamper-proof verification and traceable query of electronic cases.
(2) Support secure data sharing. We achieve secure data sharing from three aspects: using the characteristics of the Alliance chain itself to improve the access conditions of blockchain nodes; designing a user-sensitive data authorization access control policy based on eHealth codes to achieve encrypted storage of susceptible data; extracting the original data Merkle root Hash and uploading it to the chain for verifying whether the original data has been tampered with or corrupted to ensure the trustworthiness of medical data.
(3) Efficient data cross-indexing access. Develop a blockchain application based on relational data and combine it with data feature extraction algorithms to support users to efficiently index relevant electronic medical records using disease features; design separate high- and low-time data update strategies according to the timeliness of the application to improve the transaction processing performance of the system.

2   Multi-modal Healthcare Resources Collaborative Storage System

SC-Chain uses a distributed file system under the chain to support the storage of massive multi-modal raw medical data and uses blockchain technology on the chain to guarantee the credible sharing of medical data with decentralized, traceable and tamper-proof features. In addition, this collaborative storage system proposes an on-chain system that supports SQL queries and an access control strategy based on the Health QR code to protect patient privacy further while supporting complex user queries.

2.1   Overall System Architecture

As shown in Fig. 1, the proposed multi-modal medical data collaborative storage system consists of five main entities: the on-chain system, the off-chain system, the unified access interface, the medical system, and the data user DU. At the same time, the feature extraction and Hash verification algorithm is invoked to extract the data features of the raw data under the chain and the Merkle root Hash, which are combined with the data description information provided by DU to form a data block and stored in Tendermint to achieve collaborative and secure storage of data internally and provide efficient data cross-indexing access service to DU externally.

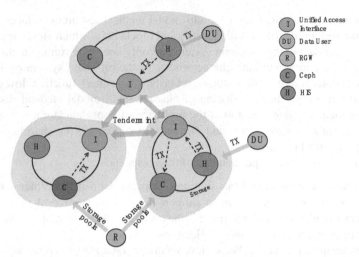

Fig. 1. Overall system architecture

(1) On-chain systems Tendermint

Tendermint is a blockchain protocol that can be used to replicate and launch blockchain applications across the Internet in a secure and consistent manner. It can tolerate any failure of 1/3 of the machine, and replicate the application safely and consistently on multiple devices, and the status of each machine running correctly is the same; it supports data tamper-proof verification that requires high access to federated chain nodes; it has good transactions Processing performance, transaction processing efficiency is high, and the maximum transaction throughput is 800 tx/s. Therefore, we use the Tendermint federated chain system as the on-chain system, and the nodes that meet the access requirements jointly maintain the encrypted data index, data description information and data characteristics of the original medical data under the chain. Utilizing key features such as decentralization, invariance, and encrypted storage of the blockchain, it ensures the safety and reliability of medical resource sharing and the efficiency of data query.

(2) Under-chain systems Ceph

Ceph is a unified distributed storage system, which has excellent storage performance, specifically manifested in high performance storage, supports TB to PB level data, adopts the CRUSH algorithm for data distribution balance and high parallelism, and realizes the copy placement of various loads Rules; high availability, no single point of failure, flexible number of copies, strong data consistency, automatic repair of multiple fault scenarios; high scalability, decentralization, positive linear growth in performance and number of nodes; rich features, support for three storage interfaces and custom interfaces [11, 12]. At present, Ceph has been supported by many cloud computing manufacturers and has been widely used. And compared with cloud storage Ceph, there is no problem such as single point of failure. This system uses Ceph as an off-chain system to store massive multi-modal raw data and return metadata to the unified access interface, providing a good underlying storage resource management service for the upper layer.

(3) Unified access interface

The Unified Access Interface supports selecting different update policies according to the application timeframe, and its specific flow is shown in Fig. 2. For low-time applications, the MerkleHash algorithm is used to calculate the Merkle root hash of the original data for data tamper-proof verification; the public-private key encryption algorithm is used to generate the public-private key according to the DU eHealth code, the public key encrypts the metadata generated from the multi-modal original data stored in Ceph, and DU retrieves the original data by decrypting the metadata information with the private key; the data feature extraction algorithm is used to extract The internal data features of the raw data are extracted using a data feature extraction algorithm to meet the data user's need to retrieve some of the data features. Finally, the Merkle root hash of packaged multi-modal medical raw data, encrypted data index, metadata and data description information generate electronic medical records to initiate transaction requests to the on-chain system; for high-time application scenarios, the unified access interface prioritizes the packaging of electronic medical records onto the chain, followed by the uploading of raw data features, and finally uses metadata to correlate two blockchain transactions.

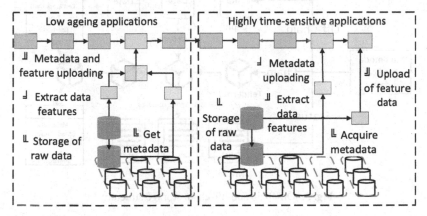

Fig. 2. Update strategy for high and low-time application data

(4) Hospital Management Information System HIS

HIS-connected mobile smart terminals collect, store, process, extract and exchange patient consultation and administrative information within the institution and are the primary data source for the collaborative storage system.

(5) Data User (DU)

The patient holds a Health QR code, which is used for authentication and authorizes the doctor to use the services of the collaborative storage system. The doctor is the direct user of this coordinated storage system and completes the storage and query operation of the medical data in the patient's local consultation and collaborative medical scenario.

2.2 Data Structure Design for On-Chain Systems

Data on a blockchain is immutable and to access historical block data it is often necessary to correlate blocks of the same type. For example, in the medical field, it is essential to correlate all blocks that record the same patient's electronic medical record for subsequent queries. However, this approach requires modifying the block structure to implement the main chain query function, which will lead to increased pressure on the operation of the main chain and the operational efficiency of the system is limited by the performance of the blockchain itself, among other issues.

Therefore, we use on-chain and off-chain collaboration to reduce the storage pressure on the on-chain system. At the same time, using the Tendermint transaction programming language, the diversity of state databases, and the decoupling of applications from the consensus engine, we developed a blockchain application based on a relational database and encapsulated SQL functions into the access interface to maintain on-chain state data in the form of relational tables to meet the needs of complex user queries.

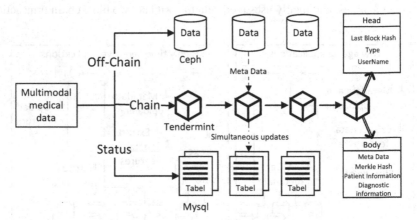

Fig. 3. On-chain and off-chain storage structure

As shown in Fig. 3, the metadata of the original data of the off-chain system is stored in the corresponding block of the on-chain system. The on-chain system data storage is mainly divided into two parts: the on-chain data block keeps the index of the original data storage location in the off-chain system, as well as the log information stored and queried by the user for subsequent queries; the on-chain status database records the final status of the blockchain execution with a table structure, maintaining a real-time updated, complete and traceable electronic medical history table, reducing the access pressure faced by the blockchain during queries.

The block is structurally divided into a block header and a block body. The Last Block Hash inside the block header is the hash of the previous block, the type indicates the type of operation performed in this block, including both add and query, and the UserName specifies the identity of the user performing the add or query operation; the block body contains the Merkle Root Hash of the data under the chain, the address index of the original medical data stored under the chain, the patient information, and the diagnosis If the operation is a query, some parts of it can default.

2.3 Access Control Policy

SC-Chain's access control solution consists of a hospital's local healthcare system HIS, a blockchain system, an off-chain storage system, a trusted authorization body, a data provider and a data requester. During this period, asymmetric encryption and authorized access control are used to ensure the security and sharing of data.

Stage 1: The patient joins the system and initializes the public-private key during the initial visit. The patient initializes the generation of their public-private key PK and SK by uploading their eHealth code. The Trusted Authorisation Centre generates the public-private key associated with the patient's eHealth code using a specific algorithm, records the private key and sends the public key to the HIS.

$$\text{Generate(HealthQRCode)} \xrightarrow{\text{TrustedAuthorisationCentre}} (PK, SK) \qquad (1)$$

Stage 2: The system encrypts and uploads the original medical data and electronic medical records generated by the patient. First, the original medical data(Data) is stored in the off-chain system and the corresponding address index (Address) is obtained, then the address index and the electronic medical record E_{data} which is encrypted with the patient's public key and uploaded to the blockchain.

$$\text{Store(Data)} \xrightarrow{\text{Ceph}} \text{address} \qquad (2)$$

$$\text{Encryption(Record, address)} \rightarrow \text{E}_{\text{data}} \qquad (3)$$

Stage 3: The data requester first queries the encrypted on-chain information through the index, then packages the data with the corresponding eHealth code and decrypts it through the Trusted Authorisation Centre to obtain the electronic medical record and the address index of the original data, and finally obtains the original off-chain data through the address index.

$$\text{Dec}(\text{E}_{\text{data}}, \text{HealthQRcode}) \rightarrow (\text{Record, address}) \qquad (4)$$

$$\text{Get(Address)} \xrightarrow{\text{Ceph}} \text{D}ata \qquad (5)$$

The following describes the workflow of SC-Chain in three major application scenarios in the healthcare system, namely local follow-up, off-site follow-up and collaborative healthcare.

Scenario 1: Patient's local follow-up
When the patient retrieves the previously generated data from the same hospital, they verify their identity by uploading an eHealth code. The system then packages the eHealth code and the encrypted data obtained from the chain and decrypts it through a trusted authorization body to obtain the address index of the previous visit's EHR and the original

data, and then uses the address index to obtain the original data stored under the chain. The private key is then used to decrypt and issue a new medical plan, and finally the initial visit is repeated to update the electronic medical record.

Scenario 2: Patient follow-up off-site

When a patient visits Hospital B, they need to access data such as the diagnosis results generated during the previous visit to Hospital A. The patient first obtains the encrypted on-chain information by querying the blockchain system, then obtains the time-sensitive token issued by the Trusted Authorisation Centre by uploading his eHealth code, packages the encrypted information and token, and sends a data request message to Hospital's RGW interface via the communication protocol, and upon receiving the data access request, Hospital A sends the packaged token and encrypted data to the Trusted Authorisation Centre for decryption. Hospital A will send the packaged token and encrypted data to the Trusted Authorisation Centre for decryption, then query the locally deployed off-chain system through the decrypted address index and return the original data to Hospital B through the RGW interface to complete the access request.

Scenario 3: Collaborative Medicine

When doctors access local or off-site patient data, they need to submit their personally identifiable information to the Trusted Authorisation Centre and subsequently wait for the patient to authorize access to the Trusted Authorisation Centre. After passing the patient's authorization, doctors can access the corresponding medical data to help with diagnosis or research through the processes in Scenarios 1 and 2. Figure 4 illustrates the process of sharing medical resources in a collaborative healthcare scenario.

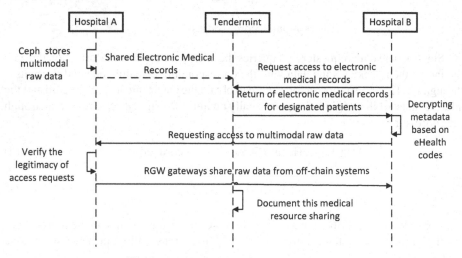

Fig. 4. Healthcare resource-sharing process

After Hospital A finishes storing the original medical data and electronic medical records on-chain, Hospital B initiates a request to the on-chain system to share the patient's medical resources. The on-chain system filters eligible electronic medical records based on the patient's information, and Hospital B uses the eHealth code to generate a private key to decrypt the actual medical diagnosis information and metadata of the off-chain system in the electronic medical records. Hospital B uses the metadata to request sharing off-chain system data from Hospital A. Hospital A receives the request and verifies the request's legitimacy, and uses Ceph's RGW gateway to share off-chain data with Hospital B for legitimate requests. Finally, the on-chain system records the medical resource sharing and updates the status database.

3   System Performance Analysis

To evaluate the performance of the proposed collaborative storage system, we implemented its prototype in the Tendermint platform and compared it with the on-chain system and the off-chain system.

Experimental environment: We simulate a blockchain network with 20 nodes by configuring 20 virtual machines on five computers and deploying a Tendermint program in each virtual machine. The five machines have the same configuration, where the operating system is Ubuntu 20.04 with an 8-core i7-12700, 2.10 GHz processor, a memory size of 32 GB, and a hard disk size of 1024 GB.

In this paper, four different modal datasets are used for multi-modal data access testing, and their details are shown in Table 1.

Table 1. Multi-modal datasets

Name	Marked content	Modal	Number	Size(K)
MSD Hippocampus	Magnetic resonance imaging	MRI	394	62.8
DRIVE	Fundus Vasculature Photo	Photo	40	423.6
COVID-chestxray	Chest X-ray	CXR	48	653.1
LNDB	Tumor Computed Tomography	CT	294	172000

Write Performance Comparison Tests

In this paper, we first test the data storage based on three smaller modal data of MRI, photo, and CXR in the off-chain system, on-chain system, and this paper system, respectively. To minimize the errors caused by external factors such as machine state, we store all the data 1000 times and take the arithmetic average of 1000 tests as the average elapsed time of one write operation, and the experimental results are shown in Fig. 5.

From the above figure, it can be seen that storing multi-modal data directly in the on-chain system is extremely time-consuming and therefore not feasible; the off-chain system has the shortest storage time, but it lacks the sharing characteristics of the on-chain system; while the system in this paper has both on-chain and off-chain system features, the storage time consumes only millisecond delay compared with the off-chain system, which is not perceptible to the users in real scenarios.

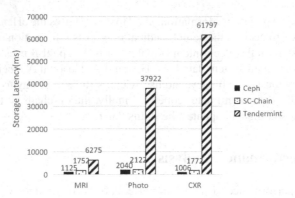

Fig. 5. MRI, CXR, Photo writing performance comparison

Secondly, larger CT data are used for storage testing, and the experimental details are the same as those for small modal data, and the results are shown in the following table (Table 2).

Table 2. CT Write Performance

Storage System	Latency (ms)
Ceph	1061
SC-Chain	1753
Tendermint	15404658

From the experimental results, it is clear that the difference in storage time of the three systems is enlarged when the data volume becomes larger. The storage time of the on-chain system leads to its complete unavailability, and the storage time of the system in this paper is about 1.7 times that of the off-chain system, but the absolute difference between them is only 0.7S, and the difference is more minor in the actual medical system.

Reading Performance Comparison Test
Like the writing experiment, the read performance experiment also uses three kinds of modal data with small data volume, and 1000 previously-stored modal data are read randomly and the time used for each read is recorded. The results of the experiment are as follows (Fig. 6).

As seen from the above figure, the difference in read performance of the three systems is relatively similar to their respective write performance. The on-chain system requires multiple read operations to perform a complete read of the modal data from the blockchain, and this leads to a sharp decrease in its read performance for multi-modal data; the average read time of the system in this paper increases by about 0.15S compared to the off-chain system, which is because the on-chain and off-chain collaborative storage require one more on-chain query to obtain the metadata.

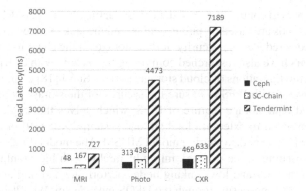

Fig. 6. MRI, CXR, photo reading performance comparison

Table 3. CT Read Performance

Storage System	Latency (ms)
Ceph	95525
SC-Chain	117213
Tendermint	1797621

In this paper, the read performance of CT data was also tested, and the performance gap between the three systems was further widened, and the results are shown in Table 3. Among them, the read time of both the system in this paper and the off-chain system is about 100S, much smaller than that of the on-chain system.

4   Related Works

Some scholars have researched how to optimize existing medical systems, and have proposed the optimization solutions of "blockchain + cloud" and "blockchain + distributed file system" in response to the difficulties in sharing data in traditional database-based medical systems and the centralization problems in cloud-based medical systems.

To solve the problem of sharing medical resources based on traditional database medical systems, Kaur H [13] et al. proposed a blockchain-based heterogeneous medical data platform, where medical data is stored in a "blockchain + cloud" storage network platform. Mei Ying [14] et al. proposed a health chain that allows patients to take ownership and control of their personal medical information while sharing medical resources. However, all of these solutions have the problem of cloud storage that may leak patients' privacy.

To address the issue of cloud storage data security, Li [15] et al. proposed a blockchain-based SSE scheme that uses blockchain as a peer-to-peer network to store data on a pay-per-use basis. Hu [16] et al. proposed an Ethernet-based SSE scheme to reduce unauthorized access to data by malicious nodes. Chen [17] et al. proposed an electronic medical record-based Ethernet-based searchable (SE) scheme for EHRs, which enables data owners to control access to data by extracting the index of EHRs. However, all the above methods are based on public chains, and the lack of access mechanisms for participating nodes reduces the security of data storage on the chain to a certain extent.

Some scholars have also researched combining blockchain with distributed file systems to address the limitations of cloud storage, such as Sun J [18] et al. who combined a blockchain system with IPFS to ensure the security of the storage platform by using the decentralized data storage feature of IPFS, which solves the single point of failure problem compared to external cloud storage systems. Xue [19] et al. proposed a blockchain-based medical data sharing model MDSM. The model divides each medical institution participating in the network into a hierarchy, with high-ranking nodes performing proxy functions and low-ranking nodes performing auditing and verification, and finally achieving consensus through the DPOS mechanism. Wu [20] et al. achieved cross-hospital sharing of medical data through authorized authentication, and through their proposed pseudonym authentication, users can access off-site data at local hospitals. Liu et al. [21] proposed a dual blockchain system based on credit data, where one chain is used to store the real-time data of multiple users, and the other chain is used to store the credit reports of a single person. However, such studies are based on blockchains with whole copy storage, which have high data storage redundancy and do not support the storage and query of massive multi-modal raw data. In this paper, the proposed collaborative storage system combines data feature extraction, MerkleHash and public-private key encryption algorithms to effectively reduce the chain's data storage burden by supporting massive multi-modal data storage and query.

5   Conclusion

This paper proposes a multi-modal medical data collaborative storage system by storing log information such as electronic medical records and data access to the chain, and multi-modal raw medical data to the distributed system under the chain, supporting the storage of massive multi-modal medical data while using the decentralization of blockchain and the non-tamperability of data to achieve the safe sharing of massive medical data; secondly, extracting the raw data data features under the chain to store on the Secondly, the original data features under the chain are extracted and stored on the chain for data retrieval and analysis, and various types of data access interfaces are developed based on relational databases to support users to access system data directly or indirectly using data description information or data features to accelerate data query efficiency and achieve efficient retrieval and access to information; on this basis, an access control strategy based on electronic health code is designed to achieve user authorised access control and real-time medical data On the basis of this, an access control strategy based on electronic health codes is designed to achieve user authorisation access control and real-time medical data sharing. Finally, the read-and-write performance analysis experiments of this collaborative storage system are carried out, and the system in this paper improves significantly in access performance compared with the traditional blockchain and has only millisecond latency with the off-chain system.

Although we have proposed corresponding data update strategies based on the timeliness of different applications, the overall transaction processing performance of the system still has much room for improvement. In the future, we will study task-aware multi-modal data collaborative storage methods, intelligently classify high and low timeliness applications based on application and data access characteristics, and combine machine learning algorithms to achieve on-chain block cache prefetching optimization to improve the application response speed.

Acknowledgments. The author is grateful for the funding of the project "Multi-modal Data Storage of Multiple Classes of Nodes" (2022YFB2702101) in the National Key R&D Program project "Key Technologies and Systems for Massive Multimodal Data Management in Blockchain Environment" (2022YFB2702100).

References

1. 李慧博,刘海涛,邬贻萍.: 基于医院大数据建设的智慧管理平台实践. 中国卫生信息管理杂志 **19**(01), 110–115 (2022)
2. Tawalbeh, L.A., Mehmood, R., Benkhelifa, E., Song, H.: Mobile cloud computing model and big data analysis for healthcare applications. IEEE Access **4**, 6171–6180 (2017)
3. 郑万松,袁军,黄志中,王占明,尹小青.: 以病人为中心的自助医疗系统研究与应用. 中国数字医学 **8**(11), 40–42 (2013)
4. Xia, Q., Sifah, E.B., Asamoah, K.O., Gao, J., Du, X., & Guizani, M.: MeDShare: trustless medical data sharing among cloud service providers via blockchain. IEEE Access **5**, 14757–14767 (2017)
5. Zhi-Ming, H., Yi-Da, X.: Electronic medical record sharing scheme based on blockchain and searchable encryption. Comput. Eng. Appl. **57**(21), 140-147 (2021)
6. Li, J., Li, X.: Privacy preserving data analysis in mental health research. In: 2015 IEEE International Congress on Big Data, pp. 95–101. IEEE (2015)
7. 侯梦薇,卫荣,陆亮,兰欣,蔡宏伟.: 知识图谱研究综述及其在医疗领域的应用. 计算机研究与发展 **55**(12), 2587–2599 (2018)
8. 阮彤,邱加辉,张知行,叶琪.: 医疗数据治理——构建高质量医疗大数据智能分析数据基础. 大数据 **5**(01), 12–24 (2019)
9. 朱承璋,刘梓汐,李文静,肖亚龙,王晗.: 分布式医疗大数据存储方案研究综述. 软件导刊 **21**(04), 7–12 (2022)
10. Buchman, E.: Tendermint: byzantine fault tolerance in the age of blockchains. University of Guelph, 2016
11. Weil, S.A., Brandt, S.A., Miller, E.L., Long, D.D., Maltzahn, C.: Ceph: a scalable, highperformance distributed file system. In: Proceedings of the 7th Symposium on Operating Systems Design and Implementation, pp. 307–320 (2006)
12. Aghayev, A., Weil, S., Kuchnik, M., Nelson, M., Ganger, G.R., Amvrosiadis, G.: File systems unfit as distributed storage backends: lessons from 10 years of Ceph evolution. In: Proceedings of the 27th ACM Symposium on Operating Systems Principles, pp. 353–369 (2019)
13. Kaur, H., Alam, M.A., Jameel, R., Mourya, A.K., Chang, V.: A proposed solution and future direction for blockchain-based heterogeneous medicare data in cloud environment. J. Med. Syst. **42**(8), 156 (2018). https://doi.org/10.1007/s10916-018-1007-5. PMID: 29987560
14. 梅颖.: 安全存储医疗记录的区块链方法研究. 江西师范大学学报(自然科学版) **41**(05), 484–490 (2017). https://doi.org/10.16357/j.cnki.issn1000-5862.2017.05.07
15. Li, H., Zhang, F., He, J.: A searchable symmetric encryption scheme using blockchain. arXiv preprint arXiv:1711.01030 (2017)

16. Hu, S., Cai, C., Wang, Q., Luo, X., Ren, K.: Searching an encrypted cloud meets blockchain: a decentralized, reliable and fair realization. In: IEEE INFOCOM 2018-IEEE Conference on Computer Communications, pp. 792–800. IEEE (2018)
17. Chen, L., Lee, W.K., Chang, C.C., et al.: Blockchain based searchable encryption for electronic health record sharing. Futur. Gener. Comput. Syst. **95**, 420–429 (2019)
18. Sun, J., Yao, X., Wang, S., Wu, Y.: Blockchain-based secure storage and access scheme for electronic medical records in IPFS. IEEE Access **8**, 59389–59401 (2020). https://doi.org/10.1109/ACCESS.2020.2982964
19. 薛腾飞,傅群超,王枞,王新宴.: 基于区块链的医疗数据共享模型研究.自动化学报**43**(09), 1555–1562 (2017). https://doi.org/10.16383/j.aas.2017.c160661
20. Wu, H.-T., Tsai, C.-W.: Toward blockchains for health-care systems: applying the bilinear pairing technology to ensure privacy protection and accuracy in data sharing. IEEE Consum. Electron. Mag. **7**, 65–71 (2018)
21. Fa-Sheng, L., Qi-Xuan, S., Jiang-Hua, L.: Fusion of double block chain credit data storage and query scheme. Comput. Eng. Appl. **58**(2), 123–128 (2022)

Congestion Control with Receiver-Aided Network Status Awareness in RDMA Transmission

Tianshi Wang[1,2], Yiran Zhang[1,2(✉)], Ao Zhou[1,2], Ruidong Li[3], Kun Zhao[3], and Shangguang Wang[1,2]

[1] Beijing University of Posts and Telecommunications, Beijing 100000, China
{tswang,yiranzhang,aozhou,sgwang}@bupt.edu.cn
[2] Beiyou Shenzhen Institute, Shenzhen 518000, China
[3] Shandong Yunhai Guochuang Innovative Technology Co., Ltd., Jinan 250000, China
{lird,zhaokunbj}@inspur.com

Abstract. Blockchain technology relies on distributed networks, and Remote Direct Memory Access (RDMA) technology, characterized by ultra-low latency, high bandwidth, has the potential to significantly improve the transmission performance of such networks. RDMA requires a underlying lossless network (usually guaranteed by link-layer flow control called PFC) to fully exploit its performance, wherein congestion control emerges as a key technology in RDMA. However, we find that existing congestion control schemes have limitations in rapidly allocating network bandwidth to eliminate congestion, thus even aggravating side effects of PFC (e.g., head-of-line blocking, unfairness, and deadlock). In this paper, we propose an RDMA congestion control scheme based on receiver-aided network state awareness (RRCC). This research introduces the following key innovations: 1) calculating congestion information through the ECN signals in data packets to achieve a more precise network state sensing method; 2) monitoring the throughput in the receiver side in real-time, and in combination with network state information, periodically adjusting the sender's rate to achieve rapid rate convergence, accurately preventing and controlling congestion, and addressing issues such as increased flow completion time and slow network congestion recovery. We evaluate RRCC using realistic traffic traces under a three-layer Clos network architecture. The results show that RRCC significantly outperforms existing congestion control schemes in terms of throughput and flow completion time while reducing the side effects of PFC.

Keywords: RDMA · lossless transmission · congestion control · blockchain · datacenter network

1 Introduction

In recent years, blockchain technology has garnered significant attention across a wide range of fields [1]. As a decentralized distributed ledger technology,

J. Chen et al. (Eds.): BlockSys 2023, CCIS 1897, pp. 223–236, 2024.
https://doi.org/10.1007/978-981-99-8104-5_17

blockchain primarily deals with the storage and transmission of a large amount of data [2,3]. By relying on a distributed network to synchronize data among all nodes [16], blockchain technology effectively improves data security and reliability [4]. However, in a distributed network environment [13], challenges such as packet loss, reordering, and network congestion have emerged, causing significant network bottlenecks that affect the blockchain's throughput and increase transaction latency and node synchronization time. In response to the demand for high throughput and low latency [12], RDMA technology offloads the transport layer to the network card and bypasses the kernel for packet processing. Furthermore, RDMA leverages lossless network technology to eliminate packet loss, improving throughput and achieving ultra-low latency while reducing CPU overhead.

RoCEv2 is an RDMA transport protocol widely used on Ethernet networks [10], which employs Priority-based Flow Control (PFC) to ensure lossless transmission. However, due to PFC's mechanism of forcibly pausing upstream device ports from sending packets, it can easily lead to issues such as congestion spreading and deadlock [9]. To reduce the risk of triggering PFC [18], RoCEv2 utilizes congestion control algorithms, such as DCQCN [19] based on ECN congestion signals and Timely [14] based on RTT congestion signals. They both react to congestion signals by adjusting sending rate to eliminate congestion.

In DCQCN, the sender controls the rate reduction based on a set of parameters, with each decrement being no more than half of the original rate, whereas Timely's sender adopts a heuristic slow rate adjustment strategy [20]. Both DCQCN and Timely employ probing rate adjustments that cannot converge rapidly, leading to slow congestion relief and failing to satisfy network demands for low latency and high throughput, which severely impacts RDMA performance. Our experiments also validate that their rate reduction components are unable to rapidly decrease the transmission rate upon detecting network congestion, resulting in poor convergence performance.

We realize that the congestion signals available for feedback from switches typically deployed in data centers are limited to ECN, whereas RTT congestion signals, not requiring switch involvement, only necessitate endpoint measurement. Other advanced solutions, such as HPCC [11] and other congestion control algorithms, achieve rapid rate convergence and high stability through precise INT information. However, the high deployment cost arises from the necessity for all network switches to support INT. Therefore, in order to improve RDMA's congestion control algorithm without making extensive changes to network equipment within the data center, innovative technologies must continue to rely on ECN or RTT as congestion signals.

Our key insight is that the receiver can provide valuable implications in congestion information. In detail, the receiving rate monitored in the receiver side is exactly the sending rate that one flow can pass through the bottleneck. Besides, due to the extremely short transmission delay and propagation delay of ACKs within data centers, the sender can determine the receiver's reception rate based on the arrival of ACKs. Recent RDMA NICs have provided hardware support,

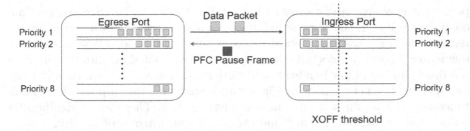

Fig. 1. The operation of PFC

enabling RDMA network cards to generate high-quality ACKs. In the Timely algorithm, the RTT is already calculated based on the ACK feedback from the receiver. These features allow the sender to measure the receiver's receiving rate from the number of ACKs returned by the receiver, without requiring explicit feedback from the receiver.

In this paper, we propose RRCC, a receiver-aided network state-aware RDMA congestion control scheme. The main innovations of this research include: 1) By calculating congestion information through the fraction ECN signals within data packets without altering the network switch equipment and configurations, we achieve a more precise network state sensing method; 2) We monitor the receiving rate of the receiver side in real-time and, in combination with link state information, periodically adjust the sender's rate, thereby achieving rapid rate convergence, accurately preventing and controlling congestion, and addressing issues such as increased flow completion time and slow network congestion recovery.

2 Background and Motivation

In this section, we first introduce the link-layer flow control that enables the underlying lossless network in RoCEv2 and why congestion control is needed. Then we describe existing congestion control schemes and analyze their limitations which motivate our work.

2.1 Link-Layer Flow Control

RoCEv2 employs Priority Flow Control (PFC) as the link-layer flow control to ensure no packet drop under normal situations. As shown in Fig. 1, when the switch buffer is about to overflow, the switch sends a PAUSE frame to notify upstream ports to cease data transmission. When the switch buffer occupancy starts to decrease, the switch notifies upstream ports again by sending a RESUME frame to restart data transmission. PFC operates on a per-priority queue basis, and thus can individually pause and resume any priority queue.

PFC can well guarantee losslessness especially when transient congestion may cause packet drop. However, PFC is not without its side effects. Specifically, when persistent excessive traffic causes PFC PAUSE frames to be triggered continuously, the traffic in the same switch queue is also affected, which brings unique issues including head-of-line blocking (i.e., congestion-unrelated flows in the same queue are innocently blocked), unfairness (i.e., without differentiating individual flows causing unfair bandwidth allocation), and even deadlock risks (i.e., all switches in the cyclic buffer loop may pause upstream switch port while simultaneously waiting for downstream port instructions). These issues significantly reduce the throughput, latency, and utilization performance of RoCEv2.

The root cause of the above negative impact introduced by PFC is the occurrence of persistent network congestion and the per-queue operation in PFC. Therefore, RoCEv2 requires a per-flow congestion control to adjust the flow rates to eliminate congestion quickly and reduce the persistent trigger of PFC.

2.2   Limitations of Existing Congestion Control Schemes

Nowadays, DCQCN [19] and Timely [14] are the two most prevalent congestion control mechanisms.

DCQCN is the first congestion control scheme designed for RoCEv2. In DCQCN, the switch acts as a Congestion Point (CP), detecting congestion by monitoring queue lengths, and conveying the congestion information via the ECN field. The receiver acts as a Notification Point (NP), generating explicit congestion notification packets (CNP) and sending them to the sender. Then the sender is the Reaction Point (RP). The sender reduces the flow rate if a CNP is received within a control period; otherwise, it increases the flow rate determined by timers and byte counters. Since DCQCN adopts a heuristic step-by-step adjustment strategy, it may require multiple RTTs to converge to the ideal rate.

Timely is a congestion control algorithm based on RTT gradients proposed by Google, which draws on the ideas of delay-based congestion control in wide-area networks and aims to provide a more optimized congestion control mechanism for lossless Ethernet RoCEv2. With Timely enabled, the sender measures the round-trip time (RTT) of data packets and heuristically reduces the transmission rate according to the gradient within a certain RTT range. However, Timely's convergence performance is may be not satisfactory in highly dynamic network environments.

In essence, both DCQCN and Timely conduct sender-based rate probing adjustments. DCQCN decreases the sending rate at most half at one time on the recipient of CNP. Timely decreases the sending rate according to gradients, with the detailed rate reduction heavily relying on the RTT range setting and gradient parameters in the algorithm. If the sending rate can not be regulated to the proper rate quickly, PFC may still be activated and negative impacts spread to the network. In summary, they both lack concrete information to guide the sender to reduce the sending rate quickly, hence may fail to achieve rapid convergence especially when severe congestion occurs.

In this work, our key insight is that more valuable information can be obtained at the receiver side to reduce sender-based probing. As one of the key indicators of RDMA network load, receiving rate can provide crucial guidance information for RDMA congestion control, because it indicates the maximum rate can pass through network when congestion. Further, by performing more refined processing and calculation of ECN, more dynamic and real-time explicit congestion information can be obtained, thereby sensing the degree of congestion. Such a design can achieve better convergence effects than existing RDMA congestion control methods, resulting in a congestion control method that adjusts the sending rate based on real-time throughput information and avoid heuristic rate reduction, and thus, achieving better network performance than DCQCN and Timely.

3   Design

In this section, we first provide an overview of the design principles behind RRCC, followed by a detailed explanation of RRCC's congestion control algorithms.

3.1   Overview

As illustrated in Fig. 2, the RRCC design is based on the following principles: In the RRCC algorithm, the sender acts as the Reaction Point (RP), the switch serves as the Congestion Point (CP), while the receiver functions as the Notification Point (NP). The CP algorithm is executed on the switch, reflecting the congestion level by marking ECN on data packets. The NP algorithm operates on the receiver's network card, measuring the reception rate, calculating the proportion of marked ECN packets and the advisory rate, and providing this information to the sender's network card through CNP feedback. The RP algorithm is implemented on the sender's network card, adjusting the transmission rate based on received CNPs and utilizing acceleration counters for rate control. These algorithms collaboratively achieve rapid rate convergence and effective congestion elimination.

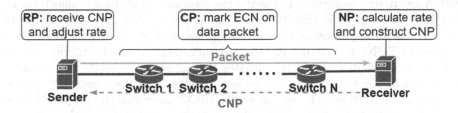

Fig. 2. RRCC framework

3.2   Algorithm

RRCC controls the rate at the flow level and does not require modifications to switches within RDMA network; it is implemented directly on RDMA NICs.

Algorithm 1. Receiver algorithm.

```
 1: function RECEIVEPACKETS(recvNum)
 2:     recvNum = recvNum + 1;
 3:     if ECN == 1 then
 4:         recvECN = recvECN + 1;
 5:     end if
 6: end function

 7: function CHECKANDSENDCNP(recvNum, recvECN, recvRate)
 8:     frac = recvECN/recvNum;
 9:     TH = BaseValue − frac;
10:     if TH ≤ TH_{High} then
11:         if TH_{medium} < TH ≤ TH_{High} then
12:             SendCNP(recvRate ∗ TH_{High}, Flag = Congested)
13:         else if TH_{Low} < TH ≤ TH_{Medium} then
14:             SendCNP(recvRate ∗ TH_{Medium}, Flag = Congested)
15:         else
16:             SendCNP(recvRate ∗ TH_{Low}, Flag = Congested)
17:         end if
18:     else
19:         SendCNP(Flag = Uncongested)
20:     end if
21:     recvNum = 0;
22:     recvECN = 0;
23: end function
```

CP Algorithm: This algorithm operates on switches, utilizing RED to mark ECN on data packets based on queue length distribution. As the RRCC receiver relies on the number of ECN marks to determine the congestion level of the link, when the queue length in the switch exceeds the threshold, the switch no longer marks ECN for data packets based on probability distribution, but instead directly marks ECN on each data packet in the queue.

NP Algorithm: Algorithm 1 presents the pseudocode of the NP algorithm for the RRCC receiver. The algorithm operates on the receiver's network card, periodically measuring throughput, calculating the proportion of received packets marked as ECN, and computing the advisory rate. At the beginning of each time period, the RRCC receiver initiates two counters, $recvRate$ and $recvECN$ which record the total number of received packets and the number of packets marked as ECN. When the period ends, RRCC calculates the proportion $frac$ of received packets marked as ECN. The parameter TH indicates the reduction factor based on $frac$ and $BaseValue$. If TH does not below the threshold, the link is considered uncongested, and a CNP is generated with the congestion notification bit $Flag$ set to false. If $frac$ belows the threshold, RRCC determines whether to use the deceleration parameters TH_{High}, TH_{Medium}, or TH_{Low} based on the interval in which the proportion falls, dynamically computing the throughput and average receiving rate for the current period. Using the deceleration param-

---

Algorithm 2. Sender algorithm.

1: **function** CONGESTED(*recvRate*)
2:     $Rate = recvRate$;
3:     $N_u = 0$;
4: **end function**
5: **function** UNCONGESTED //the increase step is first small then large
6:     **if** $N_u < 3$ **then**
7:         $RI = RI_{Low}$;
8:     **else**
9:         $RI = RI_{High}$;
10:     **end if**
11:     $Rate = Rate + \frac{(lineRate - Rate)}{lineRate} * RI$;
12:     $N_u = N_u + 1$;
13: **end function**

---

eter and reception rate, the advisory rate is calculated, a CNP is generated with *Flag* set to true, and the advisory rate is included in the CNP.

RP Algorithm: Algorithm 2 presents the pseudocode of the RP algorithm for the sender in RRCC. The algorithm runs on the sender's network card, adjusting the sending rate based on received CNPs. RRCC's sender maintains the acceleration counter *Nu* to control the sender's rate increase mode, which represents the number of consecutive uncongested periods. Upon receiving a CNP, RRCC checks *Flag* in it. If *Flag* is true, RRCC guides the sender to reduce its speed to the *recvRate* carried in the CNP, and *Nu* is reset to 0. If *Flag* is false, *Nu* increases, and RRCC probes the link bandwidth, calculating the weighted average of the current sender rate and bandwidth to increase the sending rate. RRCC sets two weights for the bandwidth: when *Nu*'s value exceeds the threshold, the sender accelerates using the high-weight parameter RI_{High}; otherwise, the low-weight parameter RI_{Low} is used.

4   Evaluation

In this section, we evaluate the performance of RRCC using typical testbeds and large-scale testbeds simulated by the NS3 simulator [6], and compare it with two common congestion control schemes, DCQCN [19] and Timely [14].

In two different scales of environments, we evaluate the performance of RRCC. Firstly, We conduct microbenchmark tests to assess the basic performance of the RRCC congestion control algorithm. Specifically, we design an incast traffic scenario to evaluate the algorithm's throughput and fairness, and a burst traffic scenario to examine its link utilization and convergence capability. Subsequently, we ran RRCC in a three-layer Clos network topology to assess its packet latency and dependency on link-layer flow control in large-scale scenarios. Based on the specific settings of the link bandwidth, we adjust the related parameters of the switch's ECN packet marking function. For DCQCN, we adopt the parameters recommended by major NIC vendors; for TIMELY, we follow the

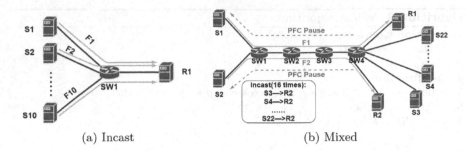

(a) Incast   (b) Mixed

Fig. 3. Incast and mixed traffic scenarios

parameters suggested in the literature [15]. In the experiments, we enable PFC as the link-layer flow control, with a static PFC threshold set to 512 KB, and the switch buffer size is 32 MB. The period of RRCC to construct CNP is 50 µs. We employ four performance metrics for evaluation: (i) Flow Completion Time (FCT); (ii) FCT slowdown, calculated by the ratio between real FCT and Ideal FCT; (iii) the number of PFC PAUSE; (iv) throughput.

4.1 Micro-benchmarks

Network Topologies. We design an incast scenario and a mixed traffic scenario. In the incast scenario, there are ten randomly selected servers S1–S10 as senders and one randomly selected server R1 as the receiver, with only one switch on the link. Each link has a capacity of 100 Gbps, a propagation delay of 3 µs, and a maximum baseline RTT of 12 µs. In the mixed traffic scenario, there are 22 randomly selected servers S1–S22 as senders and two randomly selected servers R1 and R2 as receivers, with a total of four switches SW1–SW4 on the link. Each link has a capacity of 100 Gbps, a propagation delay of 1 µs, and a maximum baseline RTT of 10 µs. Figure 3 illustrates the network topology and traffic scenarios of incast and mix traffic patterns.

Traffic Loads. In the incast experiment, we set up ten senders to simultaneously send 200 MB of data to the receiver, resulting in a total of ten concurrent connections, simulating an incast workload without any cross-traffic. In the mixed traffic experiment, we configure sender S1 sends a congested long flow F1 and sender S2 sends a victim long flow victim F2, each of these long flows carries a payload of 50 GB of data. We set up twenty sender servers S3-S22 to send bursty short flows to one receiver server R2 during long flow transmission, each of these bursty short flows carries a payload of 64 KB of data, simulating a mixed traffic workload.

Results. *RRCC quickly converges its rate when encountering congestion, maintaining stable throughput.* Figure 4 shows the throughput comparison of RRCC, DCQCN, and Timely in an incast scenario. Upon receiving the first CNP, RRCC's sender quickly converges the sending rate of each QP to the ideal rate of around 10 Gbps, with a smaller oscillation amplitude in throughput compared to

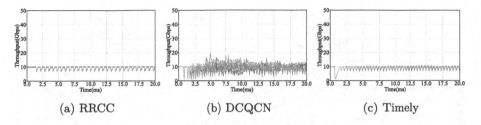

Fig. 4. Throughput among RRCC, DCQCN, and Timely in incast experiment

DCQCN and Timely, achieving faster throughput stability. RRCC adjusts the sending rate based on receiver information and real-time network conditions, rapidly adapting the sending rate to available bandwidth.

RRCC Reduces the Triggering of PFC and Alleviates Head-of-Line Blocking Issue. RRCC effectively reduces the triggering of PFC. Figure 5 presents a comparison of the throughput performance for RRCC, DCQCN, and Timely in a mixed traffic scenario, alongside the PFC PAUSE triggering conditions for each of these protocols. After incast short flows appear on the link, the path taken by congested flow F2 in DCQCN and Timely causes switches SW1–SW4 to trigger varying numbers of PFC PAUSEs, leading to a decrease in throughput for victim flow F1 sharing the same path segment with the congested flow. In contrast, the sender S2 of RRCC's F2 quickly converges its rate, avoiding the triggering of PFC PAUSE on switches SW1-4, thus F1's throughput remains unaffected.

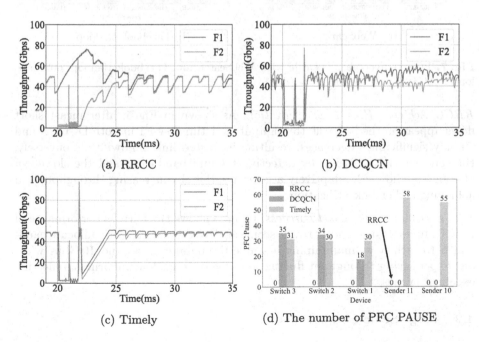

Fig. 5. Throughput among RRCC, DCQCN, and Timely in mixed traffic experiment. Both DCQCN and Timely have head-of-line blocking issue and victim flow emerges

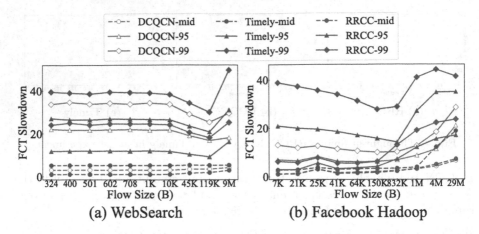

Fig. 6. FCT slowdown at average percentile, 95-percentile and 99-percentile with Web-Search and Facebook Hadoop, 60% avg. load + 20% 20-to-1 incast

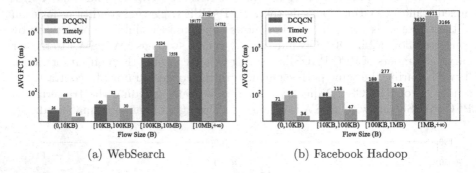

Fig. 7. FCT at average percentile with WebSearch and Facebook Hadoop, 60% avg. load + 20% 20-to-1 incast

RRCC Achieves High Link Utilization. As shown in Fig. 5, after incast short flows appear on the link, the throughput of victim flow F1 in both DCQCN and Timely significantly decreases, resulting in wasted link bandwidth. Conversely, the sender of RRCC's F1, by detecting the link bandwidth and the slowdown of congested flow F2, adaptively accelerates, thereby increasing throughput and achieving higher link utilization.

RRCC Demonstrates Good Fairness. Figure 4 shows the fairness performance of RRCC. In the 10-to-1 incast traffic scenario, RRCC is able to fairly allocate bandwidth to each flow, maintaining a stable throughput of around 10 Gbps without experiencing throughput fluctuations due to inter-flow unfairness, reflecting excellent fairness.

4.2   Large-Scale Simulations

Network Topologies. We adopt a FatTree [5] network topology, which is a structure based on a three-layer Clos architecture, consisting of 320 servers and

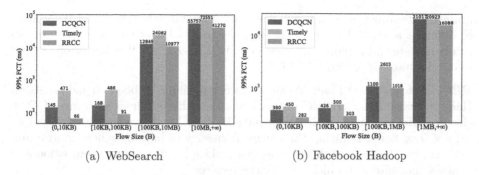

(a) WebSearch   (b) Facebook Hadoop

Fig. 8. FCT at 99-percentile with WebSearch and Facebook Hadoop, 60% avg. load + 20% 20-to-1 incast

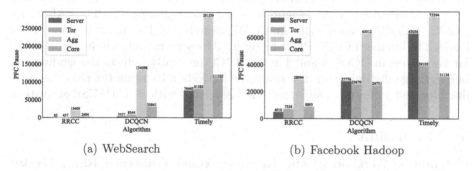

(a) WebSearch   (b) Facebook Hadoop

Fig. 9. The number of PFC PAUSE with WebSearch and Facebook Hadoop, 60% avg. load + 20% 20-to-1 incast

56 switches, including 16 core switches, 20 Agg switches, and 20 ToR switches. All servers are directly connected to the ToR switches, with a link capacity of 100 Gbps for each server-to-switch connection, and a link capacity of 400 Gbps between switches. The propagation delay for each link is set to 1 μs.

Traffic Loads. We use two typical data center traffic patterns: WebSearch [7] and Facebook Hadoop [17]. WebSearch workload is more heavy-tailed than Facebook Hadoop workload. Both traffic patterns exhibit high concurrency, high unpredictability, and high dynamics, making them common complex traffic scenarios in data centers. We set the average link load to 80%, including 60% of background traffic and 20% of incast traffic.

Results. *RRCC Demonstrates Stable FCT Slowdown.* Figure 6 presents a comparison of FCT slowdown in the incast scenario for RRCC, DCQCN, and Timely, with evaluation metrics including average, 95%, and 99% FCT slowdown. Under Facebook Hadoop traffic load, RRCC's average, 95% and 99% FCT slowdown are all significantly lower than those of DCQCN and Timely. Under WebSearch traffic load, RRCC's performance is generally better than Timely, and only slightly inferior to DCQCN in a few size ranges, with a small difference. As shown in Fig. 7, RRCC adjusts the rate based on receiver information, implementing fine-grained rate adjustments for each flow, thus improving the average FCT for flows of different sizes. Referring to the Fig. 8, RRCC adjusts the rate according to receiving rate and rapidly converges to reduce congestion, flows of different sizes maintain stable 95% and 99% FCT.

RRCC Benefits Short Flows. As shown in Fig. 6, under WebSearch and Facebook Hadoop traffic loads, RRCC outperforms the other schemes in terms of FCT slowdown for messages smaller than 800 KB. RRCC swiftly converges the sending rate of long flows, reducing the trigger frequency of link layer flow control and maintaining shorter switch queue lengths, which in turn reduces congestion and enables short flows to quickly reach the receiver.

RRCC Quickly Converges its Rate when Encountering Congestion, Thus Greatly Reducing PFC Triggering. RRCC significantly reduces the occurrence of link-layer flow control triggers. Figure 9 shows the triggering of PFC PAUSE for RRCC, DCQCN, and Timely under WebSearch and Facebook Hadoop traffic loads. The number of PFC PAUSEs received by servers and switches in RRCC is far lower than in DCQCN and Timely. RRCC promptly reduces the sending rate before triggering link-layer flow control, effectively mitigating the risks (head-to-line blocking, unfairness, and deadlock) associated with PFC PAUSE activation.

5 Discussion

Calculation Method of the Receiver-Aided Guidance Rate. The key factors in calculating the guidance rate for RRCC include ECN information from switches on the link and the statistical throughput. RRCC determines network congestion and calculates the guidance rate based on the proportion of data packets marked with ECN received by the receiver in each period. This ratio is only used to determine network congestion. If the guidance rate is calculated based on the statistical throughput and static parameters, it may result in an excessive decrease in rate and reduced link utilization. During the experiments, we set various values for the static parameters; however, in large-scale scenarios, the FCT slowdown for static calculation of guidance rate is higher than the FCT slowdown for guidance rate calculated based on the ECN ratio, resulting in worse FCT performance.

Switch ECN Configuration. In DCQCN, switches use the RED mechanism to probabilistically mark data packets with ECN based on queue length. The receiver only needs to receive any data packet with an ECN mark within each period to generate a CNP, notifying the sender of network congestion. However, in RRCC, the receiver relies on ECN information provided by switches on the link to calculate the ECN ratio, determine network congestion, and calculate the guidance rate. Therefore, more accurate ECN information from switches is required. In RRCC, switches mark all data packets in queues that exceed the threshold with ECN. The choice of threshold and parameters related to ECN in switches for RRCC is reduced, lowering operational complexity.

Deployment Feasibility. The implementation of RRCC does not require the replacement of switches within the network, and only requires programming on the RDMA network card. Therefore, the deployment cost is low, and it has good technical feasibility.

6 Related Work

HPCC [11] is a congestion control approach based on network telemetry (INT) [8] technology that accurately obtains link load information for traffic control. Compared to DCQCN and Timely, HPCC demonstrates significant advantages in fully utilizing idle bandwidth, avoiding congestion, and achieving ultra-low latency. However, HPCC requires all switches in the network to support INT technology, which may necessitate substantial replacement of existing network equipment, resulting in higher deployment costs.

IRN [15] is an RDMA proposal based on the premise of lossy networks, aiming to optimize the packet retransmission process to reduce performance degradation in RDMA networks when packet loss occurs, and to achieve RDMA networks that do not rely on PFC. RRCC significantly reduces the triggering frequency of PFC PAUSEs and mitigates the performance impact when PFC is disabled. We speculates that, with PFC disabled, RRCC can work in conjunction with IRN to achieve efficient RDMA network transmission performance in lossy networks.

7 Conclusion

In this paper, we propose RRCC, an RDMA congestion control scheme based on receiver-aided network state awareness. By utilizing ECN signals to calculate congestion information and real-time monitoring of the receiver's network card throughput in the receiver side, RRCC effectively senses the network state, thus achieving the goals of preventing and rapidly alleviating congestion while ensuring ultra-low latency and high bandwidth. Therefore, we believe that RRCC technology has broad application prospects, and can bring better performance and efficiency to the fields of distributed computing and network communication, as well as play a critical role in blockchain technology.

Acknowledgment. This work is supported by the National Key R&D Program of China (2020YFB1805500) and NSFC (62032003, U21B2016 and 62192784).

References

1. Lee, X.T., Khan, A., Sen Gupta, S., Ong, Y.H., Liu, X.: Measurements, analyses, and insights on the entire Ethereum blockchain network. In: Proceedings of The Web Conference 2020, pp. 155–166 (2020)
2. Amiri, M.J., Agrawal, D., El Abbadi, A.: SharPer: sharding permissioned blockchains over network clusters. In: Proceedings of the 2021 International Conference on Management of Data, pp. 76–88 (2021)

3. Peng, Y., Du, M., Li, F., Cheng, R., Song, D.: FalconDB: blockchain-based collaborative database. In: Proceedings of the 2020 ACM SIGMOD International Conference on Management of Data, pp. 637–652 (2020)
4. Xu, C., Zhang, C., Xu, J.: vChain: enabling verifiable Boolean range queries over blockchain databases. In: Proceedings of the 2019 International Conference on Management of Data, pp. 141–158 (2019)
5. Al-Fares, M., Loukissas, A., Vahdat, A.: A scalable, commodity data center network architecture. ACM SIGCOMM Comput. Commun. Rev. **38**(4), 63–74 (2008)
6. Alibaba-Edu: High-precision congestion control. GitHub Repository (2021). https://github.com/alibaba-edu/High-Precision-Congestion-Control
7. Alizadeh, M., et al.: Data center TCP (DCTCP). In: Proceedings of the ACM SIGCOMM 2010 Conference, pp. 63–74 (2010)
8. Broadcom: in-band network telemetry in Broadcom tomahawk 3 (2019). https://www.broadcom.com/company/news/product-releases/2372840
9. Guo, C., Wu, H., Deng, Z., Soni, G., Lipshteyn, M.: RDMA over commodity ethernet at scale. In: the 2016 Conference (2016)
10. Krawczyk, R.D., Colombo, T., Neufeld, N., Pisani, F., Valat, S.: Feasibility tests of RoCE v2 for LHCb event building. In: EPJ Web of Conferences, vol. 245, p. 01011. EDP Sciences (2020)
11. Li, Y., et al.: HPCC: high precision congestion control. In: Proceedings of the ACM Special Interest Group on Data Communication, pp. 44–58 (2019)
12. Lu, X., Shankar, D., Gugnani, S., Panda, D.: High-performance design of apache spark with RDMA and its benefits on various workloads. In: IEEE International Conference on Big Data (2016)
13. Marinos, I., Watson, R., Handley, M.: Network stack specialization for performance. In: ACM Conference on SIGCOMM (2014)
14. Mittal, R., et al.: TIMELY: RTT-based congestion control for the datacenter. In: ACM Conference on Special Interest Group on Data Communication, pp. 537–550 (2015)
15. Mittal, R., et al.: Revisiting network support for RDMA. In: Proceedings of the 2018 Conference of the ACM Special Interest Group on Data Communication, pp. 313–326 (2018)
16. Qiu, X., Chen, W., Tang, B., Liang, J., Dai, H.N., Zheng, Z.: A distributed and privacy-aware high-throughput transaction scheduling approach for scaling blockchain. IEEE Trans. Dependable Secure Comput. **01**, 1–15 (2022)
17. Roy, A., Zeng, H., Bagga, J., Porter, G., Snoeren, A.C.: Inside the social network's (datacenter) network. In: Proceedings of the 2015 ACM Conference on Special Interest Group on Data Communication, pp. 123–137 (2015)
18. Shpiner, A., et al.: RoCE rocks without PFC: detailed evaluation. In: Proceedings of the Workshop on Kernel-Bypass Networks, pp. 25–30 (2017)
19. Zhu, Y., et al.: Congestion control for large-scale RDMA deployments. ACM SIGCOMM Comput. Commun. Rev. **45**(4), 523–536 (2015)
20. Zhu, Y., Ghobadi, M., Misra, V., Padhye, J.: ECN or Delay: lessons learnt from analysis of DCQCN and TIMELY. In: Proceedings of the 12th International on Conference on emerging Networking EXperiments and Technologies, pp. 313–327 (2016)

VPBFT: Improved PBFT Consensus Algorithm Based on VRF and PageRank Algorithm

Chi Jiang, Chenying Guo, Changyi Shan, and Yin Zhang[✉]

School of Information and Communication Engineering, University of Electronic Science and Technology of China, Chengdu 610000, China
zhangyin123@uestc.edu.cn

Abstract. The PBFT consensus algorithm is widely used in the blockchain consensus, but its algorithm complexity is high and there are performance limitations. At present, the research on the supervision of the production and manufacturing process of power transmission and distribution equipment using blockchain technology lacks detailed system architecture design and function realization. This paper proposes an improved PBFT consensus algorithm VPBFT based on verifiable random function and weighted PageRank algorithm, which has better performance than PBFT. Then we implemented a power transmission and distribution consortium blockchain supervision platform and applied VPBFT to it.

Keywords: Consortium Blockchain · smart contract · PBFT · VRF · PageRank

1 Introduction

Blockchain is a decentralized and distributed database technology which basic concept is to store data in blocks and link them together to form an immutable blockchain [1], ensuring data transparency, security, and reliability. Blockchain can be classified into three types: public chain, consortium chain, and private chain. Among them, the consortium chain [2–4] is a blockchain maintained by a group of known entities, such as enterprises and government agencies, which must meet certain conditions to participate. In addition, consortium chains can achieve automated collaboration and interaction through smart contracts, improving the efficiency between participants. Currently, mainstream consortium chains adopt the PBFT algorithm. However, the high complexity and large number of nodes of the PBFT consensus algorithm create performance bottlenecks, which limits the application of consortium chains.

The construction, safety, and reliable operation of power grid rely heavily on the distribution equipment, which can effectively prevent power accidents and ensure the smooth operation of the power system. However, there are some regulatory technology problems in the distribution industry: 1. Lack of trust among

J. Chen et al. (Eds.): BlockSys 2023, CCIS 1897, pp. 237–251, 2024.
https://doi.org/10.1007/978-981-99-8104-5_18

upstream and downstream enterprises in various links. 2. Delayed speed of IoT devices sending and receiving instructions due to congested or insufficiently capable centralized server networks. 3. Unclear regulatory system, making it difficult to locate relevant responsible parties in a timely manner. 4. Preliminary ideation stage for research on the regulation of distribution equipment production processes using blockchain technology, lacking detailed architecture design, system design, and functional implementation.

To address these issues, this paper proposes an improved PBFT consensus algorithm VPBFT based on verifiable random function and weighted PageRank algorithm [5]. Experiments show that PBFT has higher throughput and lower latency. This paper implements the power transmission and distribution system based on the consortium blockchain, and realizes the real-time upload and supervision traceability process of production and circulation industry data.

Specifically, the contributions of this article are summarized into the following two points:

- we proposed an improved PBFT consensus algorithm, called VPBFT, based on verifiable random function (VRF) and weighted PageRank algorithm. VPBFT has higher security, throughput and lower consensus latency compared to the original PBFT algorithm.
- We designed and implemented a consortium blockchain for the electricity transmission and distribution industry based on the VPBFT consensus algorithm, which realizes the monitoring system for the production and manufacturing process of electricity transmission and distribution equipment.

This paper is organized as follows: Sect. 2 provides an overview of related work. Section 3 describes the structure of VPBFT consensus algorithm. Section 4 presents the architecture of the electricity transmission and distribution system based on the VPBFT consortium blockchain. Section 5 discusses the experimental results. Section 6 concludes the paper.

2   Related Work

2.1   Research on Blockchain Consensus Algorithm

The PBFT consensus mechanism was proposed by Miguel Castro and Barbara Liskov in 1999 [6]. However, the complexity and the large number of nodes in the PBFT consensus algorithm can create performance bottlenecks, limiting its application in consortium chains.

Researchers in [7] proposes an energy-efficient consensus node selection mechanism and uses VRF [8] to ensure the safety of the leader. The WRBFT algorithm proposed in [9] combines the node consistency workload with the Verifiable Random Function (VRF) to randomly select more reliable nodes that dominate the main nodes. VRF was first proposed in the Algorand consensus algorithm [8], and subsequent research [10,11] combined it with BFT to apply it to consensus algorithms. The Algorand consensus algorithm combines POS and VRF to randomly select verification nodes and consensus nodes, which can resist malicious attacks and has high security and throughput. VRF can be considered as a combination of Random Oracle (RO) [12] and Zero Knowledge Proofs [13].

2.2 Research on Smart Manufacturing Solutions Based on Blockchain

Many researchers both domestically and abroad have conducted numerous studies on blockchain-based solutions for smart manufacturing. Li et al. [14] explained how to model and develop a blockchain-supported cloud manufacturing application using a public chain network. However, designing a fully public cloud manufacturing application where all data must be stored on the public chain network is impossible due to the large amount of data and the need for too many write operations, which would greatly increase the cost. Assaqty et al. [15] designed an industrial IoT based on a private blockchain for smart manufacturing and demonstrated the feasibility of private blockchain technology in the manufacturing industry. However, the authors only proposed a model and architecture, and have yet to build a platform to validate the model using real data.

Regulatory platforms that have been successfully implemented in other industries using blockchain prove that there is great research potential in this direction. Mohaghegh et al. [16] provided a decentralized regulatory platform for recording gun ownership data and gun transactions. However, the system still requires more operational planning when it involves human interaction and regulations in order to protect user privacy. Saraiva et al. [17] designed a blockchain-based web application on the Hyperledger platform that allows relevant information required for registering regulatory medical professionals to be stored in a decentralized and reliable manner. The scarcity of reference platforms applied to the manufacturing industry in regulatory areas domestically and abroad also proves the innovation of this research to a certain extent.

3 VPBFT

3.1 VPBFT Model Assumptions

Suppose there is a VPBFT network composed of n nodes, and the set of nodes is $N = 1, 2, ..., n$, among which there are at most f Byzantine nodes, and the relationship between them satisfies $n \geq 3f + 1$. Each node i has a public-private key pair (sk_i, pk_i), where sk_i is the private key and pk_i is the public key.

In the VPBFT model, the PR value of each node in the initial stage of the PageRank algorithm is $1/N$, where N is the total number of nodes. The PageRank value of each node will be initialized at the beginning of each view. After initialization, each node will send its own PageRank value to other nodes, and at the same time receive the PageRank value sent by other nodes, and then calculate based on these values A new PageRank value and broadcast to other nodes. This process will continue for multiple rounds until the PageRank values of all nodes converge. For each node i in the PBFT network, its PageRank value $PR(p_i)_{t+1} = \alpha \sum_{p_j \in M_{p_i}} \frac{PR(p_j)_t}{L(p_j)} + \frac{1-\alpha}{N}$.

Among them, M_{p_i} is the set of all in-degree nodes of node p_i, $L(p_j)$ is the set of all out-degree nodes of node p_j, α is the damping coefficient of PageRank, which is the probability of following the out-link to this node, set to 0.85, $1 - \alpha$ represents the probability of random transfer to other nodes.

Assuming that each consensus node i has a weight value W_i, where $W_i \in [0,1]$, W_i can be evaluated based on the node's historical behavior, reputation and other factors. Isolate the 20% consensus nodes ranked by the weight value W_i, and do not participate in the master selection process. Each node i also uses its private key sk_i to generate a pseudo-random function PRF as vrf_random. In the VPBFT model, this PRF is used to select the view number and master node.

3.2   VPBFT Consensus Algorithm

Introduce PR Value to Nodes Based on Weighted PageRank Algorithm. In the PageRank algorithm, the importance of evaluating each node in the consensus network is described as the PR value. First design a triple $(source, target, weight)$, $source$ is the source node, $target$ is the target node, $weight$ is the cumulative number of times the source node sends requests or responses to the target node, and the initial value of $weight$ is 0. Each message will be written into a triplet, if $source$ and $target$ message appears multiple times, no new triplet will be generated and the weight will be increased by 1.

Figure 1 shows the transfer process of PR value. Initially, PR values of consensus nodes are equal. Nodes update their PR values based on edge weights. Weight value transmitted depends on node's own weight value and information sending frequency. Weight value passed in depends on other nodes' PR values and connectivity. PR calculation depends on node's in-degree and adjacent nodes' PR values. PR values of each node are calculated and passed until convergence.

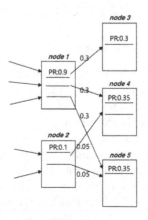

Fig. 1. PR value distribution process

The triplet records the historical consensus interaction of the node, and the initial PR value of each node is $1/N$, and the PageRank equation is used to assign a new PR value to the node according to the importance of the node in the consensus network.

Algorithm 1 describes the PageRank algorithm to calculate the PR value of participating consensus nodes.

Algorithm 1: The weighted PageRank algorithm calculates the PR value of participating consensus nodes

---

Data: Consensus node set $p_i = <p1, p2... >$, minimum error ϵ
Result: PageRank value of each node: P_k
$PR_0 \leftarrow 1/N$ //The initial PR value of each node is 1/N;
$k \leftarrow 1$ //The number of iterations is set to 1;
repeat
$\quad PR_k \leftarrow \alpha \sum_{p_j \in M_{p_i}} \frac{PR(p_j)t}{L(p_j)} + \frac{1-\alpha}{N}$ //Calculate the PR value of each
$\quad$ node separately and store it in the corresponding PR_k;
$\quad k \leftarrow k+1$ //Once per iteration, the number of iterations k+1;
until $\|P_k - P_{k+1}\| < \epsilon$ //The convergence condition is the difference between
the two changes, which is less than the given ϵ;
;
return P_k //return result

Node PR Weight Value Based on Credit Mechanism. Considering that the problem of nodes doing evil in the consortium Blockchain only depends on the PR value $PR(p_i)$ as the basis for the weight value, there will be a problem that the malicious node is very active and given a higher PR value $PR(p_i)$, so it is necessary to introduce credit The evaluation mechanism is used to improve the value of $PR(p_i)$. Based on $PR(p_i)$, nodes are rewarded or punished according to their credit status. Only nodes with higher reputation WV have the right to participate in the selection process. The weight value of the malicious node is λ, RN is the number of times to reject requests from other nodes, λ becomes larger as the proportion of malicious nodes increases, $(0 < \lambda < 0.05)$ is the penalty factor, if the master node is malicious, special treatment will be performed Direct loss of all PR values of the master node, $WV_{bad} = (1 - \lambda * RN^2) * PR(p_i)_{bad}$ is the weight value WV_{bad} node of the malicious node.

At the same time, the total PR value lost by itself is distributed to other nodes in proportion to punish the node for its evil behavior. These are distributed as rewards to normal nodes, and each normal node obtains the corresponding amount of rewards according to the proportion. $reward = \frac{PR(p_i)_{good}}{\sum PR(p_i)_{good}} * \lambda * RN^2 *$ $PR(p_i)_{bad}$ is for each normal node to get reward normal node to get reward.

The weight value of a normal node is WV_{good}, $(0 < \mu < \lambda)$ is the reward factor, RE is the number of normal and correct responses to other nodes' requests, and the final weight value $WV_{good} = (1 + \mu * RE) * PR(p_i)_{good} + reward$.

If master node is evil, WV and PR values are cleared. PR value slowly rises if node behaves well again. Frequent malicious behavior affects PR value long-term. Evil master node's PR value is distributed as a reward to other nodes. View replacement protocol initiates, selecting new master node based on highest WV. New master node broadcasts message and WV value to all replica nodes. Confirmation by other nodes enables receiving client requests for next consensus round. VRF increases unpredictability of master node selection. 20% of consensus nodes isolated, randomly selected from remaining 80% with higher weight values. Reduces master node attack possibility and excludes Byzantine nodes from candidates.

Verifiable Random Function Design. In VPBFT, nodes are classified into master nodes, replica nodes, and isolated nodes. The master node uses the weight value WV obtained by calculating PR based on the credit evaluation mechanism in the previous section as the node weight. On this basis, the VRF lottery algorithm is used to draw lots, which is independently performed by all nodes with the top 80% weight value in the network Draw lots, all consensus nodes including isolated nodes participate in the consensus. VRF scheme design is mainly composed of $GenerateKey$, $Evaluate$, $Verify$:

1) Key generation function $GenerateKey() \rightarrow (pk, sk)$: This scheme generates a public-private key pair (pk, sk), where pk is the public key and sk is the private key.

2) Random number and proof generation function $Evaluate(SK, m) \rightarrow (vrf\_random, proof)$: the input is the private key sk and the message m, and the output is the pseudo-random string vrf_random and the $proof$.

3) Verification function $Verify(pk, m, vrf\_random, proof) \rightarrow true/false$: the input is the public key pk, message m, pseudo-random string vrf_random and $proof$, and the output is $True$ or $False$, which is used to verify the pseudo-random number Whether generated by the given message and public key.

The VRF lottery algorithm flow is shown in Algorithm 2. Set an expected value σ, node i obtains the hash value vrf_random evenly distributed in the interval $[0, 2^{randomlen}]$, $randomlen$ is the bit length of vrf_random, and takes $e = vrf\_random/2^{randomlen}$.

According to the probability $\mu = \sigma/MV\_Sum$ and the weight value MV_i of the node, calculate the probability that node i succeeds k times in MV_i Bernoulli trials with probability μ, denoted as $B(k; MV_i, \mu)$. Sum the values of k from 0 to j, and find the value of j when e falls within the interval I, and $I = [\sum_{k=0}^{j} B(k; MV_i, \mu), \sum_{k=0}^{j+1} B(k; MV_i, \mu)]$. $B(k; MV_i, \mu) = \binom{w}{k} \mu^k (1-\mu)^{MV_i-k}$ is the binomial distribution followed by the probability of selecting exactly k child nodes from the node with weight MV_i, which satisfies $\sum_{k=0}^{MV_i} B(k; MV_i, \mu) = 1$. The j that meets the conditions is the lottery result of node i. When $j = 0$, it means that the lottery of node i failed, and $j > 0$ means that the lottery is successful. The encrypted lottery algorithm is shown in Algorithm 2:

Algorithm 2: VRF encrypted lottery algorithm

Data: Node private key SK_i, message m, the node weight value of the lottery
node MV_i, the weight value of the nodes participating in the consensus is
the top 80% sum MV_Sum, expectations σ

Result: node draw value j, verifiable random number vrf_random, $proof$

$vrf\_random, proof \leftarrow Evaluate(SK, m)$ //Computing pseudorandom
numbers and zero-knowledge proofs;

$e \leftarrow vrf\_random/2^{randomlen}$;

$\mu \leftarrow \sigma/MV\_Sum$;

$j \leftarrow 0$;

while $e < \sum_{k=0}^{j} B(k; MV_i, \mu)$ //draw **do**

| j++;

end

return $vrf\_random, proof, j$ //return results

During each round of consensus, we need a randomly changing message m as
the input parameter of $Evaluate()$, which can be used as a seed to make each
node generate a different random number, and avoid selecting the same node
every time. If the last generated block was Bk, we update the message m in
view v with the hash of block Bk. The initial m is generated using distributed
random numbers, and the $m_v, proof\_m = Evaluate(SK_i, m_{v-1}\|v)$. The verifi-
cation phase is shown in the Algorithm 3.

Algorithm 3: VRF Verification Algorithm

Data: The public key of the node to be verified PK_i, message m, expectations
σ, the node weight value of the lottery node MV_i, The weight value of
the nodes participating in the consensus is the top 80%sum MV_Sum,
Random number to be verified vrf_{random}, $proof$, The lottery value of
the node to be verified j

Result: Validation results $result$, the value is $true/false$

$result \leftarrow true$;

if $Verify(PK_i, m, vrf\_random, proof)$ **then**

| $result \leftarrow true$;   //verify nonce

$e \leftarrow vrf\_random/2^{randomlen}$;

$\mu \leftarrow \sigma/MV\_Sum$;

$j' \leftarrow 0$;

while $e < \sum_{k=0}^{j} B(k; MV_i, \mu)$ **do**

| j'++;

end

if $j \neq j'$ **then**

| $result \leftarrow false$;   //verify draw value

return $result$ //return results

VPBFT Consensus Process. The VPBFT consensus process is mainly divided into five stages: request, pre-prepare, prepare, commit, and reply [18], as shown in Fig. 2:

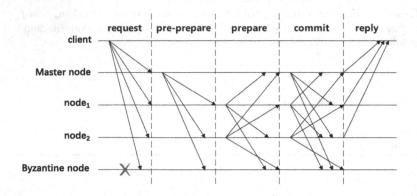

Fig. 2. VPBFT Algorithm process

Request: Client c initiates a request to all nodes. In the initial stage, the PR value of each node is $1/N$. The specific format of the request is as follows: $< REQUEST, o, t, c >_{\sigma c, sk}$, o represents operation, t represents timestamp, c Indicates the client number, σc indicates that client c signs the information, sk is the private key of client c.

Pre-prepare: In order to ensure that all normal nodes maintain a consistent state, the master node p first generates a new block, then calculates the hash value of the block and signs it. The master sends the block to the network, assigns a sequence number to the request, and sends the block's hash value and signature to other nodes. After other nodes receive the message, they regard it as a block proposal and verify it. The verification includes checking whether the block is legal, whether the hash value of the block is the same as the hash value sent by the master node, and whether the signature of the master node is legal. If it is correct, assign a unique sequence number n to the request, and then broadcast a pre-prepare message to other replica nodes in the following format: $<< PREPREPARE, v, w, n, d, s >_{\sigma p}, m >$, where, v is the sequence number of the current view, w represents the weight value calculated by the node PageRank value and credit, n is the sequence number allocated by the master node for the request, d is the hash value obtained by summarizing the request set by the request information m, which is used to prevent The request was tampered with. m represents the request information of the client, σp is the signature of the master node, and s is the lottery data, including $vrf_r andom$, $proof$ and j. Record the PR value of each node. Before malicious nodes appear, the weight value WV=PR value.

Prepare: In the prepare phase, the replica node inserts a pre-prepare message and its own prepare message in the local log, and broadcasts the prepare message to other nodes. The format of the prepare message is as follows:

$< PREPARE, v, w, n, d, i >_{\sigma i}$, Among them, i represents the number of node i, and σi is the signature of node i on the message. When the backup node (including the master node) receives the prepare message from other nodes, it will check the following information: the view number and the view number of the node itself same. n is in the range $[h, H]$. d is the same as the digest in the pre-prepar phase message. If the above checks pass, put this information in the local log. A node is considered prepared(m, v, n, i) if it receives $2f + 1$ (including itself) identical prepare messages [19], and these messages match the m, v, n of the previously received pre-prepare messages put this message in the local log and enter the commit stage. Record the PR value of each node. Before malicious nodes appear, the weight value WV = PR value.

Commit: When the replica node enters the commit phase, it sends a commit message to other nodes (including the master node), the specific format is: $< COMMIT, v, w, n, D(m), i >_{\sigma i}$, where $D(m)$ is m Message digest. After other replica nodes receive the commit message, they start to verify the following information: the signature of node i is correct; the serial number of the view is the same as that of the local view; n is in the range of $[h, H]$. Record the PR value of each node. Before malicious nodes appear, the weight WV = PR value.

Reply: After most replica nodes have submitted the commit message, the backup node will enter the REPLY stage, execute the request and send a response message to the client. Its format is as follows: $< REPLY, v, w, t, c, i, r >_{\sigma i}$, where t is the timestamp requested by the client, the client can judge the result of the request according to the timestamp, w represents the node PageRank value and The weight value obtained by credit calculation, i is the number of the replica node, and r is the response result.

The view replacement protocol consists of three steps as shown in Fig. 3.

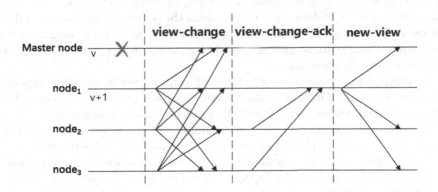

Fig. 3. VPBFT View Replacement Protocol

view-change: When the replica node thinks that there is a problem with the master node, it will send a view change message to other nodes, sort the weight values in the past period of time, and select the top 80% consensus nodes with higher weight values as the master node's candidate nodes, use VRF to randomly select from them, and the format is as follows: $< VIEW - CHANGE, v + 1, n, w, C, P, i >_{\sigma i, sk}$. Among them, $v+1$ is the number of the next representation, n is the number of the last stable checkpoint saved by the node, w represents the weight value calculated by the node PageRank value and credit, and C is the number containing $2f + 1$ correct checkpoint information Set, that is, the checkpoint is a stable checkpoint, P and each element Pm in the set is a set, sk is the private key of client c, and each Pm contains a pre-prepare message with a sequence number greater than n and $2f$ The prepare message matches.

view-change-ack: When a node receives the view-change message from $f + 1$ different nodes, it will consider that the view has entered the view-change state, and broadcast its own view-change-ack message to other nodes, which contains its own number, The number of the confirmed candidate master node, the WV value of the confirmed candidate master node and other information.

new-view: The new master node receives $2f$ view-change messages, proving that view-change is valid, and broadcasts new-view messages. The message format is: $< NEW - VIEW, v + 1, V, O, w >_{\sigma p, sk}$, where V includes $2f + 1$ (including the new primary node) view-change messages, and w represents the node PageRank value and credit calculation The obtained weight value, O is a collection of pre-prepare messages, and then the master node inserts the information in O into the log.

4   Consortium Blockchain Based on VPBFT

This paper adopts the blockchain distributed architecture, and the monitoring platform for the production and manufacturing process of power transmission and distribution equipment is realized by using the consortium Blockchain. The model is shown in Fig. 4, including data layer, network layer, business layer and application layer. The data source comes from the power transmission and distribution equipment product information obtained by spare parts manufacturers, raw material quality inspection manufacturers, manufacturers, retailers, logistics companies, etc. in the alliance.

Runtime environment: docker in Linux. The data layer includes two types: on-chain and off-chain. Off-chain data storage and caching use MySQL and Redis. On-chain data is stored using CouchDB to record product status data.

The underlying network of the consortium blockchain is based on Hyperledger Fabric 1.2 [20]. Smart contracts are used to automate the device production process and upload data onto the chain. The VPBFT consensus algorithm ensures data consistency among nodes in the consortium blockchain network.

The blockchain governance layer manages the consortium blockchain network. Node management then handles registration, deregistration, and authentication. As for smart contract management deploying and maintaining smart contracts. The data upload module uploads the production and operation data of the equipment. The data query module provides an API interface for data query on the chain. The business and application layers facilitate user interaction. Manufacturers, sellers, logistics companies, etc., enter relevant information

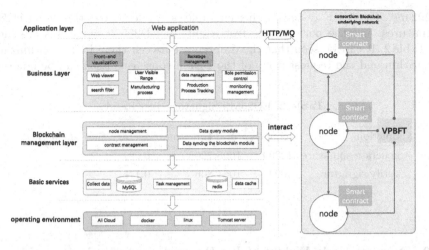

Fig. 4. Consortium chain implementation scheme for supervision of power transmission and distribution equipment based on VPBFT

into the chain. Users and regulators can use the smart contract interface to query manufacturing process information. Physical IDs are used by electrical assemblers and consumers to access complete product information. These components combine to enable lifecycle traceability, governance, and secure data sharing between users.

5 Experiment

5.1 VRF Generate and Verify Performance Analysis

From the overall process, VPBFT uses a verifiable random function to select the primary node, which may have an impact on the latency of VPBFT. In order to test the effect of VRF on VPBF, this paper tested its performance. The performance test results of VRF are shown in Table 1.

Table 1. VRF performance test results

function	requests	total time (ms)	average time spent (ms)
generate key	12000	1095.661	0.091
generating nonce and proof	1200	1004.944	0.837
verify nonce and proof	800	1033.319	1.292

The test results show that key generation takes an average of 0.091 ms, while the longest time is spent on random number and proof verification, which is only

1.292 ms. The VRF tested in this example is implemented through ED25519 signatures, and the performance test results of ED25519 signatures are shown in Table 2. It can be seen that the difference between the VPBFT optimization algorithm and the request delay of the PBFT consensus itself can be ignored.

Table 2. ED25519 Signature Test Results

function	requests	total time (ms)	average time spent (ms)
generate signature	12000	1098.726	0.091
verify signature	6000	1051.806	0.175

5.2   Normal Node Weight Value Proportion Analysis

In order to effectively increase the total weight value of ordinary nodes with VPBFT, a simulation experiment was conducted to observe the ratio of normal nodes to the total weight value under different numbers of Byzantine nodes in the VPBFT algorithm and PBFT consensus algorithm among 50 nodes. The experimental results are shown in Fig. 5.

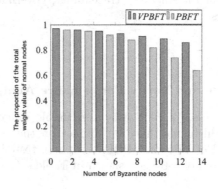

Fig. 5. Comparison of the proportion of the total weight value of normal nodes in Algorithm PBFT and Algorithm VPBFT

Although the VPBFT algorithm did not significantly increase the total weight of normal nodes in the presence of a small number of malicious nodes, the simulation experiment showed that as the number of malicious nodes increased, the VPBFT algorithm increasingly improved the proportion of the total weight of normal nodes.

5.3   Throughput Analysis

In order to test and compare the throughput of the PBFT algorithm and the VPBFT algorithm, multiple experiments were conducted both with no Byzantine nodes and with f Byzantine nodes satisfying the condition $n \geq 3f + 1$. The experimental results are shown in Fig. 6 and 7.

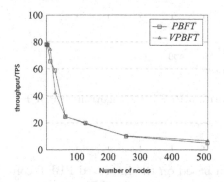

Fig. 6. Throughput comparison when the number of Byzantine nodes is 0

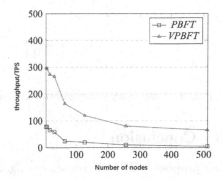

Fig. 7. Throughput comparison when the number of Byzantine nodes is not 0

It can be seen that in the presence of Byzantine nodes, VPBFT algorithm has a higher throughput than PBFT in different numbers of nodes. This is because VPBFT selects nodes that are more trustworthy and reliable to participate in the consensus.

5.4   Consensus Latency Analysis

Consensus latency refers to the time required to achieve consensus in a distributed system. The size of the consensus latency directly affects the performance and scalability of the system. The experiment tested the transaction latency during the consensus process in two cases, whether the number of Byzantine nodes was 0 or not. The comparison of the two algorithms is shown in Fig. 8.

As the number of nodes increases, the latency of both algorithms increases. When the number of Byzantine nodes is 0, the difference in latency between PBFT and VPBFT algorithms is very small. When the number of Byzantine nodes is not 0, the increase in latency of VPBFT is not significant, while the latency of PBFT increases rapidly. This is because in VPBFT, the weight of Byzantine nodes that perform malicious actions is reduced, making it difficult for them to participate in the selection of the primary node, reducing the probability of consensus failure and achieving consensus more quickly.

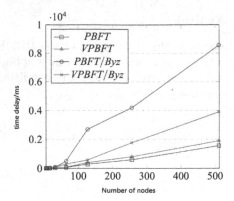

Fig. 8. Time delay comparison between algorithm PBFT and algorithm VPBFT

6 Conclusion

We propose a VPBFT consensus algorithm based on the improved PBFT consensus algorithm using verifiable random function and weighted PageRank algorithm. Experimental results show that compared to PBFT, VPBFT has higher throughput and lower latency. Furthermore, we apply the VPBFT algorithm to a production and manufacturing process supervision platform for distribution equipment based on a consortium blockchain, achieving real-time on-chain data and supervision traceability during production and flow processes.

However, we acknowledge that there are limitations in the calculation of node weights in our proposed VPBFT algorithm. We only consider the number of times a node is selected but do not take into account factors such as node performance and load. In future work, we plan to incorporate these factors into the calculation of node weights to better reflect their contribution.

Acknowledgments. This research is founded by the National Key R&D Program of China (No. 2020YFB1006002).

References

1. Zheng, Z., Xie, S., Dai, H.N., Chen, X., Wang, H.: Blockchain challenges and opportunities: a survey. Int. J. Web Grid Serv. **14**(4), 352–375 (2018)
2. Wang, T.Y., Chen, Z.S., He, P., Govindan, K., Skibniewski, M.J.: Alliance strategy in an online retailing supply chain: motivation, choice, and equilibrium. Omega **115**, 102791 (2023)
3. Christensen, T.J., Snyder, J.: Chain gangs and passed bucks: predicting alliance patterns in multipolarity. Int. Organ. **44**(2), 137–168 (1990)
4. Jung, J.J.: Service chain-based business alliance formation in service-oriented architecture. Expert Syst. Appl. **38**(3), 2206–2211 (2011)
5. Hua, Z., Fei, L., Jing, X.: An improved risk prioritization method for propulsion system based on heterogeneous information and PageRank algorithm. Expert Syst. Appl. **212**, 118798 (2023)

6. Castro, M., Liskov, B.: Practical byzantine fault tolerance. In: OsDI, vol. 99, pp. 173–186 (1999)
7. Xu, X., Sun, G., Yu, H.: An efficient blockchain PBFT consensus protocol in energy constrained IoT applications. In: 2021 International Conference on UK-China Emerging Technologies (UCET), pp. 152–157. IEEE (2021)
8. Micali, S., Rabin, M., Vadhan, S.: Verifiable random functions. In: 40th annual Symposium on Foundations of Computer Science (Cat. No. 99CB37039), pp. 120–130. IEEE (1999)
9. Huang, B., Peng, L., Zhao, W., Chen, N.: Workload-based randomization byzantine fault tolerance consensus protocol. High-Confidence Comput. **2**(3), 100070 (2022)
10. Gilad, Y., Hemo, R., Micali, S., Vlachos, G., Zeldovich, N.: Algorand: scaling byzantine agreements for cryptocurrencies. In: Proceedings of the 26th Symposium on Operating Systems Principles, pp. 51–68 (2017)
11. Leung, D., Suhl, A., Gilad, Y., Zeldovich, N.: Vault: fast bootstrapping for the algorand cryptocurrency. Cryptology ePrint Archive (2018)
12. Goldreich, O., Goldwasser, S., Micali, S.: How to construct random functions. J. ACM (JACM) **33**(4), 792–807 (1986)
13. Goldwasser, S., Micali, S., Rackoff, C.: The knowledge complexity of interactive proof-systems. In: Providing Sound Foundations for Cryptography: On the Work of Shafi Goldwasser and Silvio Micali, pp. 203–225 (2019)
14. Li, Z., Barenji, A.V., Huang, G.Q.: Toward a blockchain cloud manufacturing system as a peer to peer distributed network platform. Robot. Comput. Integr. Manuf. **54**, 133–144 (2018)
15. Assaqty, M.I.S., et al.: Private-blockchain-based industrial IoT for material and product tracking in smart manufacturing. IEEE Netw. **34**(5), 91–97 (2020)
16. Mohaghegh, M., Sakhardande, R.: A decentralised registry for firearm tracking using blockchain technology. In: 2020 5th International Conference on Innovative Technologies in Intelligent Systems and Industrial Applications (CITISIA), pp. 1–8. IEEE (2020)
17. Saraiva, R., Araújo, A.A., Soares, P., Souza, J.: MIRIAM: a blockchain-based web application for managing professional registrations of medical doctors in Brazil. In: 2021 IEEE International Conference on Blockchain and Cryptocurrency (ICBC), pp. 1–2. IEEE (2021)
18. Xie, M., Liu, J., Chen, S., Xu, G., Lin, M.: Primary node election based on probabilistic linguistic term set with confidence interval in the PBFT consensus mechanism for blockchain. Complex Intell. Syst. **9**, 1507–1524 (2022)
19. Lamport, L., Shostak, R., Pease, M.: The byzantine generals problem. In: Concurrency: The Works of Leslie Lamport, pp. 203–226 (2019)
20. Androulaki, E., et al.: Hyperledger fabric: a distributed operating system for permissioned blockchains. In: Proceedings of the Thirteenth EuroSys Conference, pp. 1–15 (2018)

Consensusless Blockchain: A Promising High-Performance Blockchain Without Consensus

Jian Zheng[1], Qing Wang[2], Jianru Lin[3], Huawei Huang[4(✉)] (iD), and Chunhua Su[1]

[1] Department of Computer Science and Engineering,
University of Aizu, Aizu 9650006, Japan
zhengj79@mail3.sysu.edu.cn, chsu@u-aizu.ac.jp
[2] School of Computer Science and Engineering, Sun Yat-sen University,
Guangzhou 510006, China
wangq79@mail.sysu.edu.cn
[3] Humi Technology Co., Ltd., Hainan 570000, China
jianru.lin@gmail.com
[4] School of Software Engineering, Sun Yat-sen University, Zhuhai 519000, China
huanghw28@mail.sysu.edu.cn

Abstract. Consensus is unnecessary when the truth is available. In this paper, we present a new perspective of rebuilding the blockchain without consensus. When the consensus phase is eliminated from a blockchain, transactions could be canonized quickly using a well-defined universal rule without consuming hashing power. Thus, the *transactions per second* (TPS) metric of such the consensusless blockchain can be largely boosted. Although consensus blockchain is promising, several technical challenges are also crucial. For example, double-spending attacks and frequent forking events must be prevented, the credit of block's minting must be carefully defined, and etc. To address those technical challenges, we propose several solutions for our consensusless blockchain (CB), including a naive monotonic scoring mechanism to calculate the ranking of each block in the chain, and a two-stage witness mechanism to add new blocks. The proposed CB chain is promising to offer a simplified and equipment-cheap infrastructure for rich real-world decentralized applications.

Keywords: Blockchain · Consensus · Consensusless · High-Performance · Blockchain Security

1 Introduction

Although Bitcoin's proof-of-work (PoW) [17] secures the transactions stored in historical blocks, it also induces extensive criticisms. The most representative criticisms include its low TPS and the extraordinary amount of energy consumption spending on mining new blocks. The Bitcoin's low TPS is induced by PoW consensus, in which miners compete with each other to win the opportunity

© The Author(s), under exclusive license to Springer Nature Singapore Pte Ltd. 2024
J. Chen et al. (Eds.): BlockSys 2023, CCIS 1897, pp. 252–265, 2024.
https://doi.org/10.1007/978-981-99-8104-5_19

of minting a new block in each round. The length expectation of each round of consensus is fixed to around 10 min. Even though such difficulty-defined mining cycle prevents frequent forking events, it also decides Bitcoin's TPS as low as 7–10. The other shortcoming of Bitcoin's blockchain is that the PoW consensus has kept encouraging miners to upgrade their hashing capability. From CPU to ASIC-assisted mining, enterprises have developed various off-the-shelf mining hardware. For example, Nvidia's GPU cards have offered full power of crypto mining. The worldwide large-scale crypto mining consumes a countless amount of energy power.

Besides the PoW-based consensus protocols and its variants [2], other popular consensus protocols have been proposed such as Proof of Stake (PoS) [1]. Although PoS or Delegated PoS (DPoS) mechanisms are believed as environmental friendly, some argue that people who pledge large amounts of coins may have a huge influence on the consensus process, and thus affecting the decentralization of a blockchain.

Given the criticisms aforementioned, various advanced consensus mechanisms [1,5,9,10,13,21] have been proposed. In those consensus protocols, either transaction throughput is improved or transaction latency is reduced. However, those studies are basically following the direction of Proof-based consensus like Bitcoin's PoW. In contrast, we argue that consensus is unnecessary if we know the truth of how to resolve conflicts about all transactions and blocks. We can setup such a truth or a universal rule in a consensusless blockchain's protocol, and then the double spending problem can be tackled with a message delivery-guaranteed method instead of a complex Proof-based consensus protocol. That means if we design a blockchain in the consensusless way, a bunch of Proof-based consensus protocols such as PoW and its variants [2,9,21], Proof of Stake [1,5,8], and byzantine consensus [10], can be dropped. Previous research has demonstrated the theoretical possibility of consensusless blockchains [12].

Without consensus, TPS can be largely boosted. This is because every block node can propose new blocks frequently in a parallel way. Those new blocks are added to the chain and do not have to experience a long consensus process.

Although Solana [22] already provides a good TPS as high as 10 thousands, it still exploits consensus protocols such as proof-of-history and DPoS. Thus, the consensus of Solana is computing-intensive. Recently, the crypto participants are talking about the frequent outages of Solana. For example, the most recent outage of Solana was occurred on May 1st. In this outage, the Solana's blockchain was down and last for 7 h due to the decentralized denial-of-service attacks from NFT mint bots. When Solana's blockchain recovered, the Solana team decided to reject any NFT minting bots. Many cryptocurrency players expressed their worries about this blasphemous censorship, which severely damages the decentralization of crypto and blockchain world.

In contrast, our proposed CB chain uses simpler and cheaper solutions than the existing blockchains. Furthermore, our CB chain does not have a centralized censorship that degrades the spirit of decentralized world. The proposed CB chain is promising to offer a green and high-performance infrastructure to various decentralized applications (DApps) in the era of Web3.

2 Related Work

The history of blockchain in the last decade has been marked by the continued development and adoption of new consensus mechanisms.

Proof-of-work (PoW) is the earliest and most widely used blockchain consensus. PoW is a consensus algorithm that was first proposed in 1993 by Cynthia Dwork and Moni Naor as a means of combating spam emails [7]. The basic idea behind PoW is that it requires computational effort to solve a mathematical puzzle, which can be verified by the network. In 2009, Bitcoin was created as the first cryptocurrency, and it used PoW as its consensus mechanism [17]. The process of mining in Bitcoin involves solving a complex mathematical puzzle to create a new block, and the first miner to solve the puzzle is rewarded with newly minted Bitcoins and transaction fees. This process helps to secure the network and prevent malicious actors from making unauthorized changes to the blockchain.

Proof of Stake (PoS) was first proposed in a whitepaper by Sunny King and Scott Nadal in 2012 as an alternative to the energy-intensive Proof of Work (PoW) algorithm used by Bitcoin [14]. In PoS, validators are chosen to validate transactions based on the number of coins they hold, rather than computational power. In 2014 Peercoin becomes the first cryptocurrency to implement PoS [20].

Practical Byzantine Fault Tolerance (PBFT) algorithm dates back to the late 1990s when its concept was first proposed by Miguel Castro and Barbara Liskov [4]. The PBFT algorithm was designed to solve the problem of Byzantine fault tolerance in distributed systems, where malicious nodes can cause the system to fail.

In addition to these consensus mechanisms, the use of sharding has also become increasingly popular in recent years, as a way to improve the scalability of blockchain networks. Sharding allows for the parallel processing of transactions, resulting in faster and more efficient validation. Elastico [16] proposed the first sharded blockchain, however, only achieves network sharding.

Overall, the last decade has seen a continued evolution of blockchain consensus mechanisms, with new innovations aimed at improving the efficiency, security, and scalability of blockchain networks.

3 Transactions

The proposed consensusless blockchain does not specify a particular transaction model. System designer can choose either the account model that is similar to Ethereum [3] or the UTXO model adopted by Bitcoin [17]. In CB chain, smart contracts are supportable, and transactions could be compatible with multiple inputs and multiple outputs.

For different account models, CB chain adopts different ways to defend against double-spending attacks. CB chain has only one valid main chain. Although sometimes forks may occur, there is only one valid block at any height in the long run. Work nodes (i.e., block proposers) can verify transaction's validity by replaying all transactions storing on the entire blockchain starting from the genesis block. For the account-based model, double-spending attacks are defended by observing whether the `nonce` of two transactions are the same. For the UTXO model, double-spending attacks can be defended by verifying whether the UTXO of a transaction has been spent in another previous transaction.

4   A Universal Rule: Ensuring the Truth of All Transactions

The universe rule is set to ensure that any honest work node maintains only a single valid chain at any time. To achieve this goal, we need to provide two basic mechanisms, i.e., *Block Scoring* and *Fork Handling*.

4.1   Block Scoring Mechanism

When there are two or more blocks at the same height, the block scoring mechanism can quickly help work nodes make a choice.

In the long run, a blockchain with only one valid chain will end up with only one block at each height. However, due to network latency, it is easy to have multiple blocks of the same height at the latest height. Work nodes need to choose one of several branches to follow. For Bitcoin, which uses the longest chain rule, the choice among multiple blocks of the same height relies on the number of following blocks. However, when the fork happens to be at the lastest height, work nodes have to wait for a following block to be generated. Before that, the worker nodes in the network would be confused by the fork. Their hashpower might be devided into different branch of forks. If there is a new fork in the next block, the distribution of computing power will become much more serious. This situation is detrimental to the security of the blockchain. Many fork attacks take advantage of this. Many fork attacks take advantage of this situation and pose a serious threat to the security of the blockchain [11,18].

According to the above analysis, we found that forks will naturally occur in the blockchain, and it is also related to the block generation speed and network delay. Bitcoin adopts a difficulty adjustment mechanism to maintain the block generation interval at about 10 min. Obviously, when the block generation interval is much longer than the network delay of block propagation, the new block has sufficient time to be transmitted to the entire network, thereby reducing the probability of fork occurrence. However, when the number of transactions contained in a block is the same, the larger the block generation interval, the lower the throughput of the blockchain system. So we designed the Block Scoring Mechanism. The block scoring mechanism no longer needs to rely on the generation of following blocks, but only relies on comparing blocks at the same height on different fork branches, so that work nodes can make consistent judgments even if the order of receiving blocks is different.

Parameter `block_score` is defined to evaluate the priority among the blocks at the same height. A block's `block_score` can be calculated by a naive monotonic function using both the inputs and outputs of all the transactions packaged in the block. The block with lowest `block_score` wins when two blocks are conflict with each other at the same height as shown in Fig. 1.

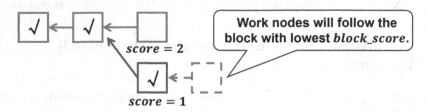

Fig. 1. Block Scoring Mechanism uses `block_score` to compare the priority of the blocks that are conflict with each other at the same height.

4.2   Fork Handling

Next we discuss *how to address two conflict blocks* at the same height when a fork forms.

Only using the block scoring mechanism does not guarantee the stability of the blockchain system. We can consider the following situation: when the block height reaches 1000, a new block with a smaller score at the height of 2 is generated, what will worker nodes do? According to the setting of the block scoring mechanism, work nodes will switch to the new block with a height of 2 follow the new block to generate the new block. This situation is similar to the "Long-Range attack" of PoS [6]. Obviously this situation is detrimental to the stability of the blockchain system. In consideration of these issues, we designed the following scheme.

We first define n_c as the number of confirmations when a newly proposed block is admitted by the entire blockchain network. When a fork appears in the CB chain, we let n_l denote the number of blocks in the longer fork branch. When $n_l \geq n_c$, work nodes must ignore the shorter branch as shown in Fig. 2. When $n_l < n_c$, work nodes must calculate `block_score` of the first blocks in two branches and choose to follow the branch whose first block has the lower `block_score`, as shown in Fig. 3. If work nodes choose to switch to the new branch of the fork, work nodes will broadcast a `fork-win` message to speed up the spread of the new branch.

The setting of n_c in a consensusless blockchain has many benefits. First of all, n_c avoids the damage of the generation of a block with a lower score at a very low block height, which may cause many blocks to be rolled back. n_c prevents attackers from using the block scoring mechanism to cause double-spending attacks or hinder the execution of normal transactions. Secondly, n_c provides a basis for the work nodes in the blockchain to judge whether a transaction is officially on the chain. Work nodes can consider that a block with n_c following blocks has been

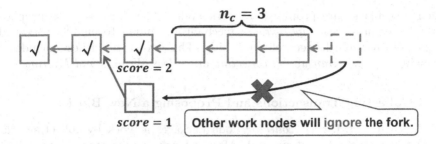

Fig. 2. When $n_l \geq n_c$, work nodes need to ignore the new fork branch no matter what the `block_score` of the first block is in the fork branch.

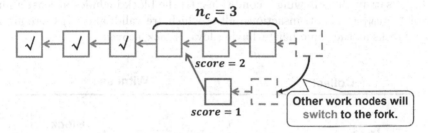

Fig. 3. When $n_l < n_c$, work nodes need to compare `block_score` of the first blocks in two branches.

confirmed on the chain, which provides a clear reference for the confirmation of transactions in the blockchain.

It is necessary to set a reasonable value for n_c. On the one hand, the value of n_c should not be too large, because in the case of the same block generation interval, the larger n_c, the greater the transaction confirmation delay, which will have a negative impact on the application of the blockchain. On the other hand the value of n_c should not be too small. Considering the block propagation delay in the actual blockchain network, there may be a hard fork. We can consider such a situation: two blocks of the same height are propagated in the network at the same time, and the block with a larger score is first received by a work node, and the block with a relatively larger score generates n_c A new area is fast. At this time, the block with a smaller score arrives at the work node, and the work node will not accept the block with a smaller score. If most of the work nodes in the network accept blocks with a smaller score, then this will cause a hard fork between the blockchain maintained by this work node and the blockchain maintained by other work nodes. Therefore, it is necessary to set a reasonable n_c according to the block generation interval, network delay and other factors.

5   Two-Stage Witness

When network latency is extremely low, the universal rule depicted in previous section is guaranteed. However, the inevitable network latency brings dynamics when new blocks are proposed by work nodes. Therefore, we also propose a carefully defined *two-stage witness* mechanism, aiming to enable work nodes to propose new blocks securely and fairly. This two-stage witness includes the following 2 stages: *transaction collecting* and *Block Witness and Minting*.

5.1   Collecting Transactions and Proposing a New Block

As shown in Fig. 4, each *collector* node packages a block by collecting transactions from the transaction pool. After a block is generated, every collector node can propose a new valid block following the previously-witnessed block and broadcast the new block to the blockchain network. A valid block proposal needs to satisfy the following 2 conditions: (i) the block includes at least a number of TX_{COUNT} ($\in \mathbb{N}_+$) transactions, all of which are valid; and (ii) there are not other blocks at the same height having lower block_scores.

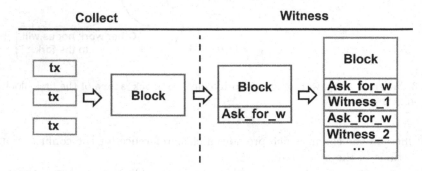

Fig. 4. The proposed *Two-Stage Witness*. We design a function Ask_for_w, aiming to allow a block's proposer to ask for endorsements (i.e., witness) from other witness nodes.

5.2   Block Witness and Minting

Work nodes continuously monitor the network. In each round of witness, each work node generates a new block by packaging valid transactions. Then, the work node broadcasts the new block and waits for a specified number of witness signed by other witness nodes.

Every valid block must be verified by a number m of witness signatures before it is added as a valid block in the chain. For any valid block, we say a witness event is successful if the following condition is satisfied.

$$\text{DistanceFunc}(\text{PK}_{\text{node}}, \text{PK}_{\text{witness}}) < \text{THRESHOLD}_{\text{witness}}, \tag{1}$$

where the DistanceFunc(PK_{node}, $\text{PK}_{\text{witness}}$) is a function used to select the qualified other witness nodes who can sign witness in a newly proposed block.

The parameters PK_{node} and $PK_{witness}$ are the public keys of the proposer node and the witness node who provides a `witness`, respectively. Parameter $THRESHOLD_{witness}$ is the customized maximum distance describing the relationship between the proposer node and another witness node who can provide a `witness` signature. Thus, `DistanceFunc(.)` makes the block minting difficult. When a new block receives a specified number m of `witness` signatures from witness nodes, the block will be accepted by the entire blockchain network and other honest work nodes will follow it. As shown in Fig. 5, when a valid witnessed block receives a number n_c of subsequent following blocks, we say that this block is eventually confirmed by the CB chain.

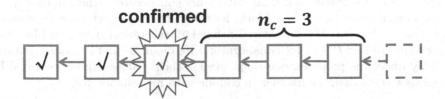

Fig. 5. When a valid witnessed block receives a number of n_c (*e.g.*, 3) subsequent following blocks, this block is eventually confirmed.

Witness has many benefits for Consensusless Blockchain. First of all, the generation of each block requires the participation of witness nodes. The selection of witness nodes is random and unpredictable, which means that it is hard for any node to complete the whole block generation procerss independently. Therefore, CB Chian can defend against various attack based on block withholding [15, 19,23]. Secondly, the specified number m of `witness` signatures from witness nodes can be reasonably set according to the network environment where the CB Chain is located. m affects the block generation interval. When the number of transactions contained in the block is the same, the block generation interval is too large to reduce the throughput of the blockchain. If the block generation interval is too small, the frequency of fork in the network will increase and the security of the blockchain will decrease. m can provide blockchain designers with a suitable parameter so that CB Chain can reach a balance between throughput and security.

6   Incentive

We deliberately decouple the incentive layer from CB chain to make the incentive mechanism neutral. Any particular incentive mechanism can be plugged into CB via the block mint hooks like the mechanism called `before_block_mint` and `after_bolck_mint`, which will be executed by the minter before or after a block's minting, respectively. For example, a Bitcoin-alike incentive method can be plugged in, by adding `coinbase` reward transactions for the collector and witnesses into the minting block in the `before_block_mint` hook. By extracting the incentive logic from the blockchain-maintenance logic, we can use CB with any economic model, even run different economic models on the same CB chain simultaneously.

We disclose more insights under the Bitcoin-alike incentive mode. Such the incentive is used to encourage collector nodes to propose new blocks. The difference is that the `coinbase` reward of CB chain is awarded to the proposer whose proposed new block has received the sufficient number of `witness` signatures. The incentive also includes the subsidy paying to the collaborators who offer `witness` signatures for any newly proposed block. The incentive helps encourage work nodes to stay honest and be willing to offer `witness` signatures for others. If a greedy attacker is able to collude with other collaborators who can offer quick `witness` signatures for his new block, he would have to select his collaborators out of all work nodes. Due to the well-defined `DistanceFunc(.)`, it would be time-consuming to find the target collaborators. He ought to find it more profitable to play under the proposed *two-stage witness* such that he can be rewarded by more new coins than the manner to collude with his collaborators.

7   Calculations

7.1   Security Analysis of Witnessing an Adversarial Block

To avoid Sybil attacks, every work node needs to pledge a certain amount of assets before participating the CB network. Let q ($\in [0,1]$) represent the proportion of adversarial nodes. Considering that the selection of witness nodes is random, the probability that a qualified witness is in fact an adversarial node is also q. That is,

$$Pr(a\ qualified\ witness\ node\ is\ an\ adversarial\ node) = q. \qquad (2)$$

We then consider an extreme adversarial case, in which an invalid block is witnessed by all adversarial collaborator nodes. The probability of such extreme case is q^m, i.e.,

$$Pr(an\ invalid\ block\ is\ witnessed) = q^m. \qquad (3)$$

Equation 3 indicates that an invalid block is almost impossible to win a successful witness when m is large enough.

7.2   The Safety of CB Chain Versus Message-Delivery Ratio

Hard forks are always undesired in a blockchain. In this part, we analyze the threat to system safety when a permanent hard fork forms. This is because a part of honest work nodes will be misled by the hard fork, when the message-delivery ratio is not high. Once any honest work node is misled by the hard fork, the safety of the blockchain will be weakened.

We then calculate the probability of the situation (denoted by $Pr_{\mathtt{misled}}$) when an honest node is misled by a hard fork. The related parameters include the message-delivery ratio r ($\in (0,1)$), the number of confirmation blocks n_c, the witness configuration parameter m, and the number of fork-win message l. Thus, the probability $Pr_{\mathtt{misled}}$ is written as follows.

$$Pr_{\mathtt{misled}} = (1 - r)^{(m+1)*(n_c+1)*(m+n_c+2)+l}. \tag{4}$$

Insight of Eq. 4: In a perfectly-connected network, the message-delivery ratio can approximate 100%. Even if r is not very high in a real-world blockchain network, Eq. 4 implicates that $Pr_{\mathtt{misled}}$ can be maintained in a very low level by choosing appropriate values of parameters n_c and m. Considering the most conservative design(the number of confirmation blocks n_c is 2 and the witness configuration parameter m is 2), the probability of hard bifurcation of a block from generation to confirmation is less than $1/10^{54}$. Table 1 shows that hard forks are almost impossible to occur naturally.

Table 1. Probability of a hard fork under the same scale of existing blockchains

Blockchain	Height	Time of existence	Probability of a hard fork in CB Chain at the same scale	Expected time for a hard fork in CB Chain
Bitcoin	751789	14 years	$< 1/10^{47}$	$> 10^{47}$ years
Ethereum	15437870	7 years	$< 1/10^{45}$	$> 10^{37}$ years
Solana	148287091	4 years	$< 1/10^{44}$	$> 10^{35}$ years

Considering that the increasing efficiency of modern network systems, the message reaching ratio r is very close to 100%. Even if there is a wide range of fluctuations in the network that causes message reaching ratio r to decrease, given appropriate n_c and m, the probability of hard-fork occurrence is guaranteed to be very low. In the worst situation that a work node suspects that it is on a hard-fork, the work node can also go back to the main chain by rejoining the network.

We conduct a simulation to verify the implication of Eq. 4. When n_c is set to 3 and the exist of fork-win message is ignored, Fig. 6 shows that the probability $Pr_{\mathtt{misled}}$ declines rapidly as the number of witness configuration parameter m increases, under different settings of message-delivery ratio $r \in \{0.6, 0.7, 0.8, 0.9\}$. When r is not high, CB can still obtain a very low $Pr_{\mathtt{misled}}$ by setting a suitable number of confirmation parameter n_c and choosing a suitable parameter m.

7.3   The Thoughput of CB Chain

Throughput is an important indicator of blockchain performance. Throughput is related to many parameters, including the system parameters of the blockchain, the number of pending transactions in the system, and the physical

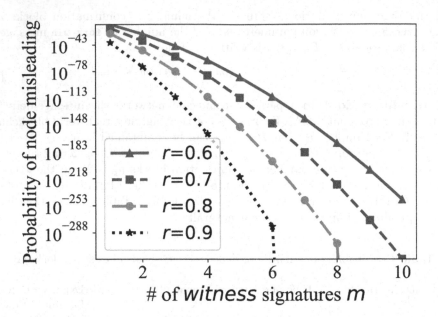

Fig. 6. The probability $Pr_{\texttt{misled}}$ versus parameter m, given different message-delivery ratio r.

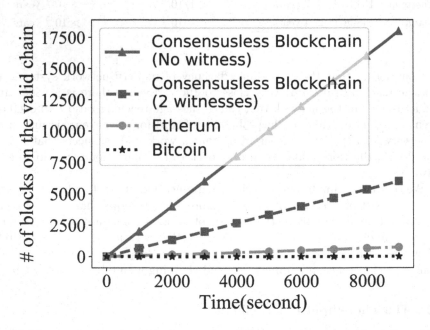

Fig. 7. The total amount of blocks on the valid chain versus time since the genesis block is generated.

network conditions. The throughput of the blockchain is constantly changing. In order to simplify the problem, we only observe the relationship between the number of blocks and the time starting from the genesis block.

We used different block intervals to simulate the block generation of Consensusless Blockchain with $m = 0$ and $m = 2$, Ethereum and Bitcoin. Assuming that the average delay in the network is 500ms (the average ping in most real network will not be so high), then it is considered that when $m = 0$, the block interval of CB Chain is 500ms, and when $m = 2$, the block interval of CB Chain is 1.5 s. The block interval of Ethereum is about 12 s and the block interval of Bitcoin is about 600 s.

As shown in Fig. 7, we can find that even if $m = 2$, the number of blocks generated by CB Chain is far more than that of Ethereum and Bitcoin. This means that the block generation speed of CB Chain is much higher than that of Ethereum and Bitcoin. Assuming that the number of transactions contained in the block is the same, the throughput of CB Chain is much higher than that of Ethereum and Bitcoin. This is because as a high-performance blockchain, CB Chain can set the block interval much smaller than that of Ethereum and Bitcoin, because according to block scoring mechanism and fork handling of CB Chain, work nodes can make consistent judgments on blocks at the same height even if the arriving order of blocks is different. Even if the block generation interval is small, CB Chain will not generate more forks. However for Ethereum and Bitcoin, when the block generation interval is very small, blockchains will generate a large number of forks, which is very harmful to the blockchain security. Therefore, CB Chain can increase throughput by greatly reducing the block generation interval, while Ethereum and Bitcoin are limited by the generation of fork and have to choose a larger block generation interval.

Comparing the number of blocks in CB Chain with different amounts of m in Fig. 7, we found that the larger m is, the more blocks generated by CB Chain. Considering the *two-stage witness* mechanism, larger m means that a block needs to spend more time in the witness step to complete the consensus. larger m means a larger block generation interval and lower throughput. CB Chain does not need m to be a large number. So the existence of m will not have a great negative impact on the throughput of CB Chain, but because of the m CB Chain obtains additional guarantees of security.

8   Conclusion

Consensusless blockchain is a game-changing design that is going to lead a new generation of blockchain protocols in the era of web3. Our proposed CB chain is promising to offer a high-performance trusted infrastructure for both research scenarios and rich real-world decentralized applications.

Acknowledgements. This Work is partially supported by the NSFC (No.62272496), Fundamental Research Funds for the Central Universities, Sun Yat-sen University (No.23lgbj019) and JSPS Grant-in-Aid for Scientific Research (C) 23K11103.

264   J. Zheng et al.

References

1. Bentov, I., Pass, R., Shi, E.: Snow white: provably secure proofs of stake. IACR Cryptology ePrint Archive 2016, 919 (2016)
2. Bhosale, J., Mavale, S.: Volatility of select crypto-currencies: a comparison of bitcoin, ethereum and litecoin. Annu. Res. J. SCMS, Pune **6**, 132–141 (2018)
3. Buterin, V.: A next-generation smart contract and decentralized application platform. White Paper **3**(37), 2–1 (2014)
4. Castro, M., Liskov, B.: Practical byzantine fault tolerance. In: OsDI, vol. 99, pp. 173–186 (1999)
5. David, B., Gaži, P., Kiayias, A., Russell, A.: Ouroboros Praos: an adaptively-secure, semi-synchronous proof-of-stake blockchain. In: Nielsen, J.B., Rijmen, V. (eds.) EUROCRYPT 2018. LNCS, vol. 10821, pp. 66–98. Springer, Cham (2018). https://doi.org/10.1007/978-3-319-78375-8_3
6. Deirmentzoglou, E., Papakyriakopoulos, G., Patsakis, C.: A survey on long-range attacks for proof of stake protocols. IEEE Access **7**, 28712–28725 (2019)
7. Dwork, C., Naor, M.: Pricing via processing or combatting junk mail. In: Brickell, E.F. (ed.) CRYPTO 1992. LNCS, vol. 740, pp. 139–147. Springer, Heidelberg (1993). https://doi.org/10.1007/3-540-48071-4_10
8. Ethereum: casper-proof-of-stake-compendium (2018). https://github.com/ethereum/wiki/wiki/Casper-Proof-of-Stake-compendium
9. Eyal, I., Gencer, A.E., Sirer, E.G., Van Renesse, R.: Bitcoin-NG: a scalable blockchain protocol. In: 13th USENIX Symposium on Networked Systems Design and Implementation (NSDI 2016), pp. 45–59 (2016)
10. Gilad, Y., Hemo, R., Micali, S., Vlachos, G., Zeldovich, N.: Algorand: scaling byzantine agreements for cryptocurrencies. In: Proceedings of the 26th Symposium on Operating Systems Principles, pp. 51–68. ACM (2017)
11. Gramoli, V.: From blockchain consensus back to byzantine consensus. Futur. Gener. Comput. Syst. **107**, 760–769 (2020)
12. Guerraoui, R., Kuznetsov, P., Monti, M., Pavlovič, M., Seredinschi, D.A.: The consensus number of a cryptocurrency. In: Proceedings of the 2019 ACM Symposium on Principles of Distributed Computing, pp. 307–316 (2019)
13. Kiayias, A., Russell, A., David, B., Oliynykov, R.: Ouroboros: a provably secure proof-of-stake blockchain protocol. In: Katz, J., Shacham, H. (eds.) CRYPTO 2017. LNCS, vol. 10401, pp. 357–388. Springer, Cham (2017). https://doi.org/10.1007/978-3-319-63688-7_12
14. King, S., Nadal, S.: PPCoin: peer-to-peer crypto-currency with proof-of-stake. Self-published paper, August 19(1) (2012)
15. Kroll, J.A., Davey, I.C., Felten, E.W.: The economics of bitcoin mining, or bitcoin in the presence of adversaries. In: Proceedings of WEIS, vol. 2013. Citeseer (2013)
16. Luu, L., Narayanan, V., Zheng, C., Baweja, K., Gilbert, S., Saxena, P.: A secure sharding protocol for open blockchains. In: Proceedings of the 2016 ACM SIGSAC Conference on Computer and Communications Security, pp. 17–30 (2016)
17. Nakamoto, S.: Bitcoin: a peer-to-peer electronic cash system. Decentralized Business Review, p. 21260 (2008)
18. Natoli, C., Gramoli, V.: The balance attack or why forkable blockchains are ill-suited for consortium. In: 2017 47th Annual IEEE/IFIP International Conference on Dependable Systems and Networks (DSN), pp. 579–590. IEEE (2017)
19. Nayak, K., Kumar, S., Miller, A., Shi, E.: Stubborn mining: generalizing selfish mining and combining with an eclipse attack. In: 2016 IEEE European Symposium on Security and Privacy (EuroS&P), pp. 305–320. IEEE (2016)

20. Vasin, P.: Blackcoin's proof-of-stake protocol v2, vol. 71 (2014) https://blackcoin. co/blackcoin-pos-protocol-v2-whitepaper.pdf
21. Wang, J., Wang, H.: Monoxide: scale out blockchains with asynchronous consensus zones. In: 16th USENIX Symposium on Networked Systems Design and Implementation (NSDI 1919), pp. 95–112 (2019)
22. Yakovenko, A.: Solana: a new architecture for a high performance blockchain v0.8.13. Whitepaper (2018)
23. Zheng, J., Huang, H., Li, C., Zheng, Z., Guo, S.: Revisiting double-spending attacks on the bitcoin blockchain: new findings. In: 2021 IEEE/ACM 29th International Symposium on Quality of Service (IWQOS), pp. 1–6. IEEE (2021)

Protocols and Consensus

Ouroboros Taktikos: Regularizing Proof-of-Stake via Dynamic Difficulty

Aaron M. Schutza[1], Hans Walter Behrens[1(✉)], Tuyet Duong[1,3],
and J. A. Aman[1,2]

[1] Topl, Austin, USA
{a.schutza,h.behrens}@topl.co
[2] Rice University, Houston, USA
james.aman@rice.edu
[3] FYEO, Inc., Jacksonville, USA
t.duong@gofyeo.com

Abstract. In any Nakamoto-style distributed ledger technology, participants must eventually come to a deterministic ordering of proposed extensions as a necessary precondition to consensus. To prevent Sybil attacks, this process encodes a bias toward selecting proposers who commit a limited resource. In proof-of-work (PoW) schemes, block proposals are secured using a hashing mechanism that preferences miners with greater computational power. In Nakamoto-style proof-of-stake (PoS) paradigms, proposers' eligibilities derive from their staked holdings, relying on a thresholding mechanism to fairly select the next block proposer by favoring those who have committed more stake. This eligibility threshold controls which parties may propose a block in a given slot, with easier thresholds increasing block density. However, higher density also increases forking – periods of uncertainty where consensus remains (temporarily) unsettled. Therefore, the selection of the PoS eligibility threshold critically affects both security and throughput in the associated chain. Previous work relies on static threshold values, which simplifies security analysis. In this work, we extend the static eligibility threshold to a dynamic one, and introduce the concept of a *local dynamic difficulty* mechanism in which thresholds follow a non-monotonic difficulty curve. We implement this mechanism in a novel PoS protocol, Ouroboros Taktikos, finding that the dynamic regime regularizes slot intervals and improves block throughput. The pseudo-predictable nature of the protocol also penalizes covert attacks, simultaneously increasing security. We compare Ouroboros Taktikos to Ouroboros Praos and show that the addition of local dynamic difficulty improves throughput by $\sim 2.9 \times$ and reduces 99th percentile block latency by $\sim 5.7 \times$ compared to the state of the art.

1 Introduction

In traditional Byzantine state machine replication (SMR), agreement typically relies on a set of fixed, known participants. In contrast, distributed ledger technologies (DLTs) leverage randomness to reach consensus with an unknown list of participants. This randomness establishes proposer eligibility for the

J. Chen et al. (Eds.): BlockSys 2023, CCIS 1897, pp. 269–283, 2024.
https://doi.org/10.1007/978-981-99-8104-5_20

consensus round, analogous to leader election in SMR, but may contain subtle bias. Attackers can leverage this bias to undermine agreement in their favor, so 'proof' schemes aim to eliminate or mitigate the issue explicitly. The most well-known of these schemes, the proof-of-work (PoW) approach popularized by Bitcoin [21], uses computational resources to secure proposer selection. Given the high power consumption of the 'work', some authors have expressed concerns [18,23,24] over the sustainability of PoW. Alternatives such as proof-of-stake (PoS) [2,5,7,9,10,12,15,17] address this criticism by drawing randomness from alternative sources and improving computational efficiency. To do so, PoS methods execute local, pseudo-random deterministic trials to establish eligibility, with constraints to limit adversarial influence. Several nodes might share eligibility to extend the chain (a *fork*), or an adversary could propose valid extensions of older chains (the so-called *nothing-at-stake* attack [19]). To address these cases, chain selection rules such as [10] limit the impact of forks, while other supplemental techniques improve bootstrapping [2] or clock synchronization [3].

PoS eligibility commonly adopts the concept of a *slot*, or a global eligibility period predicated on some underlying synchronization mechanism. Usually, time governs these slots via the generalized concept of a *time beacon* [2,4,10,17]. Participants agree on time using existing approaches such as NTP, or via more decentralized schemes as in [3]. This synchronization mechanism allows participants to locally determine a numeric eligibility for a given slot from a verifiable random test associated with that slot. The *eligibility threshold* controls whether and which participants may propose a new block. The percent of slots with valid proposals, the *active slots coefficient* f, plays a role similar to mining difficulty in PoW. By tuning f, PoS approaches can approximate existing PoW eligibility distributions [13] to more closely match their consistency bound.

In the Ouroboros family of protocols [17], honest participants discard blocks from future slots, and only share their most recent blocks; thus, the time synchronization constraint protects honest chain growth. Slot frequency typically dominates block frequency, so not every slot produces an eligibility. When the block time interval falls too low, forks become common and allow the adversary to undermine consensus. In contrast, a too-low block frequency sabotages throughput when no eligible leaders emerge for extended periods. Even a carefully-tuned static f remains susceptible to randomness, with sporadic periods of "feast or famine" arising from the uniform randomness of the eligibility threshold. Furthermore, adversaries can look ahead and test future slots associated with a given epoch nonce to determine the relative value of their private forks. This behavior, known as *grinding*, gives the adversary a small but persistent advantage within the consensus process that scales with the number of forks. We propose to address these challenges by moving from a static coefficient to a dynamic, adaptive one.

1.1   Our Contributions

Proof-of-Stake Protocol with Local Dynamic Difficulty. The protocol presented here, *Ouroboros Taktikos*[1], solves these problems and improves upon

---

[1] From the Greek τᾰκτῐκός, ordering or arranging, especially in a tactical sense.

Ouroboros Praos [10] in several surprising ways. We replace the static active slot coefficient f with a *local dynamic difficulty* (LDD) function $f(\delta)$ we call a *difficulty curve*, where eligibility depends not only on stake but also on a slot interval δ. We propose one such function, the *snowplow curve*, that offers useful properties aligning with typical blockchain desiderata. The stochastic variability introduced by Taktikos obscures forward prediction of leadership eligibility, preserving security characteristics and making covert coordination more difficult even in the context of a grinding adversary.

Security Against Grinding Attacks. The conditional probabilities introduced by dynamic slot eligibility provide an additional degree of freedom to adversarial participants. While an adversary may discover a valid eligibility, they may choose to keep it private and reveal it later, when its relative position to other proposed blocks may trigger a reorganization. To address these concerns, we approach the challenge from two directions. First, we present a novel chain selection protocol compatible with Taktikos that balances these considerations. Second, we evaluate adversarial behavior in both the bounded and unbounded cases to determine if this new freedom produces any advantage. Finally, we analyze and bound the adversarial power stemming from these changes, contextualizing the advantage relative to our consistency bound.

Implementation and Empirical Comparison. We further implement our protocol and empirically evaluate its performance against existing approaches. Specifically, we compare with Praos [10], noting that the LDD method can adapt to any eligibility game that relies on an active slot coefficient. We additionally evaluate the effects of LDD on our consistency bound under varying adversarial assumptions. We show that our procedure improves upon existing approaches in several metrics, reducing both variability and expected value of the block time interval. In aggregate, these improvements result in a $\sim 2.9\times$ increase in block throughput, and a $\sim 5.7\times$ decrease in 99th percentile block latency.

2 Related Work

Ouroboros [17] forms the foundation of Nakamoto-style probabilistic proof of stake and presents a formal framework for reasoning about blockchain consistency. Subsequent variants [2,3,10] extend the protocol to new security settings, improving the original approach and incorporating new formal techniques to tighten security bounds. However, these approaches do not consider LDD and require adaptation to our domain. We build on this foundation to introduce the local dynamic difficulty mechanism, which to the best of our knowledge does not appear in any existing PoS scheme. Similarly, our assessment of grinding extends previous work [6,16], but reframes the discussion to accommodate our modifications.

The use of time-dependent agreement for multi-agent consensus appears in other domains previously, such as control theory [20]. These ideas contain similarities to the concept of LDD as presented in this work. However, previous approaches do not consider Byzantine faults, making them impractical for adaptation to the distributed ledger domain. Other temporal approaches, such as proof-of-elapsed-time, share some similarities with our approach but rely on trusted execution modules such as Intel's SGX. Later work [8] has found that such hardware-based approaches contain vulnerabilities; our proposed approach does not require any secure hardware.

Evaluating the adversarial advantage in proof of stake systems, in particular from the perspective of the grinding adversary [5], has thus far implicitly assumed a static eligibility threshold. Markovian approaches such as those used in [17] or [14] therefore do not directly apply to the conditional probabilities that emerge from LDD. Simulation-based approaches help to bridge this gap, while leaving the door open to future work providing a stronger theoretical security analysis.

3   Design

Local Dynamic Difficulty. We first briefly recap the process of minting eligibility in Nakamoto-style proof of stake to establish context. Verifiable random function (VRF) outputs consist of a pseudo-random byte-string y of length ℓ_{VRF} and a proof π. As in Ouroboros Praos [10], a potential minter generates a test nonce $y_p \in \{0,1\}^{\ell_{\mathrm{VRF}}}/2^{\ell_{\mathrm{VRF}}}$, which represents an output from a VRF indistinguishable from uniform randomness in the range $(0, 1)$. An associated public key corresponding to the forging party p can verify each pair (y_p, π_p). We leave this functionality unaltered and model our own nonce generation on [2].

In existing approaches, the test nonce y_p is evaluated by minting parties and validators to elect slot leaders in the forging procedure by checking y_p against a static eligibility threshold. In contrast, we introduce a new eligibility paradigm based on a difficulty curve $f(\delta)$, which allows for a dynamic eligibility threshold. This concept, which we term *local dynamic difficulty* (or LDD), induces a dominant distribution with properties influenced by the choice of curve $f(\delta)$. The mechanism of LDD changes the probability of forging blocks based on how recently the previous block was observed. As with a static f, we consider $f(\delta)$ agreed upon by all parties in a global setup. We define the *slot interval* δ as a variable that measures the number of slots between consecutive blocks. More formally, the slot interval δ_ℓ for block B_ℓ is defined as the difference between slot $\mathtt{sl}_\ell$ of B_ℓ and the slot $\mathtt{sl}_{\ell-1}$ of the parent block $B_{\ell-1}$, i.e. $\delta_\ell = \mathtt{sl}_\ell - \mathtt{sl}_{\ell-1}$ where δ is used as a variable to index all possible slot intervals over the domain $\delta > 0$, since $\mathtt{sl}_\ell > \mathtt{sl}_{\ell-1} \, \forall \ell$. We treat $\mathtt{sl}_{\ell=0}$ as the genesis slot.

In the LDD forging procedure, we use a threshold function that satisfies the eligibility test for a slot interval δ with relative stake α:

$$\phi(\delta, \alpha) = 1 - \left(1 - f(\delta)\right)^\alpha \tag{1}$$

We see that independent aggregation remains valid across each slot interval:

$$1 - \phi\left(\delta_\ell, \sum_P \alpha_p\right) = \prod_P \left(1 - \phi(\delta_\ell, \alpha_p)\right) \tag{2}$$

Table 1. Key Notation

Δ	Network Delay	δ	Slot Interval
α	Relative Stake	p	Staking Party
F_A	Minimum Difficulty	F_B	Baseline Difficulty
ψ	Slot Gap	γ	Recovery Threshold

A test procedure analogous to the Praos forging procedure is carried out in each slot. A block eligibility is valid if, given nonce η, block B_ℓ in slot sl_ℓ, parent block $B_{\ell-1}$ in slot $\text{sl}_{\ell-1}$, a set of forging parties P, a specific party $p \in P$, and its relative stake α_p, the following inequality is true: $y_p(\text{sl}_\ell) < \phi(\delta_\ell, \alpha_p)$.

Before introducing our proposed difficulty curve, we first define several related terms. A *slot gap*, $\psi \geq 0 : f(\delta < \psi) = 0$, requires that no eligibilities may occur closer than ψ slots. This allows the protocol to explicitly consider network delay Δ, bounding $(\Delta < \psi)$ adversarial power derived by front-running block propagation. To compensate for the loss of chain growth induced by a slot gap, we dynamically increase forging capacity. We therefore specify a *forging window* of $\gamma - \psi$ slots where $f(\delta \leq \gamma)$ increases with δ to a maximum *amplitude* of f_A; that is, blocks become easier to mint as more empty slots occur. To retain the security properties of the underlying protocol, during bootstrapping $f(\delta)$ returns to a *baseline difficulty* f_B, independent of δ. We refer to the domain of $\delta > \gamma$ as the *recovery phase* of the LDD forging procedure. The interplay between these three domains may be finely tuned to establish new block dynamics, with completely different block time distributions and security properties (Fig. 1).

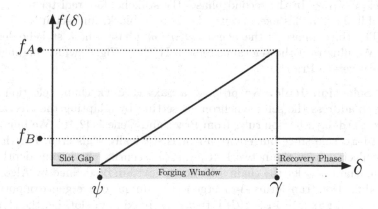

Fig. 1. Snowplow curve parameterization, visualized

We present a difficulty curve featuring a slot gap, forging window, and recovery phase defined by the 4-tuple (ψ, γ, f_A, f_B), which we call a *snowplow curve*:

$$f(\delta) = \begin{cases} 0 & \delta < \psi \\ f_A \cdot \left(\frac{\delta - \psi}{\gamma - \psi}\right) & \psi \leq \delta < \gamma \\ f_B & \gamma \leq \delta \end{cases} \tag{3}$$

where $0 \to \psi$ is the slot gap, $\psi \to \gamma$ is the forging window, f_A is the amplitude, and f_B is the baseline difficulty. Refer to Fig. 1 for a visual representation of Eq. 3. We constrain these parameters by $0 < f_B \leq f_A \leq 1$ and $0 \leq \psi < \gamma$. The Taktikos curve permits leadership eligibility to be biased by selectively extending tines with parent slots in the forging window $\delta < \gamma$, but for any $\delta \geq \gamma$ leadership returns to independent predictability [10]. A simplified form of $f(\delta)$ setting $\psi = 0$ and $\delta < \gamma < 1 + \frac{1}{c}$ is defined as $f(\delta) = c\delta$ where $c = f_A/\gamma$. This difficulty curve may be parameterized such that the proportion of blocks having slot intervals in the forging window is arbitrarily close to 1. The distribution of leader election events induced by this curve converges geometrically on $0 < \delta < \frac{1}{c} + 1$, and by choosing a $\gamma < \frac{1}{c}$ an arbitrarily small portion of blocks fall in the recovery phase on the honest-majority tine. The proportion of filled slots corresponds to the expectation value of $f(\delta)$, which we call f_{eff}.

Intuitively, this curve rewards well-synchronized nodes with increased block production without requiring additional messaging, while still allowing out-of-date participants to catch up if needed. We now use the snowplow curve to define a revised consensus protocol that leverages LDD for its leader election.

The Consensus Protocol. Using LDD, we extend Ouroboros Praos [10] to a new protocol, *Ouroboros Taktikos*. Taktikos operates in the hybrid model with the functionalities $\mathcal{F}_{INIT}$, $\mathcal{F}_{VRF}$, $\mathcal{F}_{KES}$, $\mathcal{F}_{DSIG}$. We emphasize that the modifications we make bring significant performance improvements with similar security guarantees when the difficulty curve is appropriately parameterized. The protocol consists of three phases: the first phase is the *initialization phase* where stakeholders obtain the public keys v_i^{vrf}, v_i^{kes}, v_i^{dsig} from the ideal functionalities $\mathcal{F}_{VRF}$, $\mathcal{F}_{KES}$, $\mathcal{F}_{DSIG}$. In the second phase, the stakeholders register to $\mathcal{F}_{INIT}$ with their public keys and stake, receive the genesis block, and set it as their local chain. The third phase is the *chain extension* phase where stakeholders mint blocks. We illustrate the relevant steps of Π^{Tak} in Fig. 5, which highlights key differences versus Praos.

Chain Selection Rule. We propose a `maxvalid-tk` chain selection rule, a method to address the semi-synchronous setting by adapting the `maxvalid-mc` and `maxvalid-bg` selection rules from Praos and Genesis [2,10]. We build on the `maxvalid-mc` rule since our environment is statically registered. For the set of chains collected from the network $\{\mathcal{C}_1, ..., \mathcal{C}_j\}$, security checkpoint depth $k \in \mathbb{N}$, and local chain $\mathcal{C}_{loc}$ let the chain selection algorithm be defined by Algorithm 1. This modification transforms Δ-divergences to unique convergence opportunities. The algorithm `maxvalid-slot`$(\mathcal{C})$ returns the maximum slot, i.e. the slot of the head of the chain $\mathcal{C}$. The earliest slot after each block is biased towards the honest majority with an appropriately chosen Taktikos difficulty curve.

Algorithm 1: maxvalid-tk $(k, \mathcal{C}_{\text{loc}}, \mathcal{C}_1, ..., \mathcal{C}_j)$

```
 1  C ← C_loc;
 2  for i ∈ {1, ..., j} do
 3      if IsValidChain(C_i) then
 4          if C_i forks from C at most k blocks then
 5              if |C_i| = |C| then
 6                  sl_i ← maxvalid-slot(C_i);
 7                  sl_l ← maxvalid-slot(C);
 8                  if sl_i < sl_l then
 9                      C ← C_i;
10              if |C_i| > |C| then
11                  C ← C_i;
12  return C
```

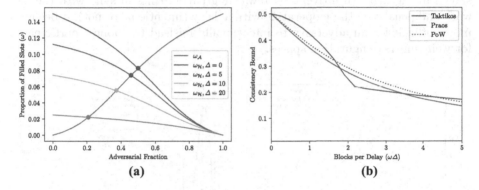

(a)   **(b)**

Fig. 2. (a) Effective honest throughput with varying network delay. (b) Consistency bound comparison in terms of blocks per delay interval, with PoW trend from [13].

4   Evaluation

Experimental Setup. The shift to LDD represents a substantial change to the eligibility test, the effects of which require careful evaluation. The conditional probabilities inherent in LDD confound exhaustive evaluation because the adversary has a new degree of freedom. Local dynamic difficulty complicates combinatorial treatments such as [6,16]. Our simulator encapsulates a superset of eligibility test behavior by adding LDD to Ouroboros Praos, emulating the behaviors of both approaches to provide an appropriate baseline for comparison.

For our chosen difficulty curve, we use $f(\delta) = (0, 15, 0.5, 0.05)$. We chose these parameters to provide similar common prefix and chain quality to [1], while also enhancing chain growth. Note that $\psi = 0$ indicates a network delay of 0 ($\Delta = 0$), an unrealistic choice in practice but suitable for our simulated context. Because $\psi \geq \Delta$ allows for tuning to observed network conditions, we can maximize both security and throughput even in the synchronous case. Our initial survey of the LDD parameter space serves as a starting point for future work exploring alternate $f(\delta)$ formulations, which may use curves of arbitrary complexity. All experiments were conducted for 10^5 slots over 30 trials.

Consistency. Figure 2(a) highlights the critical effect of network delay on *effective honest throughput*, referring to the number of blocks proposed per slot by honest participants, excluding slots in which an adversarial eligibility could supersede it. As Δ increases, out-of-band communication exclusively available to the adversary gives additional power in tie-breaking and frontrunning honest eligibilities. The points in Fig. 2(a) at which $\omega_{\mathcal{H}}$ intersects $\omega_{\mathcal{A}}$ mark the boundary beyond which the adversary produces more blocks than the honest nodes, violating consistency. This shows how long delays can substantially reduce consistency in static Nakamoto-style approaches. Under LDD we may tune $f(\delta)$ to consider delays, which mitigates the effects of network latency. When appropriately tuned, this effect actually results in a positive influence on the consistency bound as shown in Fig. 2(b). Intuitively, by rewarding participants in sync with the network and penalizing those operating with a delay (intentional or not), it becomes more difficult for an adversary to intentionally mislead the honest participants for well-tuned configuration spaces.

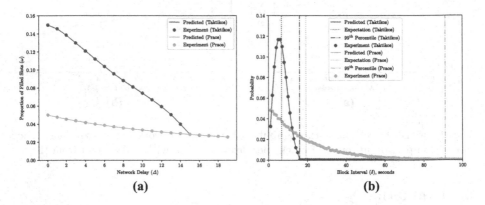

Fig. 3. Experimental comparison between Taktikos and Praos staking procedure. (a) Maximum expected chain growth as network latency increases; higher ω is better. (b) Probability density distribution of block intervals; lower δ is better.

Examining Fig. 2(b) in more detail, we see the consistency bound as a function of block production rate for several protocols. Recall that the consistency bound defines a safe upper limit for the adversarial fraction, beyond which consistency is violated. The tight bound on PoW established by [13] serves as our benchmark for comparison to the literature. Our analytic model for Praos aligns with the behavior from [10], confirming the applicability of our model for this domain. Interestingly, we find that over some regions Taktikos exceeds the consistency bound of the listed protocols for a given block production rate. For example, with a consistency bound of 0.45, the secure block production rate in Praos is approximately equivalent to PoW. At the same level of safety, Taktikos exhibits a meaningfully higher block production rate, suggestive of the potential performance benefits arising from LDD.

Performance. The Taktikos implementation of LDD offers two important improvements over existing approaches. First, it increases throughput by optimizing the usage of slot eligibilities, reducing the amount of time the chain spends idle. Second, it regularizes block production to improve block interval predictability, reducing observed variance. The dramatic effects of these changes are illustrated in Fig. 3, for the chosen parameterization of Taktikos[2] and Praos with a static threshold of $f = 0.05$ based on the real-world value used by [1].

Taktikos provides equal or substantially better effective honest throughput for all values of network delay (see Fig. 3(a)). The underlying reason for this advantage arises from the shift of the block interval distribution induced by the linear increase in the snowplow curve (from ψ to γ). In the region $\delta \geq \gamma$, Taktikos enters the recovery phase and performs identically to Praos as demonstrated in Fig. 3(a) when $\Delta \geq 15$. Over a range of realistic network latencies, $\Delta \sim 0 - 2$ seconds [22], Taktikos performs $\sim 300\%$ better than Praos. We contend that this increased chain growth is evidence of improved throughput, without the reduction in chain quality typically associated with high block production rates.

Transaction settlement relies in part on the number of blocks observed since that transactions' inclusion, an argument that relates settlement directly with chain growth. That is, as long as honest growth outpaces adversarial growth (the secure regime), the chain asymptotically approaches settlement as it grows [11].

By reducing variance in the block time interval, Taktikos increases predictability of block production and therefore in transaction settlement – a desirable property for many real-world use cases. In Fig. 3(b), we see that Taktikos shows a tight distribution of block intervals with mean, variance, and 99th percentile respectively of ($\mu = 6.67$, $\sigma^2 = 17$, 99th percentile $= 16$), where the 99th percentile is the time below which 99% of block intervals fall. All values are given in units of δ, typically seconds. In contrast, Praos shows a much wider distribution, with ($\mu = 19.3$, $\sigma^2 = 318$, 99th percentile $= 91$). Transaction settlement (which depends on block depth) therefore occurs $\sim 2.9 \times$ ($\frac{19.3}{6.67}$) more quickly and $\sim 5.7 \times$ ($\frac{91}{17}$) more predictably under Taktikos due to the shorter-tail distribution.

Grinding Adversaries. At its core, local dynamic difficulty introduces conditional probabilities that enable a new class of grinding attacks on slot eligibilities. Praos does not suffer from the same attack since the protocol determines eligibility independently of the parent block. We refer to the resulting difference in adversarial chain growth in Taktikos as the *grinding frequency*. At each eligibility, the adversary chooses to publicly use or privately save an extension, which influences their future eligibility distribution. However, the adversary may postpone that decision by maintaining both chains locally (a private fork). Consequently, the number of maintained forks scales exponentially at each adversarial eligibility.

---

[2] $f(\delta) \rightarrow (\psi = 0, \gamma = 15, f_A = 0.5, f_B = 0.05)$.

To predict the grinding frequency for a given difficulty curve, we must test every root-to-leaf path among the maintained tines. This branching structure makes it difficult to formulate an analytical solution, and computationally intractable to check exhaustively. Instead, we adopt a simulation-based approach with a cap on the number of maintained forks at a parametric depth d, which we refer to as the filtration rule. Note that $d = 1$ represents equivalence to honest behavior, where the participant extends only the longest chain.

Algorithm 2: GrindingSim1 $: \mathcal{Y}, r, f \to [0, 1]$

Require $: y_i \in [0, 1]$ for $y_i \in \mathcal{Y}$, $r \in [0, 1]$, $f : \mathbb{N} \to [0, 1]$

1 $L \leftarrow |\mathcal{Y}|$; $\ell_{\max} \leftarrow 0$; $B \leftarrow [(0, 0)]$;
2 **for** $y_i \in \mathcal{Y}$ **do**
3       $B' \leftarrow [\,]$;
4   **for** $b \in B$ **do**
5           $(s, \ell) \leftarrow b$;
6   **if** $y_i < 1 - \left(1 - f(i - s)\right)^r$ **then** $B' \leftarrow (i, \ell + 1) \| B'$;
7       $B \leftarrow B' \| B$;
8   **for** $b \in B$ **do**
9           $(s, \ell) \leftarrow b$;
10      $\ell_{\max} \leftarrow \mathsf{max}(\ell, \ell_{\max})$;
11 **return** $\ell_{\max}/L$

For the simulated staking procedure, we need only consider the VRF nonce values and the staking threshold function $\phi(\delta, r) = 1 - (1 - f(\delta))^r$, similar to Eq. 1. We can further simplify the process by assuming the adversary pools all stake into a single account, a safe assumption due to the independent aggregation property. Conceptually, we draw a series of random variables and then test the thresholds among all possible branches to see which produce valid extensions at each slot. We represent this process in Algorithm 2 for the unbounded, exhaustive evaluation, and Algorithm 3 with the filtration rule.

More formally, let $\mathcal{Y}$ be a set of i.i.d. random variables $y_i \in \mathcal{Y}$ such that $y_i \in [0, 1]$. The set $\mathcal{Y}$ will be an input and the duration of the simulation is $L = |\mathcal{Y}|$ slots. Additionally, we specify as inputs the amount of stake r that the branching adversary controls along with the difficulty curve $f : \mathbb{N} \to [0, 1]$. The grinding frequency is given by taking the limit as $L \to \infty$.

The grinding frequency is given by the limit of Algorithm 2 as $L \to \infty$ such that

$$\omega_g = \lim_{L \to \infty} \mathsf{GrindingSim1}(\mathcal{Y}, r, f) \tag{4}$$

This rate of chain growth is given by the leading branch's block number divided by the total number of slots executed by the simulation. The grinding frequency is an emergent property, varying with adversarial stake and the difficulty curve.

Algorithm 3: GrindingSim2 : $\mathcal{Y}, r, d, f \rightarrow [0,1]$

    Require : $y_i \in [0,1]$ for $y_i \in \mathcal{Y}$, $r \in [0,1]$, $d \in \mathbb{N}_1$, $f : \mathbb{N} \rightarrow [0,1]$;
1   $L \leftarrow |\mathcal{Y}|$; $\ell_{max} \leftarrow 0$; $B \leftarrow [(0,0)]$;
2   **for** $y_i \in \mathcal{Y}$ **do**
3      $B' \leftarrow []$;
4   **for** $b \in B$ **do**
5         $(s, \ell) \leftarrow b$;
6   **if** $y_i < 1 - \big(1 - f(i - s)\big)^r$ **then** $B' \leftarrow (i, \ell + 1) \| B'$;
7      $B \leftarrow B' \| B$;
8   **for** $b \in B$ **do**
9         $(s, \ell) \leftarrow b$;
10       $\ell_{max} \leftarrow \max(\ell, \ell_{max})$;
11      $B' \leftarrow []$;
12   **for** $b \in B$ **do**
13       $(s, \ell) \leftarrow b$;
14   **if** $\ell_{max} - \ell < d$ **then** $B' \leftarrow b \| B'$;
15      $B \leftarrow B'$;
16 **return** ℓ_{max}/L;

For a practical computation of grinding frequency, we use Algorithm 3 with $d > 1$ and observe that

$$\text{GrindingSim1}(\mathcal{Y}, r, f) = \lim_{d \to \infty} \text{GrindingSim2}(\mathcal{Y}, r, d, f) \tag{5}$$

and as a first-order approximation

$$\omega_g \approx \lim_{L \to \infty} \text{GrindingSim2}(\mathcal{Y}, r, d, f)\big|_{d>1} \tag{6}$$

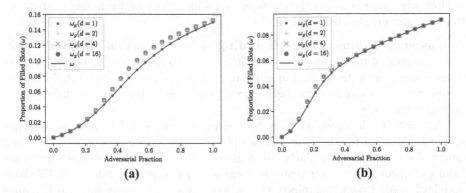

(a)   (b)

Fig. 4. Grinding advantage by adversarial fraction for (a) $\gamma = 15$. (b) $\gamma = 40$.

For comparison with honest chain growth, we predict block frequency by:

$$\omega = C\left[\sum_{\delta=0}^{\infty} \delta\pi_\delta \left(1 - \left(1 - f(\delta)\right)^r\right)\right]^{-1} \tag{7}$$

where π_δ is the stationary distribution and C is a normalization constant:

$$C = \sum_{\delta=0}^{\infty} \pi_\delta \left(1 - \left(1 - f(\delta)\right)^r\right)$$

Figure 4 presents a comparison of grinding frequency with respect to adversarial fraction for varying filtration depths, d. We verify this model by noting the equivalence of block frequency to the predicted grinding frequency when $d = 1$:

$$\omega \approx \lim_{L \to \infty} \text{GrindingSim2}(\mathcal{Y}, r, d, f)\big|_{d=1} \tag{8}$$

The honest production rate ω, is predicted with Eq. 7. While the adversarial grinding curves ω_g, are given by evaluating Eq. 6 with $L = 10^6$.

We see that as expected when $d = 1$ the grinding frequency ω_g exactly matches the block frequency ω irrespective of γ. We also see that both the magnitude and location of the adversary's benefit shift with γ. Note that, although the total AUC of $\gamma = 15$ exceeds that of $\gamma = 40$, most falls at a higher adversarial fraction beyond the consistency bound and is therefore not relevant.

As γ increases, the number of potential forks tracked by an adversary also increases, diluting the grinding advantage. As d increases the adversary's memory costs rapidly rise, as the number of tracked branch possibilities increases exponentially. However, the grinding advantage gained from tracking more branches rapidly approaches an asymptote. The added benefit in going from $d = 4$ to $d = 16$ proves negligible despite a much greater cost to the adversary. Therefore, while Taktikos does provide a small increase in adversarial power, the size of that advantage remains tightly bounded while other performance gains more than compensate for this tradeoff.

Consistency Bound Under Grinding. Direct comparison between consistency bounds of protocols poses a challenge due to differences between assumptions around both design and operation. In Fig. 2(a), we present this bound in terms of block proposals per delay interval, which varies based on block frequency and network delay.

To illustrate the challenge of direct comparison, we will describe a motivating scenario. Assume for the sake of example that all protocols assume a network delay of five seconds. Similarly, we will take the mean block frequency values from each protocol as their respective canonical frequencies: 6.67 s for Taktikos, and 19.29 s for Praos. Therefore, the ratio of blocks per delay interval becomes $\frac{5}{19.29} = 0.259$ for Praos and $\frac{5}{6.67} = 0.750$ for Taktikos.

When plotting these comparable values on Fig. 2(b), we find that Taktikos shows a consistency bound of 0.451 while Praos shows a value of 0.463. These values represent a relative difference of 2.6%; that is, Taktikos achieves 97.4% of

---

Protocol Π^{Tak}

The protocol Π^{Tak} runs by stakeholder $U_1, \cdots, U_n$ and ideal functionalities $\mathcal{F}_{\text{INIT}}, \mathcal{F}_{\text{VRF}}, \mathcal{F}_{\text{KES}}, \mathcal{F}_{\text{DSIG}}$, and random oracle H.

1. **Initialization**
   (a) The stakeholder U_i sends (KeyGen, sid, U_i) to the ideal functionalities $\mathcal{F}_{\text{VRF}}, \mathcal{F}_{\text{KES}}, \mathcal{F}_{\text{DSIG}}$ and then receives $v_i^{\text{vrf}}, v_i^{\text{kes}}, v_i^{\text{dsig}}$ from the ideal functionalities respectively.
   (b) The stakeholder U_i then registers $v_i^{\text{vrf}}, v_i^{\text{kes}}, v_i^{\text{dsig}}$ to the functionality $\mathcal{F}_{\text{INIT}}$ via command (ver-keys, $sid, v_i^{\text{vrf}}, v_i^{\text{kes}}, v_i^{\text{dsig}}$)
   (c) The stakeholder U_i in the next rounds sends (genblock-req, sid, U_i) to $\mathcal{F}_{\text{INIT}}$ and receives the stake distribution $\mathbb{S}_0$ as well as the random nonce η via the message (genblock, $sid, \mathbb{S}_0, \eta$), then sets $C_i = B_0 = (\mathbb{S}_0, \eta)$ and its initial state state$_i = H(B_0)$

2. **Chain Extension.** The stakeholder U_i with a relative stake α_i proceeds as follows. For each slot sl_j, upon receiving data d from the environment $\mathcal{Z}$, proceed as follows:
   (a) Let $\mathbb{C}$ be the set of all chains collected from network, then
       i. Prune blocks belonging to future slots and verify that for every chain $C' \in \mathbb{C}$, and every block $B_\ell = (\text{state}_\ell, d_\ell, \text{sl}_\ell, B_{\pi,\ell}, \sigma_{j,\ell}) \in C'$ with its parent block $B_{\ell-1} = (\text{state}_{\ell-1}, d_{\ell-1}, \text{sl}_{\ell-1}, B_{\pi,\ell-1}, \sigma_{j,\ell-1}) \in C'$, it holds that the stakeholder who created it is in the slot leader set of slot sl_ℓ as follows
          A. Parse $B_{\pi,\ell}$ as (U_s, y, π) for some s, and compute $\delta_\ell = \text{sl}_\ell - \text{sl}_{\ell-1}$
          B. Check that U_s is the corresponding leader of the slot sl_ℓ by sending (Verify, $sid, \eta \| \text{sl}_\ell, y, \pi, v_s^{\text{vrf}}$) to $\mathcal{F}_{\text{VRF}}$ and receiving (Verified, $sid, \eta \| \text{sl}_\ell, y, \pi, 1$) and $y < 2^{\ell_{\text{VRF}}} \phi(\delta_\ell, \alpha_s)$
          C. Check that $\sigma_{j,\ell}$ is a valid signature from U_s by sending (Verify, $sid, (\text{state}_\ell, d_\ell, \text{sl}_\ell, B_{\pi,\ell}), \text{sl}_\ell, v_s^{\text{kes}}, \sigma_{j,\ell}$) to $\mathcal{F}_{\text{KES}}$ and receiving (Verified, $sid, (\text{state}_\ell, d_\ell, \text{sl}_\ell, B_{\pi,\ell}), \text{sl}_\ell, 1$)
       ii. Run subroutine maxvalid over the set of chains from network $\mathbb{C}$ and his local chain C_i, i.e., $C' = \text{maxvalid}(\mathbb{C} \cup C_i)$, set $C_i := C'$ and state$_i = H(\text{head}(C_i))$
   (b) The stakeholder U_i sends (EvalProve, $sid, \eta \| \text{sl}_j$) to $\mathcal{F}_{\text{VRF}}$, receiving (Evaluated, sid, y, π). Let sl be the slot where the head(C_i) was mined, the stakeholder U_i then computes $\delta = \text{sl}_j - \text{sl}$, and checks if $y < 2^{\ell_{\text{VRF}}} \phi(\delta, \alpha_i)$.
   (c) If yes, then generates a new block $B = (\text{state}_i, d, \text{sl}_j, B_\pi, \sigma)$ where state$_i$ is the current state of U_i, $d \in \{0,1\}^*$, $B_\pi = (U_i, y, \pi)$ and σ is a signature of $(\text{state}_i, d, \text{sl}_j, B_\pi)$ at slot sl_j from $\mathcal{F}_{\text{KES}}$. Compute $C_i = C_i \| B$ and state$_i = H(\text{head}(C_i))$, then diffuse C'

3. **Signing Transactions.** On message (sign-tx, sid', tx) from the environment, U_i sends (Sign, sid', U_i, tx) to $\mathcal{F}_{\text{DSIG}}$ and then receives (Signature, sid', tx, σ). Then U_i sends (signed-tx, sid', tx, σ) to the environment.

Fig. 5. The Taktikos protocol. Highlights emphasize changes in construction from Ouroboros Praos [10].

Praos' consistency bound while substantially improving performance (as detailed in Sect. 4).

Note that the chosen network delay and block frequency values were selected for convenience of comparison. In practice, these values will vary dynamically based on network conditions and stochastic variability, so fixed-point comparisons provide only a small window into protocol behavior. As network delay falls, these points approach 0 and differences in consistency bound decrease while throughput improvements persist.

Finally, we provide an intuition behind the asymptotic behavior as d increases. While the adversary may track many possible tines, the value of those tines is a function of random chance and honest behavior. Each held-back tine becomes useless if either it naturally succumbs to stochastic variability – it falls too far behind the tip – or if an honest node claims that unused eligibility. Thus, even when tracking a large number of deep tines, nearly all must be discarded and the small fraction remaining provide the adversary only a modest grinding advantage.

5   Conclusion

In this work, we present Ouroboros Taktikos, a proof of stake protocol that improves the performance of Nakamoto-style probabilistic consensus. This work introduces the concept of conditional eligibility testing, termed local dynamic difficulty, and shows that adopting a time-varying difficulty curve offers advantages over the static threshold test. We propose a novel chain selection protocol and assess the effect that grinding adversaries have on protocol security in both the bounded and unbounded cases. We implement this protocol and empirically evaluate its performance against state-of-the-art, finding a $\sim 2.9\times$ improvement in block throughput and a $\sim 5.7\times$ reduction in 99th percentile block latency. The robust agreement between empirical evaluation and theoretical prediction, replicating observed real-world behavior, supports the security and throughput improvements in Taktikos and adds the powerful tool of time-based regularization to the eventual consensus toolbox.

References

1. The cardano node (2022). https://github.com/input-output-hk/cardano-node
2. Badertscher, C., Gaži, P., Kiayias, A., Russell, A., Zikas, V.: Ouroboros genesis: composable proof-of-stake blockchains with dynamic availability. In: CCS (2018)
3. Badertscher, C., Gaži, P., Kiayias, A., Russell, A., Zikas, V.: Ouroboros chronos: permissionless clock synchronization via proof-of-stake. Technical report (2019)
4. Badertscher, C., Gaži, P., Kiayias, A., Russell, A., Zikas, V.: Dynamic ad hoc clock synchronization. In: Canteaut, A., Standaert, F.-X. (eds.) EUROCRYPT 2021. LNCS, vol. 12698, pp. 399–428. Springer, Cham (2021). https://doi.org/10.1007/978-3-030-77883-5_14
5. Bagaria, V., et al.: Proof-of-stake longest chain protocols: security vs predictability (2020). https://doi.org/10.48550/arXiv.1910.02218

6. Blum, E., Kiayias, A., Moore, C., Quader, S., Russell, A.: The combinatorics of the longest-chain rule: linear consistency for proof-of-stake blockchains (2019)
7. Buterin, V., Griffith, V.: Casper the friendly finality gadget. arXiv:1710.09437 [cs] (2019)
8. Chen, L., Xu, L., Shah, N., Gao, Z., Lu, Y., Shi, W.: On security analysis of proof-of-elapsed-time (PoET). In: Spirakis, P., Tsigas, P. (eds.) SSS 2017. LNCS, vol. 10616, pp. 282–297. Springer, Cham (2017). https://doi.org/10.1007/978-3-319-69084-1_19
9. Daian, P., Pass, R., Shi, E.: Snow white: robustly reconfigurable consensus and applications to provably secure proof of stake. In: Goldberg, I., Moore, T. (eds.) FC 2019. LNCS, vol. 11598, pp. 23–41. Springer, Cham (2019). https://doi.org/10.1007/978-3-030-32101-7_2
10. David, B., Gaži, P., Kiayias, A., Russell, A.: Ouroboros praos: an adaptively-secure, semi-synchronous proof-of-stake blockchain. In: Nielsen, J.B., Rijmen, V. (eds.) EUROCRYPT 2018. LNCS, vol. 10821, pp. 66–98. Springer, Cham (2018). https://doi.org/10.1007/978-3-319-78375-8_3
11. Dembo, A., et al.: Everything is a race and Nakamoto always wins. In: CCS (2020)
12. Fan, L., Zhou, H.S.: A scalable proof-of-stake blockchain in the open setting. Cryptology ePrint Archive (2017)
13. Gaži, P., Kiayias, A., Russell, A.: Tight consistency bounds for bitcoin. In: CCS (2020)
14. Gaži, P., Ren, L., Russell, A.: Practical settlement bounds for longest-chain consensus. Cryptology ePrint Archive (2022). https://eprint.iacr.org/2022/1571
15. Gilad, Y., Hemo, R., Micali, S., Vlachos, G., Zeldovich, N.: Algorand: scaling byzantine agreements for cryptocurrencies. In: SOSP (2017)
16. Kiayias, A., Quader, S., Russell, A.: Consistency of proof-of-stake blockchains with concurrent honest slot leaders. In: ICDCS (2020)
17. Kiayias, A., Russell, A., David, B., Oliynykov, R.: Ouroboros: a provably secure proof-of-stake blockchain protocol. In: Katz, J., Shacham, H. (eds.) CRYPTO 2017. LNCS, vol. 10401, pp. 357–388. Springer, Cham (2017). https://doi.org/10.1007/978-3-319-63688-7_12
18. Küfeoğlu, S., Özkuran, M.: Bitcoin mining: a global review of energy and power demand. Energy Res. Soc. Sci. 58, 101273 (2019)
19. Li, W., Andreina, S., Bohli, J.-M., Karame, G.: Securing proof-of-stake blockchain protocols. In: Garcia-Alfaro, J., Navarro-Arribas, G., Hartenstein, H., Herrera-Joancomartí, J. (eds.) ESORICS/DPM/CBT -2017. LNCS, vol. 10436, pp. 297–315. Springer, Cham (2017). https://doi.org/10.1007/978-3-319-67816-0_17
20. Lorenz, J., Lorenz, D.A.: On conditions for convergence to consensus. IEEE Trans. Autom. Control 55, 1651–1656 (2010)
21. Nakamoto, S.: Bitcoin: a peer-to-peer electronic cash system. Technical report (2008)
22. Neudecker, T., Andelfinger, P., Hartenstein, H.: Timing analysis for inferring the topology of the bitcoin peer-to-peer network. In: IEEE UIC (2016)
23. O'Dwyer, K.J., Malone, D.: Bitcoin mining and its energy footprint (2014)
24. Ullrich, J., Stifter, N., Judmayer, A., Dabrowski, A., Weippl, E.: Proof-of-blackouts? How proof-of-work cryptocurrencies could affect power grids. In: Bailey, M., Holz, T., Stamatogiannakis, M., Ioannidis, S. (eds.) RAID 2018. LNCS, vol. 11050, pp. 184–203. Springer, Cham (2018). https://doi.org/10.1007/978-3-030-00470-5_9

Petrichor: An Efficient Consensus Protocol Leveraging DAG and Sharding for Asynchronous BFT

Song Peng, Yang Liu[✉], Jingwen Chen, Jinlong He, and Yaoqi Wang

Henan University of Technology, Zhengzhou 450001, China
liu_yang@haut.edu.cn

Abstract. As a core component of blockchain technology, the consensus mechanism provides the foundation for ensuring the trustworthiness and security of blockchain networks. However, existing consensus protocols suffer from low transaction throughput, high latency, and poor scalability. To address these challenges, we present Petrichor, an asynchronous Byzantine fault-tolerant consensus protocol based on Directed Acyclic Graph (DAG) and empowered with a sharding technique. Petrichor achieves significant performance improvements by dividing the blockchain network into multiple shards, allowing each shard to process transactions and generate blocks in parallel. We introduce the application of DAG within each shard to fully leverage its parallel propagation and multi-path confirmation properties. Within each shard, Petrichor employs a structured DAG, enabling transactions to propagate through multiple paths rather than relying on a single chain-like structure. This parallel propagation reduces transaction confirmation time and minimizes transaction latency. Furthermore, we propose a leader block election mechanism driven by random seeds, aiming to achieve fast consensus within each shard. With this mechanism, nodes within a shard can independently reach consensus without the need for direct communication, thereby facilitating efficient consensus within shards. We demonstrate the feasibility of Petrichor through theoretical analysis and validate its ability to meet the high throughput and low latency requirements of blockchain networks through extensive experiments.

Keywords: Blockchain · Asynchronous Byzantine Fault-tolerant · Consensus Protocol · DAG · Sharding

1 Introduction

Blockchain is regarded as a technology with the potential to revolutionize traditional centralized systems and business models. It offers a more efficient, transparent, and secure means of data management and transactions [1]. This technology has permeated various domains such as finance, supply chain management, the Internet of Things, and healthcare [2,3]. Consensus protocols play a pivotal

J. Chen et al. (Eds.): BlockSys 2023, CCIS 1897, pp. 284–297, 2024.
https://doi.org/10.1007/978-981-99-8104-5_21

role in blockchain by ensuring consensus among network nodes regarding the validity and order of transactions, thus upholding the security and trustworthiness of the entire blockchain network. Asynchronous consensus protocols have garnered significant attention due to their ability to accommodate asynchronous communication among nodes, providing enhanced support for the security, efficiency, and scalability of blockchain systems [4]. Compared to synchronous consensus protocols, asynchronous consensus protocols offer greater flexibility and fault tolerance, enabling them to adapt to varying communication delays and node failures.

The current consensus protocols suffer from certain limitations, such as low throughput and high latency, which hinder the widespread application and further advancement of blockchain technology [5]. To address these issues, DAG and sharding techniques have been introduced as effective solutions. Compared to traditional chain-based consensus protocols, DAG-based consensus protocols offer several advantages, including high concurrency, low latency, and high throughput [6]. Such protocols enable more flexible handling of transaction data, thereby enhancing the processing capabilities and throughput of the blockchain network. On the other hand, sharding technology allocates transactions to different shards for parallel processing of distinct transaction sets, effectively improving the overall system throughput and alleviating the burden on individual nodes [7]. By combining DAG and sharding techniques, blockchain systems can overcome the throughput limitations and scalability challenges associated with traditional consensus protocols.

Based on the aforementioned considerations, we propose Petrichor, an asynchronous Byzantine fault-tolerant consensus protocol based on DAG and empowered by sharding, aiming to leverage their advantages to address the shortcomings of existing consensus protocols. By introducing Petrichor, we bring a range of significant advantages to blockchain technology, including high throughput, low latency, and remarkable scalability. In summary, we make the following contributions:

- We present Petrichor, an asynchronous Byzantine fault-tolerant consensus protocol based on DAG and empowered by sharding. Petrichor leverages a structured DAG to achieve parallel broadcasting and transaction processing. Through sharding technology, it enables multiple shards to concurrently process different sets of transactions, thereby further enhancing transaction throughput and reducing the burden on participating nodes.
- We propose a leader block election mechanism driven by random seeds, aiming to achieve fast consensus within shards. By introducing this mechanism, each node within a shard can independently reach consensus on blocks in the DAG without the need for direct communication between nodes. This promotes efficient consensus within the shard.
- We have conducted a comprehensive theoretical analysis and experimental validation of Petrichor. Through theoretical analysis, we have demonstrated the security, consistency, and liveness properties of Petrichor. Furthermore,

extensive experiments have been conducted to verify that the Petrichor protocol exhibits outstanding throughput and low latency characteristics, even under high load conditions.

2   Related Work

DAG-Based Consensus Protocol. Hashgraph [8] achieves asynchronous Byzantine fault tolerance through a virtual voting mechanism, allowing nodes to reach consensus without incurring additional communication overhead. Aleph [9] efficiently processes and validates transactions using a DAG structure while ensuring transaction security and integrity. In this protocol, a group of nodes is responsible for maintaining and updating user-submitted transactions, organizing them in a linear sequence according to specified rules. CoDAG [10] adopts a compact DAG structure that organizes blocks into levels and widths. Additionally, the CoDAG protocol leverages the resources of Industrial Internet of Things (IIoT) devices and deploys lightweight nodes to improve the efficiency of IIoT systems. The protocol proposed by Gai et al. [11] reconstructs a blockchain system based on a single chain by sorting and merging original blocks in the DAG structure, achieving consensus on the DAG. The key idea behind Narwhal and Tusk [12] is to separate reliable transaction propagation from transaction ordering, thereby achieving high throughput and network fault recovery capability. Narwhal is a mempool protocol specifically designed for reliable propagation and storage of transaction causal history. Tusk, as an extension of Narwhal, is an asynchronous consensus protocol with DDoS resilience.

Sharding-Based Consensus Protocol. Elastico [13] is a secure sharding protocol specifically designed for open blockchain networks. It achieves a transaction rate that is nearly linearly proportional to the available computing capacity by fully harnessing computational capabilities to adjust network parallelization. Omniledger [14] employs a Verifiable Random Function (VRF) [15] for leader selection and utilizes a variant of ByzCoin [16] for consensus implementation. RapidChain [17] utilizes an optimized internal committee consensus algorithm and achieves exceptionally high throughput through block pipelining. It incorporates novel large-block propagation protocols and reconstruction mechanisms that are provably secure, ensuring system robustness. Dang et al. [18] propose to design a sharding formation protocol based on trusted random beacons and leverage trusted hardware, such as Intel SGX, to enhance performance. Meepo [19] is a sharded consortium blockchain protocol aimed at addressing critical issues in consortium blockchain systems. It achieves high cross-shard efficiency through cross-epoch and cross-call techniques, enabling more efficient interaction between multiple shards.

3   The Petrichor Protocol

System Model. Consider a peer-to-peer asynchronous network model with n nodes, where the assumption of time is removed, and the message transmission delay and node processing speeds are unknown. Meanwhile, we face an adversary with limited computational capacity, capable of controlling at most $f < n/3$ nodes ($n \geq 3f + 1$). These nodes controlled by the adversary are considered Byzantine nodes, while the remaining nodes are assumed to be honest and trustworthy. A shard refers to a collection of m nodes, where $f < m/3$ ($m \geq 3f + 1$) Byzantine nodes are present. In the subsequent discussions, f will uniformly refer to the number of Byzantine nodes in a shard. We create $k = n/m$ shards, and each shard is represented by a unique identifier S_i, where i ranges from 1 to k.

3.1 Overview

We hereby present Petrichor, a novel asynchronous Byzantine fault-tolerant consensus protocol based on DAG and empowered by sharding. This protocol allows nodes within each shard to independently achieve consensus on blocks in the DAG without the need for direct communication. By introducing a leader block election mechanism driven by random seeds and a deterministic criterion based on block hash value sorting, the Petrichor protocol ensures that every node within a shard can reach consensus. The overall architecture of the Petrichor protocol is depicted in Fig. 1.

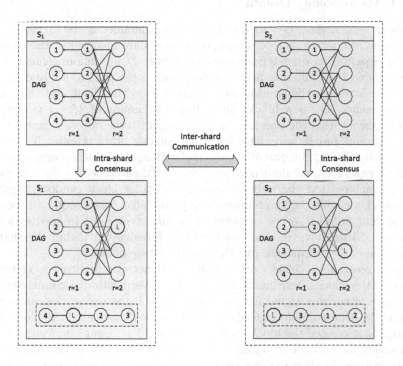

Fig. 1. The overall architecture of the Petrichor protocol.

The utilization of a DAG topology is a crucial design aspect of our protocol. In this design, each node within a shard maintains a consistent DAG constructed based on rounds. In each round, nodes broadcast two types of messages: blocks and announcements. Blocks contain specific transaction information, while announcements contain the hash values of blocks. Blocks and announcements have a one-to-one correspondence, and announcements are used to prove the legitimacy of corresponding blocks. In each round, nodes only create one block to ensure uniqueness and consistency. Through this approach, we establish the correlation between transactions, blocks, and announcements.

In the design of intra-shard consensus, we employ a randomized approach to achieve consensus on blocks within the DAG, overcoming the limitations of the FLP impossibility theory [20]. To accomplish this, we introduce the concept of a consistent random seed, which allows each node to generate a consistent random seed locally without the need for direct communication between nodes. This consistent random seed is used to determine the election of leader blocks. Once a node submits a leader block, it undergoes path validation and is sorted based on the associated path of the leader block, resulting in a consistent sequence of leader blocks. Following deterministic rules, we sort the ancestor blocks of each leader block, thereby achieving consensus within the shard.

3.2 DAG Topology Design

In this design, nodes need to receive enough announcements to move to the next round of operations to ensure enough nodes are involved in the consensus process. Specifically, when a node receives at least $2f + 1$ announcements for the current round from different nodes, it advances to the next round and creates a new block based on the transactions received from the client and the received announcements. The new block will include a minimum of $2f + 1$ references to announcements from the previous round, along with the node's signature, block source, current round, and shard identifier, among other relevant information. Additionally, during block creation, the node utilizes its identifier and the current round to generate a random number, which is then embedded into the block. This guarantees that the node generates a distinct block random number in each round, and this random number is unpredictable. In subsequent processing, this random number serves as input to a consistent random seed generation algorithm. Ultimately, the new block will be broadcasted within the shard for verification and confirmation by other participating nodes.

Upon receiving a block, other nodes conduct comprehensive verification to ensure the block's legitimacy and accuracy. Verification encompasses block uniqueness, structure, signatures, and references. If the verification process succeeds, nodes send a signature feedback to the node that created the block. When the node that created the block receives at least $2f + 1$ signature feedbacks from other nodes, indicating that a majority of nodes have confirmed the block's validity, the creating node generates an announcement corresponding to that block and broadcasts it to other nodes. Upon receiving the announcement, other nodes update their local DAG by adding the block associated with the announcement to the DAG. If a block fails to obtain a sufficient number of signature feedbacks or majority confirmations, meaning it cannot generate a corresponding announcement, the block will not be recognized, and other nodes within the shard will refrain from adding it to their local DAG. The mechanism of signature feedback and majority confirmation enhances the credibility and legitimacy of the blocks.

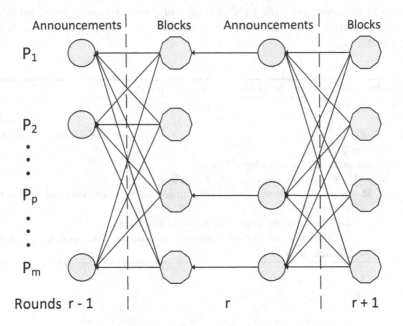

Fig. 2. The DAG structure based on rounds.

Figure 2 illustrates the DAG structure for three rounds. Nodes received $2f + 1$ announcements for round $r - 1$ from different nodes, enabling them to proceed to round r and create new blocks for broadcasting. In round r, upon receiving $2f + 1$ signature feedbacks from distinct nodes, nodes generated corresponding announcements and broadcasted them to be included in the blocks of round $r+1$. However, in round $r - 1$, node P_p did not receive a sufficient number of signature feedbacks, and in round r, node P_2 also did not receive an adequate number of signature feedbacks. As a result, both nodes did not create corresponding announcements. This indicates that these two nodes did not successfully participate in the generation and broadcasting process of announcements for that particular round.

3.3   Intra-shard Consensus

To better organize and manage the DAG, we divide it into multiple *domains*, each consisting of two consecutive rounds. We ensure the connectivity and coherence between *domains* through announcements, aiding nodes in achieving consensus throughout the shard (see Fig. 3). After the completion of each *domain*, nodes execute a random seed generation algorithm locally. This algorithm takes the random number of the block in the second round of the *domain* as input and employs a combination operation (such as XOR) to generate a consistent random seed. This consistent random seed plays a crucial role in subsequent leader block selection and serves as the initial seed for the random seed generation algorithm of the next *domain*, reducing predictability and repetitiveness between adjacent domains. The algorithm for nodes to perform random seed generation is shown in Algorithm 1.

Algorithm 1. Random Seed Generation for party p_i

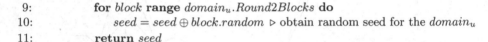

1: *Local variables* :
2:     r ▷ Round
3:     *seed*   ▷ previous domain's random seed
4:     *Round2Blocks*
5: **function** *generateRandomSeed* $(r, seed)$
6:     **if** $|DAG[announcement]|_r \geq 2f+1$ **then**
7:         **if** $r \bmod 2 = 0$ **then**   ▷ A domain consisting of two consecutive rounds
8:             $u = r \div 2$
9:             **for** *block* **range** $domain_u.Round2Blocks$ **do**
10:                 $seed = seed \oplus block.random$ ▷ obtain random seed for the $domain_u$
11:             **return** *seed*

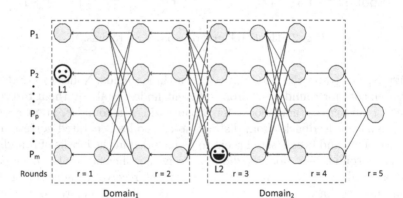

Fig. 3. Example of cross-domain path validation mechanism.

Based on the consistent random seed, in the first round of each *domain*, nodes can independently select the leader block for that *domain*. If the selected leader block has at least $f+1$ child blocks in the second round of the *domain*, it signifies sufficient support for the leader block, and nodes can commit that leader block. Committing the leader block means that its ancestor block can be sorted. Due to the collision resistance property of the hash function, different ancestor blocks will generate different hash values. Consequently, nodes can arrange the ancestor blocks in a consistent order based on their respective hash values.

Algorithm 2. Intra_Shard Consensus for party p_i

1: *Local variables* :
2:     $leader\_stack = \{\,\}$
3:     $lasted\_domain = 0$
4:     $consensus\_blocks = \{\,\}$
5:     $ancestors = \{\,\}$
6: **function** $selectLeaderBlock(r, seed)$
7:     $seed = generateRandomSeed(r, seed)$
8:     **if** $seed \neq nil$ **then**
9:         $u = r \div 2$
10:        $domain_u.seed = seed$
11:        $current\_block = getLeader(domain_u)$ ▷ Obtaining leader block of the current $domain_u$
12:        **if** $|block \in domain_u.Round2Blocks : path\,(block, current\_block)| \geq f + 1$ **then**   ▷ If the leader block has sufficient support
13:            $leader\_stack.push(current\_block)$ ▷ Commit
14:            $crossDomainValidation(u, current\_block, leader\_stack)$
15: **function** $crossDomainValidation(u, current\_block, leader\_stack)$
16:     **for** $prev\_domain$ from $domain_{u-1}$ down to $domain_{lasted\_domain+1}$ **do**
17:         $pervious\_block = getLeader(prev\_domain)$
18:         **if** $path(current\_block, pervious\_block)$ **then**   ▷ Path validation
19:             $leader\_stack.push(pervious\_block)$
20:             $current\_block = pervious\_block$
21:     $lasted\_domain = u$
22:     $shardConsensus(leader\_stack)$
23: **function** $shardConsensus(leader\_stack)$ ▷ Consensus on the blocks within a shard based on the leader block
24:     **while** $len\,(leader\_stack) > 0$ **do**
25:         $leader\_block = leader\_stack.pop()$
26:         $ancestors = \{\forall b \mid path\,(b, leader\_block) \wedge b \notin consensus\_blocks\}$ ▷ Unconsensus ancestor blocks
27:         $consensus\_ancestors = sortBlocksByHash(ancestors)$ ▷ Sort by the hash value of ancestor blocks
28:         $consensus\_blocks = consensus\_blocks.extend(consensus\_ancestors)$
29:     **return** $consensus\_blocks$

To achieve consistent leader block order and block order among nodes, we introduce a cross-domain path validation mechanism. This mechanism ensures that after a node submits a leader block for a *domain*, in the range between the current *domain* and the *domain* where the leader block was last submitted, the node verifies the dependencies between the leader blocks level by level and submits the leader blocks in the correct order. Specifically, after a node submits a leader block *current_block* of a domain, the node verifies whether there is at least one association path between *current_block* and the leader block *previous_block* of the previous *domain*. If an association path exists, the node will submit the leader block *previous_block* and order it before *current_block*. Then, the node will proceed to the previous domain for path validation starting from *previous_block*. This iterative process guarantees that nodes possess a consistent sequence of leader blocks, ensuring a consistent block order within the shard. The algorithm for intra-shard consensus executed by nodes is presented in Algorithm 2.

Figure 3 illustrates an example of the cross-domain path validation mechanism. $L1$ and $L2$ represent the leader blocks in $domain_1$ and $domain_2$, respectively. According to the consensus rules, $L1$ did not receive sufficient support and therefore was not submitted. On the contrary, $L2$ obtained sufficient support in the 4th round, as indicated by the blue color in the figure, allowing it to be submitted. During the cross-domain path validation stage, the node verifies whether there exists at least one associated path between $L2$ and $L1$. Since such a path exists (indicated by the red color), the node submits $L1$ and arranges it before $L2$ in the sequence.

4   The Theoretical Analysis of Petrichor

Lemma 1 *(Safety).* If the number of malicious nodes in the shard does not exceed $f < m/3$, the protocol can achieve security.

Proof. For each block created by a node, it is necessary to receive at least $2f+1$ signature feedbacks to generate the corresponding announcement, proving its legitimacy. If a malicious node proposes an illegitimate block, it will receive at most f signature feedbacks, which means that the malicious node cannot generate the announcement corresponding to this block. Therefore, honest nodes will not acknowledge this block.

Lemma 2 *(Safety).* Attackers are unable to accurately predict and prevent the propagation of specific leader blocks.

Proof. The random seed is obtained through a combination operation based on the random number in the second-round block of the *domain* and the random seed of the previous *domain*. This random seed determines which block is chosen as the leader block in the first round of the *domain*. Attackers are unable to predict the exact value of this random seed in the first round because it depends on the random number in the second-round block, which attackers cannot know before the end of the second round. Therefore, in the first round, attackers cannot accurately determine which block's propagation to prevent.

Lemma 3 *(Agreement).* Within the same shard, honest nodes can achieve consistency in the order of leader blocks and block sequences.

Proof. When an honest node submits the leader block b^u in $domain_u$, it performs path validation using the cross-domain path validation mechanism for the leader blocks of previous *domains*. Since each block references at least $2f + 1$ announcements from the previous round, and each announcement corresponds to a block, it means that each block references at least $2f + 1$ blocks from the previous round. By using induction, we can deduce that for the leader block b^v in a subsequent *domain*$_v$, b^v references at least $2f + 1$ blocks in the second round of *domain*$_u$. Moreover, since b^u has at least $f + 1$ blocks supporting it in the second round of *domain*$_u$, there must be at least one intersection between $2f + 1$ and $f + 1$, indicating that there is at least one path connecting leader blocks from different *domains*. Therefore, honest nodes within the same shard can achieve consistent ordering of leader blocks. Additionally, since the DAG includes a block, it should also include its corresponding ancestor blocks. By applying the deterministic rules to sort the ancestor blocks of leader blocks, honest nodes can obtain consistent block ordering within the shard.

Lemma 4 *(Liveness)*. All blocks created by honest nodes will eventually be outputted.

Proof. If a block can generate an announcement, it is considered valid. This announcement can be included in the next round of blocks, and due to the one-to-one correspondence between announcements and blocks, the corresponding block will be confirmed and outputted according to the consensus rules. Therefore, it is only necessary to prove that a block created by an honest node can generate a corresponding announcement to prove the Lemma. Each block requires at least $2f + 1$ signature feedbacks to generate the corresponding announcement. Even if f malicious nodes collude to withhold signature feedback for a block proposed by an honest node, as long as the other $2f + 1$ honest nodes sign and confirm the block, the corresponding announcement can be generated.

5 Performance Evaluation

Experimental Setup. We have set up a local experimental environment consisting of four servers based on the Petrichor protocol. Each server is equipped with an Intel(R) Xeon(R) 5218R CPU 2.10 GHz 128 GB of memory 40 CPUs to ensure sufficient computing and storage resources to support the experiments. TCP protocol has been adopted as the communication protocol to ensure reliable point-to-point message transmission. Additionally, we have limited the bandwidth between nodes to 20 Mbps to reflect the communication conditions in real network environments. To simulate network latency, we have set a delay of 100 ms for each message to examine the protocol's performance under limited communication speed.

In this study, we conducted a comprehensive evaluation of the performance of the Petrichor protocol, with a particular focus on throughput and latency, two key metrics. Fig. 4 illustrates the variations in throughput and latency observed in a network consisting of 64 nodes, tested under different shard numbers (2, 4, 8, 16) and different input rates (50000tx/s, 100000tx/s, 150000tx/s, 200000tx/s). Here, the input rate represents the rate at which clients submit transactions to the system (tx/s). The experimental results demonstrate that as the shard number and input rate increase, Petrichor is capable of effectively parallel processing a greater number of transactions, thereby enhancing the overall system throughput. Additionally, Petrichor manages to maintain transaction latency at an acceptable level, ensuring users can obtain swift transaction confirmation and response. Particularly noteworthy is the exceptional performance achieved by Petrichor in a configuration involving 16 shards, each consisting of 4 nodes. It achieves a throughput exceeding 170000tx/s with a latency of less than 3 s. These results showcase the advantages of Petrichor in terms of throughput and latency, especially in high-load environments.

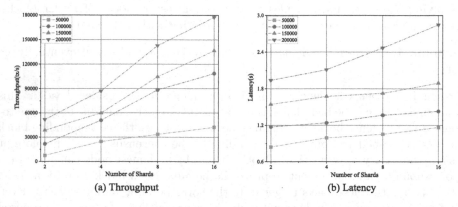

(a) Throughput   (b) Latency

Fig. 4. The performance evaluation of Petrichor across varying shard numbers and different input rates.

Moreover, we have conducted a thorough investigation into the throughput and latency of the Petrichor protocol across varying shard numbers and different transaction sizes (512B, 1024B, 2048B, 4096B, 8192B), and present the related results in Fig. 5. The findings demonstrate that as the shard quantity and transaction size escalate, Petrichor experiences a commensurate amplification in both throughput and latency. It is particularly noteworthy that within the domain of transaction sizes smaller than 1024B, we have discerned a comparatively modest escalation in throughput and latency. However, once the transaction size surpasses the threshold of 1024B, the escalation in throughput becomes conspicuously pronounced, mirroring a similar trend in latency. This suggests that by increasing the transaction size, Petrichor can accommodate more transaction data and associated information, thereby enabling the possibility of processing a greater number of transactions within a given temporal unit. However, as the transaction size expands, the required resources per transaction, including computation, processing, and network bandwidth, also increase accordingly, which may lead to longer confirmation times for transactions.

In addition to conducting performance tests under normal conditions, it is essential to evaluate the protocol's behavior in the event of node failures to study

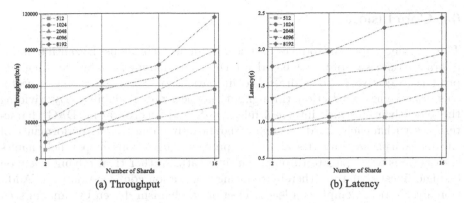

Fig. 5. The performance evaluation of Petrichor across varying shard numbers and different transaction sizes.

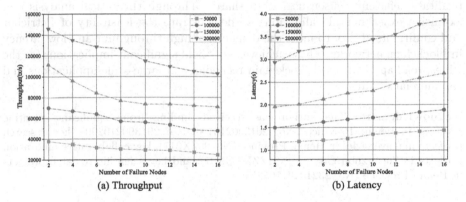

Fig. 6. The performance evaluation of Petrichor across varying numbers of faulty nodes and different input rates.

its robustness and fault-tolerance capabilities. To accomplish this, we simulated various numbers of faulty nodes and observed the protocol's performance in such scenarios. The simulated faulty nodes may experience node crashes, delays, or malicious collusion. We divided the entire network into 16 shards, each containing 4 nodes. Subsequently, we executed the protocol under different numbers of faulty nodes and different input rates (50000tx/s, 100000tx/s, 150000tx/s, 200000tx/s), and the experimental results are depicted in Fig. 6. The results indicate that the number of faulty nodes significantly affects the protocol's performance. The presence of faulty nodes reduces the overall throughput of the protocol and increases the message propagation and protocol execution latency. Moreover, the impact of faulty nodes is more pronounced at higher input rates.

6   Conclusion

The present paper introduces Petrichor, an asynchronous Byzantine fault-tolerant consensus protocol based on DAG and empowered by sharding. Its primary objective is to address the limitations of existing consensus protocols concerning transaction throughput, latency, and scalability. By dividing the blockchain network into multiple shards and incorporating DAG characteristics within each shard, Petrichor significantly enhances the performance of the blockchain network. Its ability to process transactions in parallel enables transactions to propagate through multiple paths, rather than relying solely on a single linear structure, thereby reducing transaction confirmation time. Additionally, Petrichor employs a leader election mechanism driven by random seed to achieve rapid consensus within shards, enabling each node to independently participate in consensus without requiring direct communication. This further facilitates efficient consensus within shards. Through theoretical analysis and extensive experimental validation, we demonstrate the feasibility of Petrichor and confirm its ability to meet the demands of high throughput and low latency in blockchain networks. These achievements hold significant implications for the widespread application of blockchain technology in large-scale applications and commercial scenarios.

Acknowledgment. The author has received funding from significant scientific projects in Henan Province (No. 201300210100, No. 201300210200), key research projects in universities in Henan Province (No. 23ZX017), key collaborative innovation projects in Zhengzhou City (No. 21ZZXTCX07), and key scientific research projects in Henan Province (No. 232102211082).

References

1. Yu, Y., Li, Y., Tian, J., Liu, J.: Blockchain-based solutions to security and privacy issues in the internet of things. IEEE Wirel. Commun. **25**(6), 12–18 (2018)
2. Yao, H., Mai, T., Wang, J., Ji, Z., Jiang, C., Qian, Y.: Resource trading in blockchain-based industrial internet of things. IEEE Trans. Industr. Inf. **15**(6), 3602–3609 (2019)
3. Majeed, U., Khan, L.U., Yaqoob, I., Kazmi, S.A., Salah, K., Hong, C.S.: Blockchain for IoT-based smart cities: recent advances, requirements, and future challenges. J. Netw. Comput. Appl. **181**, 103007 (2021)
4. Xiao, Y., Zhang, N., Lou, W., Hou, Y.T.: A survey of distributed consensus protocols for blockchain networks. IEEE Commun. Surv. Tutor. **22**(2), 1432–1465 (2020)
5. Wan, S., Li, M., Liu, G., Wang, C.: Recent advances in consensus protocols for blockchain: a survey. Wireless Netw. **26**, 5579–5593 (2020)
6. Wang, Q., Yu, J., Chen, S., Xiang, Y.: SoK: DAG-based blockchain systems. ACM Comput. Surv. **55**(12), 1–38 (2023)
7. Hashim, F., Shuaib, K., Zaki, N.: Sharding for scalable blockchain networks. SN Comput. Sci. **4**(1), 2 (2022)

8. Baird, L.: The swirlds hashgraph consensus algorithm: fair, fast, byzantine fault tolerance. Swirlds Tech Reports SWIRLDS-TR-2016-01, Technical report 34, 9–11 (2016)
9. Gągol, A., Leśniak, D., Straszak, D., Świętek, M.: Aleph: efficient atomic broadcast in asynchronous networks with byzantine nodes. In: Proceedings of the 1st ACM Conference on Advances in Financial Technologies, pp. 214–228 (2019)
10. Cui, L., Yang, S., Chen, Z., Pan, Y., Xu, M., Xu, K.: An efficient and compacted DAG-based blockchain protocol for industrial internet of things. IEEE Trans. Industr. Inf. **16**(6), 4134–4145 (2019)
11. Gai, K., Hu, Z., Zhu, L., Wang, R., Zhang, Z.: Blockchain meets DAG: a BlockDAG consensus mechanism. In: Qiu, M. (ed.) ICA3PP 2020. LNCS, vol. 12454, pp. 110–125. Springer, Cham (2020). https://doi.org/10.1007/978-3-030-60248-2_8
12. Danezis, G., Kokoris-Kogias, L., Sonnino, A., Spiegelman, A.: Narwhal and tusk: a DAG-based mempool and efficient BFT consensus. In: Proceedings of the Seventeenth European Conference on Computer Systems, pp. 34–50 (2022)
13. Luu, L., Narayanan, V., Zheng, C., Baweja, K., Gilbert, S., Saxena, P.: A secure sharding protocol for open blockchains. In: Proceedings of the 2016 ACM SIGSAC Conference on Computer and Communications Security, pp. 17–30 (2016)
14. Kokoris-Kogias, E., Jovanovic, P., Gasser, L., Gailly, N., Syta, E., Ford, B.: OmniLedger: a secure, scale-out, decentralized ledger via sharding. In: 2018 IEEE Symposium on Security and Privacy (SP), pp. 583–598. IEEE (2018)
15. Micali, S., Rabin, M., Vadhan, S.: Verifiable random functions. In: 40th Annual Symposium on Foundations of Computer Science (cat. No. 99CB37039), pp. 120–130. IEEE (1999)
16. Kokoris Kogias, E., Jovanovic, P., Gailly, N., Khoffi, I., Gasser, L., Ford, B.: Enhancing bitcoin security and performance with strong consistency via collective signing. In: 25th USENIX Security Symposium (USENIX Security 2016). USENIX Association (2016)
17. Zamani, M., Movahedi, M., Raykova, M.: RapidChain: scaling blockchain via full sharding. In: Proceedings of the 2018 ACM SIGSAC Conference on Computer and Communications Security, pp. 931–948 (2018)
18. Dang, H., Dinh, T.T.A., Loghin, D., Chang, E.C., Lin, Q., Ooi, B.C.: Towards scaling blockchain systems via sharding. In: Proceedings of the 2019 International Conference on Management of Data, pp. 123–140 (2019)
19. Zheng, P., Xu, Q., Zheng, Z., Zhou, Z., Yan, Y., Zhang, H.: Meepo: multiple execution environments per organization in sharded consortium blockchain. IEEE J. Sel. Areas Commun. **40**(12), 3562–3574 (2022)
20. Fischer, M.J., Lynch, N.A., Paterson, M.S.: Impossibility of distributed consensus with one faulty process. J. ACM (JACM) **32**(2), 374–382 (1985)

A Kind of Optimization Method for Committee and Reward Mechanism

Zhiruo Zhang[ID], Feng Wang[✉], Yang Liu[✉], Yang Lu, and Xinlei Liu

Henan University of Technology, Zhengzhou 450001, China
wfmail@sina.com, liu_yang@haut.edu.cn

Abstract. Consensus protocols play a vital role in blockchain by determining block generation speed and ensuring blocks' consistency and security. To address issues such as low efficiency and inadequate throughput in consensus algorithms, we have conducted research and proposed a novel Byzantine Fault Tolerant (BFT) protocol called CF-BFT, which operates in a dual-mode fashion and relies on node identity authentication. The CF-BFT protocol encompasses two sub-protocols: CheckBFT and FastBFT. Initially, the system assumes a pessimistic environment and executes the CheckBFT protocol, wherein a committee verifies the current environment's safety and the integrity of the leader node. Upon confirming the safety of the current environment, the CF-BFT protocol transitions to the FastBFT protocol for message handling. By optimizing the number of participating nodes, we optimized and reduced the participant nodes from the conventional $3f+1$ to a more efficient $2f+1$ committee members. This mitigates the communication overhead. By incorporating a hash-based selection mechanism for choosing the primary, we have enhanced the decentralization and randomness of the protocol. Moreover, the adoption of a ring topology for selecting primary nodes and committee members greatly enhances the scalability of the blockchain network. Furthermore, we introduce the concepts of cumulative reputation value and consumable reputation value to optimize the reward mechanism, resulting in a more rational tenure of the primary node within the FastBFT sub-protocol. Experimental results demonstrate that the proposed algorithm outperforms traditional BFT algorithms and other dual-mode algorithms across various performance indicators. While ensuring consistency and security, it significantly reduces communication costs and improves consensus efficiency. The experiment showed that in the best-case scenario, we improved by 47% to 2.5 times compared to SAZyzz, while in the worst-case environment, we achieved a maximum performance increase of 20% to 70%.

Keywords: Blockchain · Consensus Protocol · Dual-mode · Byzantine Fault Tolerance · Distributed System

1 Introduction

In recent years, blockchain and distributed technologies, with their decentralized and tamper-proof characteristics, have gradually become the focus of atten-

J. Chen et al. (Eds.): BlockSys 2023, CCIS 1897, pp. 298–310, 2024.
https://doi.org/10.1007/978-981-99-8104-5_22

tion for worldwide government agencies and large internet companies. Since the advent of Bitcoin [1], this technology has achieved breakthrough developments and widespread application in fields such as government affairs, healthcare, asset verification, provenance tracking, ect [2–7]. Consensus protocols, as a key component of blockchain, determine the methods and rules for establishing consensus. This includes determining the success of transactions, selecting nodes to have the right to package blocks (or called bookkeeping rights), obtaining those blocks, as well as how to define malicious nodes and punish them accordingly.

Consensus protocols can be divided into two categories: Crash Fault Tolerant (CFT) and Byzantine Fault Tolerant (BFT). Most CFT protocols, such as Paxos [8] and Raft [9], are primarily used in distributed systems and focus on issues like communication delays and node failures. On the other hand, BFT protocols, such as PBFT [10] and BFT-SmaRt [11], specifically address the problem of malicious nodes attempting to disrupt consensus. As a result, BFT protocols often exhibit lower consensus efficiency and higher communication overhead. In blockchain consensus protocols, ensuring consistency and security under worst-case conditions leads to lower efficiency. However, blockchain systems are not always operating under the worst conditions, which led to the concept of dual-mode consensus protocols. Dual-mode consensus protocols were initially proposed by Ramakrishna Kotla and Lorenzo Alvisi in 2007 [12]. They typically consist of two sub-protocols: a complex but secure backup sub-protocol for pessimistic environments and a simple and efficient fast sub-protocol for optimistic environments, for improving consensus efficiency. In general, the protocol assumes the blockchain is in a secure environment by default and actively uses the fast sub-protocol to commit transactions. If a blockchain inconsistency is detected, the protocol falls back to the backup sub-protocol.

We propose CF-BFT protocol, which is a dual-mode synchronous consensus protocol based on node authentication. It is applicable to private chains, consortium chains, and public chains. Unlike the assumption made by most dual-mode protocols that the blockchain is in a secure environment by default, CF-BFT verifies the safety of the environment and the honesty of the primary by examining the Check_BFT sub-protocol. When the check protocol determines that the environment is secure, CF-BFT activates the Fast_BFT sub-protocol for fast and efficient consensus. In the Fast_BFT protocol, only the primary processes messages, and the replicas do not need to communicate with each other but only receive messages from the primary. We present a series of enhancement techniques to elevate the performance of the protocol. Our contributions can be summarized as follows:

- Reduce the number of participating nodes from $3f + 1$ to $2f + 1$. The CF-BFT protocol divides the replica nodes into active replicas and passive replicas. Only $2f + 1$ nodes (1 primary and $2f$ active replicas) participate in the consensus, and as long as $f + 1$ votes are received, a message is considered validated. Other passive nodes simply replicate the consensus. This significantly reduces the communication overhead in the CheckBFT phase and improves consensus efficiency. In the FastBFT phase, it alleviates the pressure on the primary to process transactions.

- Introduce a new node selection method that increases decentralization by randomly selecting the primary, whcih reduce the likelihood of attackers finding and targeting the primary.
- A more reasonable reward mechanism is designed, which rewards honest nodes through token incentives and reputation value enhancements. And we design the selection method and computation range of $FastTime$, resulting in a more reasonable range for $FastTime$ settings.
- Discuss the impact of revalidating messages after the primary is attacked on performance, as well as the application scenarios, limitations, and further improvement approaches of the protocol.

2   Related Work

In 1999, the Practical Byzantine Fault Tolerance (PBFT) protocol was proposed, which not only tolerates Byzantine nodes in distributed systems but also reduces the complexity of previous Byzantine fault-tolerant protocols from exponential to polynomial level. Moreover, PBFT significantly improves the response time of the protocol by an order of magnitude. The consensus process of PBFT consists of three phases: the primary receives transactions and broadcasts them to other nodes in the first phase, nodes broadcast their vote results to each other in the second phase, and nodes broadcast their decision opinions to each other in the third phase. HotStuff [13] introduced a BFT-based consensus protocol with a three-phase voting scheme, where replica nodes do not need to vote with each other but simply respond to the messages from the primary. By introducing threshold signatures to validate the voting results of replica nodes, it achieves $O(n)$ message verification complexity. BFT-SMaRt is a distributed consensus engine implemented in the Java programming language. It improves modularity, reliability, and provides a flexible programming interface.

In 2007, Ramakrishna Kotla and Lorenzo Alvisi proposed the Zyzzyva dual-mode consensus protocol. This protocol assumes an optimistic environment by default, where it actively processes client-initiated requests but requires all nodes to be honest. If the primary fails, messages among replica nodes may become inconsistent, but the client detects this and assists in converging the correct replica nodes onto a total order of a single request, and subsequently only responds to orders consistent with that total order. SAZyzz [14] utilizes a tree-based communication model, effectively enhancing the protocol's scalability by reducing the communication complexity of both modes to $O(logN)$. ASAZyzz comprises two components: the fast-path and the backup-path, each incorporating two protocols: a simple protocol and an extensible protocol. This design significantly improves the scalability of the blockchain system. CheapBFT [15] consists of three sub-protocols: CheapTiny for normal scenarios, CheapSwitch for transitions, and MinBFT for rollbacks. In the optimistic scenario, Cheap-Tiny only requires the participation of $f+1$ active replica nodes in the protocol phases. Thunderella [16] introduces the concept of optimistic responsiveness, where a committee and a primary named accelerator are selected. If more than 3/4 of the committee nodes are honest and the primary is also honest, the optimistic scenario is achieved. In the optimistic scenario, the protocol can efficiently process requests.

3   CF-BFT Protocol

This chapter provides a detailed description of the CF-BFT protocol and introduces the optimizations made to it. It covers the selection of primary and consensus nodes, the new reward mechanism for nodes, and the range of $FastTime$ selection.

3.1   CF-BFT Protocol Overview

The CF-BFT protocol consists of two sub-protocols: CheckBFT and FastBFT, as illustrated in the diagram. As shown in Fig. 1, the sub-protocols differ in terms of the nodes involved in message processing and the communication among nodes. Additionally, the protocol introduces the concept of a committee, where only committee members are required to participate in the consensus on messages, while non-committee nodes can passively replicate the messages.

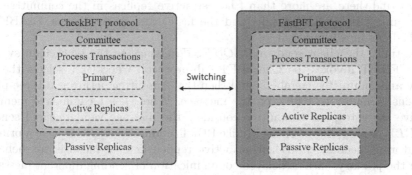

Fig. 1. Consensus nodes and committee for FastBFT and CheckBFT sub-protocols.

The CF-BFT protocol maintains a network of $n = 3f+1$ nodes. The protocol divides the replica nodes, excluding the primary, into active replicas and passive replicas, comprising $2f$ active replicas and f passive replicas. The committee consists of the primary and the active replicas, totaling $2f + 1$ nodes. During the consensus process, only committee nodes participate actively, while passive replicas passively receive messages from the committee. The message handling differs for committee nodes in the two sub-protocols. In CheckBFT, both the primary and active replicas engage in mutual voting to verify the correctness of transactions. In FastBFT, active replicas only communicate and vote with the primary, without engaging in inter-replica communication. As shown in Fig. 2.

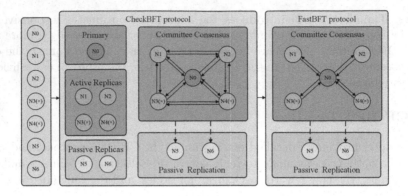

Fig. 2. Architectural paradigm of CF-BFT.

3.2   Protocol Workflow

The CF-BFT protocol consists of two sub-protocols, unlike other dual-mode protocols that assume the environment is secure and proactively submit messages. CF-BFT initially assumes a pessimistic environment and invokes the CheckBFT sub-protocol. In the consensus process of CheckBFT, the identity of the primary and the safety of the environment are verified. Only when the primary is deemed honest and there are more than f honest active replicas in the committee, the environment is considered safe, and the faster and more efficient FastBFT is invoked. As shown in Fig. 3.

Initially, the client sends a *REQUEST* message to the blockchain system, and CF-BFT invokes the CheckBFT sub-protocol. CheckBFT selects the primary and committee members, and then the committee performs a three-phase consensus similar to PBFT on the message. When $f+1$ committee members receive the votes, the committee considers the message validated and sends a *REPLY* message to the client. Unlike PBFT, committee replicas have a primary monitoring mechanism. When an active replica detects inconsistent behavior from the primary, such as delayed communication or sending different messages, it packages the evidence and sends it to other committee members to select a new primary. During the Node authentication process, if no malicious behavior is detected from the primary by the active replicas during the consensus process, the primary is considered honest. When $f+1$ committee members agree that the primary is honest, the current environment is considered safe, and the FastBFT sub-protocol is invoked.

In the FastBFT sub-protocol, the active replicas in the committee only communicate with the primary and not with each other. CF-BFT introduces *FastTime* to represent the number of fast consensus rounds, randomly determined by the reputation of the primary. Once the fast consensus phase is completed, FastBFT enters the *Verification* phase, where the committee calculates the total hash value of all messages submitted in FastBFT and performs a reverification through mutual communication. Only when receiving votes from more than $f + 1$ committee members, the messages in the fast consensus phase are considered correct, and the reputation of the primary is increased.

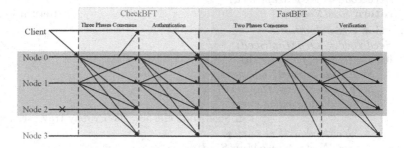

Fig. 3. Consensus process of CF-BFT.

Additionally, in FastBFT, both active replicas and passive replicas do not need to communicate with each other. However, active replicas are responsible for processing messages and sending replies to the primary, while passive replicas only need to passively replicate messages without processing them.

3.3 Primary and Committee Formation

To increase the randomness in selecting the primary and simplify the formation process of the committee, we introduce a structure called Consistent Circular Mesh Topology [17], as shown in Fig. 4. Unlike traditional network structures, replicas in the circular mesh structure maintain information about their predecessor and successor. When a node joins or leaves the network, it needs to communicate with its predecessor and successor to update the corresponding information.

The CF-BFT protocol utilizes a hash-based method for selecting the primary, aiming to avoid attacks that can exploit vulnerabilities in conventional approaches such as using the Remainder of view number and node. Specifically, when the protocol receives a message from a client, it initiates the CheckBFT sub-protocol and employs the formula $p = h_m \ mod \ n$ to determine the primary, where h_m represents the hash value of the message m. The primary selects active replicas to form the committee by traversing f successor nodes. If any node failures occur during the selection of committee members, the current active replica sends a message to the primary, and the primary then traverses the remaining predecessor nodes to complete the committee formation. When a node detects that both its predecessor and successor have failed, it broadcasts a global message to other nodes, seeking assistance in finding new predecessor and successor.

Algorithm 1 Random Selection Primary and Committee

1: **function** $CreatSeedAndPrimary$
2:     $Seed = H(Message.Content + Timestamp + View)$ ▷ Hash operation
3:     $SeedNode \Leftarrow NodeMap(Seed)$
4:     **return** $SeedNode$ ▷ Return Primary
5: **function** $CreatCommittee$
6:     $SeedNode \Rightarrow OrgMap(Seed)$
7:     **for** $i = 0, \ i < 2f, \ i++$ **do**
8:         $SeedNode = SeedNode.next$
9:         $SeedNode \Rightarrow OrgMap(Seed)$
10:        **if** $SeedNode_c rashes$ **then**
11:                        ▷ If SeedNode crashes, the Primay traverses forward
12:            $SeedNode = Primary.pre$
13:            $SeedNode \Rightarrow OrgMap(Seed)$
14:            **for** $j = 2f - i - 1, \ j > 0, \ j--$ **do**
15:                $SeedNode = SeedNode.pre$
16:                $SeedNode \Rightarrow OrgMap(Seed)$
17:        **break**
18:     **return** $OrgMap$

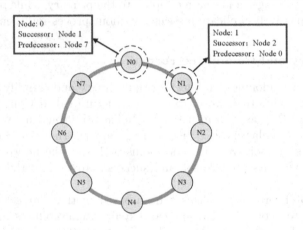

Fig. 4. Circular topology.

3.4 Optimization of Reward Mechanism

This section introduces optimizations to the reward mechanism by introducing the concept of tokens, whereby the master node receives dual rewards in the form of tokens and reputation boost when successfully completing tasks within a term and passing the $Verification$ phase. This enhances the rationality of the reward mechanism and enables the protocol to be applicable in a wider range of blockchain scenarios. Our research also sets values for $FastTime$, which determines the number of transactions a master node is allowed to process independently during its term. By introducing the concepts of cumulative reputation

RA and consumable reputation RC, it is expected that upon becoming a primary, the primary's previously earned reputation should decrease based on the term served, while being provided with new reputation. The longer the term, the higher the cumulative reputation RA and consumable reputation RC, resulting in a more reasonable selection of $FastTime$ values.

In the CF-BFT protocol, when a primary node successfully completes the FastBFT consensus process and verifies the correctness of all messages during the verification phase, it is rewarded with tokens cn and its cumulative reputation RA is increased. The value of cn is calculated based on the value of the transactions processed by the node during its term and can be customized.

$$RA = t \times cn \tag{1}$$

where t represents the timestamp when the node's term begins.

In the CF-BFT protocol, the selection process for FastTime is currently based on a simple approach of generating a random number within a given range of reputation values. However, this approach overly relies on luck and does not consider the efficiency of honest nodes in handling messages. To address this, this paper introduces the concepts of consumable reputation RC and effective reputation value R.

$$RC = t \times FastTime \tag{2}$$

To calculate the effective reputation value R, it is defined as follows:

$$R_i = \lambda_1 \times RA_i - \lambda_2 \times RC_i - t_g \tag{3}$$

where R can have negative values, λ_1 and λ_2 is a user-defined ratio, and t_g represents the timestamp of the genesis block in the protocol.

Assuming the base $FastTime$ value is μ, and the random $FastTime$ value is chosen from the interval $[\mu, \mu + \lambda_3 \times R_i]$ (or $[\mu + \lambda_3 \times R_i, \mu]$ when $R_i < 0$).

By making the random $FastTime$ larger, the RC increases, while the R decreases further. This setting prevents nodes with the same cumulative reputation from obtaining significantly different $FastTime$ and ensures that nodes with high cumulative reputation from previous high efficiency but recent frequent disconnections are not allocated excessive message processing pressure.

4   Performance Evaluation

This section presents the testing and comparison experiments conducted on the CF-BFT, as well as traditional BFT and the SAZyzz dual-mode protocol.

Performance tests and node simulations were conducted on a server with the following specifications: Intel(R) Xeon(R) Gold 5218R CPU @ 2.10 GHz, 8 GB RAM, 8 cores, running CentOS 7.5. The latency between servers was less than 1.5 ms. We use the Go programming language to create a program entity that represents an actual node. By simulating nodes on a virtual machine, we can simulate the behavior, interaction, and state of nodes in order to test, validate, or study complex distributed systems or networks.

4.1   Performance Comparison with BFT Protocols

This section tests the throughput of PBFT, CF-BFT, BFT-SMaRt, and HotStuff protocols under the Bitcoin standard (with 256 KB per transaction and 1024 transactions per block) with 4–64 nodes, as shown in Fig. 5. It can be observed that under optimal conditions, when the number of nodes exceeds 8 and even under worst-case scenarios, when the number of nodes exceeds 32, CF-BFT consistently outperforms other protocols in terms of throughput.

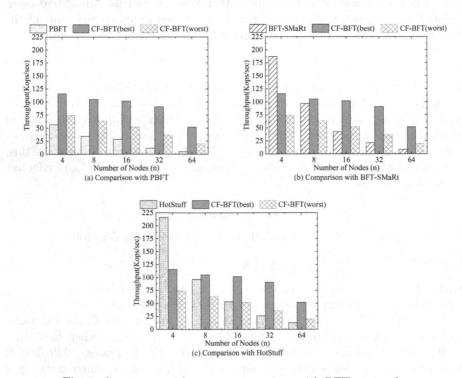

Fig. 5. Consensus performance comparison with BFT protocols.

4.2   Performance Comparison with SAZyzz

In this section, the throughput of the CF-BFT and SAZyzz protocols was tested under both best and worst-case scenarios, with a range of 4–46 nodes and block sizes ranging from 100 KB to 400 KB, as depicted in Fig. 6. It can be observed that our protocol consistently outperforms SAZyzz in the best-case scenario. In the worst-case scenario, particularly for block sizes between 100 KB and 200 KB, our protocol consistently exhibits superior performance, with throughput improvements ranging from 47% to 2.5 times. However, for block sizes of 300-300KB, the performance improvement diminishes when the number of nodes is either excessive or insufficient. Notably, with 10–25 nodes, the performance improvement ranges from 20% to 70%.

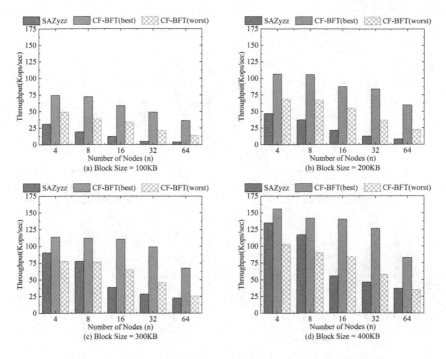

Fig. 6. Consensus performance comparison with SAZyzz protocol.

5   Discussion and Analysis

This chapter discusses the impact of message rollback due to Byzantine attacks on the performance of CF-BFT. It also explores the challenges that CF-BFT may face in applications and presents directions for further improvement.

5.1   Performance Degradation

This section focuses on the influence of CF-BFT protocol on throughput under the worst-case scenario. Firstly, the environmental definitions are clarified, where the best condition assumes all nodes are honest, and the worst condition considers the existence of f Byzantine nodes that are attacked and controlled by adversaries during their primary tenure, leading to message rollback and reverification within the FastBFT sub-protocol. As shown in Fig. 7, it can be observed that as the number of nodes increases, the proportion of performance degradation increases form 30% to 55%.

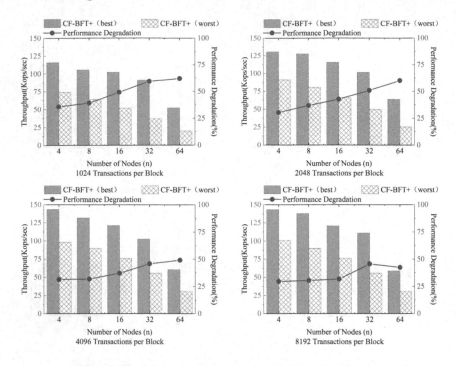

Fig. 7. Consensus performance comparison of rollback.

5.2   Application and Prospect

This section discusses the application scenarios, limitations, and future improve-ment directions of the CF-BFT protocol. The CF-BFT protocol is a dual-mode fault-tolerant Byzantine protocol that achieves consensus through inter-node communication. It is suitable for almost all private and consortium blockchain scenarios. Additionally, the protocol adopts a ring network topology, which greatly enhances the scalability of the blockchain through node connections. The token reward mechanism introduced in the protocol also makes it applicable to many public blockchain scenarios. The node identity authentication in CF-BFT does not require client participation, making it particularly suitable for Internet of Things (IoT) environments.

However, as the number of nodes increases, the performance of the CF-BFT gradually decreases, and the pressure on the primary also increases. Therefore, when applied to large-scale IoT and public blockchain environments, CF-BFT faces greater challenges. To address this, we will further optimize the number of primary and committees, and parallelize message processing by selecting multi-ple committees. This approach aims to improve the protocol's throughput and reduce the message processing pressure on each primary.

6 Conclusion

In this paper, we introduced a new blockchain protocol called CF-BFT, which consists of two sub-protocols, CheckBFT and FastBFT, forming a dual-mode consensus protocol. We first introduced the concept of committees, dividing replicas into active replicas and passive replicas, and reduced the number of participating nodes to $2f + 1$, thereby improving the protocol's throughput and reducing communication costs. Secondly, we optimized the selection process for primary by randomly selecting them based on hash calculations. This improved the decentralization characteristics of the protocol and reduced the likelihood of primary attacks. Finally, by modifying the reward mechanism, we introduced the concepts of consumable reputation value and cumulative reputation value, making the selection of primary in FastBFT more reasonable. The experimental results demonstrated that in the best-case scenario, the CF-BFT protocol achieved a throughput improvement of 47% to 2.5 times compared to SAZyzz, while in the worst-case scenario, the improvement ranged from approximately 20% to 70%.

Acknowledgments. The authors are supported by the Key Laboratory of Network Password Technology in Henan Province, China (LNCT2022-A20) in 2022; the Major Science and Technology Special Project of Henan Province, China (No.201300210100, No.201300210200); the Key Scientific Research Project of Higher Education Institutions in Henan Province, China (No.23ZX017); the Key Special Project for Science and Technology Collaborative Innovation in Zhengzhou City, Henan Province, China (No.21ZZXTCX07); and the Key Science and Technology Project of Henan Province, China (No.232102211082).

References

1. Nakamoto, S.: Bitcoin: A peer-to-peer electronic cash system. Decentralized business review, p. 21260 (2008)
2. Li, X., Liu, Y.: Research and implementation of intellectual property trading platform based on blockchain. Comput. Eng. Appl. **59**(3), 308–316 (2023)
3. Lu, J., Shen, J., Vijayakumar, P., Gupta, B.B.: Blockchain-based secure data storage protocol for sensors in the industrial internet of things. IEEE Trans. Ind. Inf. **18**(8), 5422–5431 (2021)
4. Nguyen, G.N., Le Viet, N.H., Elhoseny, M., Shankar, K., Gupta, B., Abd El-Latif, A.A.: Secure blockchain enabled cyber-physical systems in healthcare using deep belief network with ResNet model. J. Parallel Distrib. Comput. **153**, 150–160 (2021)
5. Gupta, B.B., Li, K.C., Leung, V.C., Psannis, K.E., Yamaguchi, S., et al.: Blockchain-assisted secure fine-grained searchable encryption for a cloud-based healthcare cyber-physical system. IEEE/CAA J. Automatica Sinica **8**(12), 1877–1890 (2021)
6. Cvitić, I., Peraković, D., Periša, M., Gupta, B.: Ensemble machine learning approach for classification of IoT devices in smart home. Int. J. Mach. Learn. Cybern. **12**(11), 3179–3202 (2021)

7. Liu, Y., Yang, W., Wang, Y., Liu, Y.: An access control model for data security sharing cross-domain in consortium blockchain. IET Blockchain **3**(1), 18–34 (2023)
8. Lamport, L.: Paxos made simple. ACM SIGACT News (Distrib. Comput. Column) **32**(4) (Whole Number 121), 51–58 (2001)
9. Ongaro, D., Ousterhout, J.: In search of an understandable consensus algorithm. In: 2014 {USENIX} Annual Technical Conference ({USENIX}{ATC} 14), pp. 305–319 (2014)
10. Castro, M., Liskov, B.: Practical byzantine fault tolerance. In: OsDI. vol. 99, pp. 173–186 (1999)
11. Bessani, A., Sousa, J., Alchieri, E.E.: State machine replication for the masses with BFT-smart. In: 2014 44th Annual IEEE/IFIP International Conference on Dependable Systems and Networks, pp. 355–362. IEEE (2014)
12. Kotla, R., Alvisi, L., Dahlin, M., Clement, A., Wong, E.: Zyzzyva: speculative byzantine fault tolerance. In: Proceedings of Twenty-first ACM SIGOPS Symposium on Operating Systems Principles, pp. 45–58 (2007)
13. Yin, M., Malkhi, D., Reiter, M.K., Gueta, G.G., Abraham, I.: HotStuff: BFT consensus with linearity and responsiveness. In: Proceedings of the 2019 ACM Symposium on Principles of Distributed Computing, pp. 347–356 (2019)
14. Sohrabi, N., Tari, Z., Voron, G., Gramoli, V., Fu, Q.: SAZyzz: Scaling AZyzzyva to meet blockchain requirements. IEEE Trans. Serv. Comput. **16**, 2139–2152 (2022)
15. Kapitza, R., et al.: CheapBFT: resource-efficient byzantine fault tolerance. In: Proceedings of the 7th ACM European Conference on Computer Systems, pp. 295–308 (2012)
16. Pass, R., Shi, E.: Thunderella: blockchains with optimistic instant confirmation. In: Nielsen, J.B., Rijmen, V. (eds.) EUROCRYPT 2018. LNCS, vol. 10821, pp. 3–33. Springer, Cham (2018). https://doi.org/10.1007/978-3-319-78375-8_1
17. Liu, X., Liu, Y., Li, X., Cao, H., Wang, Y.: FP-BFT: a fast pipeline byzantine consensus algorithm. IET Blockchain (2023)

MagpieBFT: An Efficient Asynchronous BFT Protocol for Blockchain

Yaoqi Wang, Yang Liu$^{(\boxtimes)}$, Song Peng, and Jingwen Chen

Henan University of Technology, Zhengzhou 450001, China
liu_yang@haut.edu.cn

Abstract. Asynchronous Byzantine fault tolerance (BFT) protocols have received increasing attention due to their better real network adaptation and non-leader model. Synchronous BFT protocols, such as the PBFT, may perform better but lose their liveness if the network turns unstable. In this paper, we propose MagpieBFT, a three-stage efficient asynchronous BFT protocol, which exhibits more throughput and less latency than HoneyBadgerBFT, DumboBFT and DispersedLedger. We adopt the heterogeneous transaction execution mode that allows each proposer processing separate transactions asynchronously to release the concurrent execution capability of the system. We lower the verification overhead of threshold signatures to improve the throughput of the system. We remove the asynchronous binary agreement stage to decrease the transaction latency. Experimental results demonstrate that when the node size reaches 80, the throughput of our protocol is 7.9 times of that in HoneyBadgerBFT, 2.5 times of that in DumboBFT, and 3.5 times of that in DispersedLedger.

Keywords: Blockchain · byzantine fault tolerance · asynchronous BFT

1 Introduction

In distributed systems, the consensus mechanism refers to the nodes in the system agreeing on the order of transactions. Byzantine Fault Tolerance (BFT) [16] refers to the ability of a system that can tolerate arbitrary failures, including Byzantine attacks. A BFT protocol is used to ensure that non-faulty replicas can agree on a value despite the efforts of Byzantine nodes.

1.1 Related Work

Byzantine fault tolerance protocols provide safety and liveness constraints, allowing a distributed system to function normally even if some nodes are malicious. However, in the asynchronous settings, Fisher et al. [12] demonstrated that no deterministic consensus protocol could address the consistency with one faulty node. The asynchronous binary agreement protocols [4,8,19] illustrated that the FLP impossibility theory could be circumvented by employing randomization. The state machine replication system is constructed by using the state-of-the-art

© The Author(s), under exclusive license to Springer Nature Singapore Pte Ltd. 2024
J. Chen et al. (Eds.): BlockSys 2023, CCIS 1897, pp. 311–324, 2024.
https://doi.org/10.1007/978-981-99-8104-5_23

asynchronous BFT protocols [2,11,13,17] in an asynchronous network environment. The DAG-based asynchronous BFT protocols [3,14] allow nodes to agree on the order of transactions represented with the Directed Acyclic Graph (DAG).

HoneyBadgerBFT [17] is the first practical asynchronous BFT protocol, which does not require time assumptions like the Timeout mechanism to build a state machine replication system in the asynchronous network environment. The protocol optimizes the asynchronous binary Byzantine agreement (ABBA) [6] and adopts the asynchronous common subset (ACS) proposed by Ben-or [5] to build blocks. The ACS protocol includes two sub-protocols: reliable broadcast (RBC) protocol and asynchronous binary agreement (ABA) protocol. Each node broadcasts the transaction through the RBC protocol and then executes the ABA protocol to decide whether or not to commit the transaction.

According to DumboBFT, the performance bottleneck of HoneyBadgerBFT results from the ABA protocol. There must have N ABA instances launched per round, and each instance has to verify $O(n^2)$ threshold signatures, therefore the algorithm complexity goes to $O(n^3)$. Some ABA instances may take a long to reach an agreement if the network becomes unstable or the number of nodes bumps up. Minimizing the number of ABA instances of each round becomes the key to improving system efficiency. DumboBFT provides two solutions, which are Dumbo1 and Dumbo2.

Dumbo1 decreases the rounds of ABA running from n to k. Since a committee composed of k members is randomly selected ($k < n$ and k is independent of n) to participate in the consensus, the ABA protocol only needs to run k times to determine the consistency.

Dumbo2 lowers the number of times the ABA protocol is executed to a constant value independent of the scale of nodes by using the multi-valued Byzantine agreement (MVBA) [7]. In Dumbo2, each node broadcasts transactions through the provable reliable broadcast (PRBC) protocol and executes the MVBA to determine which transactions should be committed.

Although Dumbo2 has decreased the number of ABA instances to a constant value mostly less than three, the verification overhead caused by threshold signatures remains the same with HoneyBadgerBFT, which is still significant, according to our findings.

1.2 Our Contributions

We propose an efficient asynchronous BFT protocol, namely MagpieBFT, which provides a three-stage commitment model to reach the agreement. We decrease the verification overhead of the threshold signature and the number of communication rounds between the nodes.

The features and advantages of the protocol are as follows:

- In MagpieBFT, we adopt a heterogeneous transaction execution mode to release the system's concurrent execution capability, which means each node can execute the transactions in concurrency and yield the block requests asynchronously. In HoneyBadgerBFT, the transaction requests proposed by each node will generate an individual block, which increases the frequency of reaching agreement. However, since each block generation requires voting, the frequent broadcast of votes hinders the throughput of the system. In MagpieBFT, the number of voting is decreased by generating a total block for all the transaction requests proposed by each node to improve the throughput of the system.

- In the transaction broadcast stage of the MagpieBFT, the proposer gathers all partial signatures without propagating them. In contrast, in Dumbo2, all nodes broadcast the partial signatures which increases the algorithm complexity. During the MagpieBFT's vector broadcast stage, each node only verifies the proofs in the vectors that it has not verified, rather than verifying all proofs in the vectors like Dumbo2. By lowering the verification overhead of threshold signatures from $O\left(n^3\right)$ to asymptotically optimal $O\left(n^2\right)$, we further improve the throughput of the system.

- The VABA [2] algorithm is utilized to eliminate the ABA phase, ensuring rapid termination of the algorithm while satisfying the FLP impossibility theorem. Moreover, we employ the three-phase commit architecture of PBFT to decrease communication rounds in the VABA algorithm.

2   MagpieBFT Model

2.1   Key Notations

See Table 1.

Table 1. Notations

Notation	Meaning
P_s	node identifier
P_p	the producer
v_s	the value proposed by P_s
$\rho_{\langle j, v_s \rangle}$	the partial signature generated by P_j based on v_s
h_{v_s}	the hash value of v_s
σ_{v_s}	the threshold signature of v_s
TX_s	the transactions proposed by P_s
V_s	the transaction sequence vector proposed by P_s
$\sigma_{\langle preprepare, V_s \rangle}$	the preprepare signature for V_s
$\sigma_{\langle prepare, V_s \rangle}$	the prepare signature for V_s
$\sigma_{\langle commit, V_s \rangle}$	the commit signature for V_s

2.2   System Model

We consider a system involving a set of $n = 3f + 1$ nodes, indexed by $i \in n$ where $[n] = \{1, 2, \ldots, n\}$.

Setup. Each node interacts with a trusted dealer during the initialization stage to obtain a public key and its private key.

Static Byzantine faults. A set of $F \in [n]$ of up to $f = |F|$ nodes are faulty, which are the Byzantine nodes controlled by the adversary, who learns all internal states kept by the Byzantine nodes.

Asynchronous network. Network communication consists of point-to-point (P2P), authenticated, and reliable channels. An authenticated P2P channel connects each pair of nodes.

3   MagpieBFT Protocol

Any miner can propose a block request in a public blockchain system like the Bitcoin system after executing the homogeneous transactions. However, in the public blockchain system, PoX consensus protocols [15,18] require a significant amount of computing power to compete for the accounting rights, resulting in the low performance of the public blockchain system. Despite multiple endorsers being able to execute transactions concurrently in the consortium blockchain system, the system's overall efficiency has not been greatly improved. The reason is that the partially synchronous BFT protocols [1,9,10,20] employed in the existing consortium blockchain systems are using a strong leader model. Although each node may process transactions concurrently, the block request can't be yielded asynchronously to fully release the concurrent execution capacity of the system. Therefore, it is recognized that the asynchronous BFT protocols quite fit in both the public blockchain and the consortium blockchain systems due to their no-leader model and unstable network adaptation capability, in which any node can launch a block request to keep consistent with the architecture for the public blockchain systems and release the concurrency performance for the consortium blockchain systems.

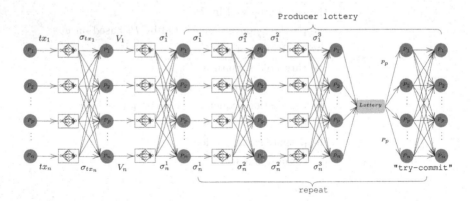

Fig. 1. Three-stage commitment model of MagpieBFT. σ_j^1 is the *preprepare* signature for V_j. σ_j^2 is the *prepare* signature for V_j. σ_j^3 is the *commit* signature for V_j.

3.1 Overview

We propose an efficient three-stage asynchronous BFT protocol, MagpieBFT, that supports each node concurrently initiating a block request, which can fully release the concurrency capability of the system.

The architecture of the protocol is shown in Fig. 1.

MagpieBFT works in a round-based manner, in which each round consists of three stages: transaction broadcast stage, vector broadcast stage, and producer lottery and decision stage.

Each node broadcasts its transaction request to all the other nodes in the transaction broadcast stage. All nodes in our protocol could broadcast transactions to release the system's concurrent execution capacity entirely.

Algorithm 1. The MagpieBFT protocol (for party P_i)

1: **Local variables Initialization:**
2:     $V_i = \{(s_1, \sigma_{tx_1}), (s_2, \sigma_{tx_2}), \cdots, (s_n, \sigma_{tx_n})\}$, where $(s_j, \sigma_{tx_j}) \leftarrow (\bot, \bot)$ for all $1 \le j \le n$; ▷ The order in which P_i executes transactions is stored in V_i, where s_j is the identifier of the node, and σ_{tx_j} is the proof of the transaction(indicates that the proposer P_j of tx_j is an honest node).
3:     $Len \leftarrow 0$
4:     $D_i \leftarrow \{\}$ ▷ D_i is used to store the valid transaction order vector V.
5: **upon** receiving transaction tx_i from the client **do**
6:     broadcast tx_i to all nodes
7: **upon** delivery of (j, σ_j) from P_j **do**
8:     $(s_j, \sigma_j) \leftarrow (j, \sigma_j)$ ▷ Store valid proof of the transaction.
9:     $Len = Len + 1$
10: **upon** $Len = n - f$ **do**
11:     participate the vector broadcast stage with V_i
12: **upon** delivery $\sigma_{\langle preprepare, V_i \rangle}$ from the vector broadcast stage **do**
13:     participate the producer lottery selection and decision stage
14: **upon** delivery of V_p from the producer lottery selection and decision stage
15:     **for each** $\sigma_{tx_j} \in V_p$ **do**
16:         **if** P_i has delivered tx_j **then**
17:             **continue**
18:         **else**
19:             Call for help from other parties to recover the missing transaction tx_j.

In the vector broadcast stage, each node broadcasts the received proofs to all the other nodes through a vector, in which is the order of the proofs corresponding to the sequence of transactions delivering by each node. The vector broadcast by the producer will determine the order of transactions within our final commit block. After each node receives the vector broadcast from other nodes, it only verifies the proof that it has not verified in the vector, rather than verifying all proofs in the vector, lowering the verification overhead of the threshold signature. Each node P_i will get the *preprepare* signature of the transaction sequence vector V_i once the vector broadcast phase is completed.

In the producer lottery and decision stage, two additional threshold signatures for each V_i are constructed: the *prepare* signature and the *commit* signature. Safety is achieved through the marriage of the *prepare* signature and the *commit* signature. Once an honest node commits V_i, then all honest nodes will lock themselves on V_i. The combination of the *preprepare* signature and the *prepare* signature meets liveness. If an honest node locks itself on V_i, then all honest nodes will have a key to unlock the "*locked*" nodes, allowing the "*locked*" nodes to take part in the following step. After each node P_i obtaining the *commit* signature for V_i, an unique producer P_p is randomly picked out via the threshold coin-tossing schema. The *preprepare*, *prepare*, and *commit* signatures for V_p that each node has acquired will be broadcast. Each node makes a decision depending on whether it receives the *preprepare*, *prepare*, or *commit* signature of V_p. The probability of the chosen producer to be an honest node is greater than $2/3$, so the exception of the number of lotteries is less than $3/2$. The protocol is shown in Algorithm 1.

Algorithm 2. Provable broadcast, with identifier ID and sender P_s

---

Input: v_s; *VAL*   ▷ *VAL* is a function used to verify v_s.
Output: ID; σ_{v_s}
1: **Local variables Initialization:**
2:    $Shares \leftarrow \{\}$ ▷ *Shares* is used to cache partial signatures sent from other nodes.
3:    $v_s \leftarrow v_s$
4:    $VAL \leftarrow VAL$
      ▷ Protocol for the sender P_s
5: broadcast v_s to all nodes
6:    wait until $|Shares| = 2f + 1$
7:       $\sigma \leftarrow$ Combine$_{2f+1}$ (ID, *Shares*)   ▷ Compute the proof σ_{v_s}.
8:       multicast(Done, ID, σ_{v_s})
9: **upon** receiving $\left(\text{Vote, ID}, \rho_{\langle j,v_s\rangle}\right)$ from P_j for the first time **do**
10:    **if** ShareVerify$_{2f+1}$ $\left(\text{ID}, \rho_{\langle j,v_s\rangle}\right) = 1$ **then**   ▷ Verify the partial signature $\rho_{\langle j,v_s\rangle}$.
11:       $Shares \leftarrow Shares \cup \{j, \rho_j\}$
      ▷ Protocol for each party P_i
12: **upon** receiving transactions from the sender P_s **do**
13:    **if** $VAL\,(v_s) = true$ **then**
14:       $\rho_i \leftarrow$ SigShare (ID, sk_i)   ▷ Generate the partial signature $\rho_{\langle i,v_s\rangle}$.
15:       send $\left(\text{Vote, ID}, \rho_{\langle i,v_s\rangle}\right)$ to P_s
16: **upon** receiving (Done, ID, σ_{v_s}) from P_s
17:    **if** Verify (ID, σ_{v_s}) $= true$ **then**   ▷ Verify the proof σ_{v_s}.
18:       **return** (ID, σ_{v_s})

3.2   Detailed TortoiseBFT Protocol Description

Transaction Broadcast Stage. The provable broadcast protocol is employed to broadcast the transactions. The provable broadcast protocol consists of three

---

Algorithm 3. Transaction broadcast stage, with identifier ID and sender P_s

1: **function** $VAL(TX_s)$
2: **for each** $tx \in TX_s$ **do**   ▷ Each transaction consists of three parts, an application payload, an ECDSA signature and two public keys.
3:    **if** ECDSA signature is invalid **then**
4:      **return** false
5:    **return** true
6: **end function**

7: **upon** receiving TX_s from the client **do**
8: $PB_{\langle TX_s, P_s \rangle}(TX_s, VAL)$ ▷ Take TX_s and VAL as input to PB.

---

rounds. Initially, the proposed P_s broadcasts his proposed value v_s to all nodes. After receiving v_s from the proposer, each node will verify v_s through the VAL function. If v_s is valid, partial signature $\rho_{\langle i, v_s \rangle}$ of v_s will be generated and sent back to the proposer. If the proposer could receive $2f+1$ valid partial signatures, it will combine them into a threshold signature σ_{v_s} and broadcast it to all the other nodes. If σ_{v_s} is valid after verification, which means at least $2f + 1$ nodes have endorsed v_s. The provable broadcast protocol is shown in Algorithm 2.

Algorithm 4. Vector broadcast stage, with identifier ID and sender P_s

1: **function** $EX\text{-}VAL(\text{ID}, V)$ ▷ Verify the proofs in the transaction sequence vector V.
2: **if** $|V| < n - f$
3:    **return** false
4: **for each** $(j, \sigma_j) \in V$ **do** ▷ j is the identifier of the node, and σ_j is the proof of the transaction.
5:    **if** P_i delivered σ_j **then**
6:      **continue**
7:    **else if** $\text{ShareVerify}_{2f+1}(j, \sigma_j) = true$ **then**
8:      **return** false
9: **return** true
10: **end function**

11: **upon** delivering $n - f$ distinct $PB_{\langle TX_j, P_j \rangle}$ output at the transaction broadcast stage **do**
12: $PB^{preprepare}_{\langle V_s, P_s \rangle}(V_s, EX\text{-}VAL)$ ▷ Take V_s and $EX\text{-}VAL$ as input to PB.

After receiving the transaction requests TX_s from the near clients, each proposer P_s passes TX_s and the VAL function as parameters into the provable broadcast protocol, where the VAL function is utilized to verify each transaction tx in TX_s. The transaction broadcast stage is shown in Algorithm 3.

Vector Broadcast Stage. It is noticed that each node may have different sequence of transactions it has received during the transaction broadcast stage. The purpose of the vector broadcast stage is to make each node aware of the sequences of the other nodes.

Algorithm 5. Producer lottery and decision stage, with identifier ID and sender P_s

1: **Local variables Initialization:**
2:    $r \leftarrow$ current round
3:    $k \leftarrow 1$
4:    $lock \leftarrow \perp$

5: **function** $VAL\big(\text{ID}, \sigma_{\langle \perp, V_j \rangle}, k\big)$
6:    **if** input is $\perp$ **then**
7:       **return** true
8:    **if** Verify $\big(\text{ID}, \sigma_{\langle \perp, V_j \rangle}\big) = true$ **and** $k = 1$ **then**
9:       **return** true
10:    **if** $lock = \perp$ **and** Verify $\big(\text{ID}, \sigma_{\langle \perp, V_j \rangle}\big) = true$ **then**
11:       **return** true
12:    **if** $lock \neq \perp$ **and** $lock$ extends from $\sigma_{\langle \perp, V_j \rangle}$ **then**
13:       **return** true
14:    **return** false
15: **end function**

16: **for each** $k \in \{1, 2, ..., n\}$ **do**
17:    **upon** delivering $\big(\text{ID}, \sigma_{\langle preprepare, V_s \rangle}\big)$ from $PB^{preprepare}_{\langle V_s, P_s \rangle}$ **do**
18:       $PB^{prepare}_{\langle V_s, P_s \rangle} \big(\sigma_{\langle preprepare, V_s \rangle}, VAL\big)$
19:    **upon** delivering $\big(\text{ID}, \sigma_{\langle prepare, V_s \rangle}\big)$ from $PB^{prepare}_{\langle V_s, P_s \rangle}$ **do**
20:       $PB^{commit}_{\langle V_s, P_s \rangle} \big(\sigma_{\langle prepare, V_s \rangle}, VAL\big)$
21:    **upon** delivering $n - f$ distinct $PB^{Commit}_{\langle V_j, P_j \rangle}$ output **do**
22:       $P_p \leftarrow \text{Lottery}_{\langle r, k \rangle}$
23:       multicast$\big(\text{try-commit}, \sigma_{\langle latest, V_p \rangle}\big)$
24:       **upon** receiving $n - f$ try-commit messages from distinct parties **do**
25:          **if** receives a valid $\sigma_{\langle commit, V_p \rangle}$ **then**
26:             **return** V_p
27:          **if** receives a valid $\sigma_{\langle prepare, V_p \rangle}$ **then**
28:           **if** $lock = \perp$ **then**
29:             $lock \leftarrow \sigma_{\langle prepare, V_p \rangle}$
30:          **if** receives a valid $\sigma_{\langle preprepare, V_p \rangle}$ **then**
31:             $PB^{prepare}_{\langle V_s, P_s \rangle} \big(\sigma_{\langle preprepare, V_p \rangle}, VAL\big)$
32:          **if** no valid signature on V_p is received **then**
33:             **if** $\sigma_{\langle preprepare, V_p \rangle} = \perp$ **then**
34:                $PB^{prepare}_{\langle \perp, P_s \rangle} \big(\sigma_{\langle \perp, \perp \rangle}, VAL\big)$
35:             **else**
36:                $PB^{prepare}_{\langle V_s, P_s \rangle} \big(\sigma_{\langle preprepare, V_s \rangle}, VAL\big)$

After the proposer receiving $n - f$ threshold signatures from the other nodes during the transaction broadcast stage, it will place the threshold signatures with a sequence into a transaction sequence vector V_s and broadcast V_s. Each proposer P_s passes V_s and the *EX-VAL* function as parameters into the provable broadcast protocol, where the *EX-VAL* function is utilized to verify each threshold signature σ_{v_s} in V_s. During the verification, each node only verifies the threshold signature that it has not been confirmed in the vector before to overcome the problem of repeated verification. The detail of the vector broadcast stage is shown in Algorithm 4.

Producer Lottery and Decision Stage. After each node verifying $n - f$ valid vectors, then the producer lottery and decision stage is coming. Before the producer is selected, two additional threshold signatures for each V_i are generated: the *prepare* signature $\sigma_{\langle prepare, V_i \rangle}$ and the *commit* signature $\sigma_{\langle commit, V_i \rangle}$.

The *preprepare* signature is utilized as the input of provable broadcast protocol to acquire the *prepare* signature once each node P_i obtains the *preprepare* signature of the V_i during the vector broadcast stage. Immediately afterward, the *prepare* signature is employed as the input of provable broadcast protocol to acquire the *commit* signature. For each V_i, its $\sigma_{\langle preprepare, V_i \rangle}$, $\sigma_{\langle prepare, V_i \rangle}$ and $\sigma_{\langle commit, V_i \rangle}$ signatures satisfy the following relation constraint:

1. If an honest node receives $\sigma_{\langle commit, V_i \rangle}$, then at least $f + 1$ honest nodes have received $\sigma_{\langle prepare, V_i \rangle}$.
2. If an honest node receives $\sigma_{\langle prepare, V_i \rangle}$, then at least $f + 1$ honest nodes have received $\sigma_{\langle preprepare, V_i \rangle}$.

In comparison to VABA, constructing only three signatures for the proposal values of each node suffices. Consequently, this reduces the communication rounds of the VABA algorithm.

An unique producer is randomly picked out via the threshold coin-tossing schema. Each node will broadcast partial signatures, and when each node receives $2f + 1$ partial signatures, it will form a threshold signature. To maintain randomness, we hash the threshold signature and take the remainder according to the number of nodes, so that all nodes can get the common producer P_p.

Once P_p is extracted, all nodes will move to the "try-commit" stage. Each node broadcasts the latest signature of V_p to all nodes in the "try-commit" message. Each node P_i needs to make the following choices after receiving $n - f$ "try-commit" messages:

1. If P_i receives a $\sigma_{\langle commit, V_p \rangle}$, P_i will commit V_p.
2. If P_i receives a $\sigma_{\langle prepare, V_p \rangle}$, P_i will *lock* on V_p.
3. If P_i receives a $\sigma_{\langle preprepare, V_p \rangle}$, $\sigma_{\langle preprepare, V_p \rangle}$ is employed as the input by P_i for the next round.
4. If P_i has not received any signature, P_i will hold its point of view (still use $\sigma_{\langle preprepare, V_i \rangle}$ as the input for the next round, if $\sigma_{\langle preprepare, V_i \rangle}$ is not generated, P_i will use a null value as the input for the next round).

We only broadcast the latest signature of V_p (the latest signature refers to the last signature generated among the three signatures) when broadcasting its signature. This leads to reduced communication overhead compared to VABA. Nodes are permitted to propose empty operations during the producer lottery and decision stage, facilitating its swift termination.

The detail of the producer lottery and decision broadcast stage is shown in Algorithm 5.

4   Theoretical Analysis of the Protocol

Claim 1. The threshold signature verification overhead in MagpieBFT is $O(n^2)$.

Proof. In the transaction broadcast stage, only the proposer gathers partial signatures and broadcasts σ to all nodes after calculating the threshold signature σ. As a result, in the transaction broadcasting stage, the verification cost of the threshold signature is $O(n^2)$.

The maximum number of valid threshold signatures that may be generated is n since there are only n nodes in the system. Each node should validate the threshold signature at most n times, and once the threshold signature has been validated, the node does not need to verify it repeatedly. The verification cost of the threshold signature is $O(n^2)$ at the vector broadcast stage.

In conclusion, the total threshold signature verification overhead of the MagpieBFT is $O(n^2)$.

Lemma 1. Assuming that the proposer is an honest node, if one honest node outputs v and another honest node outputs v', then $v = v'$.

Proof. To show a contradiction, suppose $v \neq v'$. Because each proposed value has to get $2f + 1$ votes to be confirmed, there must be at least one honest node who voted twice for the same proposer. This condition would be impossible because the honest nodes shall vote for the proposer only once.

Lemma 2. *(Liveness)* An honest node will still participate in the subsequent decision even if it has a *lock*.

Proof. Assume that an honest node locks itself on V_p after receiving $\sigma_{\langle prepare, V_p \rangle}$ in the k round of the producer lottery and decision stage. It implies that at least $f+1$ honest nodes in the system have received $\sigma_{\langle preprepare, V_p \rangle}$. Each honest node will get $\sigma_{\langle preprepare, V_p \rangle}$ at the "try-commit" stage and use $\sigma_{\langle preprepare, V_p \rangle}$ as the proposed value for the following round.

As all honest nodes have $\sigma_{\langle preprepare, V_p \rangle}$ in the round j $(j \geq k+1)$, the honest nodes holding the *lock* will continue to vote after obtaining $\sigma_{\langle preprepare, V_p \rangle}$, so as to maintain the liveness of the system.

Lemma 3 *(Agreement).* If an honest node outputs the transaction sequence vector V_p, all honest nodes will eventually output the transaction sequence vector V_p.

Proof. Assume that an honest node outputs the transaction sequence vector V_p upon acquiring $\sigma_{\langle commit,V_p \rangle}$ in the k round of the producer lottery and decision stage. It implies that at least $f + 1$ honest nodes in the system have received $\sigma_{\langle preprepare,V_p \rangle}$ for the reason that there exists the progressive relationship between $\sigma_{\langle commit,V_p \rangle}$ and $\sigma_{\langle preprepare,V_p \rangle}$. Since the adversary can only control at most f nodes, each honest node will receive $\sigma_{\langle preprepare,V_p \rangle}$ in the "try-commit" stage and use $\sigma_{\langle preprepare,V_p \rangle}$ as the proposed value for the next round.

In the round j ($j \geq k + 1$), since all honest nodes have $\sigma_{\langle preprepare,V_p \rangle}$, the Byzantine producer cannot persuade all honest nodes to submit V_p' ($V_p' \neq V_p$). As the rounds continue to iterate, all honest nodes will eventually output the transaction sequence vector V_p.

Lemma 4 *(Total Order).* If the transaction sequence output by one honest node is $tx_1, tx_2, \cdots, tx_j$, and the transaction sequence output by another honest node is $tx_1', tx_2', \cdots, tx_j'$, then for all $i \leq j$, there is $tx_i = tx_j'$.

Proof. All honest nodes will deliver the same transaction sequence vector V_p, according to Lemma 3. For each valid threshold signature in V_p, according to Lemma 1, all honest nodes will output the same transaction (even if an honest node may not receive the corresponding transaction, the node can seek the help of other nodes to restore the missing transaction).

Lemma 5 *(Totality).* If $n - f$ honest nodes have received an input, then all honest parties will produce an output.

Proof. Assume there are $n - f$ honest nodes in the system that receive the transaction requests from the near clients, each node will participate in the vector broadcast stage after receiving $n - f$ threshold signatures in the transaction broadcast stage. Then, each honest node will broadcast the transaction sequence vector in the vector broadcast stage. All honest nodes will participate in the producer lottery and decision stage after receiving $n - f$ valid vectors in the vector broadcast stage. Following *agreement* of MagpieBFT, all honest nodes can get the same output.

5   Experimental Evaluations

We implement our MagpieBFT, DispersedLedger, Dumbo2, and HoneyBadgerBFT to evaluate their performance with the same parameters as in HoneyBadgerBFT.

Setup. We deployed the protocols on the two local servers. Each server had 40 CPUs supported by Intel(R) Xeon(R) Gold 5218R processors. All cores sustained a Turbo CPU clock speed of up to 2.1 GHz. The four protocols are run in the same environment with the same parameters.

Evaluation. We do experiments by altering the size of transactions and the scale of nodes. We varying the batch size from 4 to $1 \cdot 10^6$ transactions.

322   Y. Wang et al.

Latency. Latency is measured as the time difference from the nodes proposed the transactions to the time that $n - f$ nodes produced the block. The transactions scale and the node scale have an implication on the latency. The basic latency refers to the latency at the circumstances of the number of transactions equals to 1.

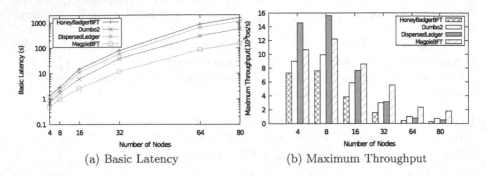

(a) Basic Latency   (b) Maximum Throughput

Fig. 2. Basic Latency and Maximum Throughput

Figure 2(a) depicts the basic latency of the target protocols including Honey-BadgerBFT, Dumbo2, DispersedLedger, and MagpieBFT with the nodes scale varying. The basic latency gap among them increases as the nodes scale grows. We can see that MagpieBFT has 9.9 times less latency than HoneyBadgerBFT, 3.4 times less latency than Dumbo2, and 7.3 times less latency than DispersedLedger when the node size is 64, due to the time-consuming ABA stage in MagpieBFT being removed.

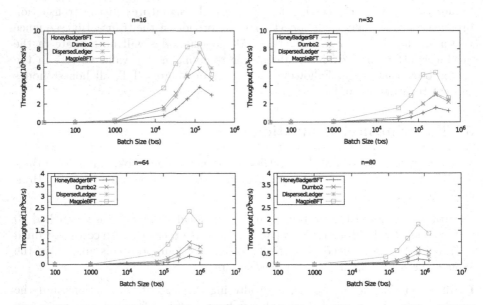

Fig. 3. Throughput of HoneyBadgerBFT, Dumbo2, DispersedLedger, and MagpieBFT

Throughput. The number of transactions committed by the system per second is known as the throughput. Comparison experiments are conducted to evaluate the throughput of the target protocols as the number of transactions varying. The experimental results of the throughput are listed in Fig. 3.

Figure 2(b) depicts the maximum throughput of the target protocols including HoneyBadgerBFT, Dumbo2, DispersedLedger, and MagpieBFT with the nodes scale varying. The communication overhead will rise along with the node's scale, reducing the throughput of HoneyBadgerBFT, Dumbo2, DispersedLedger, and MagpieBFT.

The maximum throughput gap among the four protocols increases as the scale of the node grows. We can see that MagpieBFT has 2.5 times more throughput than Dumbo2, 3.5 times more throughput than DispersedLedger, and 6.2 times more throughput than HoneyBadgerBFT when the node size is 64, since the verification overhead of the threshold signature in MagpieBFT is lowered.

6 Conclusions

In this paper, we present an efficient asynchronous BFT protocol-MagpieBFT to further improve the performance of asynchronous BFT protocols, such as Honey-BadgerBFT and DumboBFT. The comparison experimental results demonstrate the superiority of the MagpieBFT with the following improvement and optimization of the system. (1) MagpieBFT adopts the heterogeneous execution architecture that enables each node processing separate transactions concurrently and proposing the block requests asynchronously, thus the concurrent execution capability of the system can be released to complement the performance loss in public blockchain and consortium blockchain system. (2) MagpieBFT minimizes the threshold signature verification overhead in HoneyBadgerBFT, DumboBFT, and DispersedLedger from $O\left(n^3\right)$ to asymptotically optimal $O\left(n^2\right)$. (3) MagpieBFT removes the asynchronous binary agreement stage of to improve the transaction latency while maintaining safety constraints of the system consistency.

Acknowledgments. The authors are supported by the significant scientific and technological project of Henan Province (No. 201300210200, 201300210100), the Collaborative innovation Key Project of Zhengzhou city (No. 21ZZXTCX07), the Fundamental research project of key scientific research project plan of colleges and universities of Henan Province (No. 23ZX017), the Key scientific and technological research project of Henan Province (No. 232102211082).

References

1. Abraham, I., Malkhi, D., Nayak, K., Ren, L., Yin, M.: Sync HotStuff: simple and practical synchronous state machine replication. In: 2020 IEEE Symposium on Security and Privacy (SP), pp. 106–118. IEEE (2020)
2. Abraham, I., Malkhi, D., Spiegelman, A.: Asymptotically optimal validated asynchronous byzantine agreement. In: Proceedings of the 2019 ACM Symposium on Principles of Distributed Computing, pp. 337–346 (2019)

3. Baird, L., Luykx, A.: The Hashgraph protocol: Efficient asynchronous BFT for high-throughput distributed ledgers. In: 2020 International Conference on Omnilayer Intelligent Systems (COINS), pp. 1–7. IEEE (2020)

4. Ben-Or, M.: Another advantage of free choice (extended abstract) completely asynchronous agreement protocols. In: Proceedings of the Second Annual ACM Symposium on Principles of Distributed Computing, pp. 27–30 (1983)

5. Ben-Or, M., Kelmer, B., Rabin, T.: Asynchronous secure computations with optimal resilience. In: Proceedings of the Thirteenth Annual ACM Symposium on Principles of Distributed Computing, pp. 183–192 (1994)

6. Cachin, C., Shoup, V.: Random oracles in constantinople: practical asynchronous byzantine agreement using. In: Proceedings of the 19th ACM Symposium on Principles of Distributed Computing, pp. 1–26 (2000)

7. Cachin, C., Kursawe, K., Petzold, F., Shoup, V.: Secure and efficient asynchronous broadcast protocols. In: Kilian, J. (ed.) CRYPTO 2001. LNCS, vol. 2139, pp. 524–541. Springer, Heidelberg (2001). https://doi.org/10.1007/3-540-44647-8_31

8. Cachin, C., Kursawe, K., Shoup, V.: Random oracles in constantinople: practical asynchronous byzantine agreement using cryptography. J. Cryptol. **18**(3), 219–246 (2005)

9. Castro, M., Liskov, B.: Practical byzantine fault tolerance. In: OsDI. vol. 99, pp. 173–186 (1999)

10. Chan, T.H., Pass, R., Shi, E.: PaLa: a simple partially synchronous blockchain. Cryptology ePrint Archive (2018)

11. Duan, S., Reiter, M.K., Zhang, H.: Beat: Asynchronous BFT made practical. In: Proceedings of the 2018 ACM SIGSAC Conference on Computer and Communications Security, pp. 2028–2041 (2018)

12. Fischer, M.J., Lynch, N.A., Paterson, M.S.: Impossibility of distributed consensus with one faulty process. J. ACM (JACM) **32**(2), 374–382 (1985)

13. Guo, B., Lu, Z., Tang, Q., Xu, J., Zhang, Z.: Dumbo: faster asynchronous BFT protocols. In: Proceedings of the 2020 ACM SIGSAC Conference on Computer and Communications Security, pp. 803–818 (2020)

14. Keidar, I., Kokoris-Kogias, E., Naor, O., Spiegelman, A.: All you need is DAG. In: Proceedings of the 2021 ACM Symposium on Principles of Distributed Computing, pp. 165–175 (2021)

15. King, S., Nadal, S.: Ppcoin: peer-to-peer crypto-currency with proof-of-stake. Self-published Paper, August 19(1) (2012)

16. Lamport, L., Shostak, R., Pease, M.: The byzantine generals problem. In: Concurrency: The Works of Leslie Lamport, pp. 203–226 (2019)

17. Miller, A., Xia, Y., Croman, K., Shi, E., Song, D.: The honey badger of BFT protocols. In: Proceedings of the 2016 ACM SIGSAC Conference on Computer and Communications Security, pp. 31–42 (2016)

18. Nakamoto, S.: Bitcoin: a peer-to-peer electronic cash system. Decentralized Business Review, p. 21260 (2008)

19. Rabin, M.O.: Randomized byzantine generals. In: 24th Annual Symposium on Foundations of Computer Science (SFCS 1983), pp. 403–409. IEEE (1983)

20. Yin, M., Malkhi, D., Reiter, M.K., Gueta, G.G., Abraham, I.: HotStuff: BFT consensus with linearity and responsiveness. In: Proceedings of the 2019 ACM Symposium on Principles of Distributed Computing, pp. 347–356 (2019)

A Hierarchical Blockchain Framework with Selectable Consensus Scope for Data Sharing in Internet of Vehicles

Xi Lou[1], Ke Zhang[1,2](✉), Fan Wu[1,2], Xiaoyan Huang[1,2], and Luyang Wang[1]

[1] School of Information and Communication Engineering, University of Electronic Science and Technology of China, Chengdu 611731, China
zhangke@uestc.edu.cn
[2] Shenzhen Institute for Advanced Study, University of Electronic Science and Technology of China, Shenzhen 518000, China

Abstract. With the development of Internet of Vehicles (IoVs), data sharing has become a crucial means to improve driving safety and travel efficiency. In the process of data sharing, ensuring the security of the sharing process is of paramount importance. Using blockchain technology to ensure the security of data sharing in vehicular networking scenarios is a promising approach. However, there are some issues in applying blockchain to data sharing in vehicular networking scenarios. On the one hand, the consensus of blockchain requires multiple full network broadcasts, and as the number of nodes in the network increases, system overhead will grow rapidly. On the other hand, malicious nodes in blockchain may affect system security. To address these problems, we propose a hierarchical blockchain framework with selectable consensus scope. We dynamically select the consensus scope of data according to its impact range, avoiding consensus on the entire network. In addition, we propose a trust model to compute the reliability of Roadside units (RSUs) in the area, assigning different permissions to different RSUs in the system. We also improve the PBFT algorithm based on this reputation model, further reducing the cost of consensus. Simulation results show that the proposed approach can reduce consensus consumption and identify malicious nodes more quickly, ensuring the efficiency and security of the data sharing process.

Keywords: Blockchain · Internet of Vehicles · Data Sharing · Trust Model · PBFT

1 Introduction

With the development of technology, The Internet of Things (IoT) technologies, including the IoVs, have been rapidly developing [1,2]. People pay more attention to their travel experience during the travel process. Nowadays, data plays an increasingly important role in various domains [3], and data sharing

J. Chen et al. (Eds.): BlockSys 2023, CCIS 1897, pp. 325–338, 2024.
https://doi.org/10.1007/978-981-99-8104-5_24

provides powerful guarantees for improving traffic efficiency [4]. Vehicles perceive surrounding information through sensors and share this information with other vehicles, enabling other vehicles to quickly grasp the surrounding environment information. However, malicious vehicles can mislead other vehicles' driving judgments by sharing false data or tampering with shared data, thereby endangering traffic safety. Therefore, how to ensure the security and efficiency of data sharing in the IoVs is a key problem to be solved.

Blockchain technology relies on distributed ledgers, consensus mechanisms, smart contract and digital signature technology, which can guarantee the security, traceability, and privacy protection of transaction processes in distributed scenarios [5–7]. In recent years, it has been widely applied in IoT, intelligent transportation and other fields [8]. Although using blockchain technology for data sharing in the IoV can effectively solve the security problems [9], it also brings some issues. As a distributed system, blockchain requires ensuring consensus among all nodes within the system. Therefore, consensus algorithms play a critical role in blockchain technology, directly impacting the performance and scalability of blockchain systems. The traditional blockchain consensus mechanism relies on mining algorithms [10], which will result in excessively high overall computing power consumption of the system. Some other voting-based consensus algorithms such as PBFT [11] will bring huge communication overhead with the increase of network size. Moreover, in the process of data sharing, the impact scope of each data is not consistent. Consensus on different types of data across the entire network will bring a lot of useless system consumption.

Therefore, we propose an efficient hierarchical blockchain framework. In order to ensure the security of this framework, we propose a trust model, and based on this trust model, we propose an improved PBFT algorithm, which further reduces the consumption of the consensus process. Our contributions of this paper are as follows:

- We propose a hierarchical blockchain framework with selectable consensus scope, where the consensus scope list of each transaction is recorded and transactions are only validated within the specified scope instead of the entire network. The proposed framework allows for flexible data sharing within designated ranges and avoids the cost of widespread consensus.
- We introduce a trust model for consensus nodes in this framework, which considers the performance of RSUs in the consensus process and the quality of services provided by RSUs to vehicles. The trust model can rapidly detect malicious nodes and serves as the basis for selecting global blockchain consensus nodes for each sub-area, ensuring the security of the blockchain framework.
- Based on the trust reputation model, we improve the PBFT algorithm, where the reputation value of each node determines its authority in the PBFT consensus process. The improved PBFT algorithm reduces the probability of malicious nodes disrupting the consensus and also reduces the cost of the consensus process.

2   System Model and Hierarchical Blockchain Framework

The proposed system model is illustrated in Fig. 1, where blockchain serves as a secure and tamper-proof data sharing platform. We divide the entire graphical area into multiple sub-areas based on geographic conditions. There are a certain number of RSUs in each sub-area, provide services to vehicles within their communication range. RSUs maintain the blockchain ledger as the consensus nodes of the blockchain. Vehicles share their own information or the road information collected with RSUs, which encapsulate the information into blockchain transactions and perform block packaging and consensus operations on the transactions. When a vehicle needs to obtain corresponding information, it only needs to send a corresponding request to the RSU, the request contains the characteristics of the expected data, RSU will querie the information in the blockchain ledger and returns it. As an immutable distributed ledger, blockchain ensures the traceability of shared information, prevents vehicles from maliciously sharing false information, and avoids the single-point attack problem on databases in traditional data sharing scenarios. In this section, we will explain in detail the proposed hierarchical blockchain framework with selectable consensus scope and the sharing process of different types of data.

As is shown in Fig. 1, there are two types of blockchains in the proposed blockchain, namely the local blockchain and the global blockchain. The local blockchain ledger is jointly maintained by all RSUs in each sub-area, and the global blockchain is jointly maintained by the entire road network area, where a small part of the nodes in each sub-area jointly maintain a global blockchain ledger. We categorize the data that needs to be shared into two types: one type of data has a small impact range and does not need to be disseminated to the entire network, which we call local data; the other type of data has an impact range spanning multiple areas, which we call cross-domain data. We will then provide a detailed description of the sharing process for local data and cross-domain data in the proposed blockchain framework.

2.1   The Sharing Process of Local Data

Local data refers to the data with an impact range limited to a sub-area, such as local traffic information. After collecting local data, vehicles send it to nearby RSUs. Upon receiving the data sent by the vehicle, the RSU encapsulates the local data as transactions of the local blockchain, packages the transactions into local blocks, and participates in the local consensus process to add the block to the local blockchain. Specifically, the format of local transactions can be expressed as

$$TX = \{D, S_{local}, uid_v\} \tag{1}$$

where D represents the data content to be shared, S_{local} is an identifier, which indicates that the consensus scope of this transaction is only the local underlying chain. uid is the unique identity of the vehicle in the network, and uid_v indicates that the data is shared by vehicle v. After the transaction completes

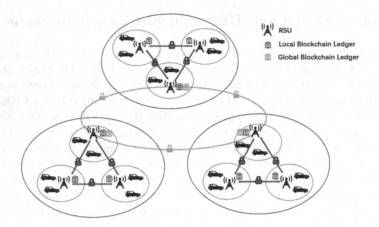

Fig. 1. System model

the consensus in the local blockchain, the data sharing is completed, and then the vehicles in this sub-area can obtain the shared data by sending a request to any RSU in this sub-area.

2.2 The Sharing Process of Cross-Domain Data

Cross-domain data refers to data whose scope of influence is not limited to a specific sub-area. For instance, a legitimate vehicle in a certain sub-area that intends to enter a different sub-area needs to migrate its identity information from the current sub-area to the next sub-area. The vehicle can send its area switching request to a RSU, and upon receiving the request, the RSU encapsulates the vehicle's data and driving behavior information as a transaction. The RSU then selects the consensus scope to be the sub-area from which the vehicle will exit and the sub-area it will enter. Once the transaction completes the consensus in local blockcains in these two sub-areas, the migration of the vehicle's identity information is complete, which that the vehicle can directly function as a legitimate vehicle in the destination sub-area after entering it. Specifically, the format of the cross-domain transaction can be expressed as

$$TX = \{D, S_{corss}, range = [l_1, \cdots, l_n], uid_v\} \qquad (2)$$

where D represents the data content to be shared, S_{corss} is an identifier, which indicates that the consensus scope of this transaction is not limited to this sub-area. $range$ is the list of consensus regions for this transaction. uid_v indicates that the data is shared by vehicle v.

When an RSU in a sub-area receives cross-domain data, it firstly determines the impact scopes of the data through the smart contract and generates a list of consensus regions for the data, and then encapsulates the data and the list of consensus regions into a cross-domain transaction on the blockchain. The RSU then packages the transaction into a block and initiates the consensus process in the local blockchain in this sub-area. The global blockchain nodes in the sub-area will check the transactions included in the new blocks in the local blockchain. If a cross-domain transaction is detected, one global node will initiate the consensus process in the global blockchain for this cross-domain transaction. Once the consensus is reached in the global blockchain, the transaction is added to the blockchain ledger of all the sub-areas' global nodes. The global nodes of the other sub-areas check this transaction added to the global blockchain ledger. If the consensus region list of the transaction contains a certain sub-area, the global blockchain node in this sub-area will consensus this transaction on the local blockchain.

In conclusion, the consensus process of cross-domain data can be divided into three stages: first, the consensus in the local blockchain of the initial sub-area; second, the consensus in the global blockchain; and third, the consensus in the local blockchains of selected sub-areas. After cross-domain data complete consensus, vehicles in the selected sub-areas can send requests to RSUs in their sub-areas to obtain the corresponding data.

3   The Trust Model of RSU

In the proposed framework, RSUs serve as consensus nodes of the blockchain, maintaining the ledger of the blockchain and providing data sharing services as servers to vehicles. Therefore, the role played by RSUs is intuitively important. However, as RSUs need to expose their wireless interface in the public environment, they are not entirely trustworthy and are vulnerable to external network attacks. Malicious RSUs may disrupt the consensus process and provide worng information to vehicles, jeopardizing traffic safety. To address this issue, this paper proposes a reputation model for RSUs, which takes into account the behavior of RSUs in the consensus process and the quality of services provided by RSUs to vehicles. The role of this trust model includes:

- Detecting malicious nodes and limiting the permissions of RSUs with low reputation values, which can reduce the losses caused by malicious behavior.
- On the basis of this trust model, the consensus algorithm is improved to enhance the security of consensus and reduce the consumption. The improved algorithm will be detailed in Sect. 5.
- The turst model will serve as the basis for selecting global blockchain nodes in each sub-area. Selecting RSUs with better reputation as global blockchain nodes can improve the security of the proposed blockchain framework.

The reputation value of RSU is recorded and updated regularly in the local blockchain, so that each RSU in the sub-area knows the reputation value of all RSUs in this sub-area. The reputation value of RSU consists of two parts: the first part is the behavior of RSU in the local blockchain consensus process, which is generated by mutual evaluation between RSUs. The second part is the service provided by RSU for vehicles, which is generated by the evaluation of vehicles for RSUs. This section will elaborate on these two parts of reputation value and introduce the calculation of the overall reputation value.

3.1   The Reputation Value of the Consensus Process

The reputation value of RSU in the consensus process refers to subjective logic [12,13], subjective logic is to formulate an individual's evaluation of reputation based on past interactions and recommendations. In a sub-area with n RSUs, the reputation value of the consensus process of RSU i can be given by the following formula:

$$O_i = \frac{O_{1 \to i} + \cdots + O_{n \to i}}{n - 1} \tag{3}$$

$$T_i = \frac{O_{1 \to i} O_1 + \cdots + O_{n \to i} O_n}{O_1 + \cdots + O_n} \tag{4}$$

where T_i represents the reputation value of RSU i in the consensus process in the sub-area, $O_{i,j}$ is the evaluation value of RSU i to RSU j and O_i represents the average evaluation value of the remaining RSUs in the sub-area to RSU i. $O_{i,j}$ is calculated based on the direct interactions between RSU i and RSU j and the recommendations of other RSUs, the following will provide a detailed explanation of the calculation of $O_{i,j}$.

Direct Reputation of RSU i to RSU j. At a certain time t, the direct reputation value of RSU i to RSU j is related to their interation history within a time window of length T. This time window can be divided into a series of time slots $\{t_1, \cdots, t_x, \cdots, t_X\}$. In a time slot t_x, the direct reputation of RSU i to RSU j can be represented as a three-dimensional vector

$$p_{i \to j}^{t_x} = \left\{ g_{i \to j}^{t_x}, b_{i \to j}^{t_x}, u_{i \to j}^{t_x} \right\} \tag{5}$$

where $g_{i \to j}^{t_x}$ represents trust, $b_{i \to j}^{t_x}$ represents distrust and $u_{i \to j}^{t_x}$ represents uncertainty. $g_{i \to j}^{t_x}, b_{i \to j}^{t_x}, u_{i \to j}^{t_x} \in (0, 1]$ and $g_{i \to j}^{t_x} + b_{i \to j}^{t_x} + u_{i \to j}^{t_x} = 1$. As follows, $g_{i \to j}^{t_x}$, $b_{i \to j}^{t_x}$ and $u_{i \to j}^{t_x}$ can be calculated according to the interactions between RSU j and RSU i in consensus process in time slot t_x.

$$\begin{cases} g_{i \to j}^{t_x} = (1 - u_{i \to j}^{t_x}) \dfrac{\mu \alpha_{i \to j}^{t_x}}{\mu \alpha_{i \to j}^{t_x} + \upsilon \beta_{i \to j}^{t_x}} \\[2ex] b_{i \to j}^{t_x} = (1 - u_{i \to j}^{t_x}) \dfrac{\upsilon \beta_{i \to j}^{t_x}}{\mu \alpha_{i \to j}^{t_x} + \upsilon \beta_{i \to j}^{t_x}} \\[2ex] u_{i \to j}^{t_x} = \dfrac{\gamma_{i \to j}^{t_x}}{\alpha_{i \to j}^{t_x} + \beta_{i \to j}^{t_x} + \gamma_{i \to j}^{t_x}} \end{cases} \tag{6}$$

where $\alpha_{i \to j}^{t_x}$ represents the number of positive interactions that RSU i perceives from RSU j in consensus process during time slot t_x, $\beta_{i \to j}^{t_x}$ represents the number of malicious interactions that RSU i perceives from RSU j in consensus process during time slot t_x, $\gamma_{i \to j}^{t_x}$ represents the number of uncertain interactions that RSU i perceives from RSU j in consensus process during time slot t_x. μ is the influence power of positive interactions, υ is the influence power of malicious interactions and $\mu + \upsilon = 1$. In order to punish the malicious behavior of RSU in the consensus process, we define that the influence power of malicious interactions is greater than the influence power of positive interactions, that is, $\upsilon > \mu$.

When calculating the reputation value, it is also necessary to take into account the impact of reputation freshness, as the impact of more recent interaction records on reputation values should be greater. Therefore we define the freshness function

$$\tau_x = e^{x-X} \tag{7}$$

where $x \in [1, X]$ indicates the xth time slot within the time window, The larger x represents the closer to the current moment. By introducing the freshness function, we can calculate the triple $p_{i \to j} = \{g_{i \to j}, b_{i \to j}, u_{i \to j}\}$ as follow.

$$\begin{cases} g_{i \to j}^{direct} = \frac{1}{\sum_{x=1}^{X} \tau_x} \sum_{x=1}^{X} (\tau_x g_{i \to j}^{t_x}) \\ b_{i \to j}^{direct} = \frac{1}{\sum_{x=1}^{X} \tau_x} \sum_{x=1}^{X} (\tau_x b_{i \to j}^{t_x}) \\ u_{i \to j}^{direct} = \frac{1}{\sum_{x=1}^{X} \tau_x} \sum_{x=1}^{X} (\tau_x u_{i \to j}^{t_x}) \end{cases} \tag{8}$$

According to the three-dimensional vector calculated before, we can calculate the direct reputation of RSU i to RSU j in time slot t_x as

$$O_{i \to j}^{direct} = g_{i \to j}^{direct} + \delta u_{i \to j}^{direct} \tag{9}$$

where $\delta \in (0, 1)$, which represents the degree of uncertainty effect on reputation.

Recommended Reputation of RSU i to RSU j. In the proposed trust model, the reputation of RSU i to RSU j not only considers the interaction records between these two RSUs, but also takes into account the reputation values of other RSUs in this sub-area to RSU j. We use the gossip protocol to broadcast the reputation triples in the sub-area, so that the reputation value of malicious nodes can quickly decrease in the sub-area. Similar to social networks, the higher the direct reputation value between two RSUs, the greater the credibility of the indirect reputation. For RSU i, once it obtains the reputation triples of RSU j from other RSUs in the sub-area, RSU i can calculate the recommended reputation triple as follow.

$$\begin{cases} g_{i \to j}^{rec} = \frac{1}{\sum_{y \in Y} O_{i \to y}^{direct}} \sum_{y \in Y} (O_{i \to y}^{direct} g_{y \to j}^{direct}) \\ b_{i \to j}^{rec} = \frac{1}{\sum_{y \in Y} O_{i \to y}^{direct}} \sum_{y \in Y} (O_{i \to y}^{direct} b_{y \to j}^{direct}) \\ u_{i \to j}^{rec} = \frac{1}{\sum_{y \in Y} O_{i \to y}^{direct}} \sum_{y \in Y} (O_{i \to y}^{direct} u_{y \to j}^{direct}) \end{cases} \tag{10}$$

where Y is the set of RSUs in the sub-area except RSU i and RSU j.

The Combined Reputation of RSUi to RSU j. Combining the subjective reputation triple and the recommended reputation triple, we can obtain the combined reputation triple of RSUi to RSUj, as follow:

$$
\begin{cases}
g_{i \to j} = \frac{g_{i \to j}^{rec} u_{i \to j}^{direct} + g_{i \to j}^{direct} u_{i \to j}^{rec}}{u_{i \to j}^{rec} + u_{i \to j}^{direct} - u_{i \to j}^{rec} u_{i \to j}^{direct}} \\[2mm]
b_{i \to j} = \frac{b_{i \to j}^{rec} u_{i \to j}^{direct} + b_{i \to j}^{direct} u_{i \to j}^{rec}}{u_{i \to j}^{rec} + u_{i \to j}^{direct} - u_{i \to j}^{rec} u_{i \to j}^{direct}} \\[2mm]
u_{i \to j} = \frac{u_{i \to j}^{rec} u_{i \to j}^{direct}}{u_{i \to j}^{rec} + u_{i \to j}^{direct} - u_{i \to j}^{rec} u_{i \to j}^{direct}}
\end{cases}
\tag{11}
$$

After getting the combined reputation triple, we can calculate the final evaluation value of node i to node j, as follow.

$$
O_{i \to j} = g_{i \to j} + \delta u_{i \to j}
\tag{12}
$$

In each sub-area, each RSU regularly packages its evaluation values of all other RSUs as a transaction and adds it to the local blockchain ledger through consensus. Based on (3), the smart contract will calculates the reputation value of consensus process for each RSU in the sub-area.

3.2 Reputation Value of Vehicles to the RSU

In a sub-area, a vehicle requests service from a specific RSU, and then evaluates the quality of the service provided by the RSU. The evaluation of the RSU's service by the vehicle will be encapsulated into a transaction and added to the blockchain ledger. The evaluation will be classified into three categories: positive, negative, and uncertain. A positive evaluation indicates that the RSU provided timely and safe services to the vehicle after receiving the service request. A negative evaluation means that the RSU provided malicious or false information to the vehicle, intentionally damaging traffic safety after receiving the service request. An uncertain evaluation means that the vehicle did not receive a response from the RSU after sending a service request due to reasons such as poor network conditions or a high volume of service requests. These three types of evaluations will have different impacts on the reputation value.

When calculating the reputation value of vehicles to RSU i, we consider the most recent M evaluations for it. For a given time point t, assuming that among the most recent M evaluations, there are M_1 positive evaluations occurring at time points $\{t - t_1^{pos}, \cdots, t - t_{M_1}^{pos}\}$, M_2 negative evaluations occurring at time points $\{t - t_1^{pos}, \cdots, t - t_{M_2}^{pos}\}$, and M_3 negative evaluations occurring at time points $\{t - t_1^{pos}, \cdots, t - t_{M_3}^{pos}\}$. Similar to the reputation value of the consensus process, the impact of vehicle evaluations on reputation values also needs to consider the freshness of the evaluations, where more recent evaluations will have a greater impact on reputation values. The reputation value of vehicles to RSU i can be calculated as follow.

$$
V_i = \frac{\zeta \sum_{m=1}^{M_1} e^{-t_m^{pos}} - \eta \sum_{n=1}^{M_3} e^{-t_n^{neg}}}{\zeta \sum_{m=1}^{M_1} e^{-t_m^{pos}} + \eta \sum_{n=1}^{M_3} e^{-t_n^{neg}} + \theta \sum_{k=1}^{M_2} e^{-t_k^{unc}}}
\tag{13}
$$

where ζ, η and θ represent the influence power of positive, negative, and uncertain respectively. Generally speaking, the impact of malicious behavior on reputation is greater than that of uncertain behavior, which is greater than that of positive behavior, so we define $\eta > \theta > \zeta$.

3.3 Calculation of RSU Reputation Value

In the proposed RSU trust model, the trust value of an RSU is determined by two factors: the reputation value of RSU in the consensus process and the evaluation from vehicles on the quality of service provided by the RSU. By combining these two types of reputation values, the trust value of RSU i in the sub-area can be calculated as follow.

$$R_i = \omega T_i + (1 - \omega)V_i \tag{14}$$

where ω is a weight parameter manually set to indicate impact of reputation in the consensus process on the overall trust value in the proposed RSU trust model.

The reputation value of RSU will be regularly updated in the local blockchain ledger through the smart contract. The reputation value of RSU will affect its permissions in the system. The proposed trust model is capable of quickly responding to malicious behaviors of nodes. When a node is identified as a malicious node, system administrators can perform security maintenance on that node to ensure the security of the entire blockchain framework.

4   Improved PBFT Base on the Trust Model

In common blockchain consensus protocols, PBFT has many advantages. Compared to traditional PoW consensus algorithms, the PBFT algorithm does not require mining or competing for consensus, thus saving a lot of computing and energy resources. Compared to other consensus algorithms such as Raft [14] or Kafka [15], PBFT has Byzantine fault tolerance and higher security. Therefore, the PBFT consensus algorithm is very suitable for the low computing power and high security requirements of the Internet of Vehicle scene. In the proposed blockchain framework, we adopt PBFT as the consensus protocol for both the local and global blockchains. However, traditional PBFT also has some problems:

- When a view change occurs, the new primary node's number is the current failed primary node's number plus one, which may cause some problems. First, Byzantine nodes can launch denial-of-service attacks on nodes with lower numbers than themselves, thus increasing their chances of being elected as the primary node. Second, the reputation of the next primary node cannot be guaranteed, and it may continue to select Byzantine nodes, causing frequent view changes.
- In the three-phase broadcast protocol of PBFT, a large number of messages need to be broadcasted throughout the network, which will generate a large amount of message passing and consume system bandwidth, resulting in system blockage.

To address the above issues, we have made improvements to the PBFT algorithm used in the local and global blockchains.

4.1 Improved PBFT Algorithm for Local Blockchain

In this paper, a new scheme for selecting the primary node is proposed during the process of view change in the local blockchain PBFT algorithm. Assuming there are N RSUs in a certain sub-area, we sort the reputation values of all RSUs from high to low based on the proposed trust model, and select the top $N/3$ RSUs with the highest reputation values as candidate primary nodes. When selecting the next primary node during view change, it will be randomly generated from all candidate primary nodes. Nodes with higher reputation values perform better in the system, have higher security, and have a lower probability of being attacked as Byzantine nodes. Therefore, selecting nodes with higher reputation values as primary nodes can reduce the probability of view change. In the proposed primary node selection scheme, since the primary node is randomly generated from the candidate primary node group, other nodes cannot predict whether they can be elected as the primary node, so they cannot launch a denial-of-service attack against honest nodes to achieve the goal of being elected as the primary node.

The proposed improvement scheme also categorizes all RSUs in the sub-region according to their reputation values. Assuming there are N RSUs in a certain sub-region, we select the top $2N/3$ nodes in reputation value as consensus nodes, and the remaining nodes as accounting nodes. Accounting nodes do not participate in the consensus process but only participate in the record of the blockchain ledger. This can exclude RSUs with lower reputation values from the consensus process, reduce the probability of being attacked by Byzantine during the consensus process, and improve system security. It can also reduce the number of consensus nodes and the consumption of the consensus process.

4.2 Improved PBFT Algorithm for Global Blockchain

The nodes in the global blockchain are composed of K RSUs with the highest reputation selected by each subregion at regular intervals. We propose a new scheme for selecting the primary node in the PBFT consensus algorithm applied in the global blockchain. To address the scenario where an RSU in a subregion is targeted by a range attack, we adopt a scheme where the sub-areas take turns to provide the primary node. When changing views, a new primary node is randomly selected from the next subregion. This scheme avoids the situation where nodes in a sub-area are continuously elected as primary nodes when all RSUs in the subregion are compromised as Byzantine nodes. The selection of the primary node maintains a certain level of randomness, thus preventing the previously mentioned denial-of-service attacks. This approach effectively reduces the probability of view switching and minimizes system consumption.

5   Performance Evaluation

In this section, we use numerical simulations to evaluate the performance of the reputation model proposed in this paper and the proposed hierarchical blockchain framework.

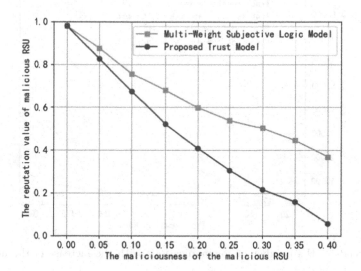

Fig. 2. Trend of reputation value with the deepening of maliciousness degree

5.1   Performance of the Proposed Trust Model

In the proposed trust model, the reputation of the RSU is calculated by considering its performance in the consensus process and the quality of services provided by the RSU to vehicles. We compared our reputation model with the Multi-Weighted Subjective Logic Reputation Model [12]. The major parameters settings are as follows: There are 20 RSUs in the simulation, and the influence power of malicious interactions in consensus process $v = 0.7$ and the influence power of positive interactions $\mu = 0.3$; the degree of uncertainty effect on reputation $\delta = 0.5$; the influence power of positive, negative and uncertain in the reputation value of vehicles to RSU are respectively $\zeta = 0.3$, $\eta = 0.7$ and $\theta = 0.5$; the weight parameter that indicates the impact of reputation in the consensus process $\omega = 0.5$.

Figure 2 shows the changes in reputation values in sub-areas under different reputation models for varying degrees of maliciousness of RSUs. The degree of maliciousness indicates the probability of an RSU sending malicious behavior. When the degree of maliciousness of an RSU is 0.3, the malicious RSU will interact with vehicles or other RSUs with a probability of 0.3. It can be observed from the figure that the proposed reputation model considers more factors, is more sensitive to malicious behavior of RSUs, and can detect malicious behavior of RSUs faster.

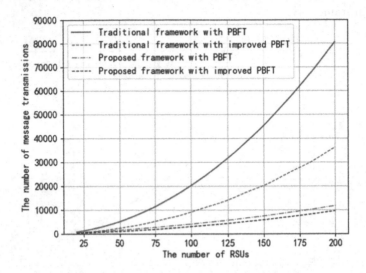

Fig. 3. Trends of the number of communications with the increase of the number of RSUs

5.2 Performance of the Proposed Hierarchical Blockchain Framework and the Improved PBFT

To verify the superiority of the proposed blockchain framework and the improved PBFT algorithm, four different scenarios were compared: the first scenario used the traditional blockchain framework with PBFT, the second used the traditional blockchain framework with improved PBFT, the third used the proposed blockchain framework with PBFT, and the fourth used the proposed blockchain framework with improved PBFT. In the proposed framework, each sub-area was simulated with 10 RSUs, and 3 RSUs with the highest reputation in each sub-area were selected as consensus nodes for the global blockchain.

Figure 3 shows the number of communication rounds required for consensus for different numbers of consensus nodes in the frameworks. It can be observed that as the number of RSUs in the network increases, the communication rounds in the traditional blockchain framework exhibit quadratic growth, while the communication rounds in the proposed blockchain framework increase more slowly. Moreover, when the improved PBFT algorithm is used, the overall number of communication rounds in both frameworks is further reduced.

6   Conclusion

In this paper, we propose a hierarchical layered blockchain framework in which each transaction can choose a different consensus range based on its own impact scope. To ensure the security of the proposed blockchain framework, a trust model for RSUs is proposed, and based on this model, we propose the improve PBFT algorithm. Simulation results show that compared with the traditional reputation model, the proposed reputation model can more quickly detect malicious nodes, and the proposed blockchain framework combined with the improved PBFT can bring smaller consensus consumption.

Acknowledgments. This work was supported in part by the National Key R&D Program of 2022YFB2702303, and in part by the National Natural Science Foundation of China under Grant 62071092.

References

1. Wang, R., Zhang, Y., Fortino, G., Guan, Q., Liu, J., Song, J.: Software escalation prediction based on deep learning in the cognitive internet of vehicles. IEEE Trans. Intell. Transp. Syst. **23**(12), 25408–25418 (2022)
2. Zhang, Y., Sun, Y., Jin, R., Lin, K., Liu, W.: High-performance isolation computing technology for smart IoT healthcare in cloud environments. IEEE Internet Things J. **8**(23), 16872–16879 (2021)
3. Zhang, Y., Lu, H., Jiang, C., Li, X., Tian, X.: Aspect-based sentiment analysis of user reviews in 5G networks. IEEE Netw. **35**(4), 228–233 (2021)
4. Cao, J., Leng, S., Zhang, L., Imran, M., Chai, H.: A V2V empowered consensus framework for cooperative autonomous driving. In: GLOBECOM 2022 - 2022 IEEE Global Communications Conference, pp. 5729–5734 (2022)
5. Jiang, Z., Zheng, Z., Chen, K., Luo, X., Tang, X., Li, Y.: Exploring smart contract recommendation: towards efficient blockchain development. IEEE Trans. Serv. Comput. 1–12 (2022)
6. Zheng, Z., Chen, W., Zhong, Z., Chen, Z., Lu, Y.: Securing the ethereum from smart Ponzi schemes: identification using static features. ACM Trans. Softw. Eng. Methodol. **32**, 1–28 (2022)
7. Jiajing, W., Liu, J., Chen, W., Huang, H., Zheng, Z., Zhang, Y.: Detecting mixing services via mining bitcoin transaction network with hybrid motifs. IEEE Trans. Syst. Man Cybern.: Syst. **52**(4), 2237–2249 (2022)
8. Wen, H., Fang, J., Wu, J., Zheng, Z.: Hide and seek: an adversarial hiding approach against phishing detection on ethereum. IEEE Trans. Comput. Soc. Syst. 1–12 (2022)
9. Chai, H., Leng, S., Zhang, K., Mao, S.: Proof-of-reputation based-consortium blockchain for trust resource sharing in internet of vehicles. IEEE Access **7**, 175744–175757 (2019)
10. Nakamoto, S.: A Bitcoin. A peer-to-peer electronic cash system. Bitcoin, vol. 4, p. 2 (2008). https://bitcoin.org/bitcoin.pdf
11. Castro, M., Liskov, B., et al.: Practical byzantine fault tolerance. In: OsDI, vol. 99, pp. 173–186 (1999)

12. Huang, X., Rong, Yu., Kang, J., Zhang, Y.: Distributed reputation management for secure and efficient vehicular edge computing and networks. IEEE Access **5**, 25408–25420 (2017)
13. Kang, J., Xiong, Z., Niyato, D., Xie, S., Zhang, J.: Incentive mechanism for reliable federated learning: a joint optimization approach to combining reputation and contract theory. IEEE Internet Things J. **6**(6), 10700–10714 (2019)
14. Ongaro, D., Ousterhout, J.: In search of an understandable consensus algorithm. In: 2014 {USENIX} Annual Technical Conference ({USENIX}{ATC} 14), pp. 305–319 (2014)
15. Kreps, J., Narkhede, N., Rao, J., et al.: Kafka: a distributed messaging system for log processing. In: Proceedings of the NetDB, Athens, Greece, vol. 11, pp. 1–7 (2011)

An Improved PBFT Consensus Algorithm for Supply Chain Finance

Guoqing Zhang[1], Shunhui Ji[1], Hai Dong[2], and Pengcheng Zhang[1](✉)

[1] College of Computer and Information, Hohai University, Nanjing 211100, China
{guoqingzhang,shunhuiji,pchzhang}@hhu.edu.cn
[2] School of Computing Technologies, RMIT University, Melbourne 3001, Australia
hai.dong@rmit.edu.au

Abstract. Supply chain finance is a financing scheme to provide financial services for the enterprises of supply chain. Blockchain technology, with distributed, traceable and non-tamperable characteristics, offers opportunities to solve problems in the development of supply chain finance. Consensus algorithms are the key to ensuring the efficient cooperation of the blockchain, among which the Practical Byzantine Fault Tolerance (PBFT) algorithm has a wide range of applications in consortium chains which solves the core issue of how to make nodes keep their data consistent. However, the PBFT algorithm has a higher communication overhead and does not support the nodes join or exit. It is difficult to meet the requirement of supply chain finance. Therefore, this paper proposes an improved PBFT algorithm for Supply Chain Finance, named PBFT-SCF. Firstly, a dynamic node entry and exit mechanism be designed for dynamically changing the number of nodes at runtime. Secondly, the scoring model is established to build an appropriate consensus node group, which replaces the original that all nodes participate in consensus so that the resource consumption can be reduced. Finally, the consistency protocol of the PBFT algorithm is optimized to achieve higher efficiency. Results indicate that the PBFT-SCF algorithm has better characteristics in terms of consensus efficiency and communication overhead. Specifically, when the number of node is 46, the transaction latency is reduced to 3.5% and the number of communication times is 2.8% of the PBFT algorithm.

Keywords: Supply Chain Finance · Blockchain · Consortium Chain · Consensus Algorithm · PBFT Algorithm

1 Introduction

Supply chain finance is a new financing scheme in the new era, which is caused by the financing difficulties of small and medium-sized enterprises [1]. At present, the main problem in the development of supply chain finance comes from information asymmetry. Supply chain finance business is usually concentrated in the first and second tier suppliers or distributors of core enterprises, and banks do not

J. Chen et al. (Eds.): BlockSys 2023, CCIS 1897, pp. 339–352, 2024.
https://doi.org/10.1007/978-981-99-8104-5_25

know the business operation information. This constrains the financing capacity of the whole supply chain [2]. Blockchain technology, as a technology that can transmit information, has the characteristics of decentralization, transparency, and traceability [3]. The application of this technology can build a federated platform where all parties share information, which can effectively solve existing problems in supply chain finance [4]. Consortium chains are a compromise between public and private chains, which can better meet the needs of enterprises [5]. Consensus algorithms are the key to ensuring the efficient cooperation of the blockchain, among which the Practical Byzantine Fault Tolerance (PBFT) algorithm has a wide range of applications [6] in consortium chains. However, adopting the PBFT algorithm for consensus in supply chain finance is not effective enough and will face the following critical issues. Firstly, the number of nodes in supply chain finance is relatively large. While the communication complexity of the PBFT algorithm is $O(n^2)$ [7], as the number of nodes in the network increases, it is easy to experience system failure or consensus timeout due to excessive communication overhead. Secondly, in the scenario of supply chain finance, there may be some nodes joining and exiting dynamically, but the PBFT algorithm does not provide this capability.

In order to solve these problems, an improved PBFT consensus algorithm for Supply Chain Finance, called PBFT-SCF, is proposed in this paper. The PBFT-SCF algorithm is optimized based on the PBFT algorithm, which inherits all advantages of the PBFT algorithm. Besides, PBFT-SCF has lower communication overhead and higher dynamic scalability. Overall, the key points of contribution in this paper are summarized as follows.

(1) A dynamic node entry and exit mechanism is proposed for dynamically changing the number of nodes at runtime. Nodes can freely join and exit in the consensus network as needed.
(2) A scoring model is designed to build a trustworthy consensus group and find the byzantine node. This can narrow down the number of nodes participating in the consensus process while maintaining the original security.
(3) The consistency protocol is enhanced to reduce the overhead of two whole network broadcast communication, which could reach consensus with less communication traffic.
(4) The simulation experiments are conducted to evaluate the performance of PBFT-SCF by comparing with the PBFT [6], CPBFT [8] and G-PBFT [9]. Results illustrate that the superiority of the PBFT-SCF algorithm in terms of consensus latency and transaction throughput.

The remaining sections have the following structure. Section 2 describes the background knowledge of the PBFT algorithm and supply chain finance. Section 3 elaborates on the detail of the PBFT-SCF algorithm. Section 4 analyzes the performance of the PBFT-SCF algorithm by a series of experiments. Section 5 summarizes the related works of the improved PBFT algorithm. Section 6 concludes our work. Section 7 thanks to our funding agencies.

2 Background

Before elaborating on the design of PBFT-SCF, we introduce some preliminary knowledge in this section, including the PBFT consensus algorithm and supply chain finance.

2.1 PBFT Algorithm

The PBFT algorithm [6] is designed to address the problem of ensuring ultimate consistency and correctness despite the presence of malicious nodes in the network. Assume that there are n nodes in the system, of which there are f byzantine nodes where malicious behavior may occur. The system can only behave perfectly if $n \geq 3f + 1$ is guaranteed.

To reach a consensus, nodes need to perform the following three protocols: the consistency protocol, the view change protocol and the checkpoint protocol. The consistency protocol ensures the consistency of data stored on nodes. If an error occurs in the primary node during system operation, a view switch is performed. The checkpoint protocol refers to the periodic processing of logs [10].

The PBFT algorithm consists of a series of communication flows, which mainly involve five phase, as shown in Fig. 1.

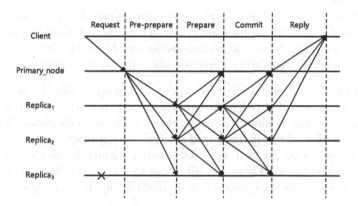

Fig. 1. The communication flows of the PBFT algorithm.

1) Request phase: The primary node waits for the client to initiate a request, which packages the transaction to generate the request.
2) Pre-prepare phase: After receiving a request message from the client node, the primary node constructs a pre-prepare message and broadcasts.
3) Prepare phase: The replica node checks the pre-prepare message it receives. If the message passes the check, it is transmitted to the network until the node receives $2f$ valid prepare messages from other different nodes.

4) Commit phase: Each node transmits commit message in the whole network, and when the node receives $2f$ valid commit messages from other different nodes, it means that this phase has been completed.

5) Reply phase: Once the node has completed the commit phase, it feeds back a reply message to the client. Only when the client receives $f+1$ valid reply message can the client successfully accepts the execution result.

2.2 Supply Chain Finance

Supply chain finance is a financing scheme that relies on the credit of core enterprises and the real trade relationship of enterprises in the supply chain [11]. In the supply chain finance field, there exist two business roles. One is the enterprises in the chain including core enterprises, suppliers, dealers and capital institutions. The other is the regulatory agencies which have high credibility. Based on the business role, the nodes of blockchain in supply chain finance are usually divided into two categories: consensus working nodes and supervisory nodes.

1) Consensus working nodes: Consensus working nodes are responsible for completing the whole consensus process. Their ultimate goal is to achieve data consistency. Generally, they are composed of all enterprises in the supply chain which are verified offline by banks, with a relatively high degree of credibility.

2) Supervisory nodes: Supervisory nodes are responsible for supervising the process of reaching a consensus. They act as the top level overseers of the system, watching what the consensus nodes are doing. Generally, they are held by relevant regulatory departments, with high credibility.

In order to make full use of the supervisory node and reduce the burden of the consensus working node, we let the supervisor node take charge of the review of node entry and exit. Besides, the supervisory node also calculates the comprehensive score of working nodes based on the scoring model in the supervising process of consensus. To be noted, This paper mainly focuses on the process of reaching a consensus. Therefore, all nodes in the rest of this paper represent consensus working nodes, except those indicating supervisory nodes.

3   PBFT-SCF Consensus Algorithm

In this section, we elaborate on the design of the PBFT-SCF algorithm in detail. We first present an overview of the PBFT-SCF consensus algorithm. Then, we describe the design of the dynamic entry and exit mechanism. Next, we introduce the scoring model and relevant definitions. Finally, we describe the standard of node classification and the optimized consistency protocol.

3.1 Overview of PBFT-SCF Algorithm

The PBFT-SCF algorithm is based on the PBFT algorithm and is optimized in combination with the business scenario of supply chain finance. Firstly, we design the dynamic node entry and exit mechanism to freely change the number of nodes at runtime. As part of the PBFT-SCF consensus algorithm, the mechanism works when a node requests to join or exit, or when a byzantine node is removed from the network. Moreover, the scoring model is designed based on the activity, completion rate, and specific behavioral performance of nodes. The supervisory node score the nodes based on the scoring model in its consensus observation process. According to the score, appropriate nodes to participate in the consensus process are selected and byzantine nodes are removed. Finally, the consistency protocol changes the way messages are delivered such as the replica node sends the prepare message to the primary node and the primary node broadcasts a commit message to the replica nodes.

3.2 Dynamic Node Entry and Exit Mechanism

For dynamically changing the number of nodes at run time, the dynamic node entry and exit mechanism be designed. Nodes can join and exit the consensus network freely, and in this process, there is no need to restart the blockchain network. Besides, when a byzantine node needs to be cleared out from the network, the mechanism also works.

Node Join. When a new node wants to join the consensus network, the node entry/exit protocol is executed.

Node Exit. When a node wants to exit the consensus network, or when a byzantine node is cleared from the network due to malicious behavior, the node entry/exit protocol is executed.

The node entry/exit protocol consists of the following five stages, as shown in Fig. 2.

1) Apply stage: A node applies to join/exit the network and sends an apply message to the supervisory node.
2) Agree stage: After the supervisory node receives the apply message and approves it, it broadcasts an agree message to all nodes in the network.
3) Confirm stage: The node confirms the received agree message. After the confirmation is correct, a confirm message will broadcast to the network nodes. When a node receives $2f$ valid confirm message from other different nodes, it enters the update-net stage.
4) Update-net stage: The supervisory node recalculates the number of nodes in the network and updates the view, which then transmits to all network nodes.
5) Update-done stage: After receiving the update-net message, the node updates local information including the number of nodes and the view. Then it sends the update-done message to the supervisory node.

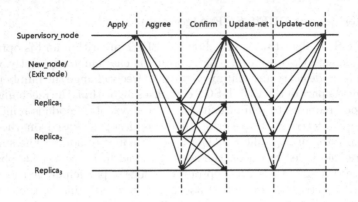

Fig. 2. The communication flows of the node entry/exit protocol.

3.3   Scoring Model

In order to build a trustworthy consensus group, the scoring model to evaluate the node credibility is designed. Besides, a byzantine node can be found by it. After each round of consensus, the supervisory node calculates the scores of working nodes based on the scoring model.

The behavior of the nodes in the system can be divided into three categories: normal behavior, interrupt behavior and malicious behavior, as shown in Table 1.

Table 1. The behavior of nodes.

Node behavior	Performance of behavior
Normal behavior	Complete the consensus process successfully
Interrupt behavior	Timeout, information missing
Malicious behavior	Tamper with information

Aiming at the above behaviors, the scoring model is designed around the activity degree, completion rate and behavior performance. The relevant definitions of the scoring model are as follows:

Definition 1 (Comprehensive score). *The comprehensive score represents the credibility of the node, and the comprehensive score of node i is defined as* S_i:

$$S_i = \alpha H_i + \beta A_i + \gamma C_i + \theta_i \tag{1}$$

Where, H_i is historical score, A_i is activity degree, C_i is completion rate, θ_i is behavior performance. α, β, γ are the weight parameters, and $\alpha + \beta + \gamma = 1$. α, β, γ can be assigned according to the needs of different business scenarios of supply chain finance.

The higher the comprehensive score is, the higher credibility of the node. However, when the comprehensive score is non-positive, it indicates that the node has inconsistent behavior with other nodes, and this node will be identified as a byzantine node clearing out of the network.

Definition 2 (Historical score). *Define the time from the beginning to the present as* T. *Let* $\triangle T$ *represents a certain time, and* $T = (m-1)\triangle T + \triangle T'_m$. *Where,* $\triangle T'_m$ *represents the current period of time. The comprehensive score of the node in the past* $(m-1)\triangle T$ *time period will affect the score in the current period of time. The historical score of node* i *is defined as* H_i:

$$H_i = \begin{cases} S_{init} & m = 1 \\ \sum_{j=0}^{m-1} (\frac{1}{2})^{m-j} S_{i\triangle T_j} & m > 1 \end{cases} \qquad (2)$$

Where, S_{init} is the system initial score and the default value is 1. $S_{i\triangle T_j}$ is the comprehensive score of node i in the time period $\triangle T_j$.

Definition 3 (Activity degree). *The activity degree of node* i *is defined as* H_i:

$$A_i = e^{-a(P-P_i)} \qquad (3)$$

Where, P is the total number of consensus times at a certain time, P_i is the number of times node i participates, and a is the adjustment parameter.

Definition 4 (Completion rate). *The completion rate of node* i *is defined as* C_i:

$$C_i = \frac{P_{ic}}{P} \qquad (4)$$

Where, P_{ic} is the number of times node i has successfully logged a message locally.

Definition 5 (Behavior performance). *After each round of consensus, the supervisory node checks the message list of the node. When the behavior of a node is inconsistent with that of most other nodes, the node is considered to have malicious behavior. The behavior performance of node* i *is defined as* θ_i:

$$\theta_i = \begin{cases} 0 & no\ malicious\ behavior\ occurs \\ -1 & malicious\ behavior\ occurs \end{cases} \qquad (5)$$

3.4   Node Classification

The consensus working nodes can be classified into four states according to the order of S_i from small to large. Assume that there are n nodes in the system and $f = \lfloor \frac{n-1}{3} \rfloor$, the specific definitions of the node state are shown in Table 2.

Among them, byzantine node does not have authority and will be kicked out of the system after the end of this round of consensus. The authorities of the remaining three types of nodes are shown in the Table 3.

Table 2. The state of nodes.

Node state	Description
Priority node	The order of S_i in $(2f - n]$ and $S_i > 0$
Ordinary node	The order of S_i in $(f - 2f]$ and $S_i > 0$
Backup node	The order of S_i in $(0 - f]$ and $S_i > 0$
Byzantine node	$S_i \leq 0$

Table 3. The authority of nodes.

Node authority	Priority node	Ordinary node	Backup node
Become primary node	√	×	×
Reach consensus	√	√	×
Record ledger	√	√	√

Consensus Node Selection. In PBFT-SCF algorithm, priority nodes and ordinary nodes form the consensus group, whose size is S. Only the node in the consensus group take part in reaching a consensus, which could reduce the number of nodes involved in the consensus process. Although the number of consensus nodes is reduced, the consistency also can be reached. Since there are $S \geq 2f + 1$ nodes responsible for reaching consensus, even if there are f Byzantine nodes, there will be more than f reliable nodes left. As a result, this makes it possible to obtain consistent final performance.

Primary Node Selection. The original PBFT algorithm selects the primary node according to the view number. The primary node may have unstable performance or be vulnerable to attacks, which will affect the overall performance of the algorithm. Verifiable Random Function (VRF) is a cryptographic function that processes inputs to verifiable pseudorandom outputs and appropriate to select a primary node. In PBFT-SCF, all priority nodes form the primary node contention list and the primary node is selected in the contention list based on the VRF function. The details of the specific selection process are available in [12].

3.5 Optimized Consistency Protocol Process

The original consistency protocol in the PBFT algorithm needs to broadcast two times in the whole network, resulting in lower consensus efficiency. In order to reduce communication overhead, the PBFT-SCF algorithm optimizes the consistency protocol. In the PBFT-SCF algorithm, consensus nodes send a prepare message to the primary node instead of broadcasting it to other nodes, similarly a commit message is passed one-way from the master node to the consensus node. The reason why this method can ensure the final consistency is that the primary node broadcasts the commit message only after receiving the consistent prepare message from all consensus nodes. Otherwise, the primary node does nothing and waits for launching a new consensus. The optimized consistency protocol process also consists of five phases like the PBFT algorithm, as shown in Fig. 3.

1) Request phase: The primary node waits for the client to initiate a request, which packages the transaction to generate the request.
2) Pre-prepare phase: After receiving a request message from the client node, the primary node constructs a pre-prepare message and broadcasts the pre-prepare message to all consensus nodes.
3) Prepare phase: The consensus node sends the prepare message to the primary node after verifying the pre-prepare message.
4) Commit phase: After receiving the consistent preparation message from all consensus nodes, the primary node enters the commit phase and broadcasts the commit message to all nodes in the network.
5) Reply phase: When the node receives the commit message, the node performs the appropriate action and writes the ledger to the local. And if the node is a consensus node, it responds to the client with execution results. Only when the client receives $f + 1$ valid reply message can the client successfully accept the execution result.

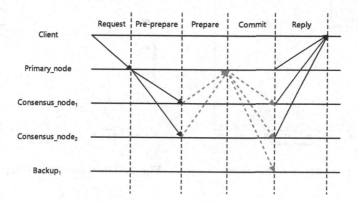

Fig. 3. The communication flows of the optimized consistency protocol.

4   Simulation Experiments and Analysis

In this section, we simulate the performance of PBFT-SCF, PBFT [6], CPBFT [8] and G-PBFT [9] consensus algorithm by Java language. In the experiment, we use Java Multithreading and Jedis technology to simulate the communication process of different nodes. The PC used in the experiment were equipped with 11th Gen Intel(R) Core(TM) i7-11800H@2.30 GHz. We compare and analyze the four consensus algorithms from the following three aspects: transaction latency, throughput and communication overhead.

4.1 Transaction Latency

Transaction latency refers to the time interval between the client sending a transaction request to the primary node and the client confirming the completion of the consensus. In order to not lose generality, the consensus latency is taken as the average value of 200 transactions, under the condition of different number of nodes. As can be seen from Fig. 4, the transaction latency of PBFT-SCF is obviously lower than that of PBFT, CPBFT and G-PBFT. Specifically, When the number of nodes is 46, the PBFT-SCF reduces the transaction latency to 3.6%, 6.9% and 7.6%, compared with PBFT, CPBFT and G-PBFT respectively. Experimental results show that PBFT-SCF has obvious advantages over the other three methods in transaction latency.

The main reason for the above results is that our PBFT-SCF algorithm reduces the amount of nodes participating in consensus. Besides, the consistency protocol is optimized, which reduces the communication times in the prepare and commit phase.

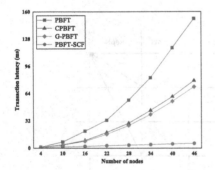

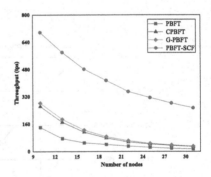

Fig. 4. The latency comparison.   **Fig. 5.** The throughput comparison.

4.2 Throughput

The transaction processing capacity of the system depends on the throughput, which denotes the number of transactions processed in a certain time. We test the transaction throughput of four consensus algorithms respectively under different numbers of nodes. Figure 5 depicts the throughput of the four algorithms. With the increase of the number of nodes in the network, the throughput of all algorithms presents a trend of decline, but in general, the throughput of the PBFT-SCF algorithm is much higher than the other three algorithms. When

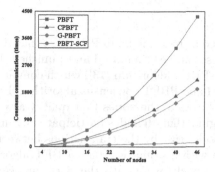

Fig. 6. The communication comparison.

the number of nodes is 46, the transaction of PBFT-SCF is 182.12(TPS), while that of PBFT, CPBFT and PBFT is 6.58(TPS), 12.65(TPS) and 13.92(TPS), respectively.

The main reason for this phenomenon is that the latency of PBFT-SCF is smaller than other algorithms. Therefore, in a unit of time, PBFT-SCF can complete more transactions and the throughput is higher than the other three algorithms.

4.3 Communication Overhead

This paper mainly calculates the communication frequency in the process of consensus as the communication cost. According to the description of the PBFT algorithm in Sect. 2, we can know that when the total number of nodes is n, the total number of communication times is $2n \cdot (n - 1)$. It can be inferred that the number of communications required to complete a consensus based on the CPBFT [8] algorithm is about $n \cdot (n - 1)$. And the G-PBFT [9] consensus algorithm requires $(n + 3) \cdot n/2$ times to complete a consensus. In contrast, the PBFT-SCF algorithm reduces the number of nodes participating in consensus and simplifies the consistency protocol process, so the total number of communication times is approximately $4(n - 1)/3$. As can be seen from Fig. 6, the communication overhead of our PBFT-SCF algorithm increases linearly, while the other three algorithms present the trend of exponential growth as the number of nodes increases.

5 Related Works

In this section, we summarize the related works of those improved PBFT consensus algorithms. Many scholars have made improvements to the traditional PBFT algorithm from various aspects. We roughly divide them into three categories: credit model, consensus process optimization and consensus node group.

5.1   Credit Model

Many papers introduced a credit model in PBFT, so that the nodes participating in the consensus process can be stimulated and punished. For example, Tong et al. proposed the Trust-PBFT algorithm [13], which combined the PeerTrust p2p trust calculation model and PBFT consensus algorithm. By PeerTrust model to evaluate the trustworthiness of the nodes that qualify as participants of PBFT, which replaced the original that all nodes participate in. Similarly, T-PBFT algorithm [14] evaluated node trust by the transactions between nodes and replaced a single primary node with a primary group. RBFT algorithm [15] that incorporated a reputation model to evaluate the performance of each node in the consensus process. The node with a higher reputation obtained greater opportunities to be a primary node to generate new valid blocks, which reduced the security risk of the primary node.

5.2   Consensus Process Optimization

PBFT algorithm communication complexity is $O(n^2)$, which has a higher resource consumption and lower consensus efficiency. Many scholars work to simplify the PBFT algorithm process. He et al. proposed the ePBFT algorithm [16], which removed the process of selecting the master node. All the nodes in the consortium chain can broadcast the signed transaction data to the whole network. Only need request and prepare-response phase that the consensus can be reached. EZBFT algorithm [17] provided a three-step consensus in the common case. A client can send a request to any replicas, then the replica forwarded the request to other replicas and every replica sent a reply to the client. In HSBFT algorithm [18], the primary is not only the initiator of the new message, but also the coordinator of the consensus process. In normal case operation, the communication complexity of prepare and commit stage will all be reduced to $O(n)$, which makes it possible to form a larger consensus network.

5.3   Consensus Node Group

By grouping consensus nodes, the algorithm can reduce the number of nodes in the consensus process, such as GH algorithm [19] divided all replicas in a distributed system into groups, each of which had a primary node. The replicas reach consensus in the group first, then reach global consensus in the end. Wang et al. proposed vPBFT algorithm [20] which introduced the vote algorithm into the PBFT algorithm. The nodes of different types have different responsibilities, and the nodes of different types have a certain quantitative relationship. EBFT proposed by Li et al. [21] divided all nodes in the system into different groups based on a clustering algorithm and provided an $O(n)$ communication complexity. SHBFT algorithm [22] designed a hierarchical structure to speed up the consensus process, and achieved a global consensus through local consensus.

6   Conclusion

In this paper, we propose the PBFT-SCF algorithm to optimize that the PBFT consensus algorithm is not suitable for the supply chain finance environment. In our PBFT-SCF algorithm, we design the node dynamic entry and exit mechanism, which solves the problem of the PBFT algorithm that nodes can not join or exit in the consensus at runtime. Moreover, we design the scoring model of the nodes, which could build a trustworthy consensus group and find the byzantine node. In addition, based on the trustworthy consensus group, we optimize the consistency protocol of the PBFT algorithm to reduce the communication overhead. Overall, our PBFT-SCF algorithm not only greatly reduces the communication overhead in the consensus process but also provides dynamic scalability. A series of experiments are performed to demonstrate the outstanding capability of PBFT-SCF over the traditional PBFT consensus algorithm. To be more precise, when the number of nodes is 46, the throughput of PBFT-SCF is 27 times that of the PBFT algorithm.

Acknowledgments. The work is supported by the National Natural Science Foundation of China (No.62272145 and No.U21B2016), the Fundamental Research Funds for the Central Universities of China (B220202072, B210202075), the Natural Science Foundation of Jiangsu Province (BK20191297), the CloudTech RMIT Green Bitcoin Joint Research Program/Laboratory, and the Cooperative Research Centres Projects (CRC-P) funding scheme "Fast and Secure Crypto Payments for E-Commerce Merchants" (CRCPXIII000145).

References

1. Wang, R.: Application of blockchain technology in supply chain finance in Beibu gulf region. In: 2021 International Wireless Communications and Mobile Computing (IWCMC), pp. 1860–1864. Harbin City, China (2021)
2. Zhang, F., Ding, Y.: Research on anti-tampering simulation algorithm of block chain-based supply chain financial big data. In: 2021 IEEE 2nd International Conference on Big Data, Artificial Intelligence and Internet of Things Engineering (ICBAIE), pp. 63–66 (2021)
3. Acharjamayum, I., Patgiri, R., Devi, D.: Blockchain: a tale of peer to peer security. In: 2018 IEEE Symposium Series on Computational Intelligence (SSCI), pp. 609–617. IEEE (2018)
4. Shao, Q., Jin, C., Zhang, Z., Qian, W., Zhou, A.: Blockchain technology: architecture and progress. J. Comput. **41**(05), 969–988 (2018)
5. Wan, S., Li, M., Liu, G., Wang, C.: Recent advances in consensus protocols for blockchain: a survey. Wireless Netw. **26**(03), 5579–5593 (2020)
6. Castro, M., Liskov, B.: Practical byzantine fault tolerance. In: Procedings of the Third Symposium on Operating Systems Design and Implementation (OSDI), pp. 173–186. New Orleans, USA (1999)
7. Li, Y., et al.: An extensible consensus algorithm based on PBFT. In: 2019 International Conference on Cyber-enabled Distributed Computing and Knowledge Discovery (CyberC), pp. 17–23 (2019)

8. Wang, Y., Song, Z., Cheng, T.: Improvement research of PBFT consensus algorithm based on credit. In: Zheng, Z., Dai, H.-N., Tang, M., Chen, X. (eds.) BlockSys 2019. CCIS, vol. 1156, pp. 47–59. Springer, Singapore (2020). https://doi.org/10.1007/978-981-15-2777-7_4

9. Lao, L., Dai, X., Xiao, B., Guo, S.: G-PBFT: a location-based and scalable consensus protocol for IoT-blockchain applications. In: 2020 IEEE International Parallel and Distributed Processing Symposium (IPDPS), pp. 664–673 (2020)

10. Xue, Q., Zhang, T., Sun, Y.: PBFT algorithm for internet of things. In: 2022 7th International Conference on Computer and Communication Systems (ICCCS), pp. 684–689. IEEE (2022)

11. Sun, W.: Application of blockchain technology in the supply chain finance. In: 2022 7th International Conference on Cloud Computing and Big Data Analytics (ICCCBDA), pp. 205–209. IEEE, Chengdu, China (2022)

12. Xu, X., Sun, G., Yu, X.: An efficient blockchain PBFT consensus protocol in energy constrained IoT applications. In: 2021 International Conference on UK-China Emerging Technologies (UCET), pp. 152–157 (2021)

13. Tong, W., Dong, X., Zheng, J.: Trust-PBFT: a peertrust-based practical byzantine consensus algorithm. In: 2019 International Conference on Networking and Network Applications (NaNA), pp. 344–349. Daegu, Korea (South) (2019)

14. Gao, S., Yu, T., Zhu, J., Cai, W.: T-PBFT: an eigentrust-based practical byzantine fault tolerance consensus algorithm. China Commun. 16(12), 111–123 (2019). https://doi.org/10.23919/JCC.2019.12.008

15. Lei, K., Zhang, Q., Xu, L., Z., Q.: Reputation-based byzantine fault-tolerance for consortium blockchain. In: 2018 IEEE 24th International Conference on Parallel and Distributed Systems (ICPADS), pp. 604–611. IEEE (2018)

16. He, L., Hou, Z.: An improvement of consensus fault tolerant algorithm applied to alliance chain. In: 2019 IEEE 9th International Conference on Electronics Information and Emergency Communication (ICEIEC), pp. 1–4 (2019)

17. Arun, B., Peluso, S., Ravindran, B.: ezBFT: decentralizing byzantine fault-tolerant state machine replication. In: 2019 IEEE 39th International Conference on Distributed Computing Systems (ICDCS), pp. 565–577 (2019)

18. Jiang, Y., Lian, Z.: High performance and scalable byzantine fault tolerance. In: 2019 IEEE 3rd Information Technology, Networking, Electronic and Automation Control Conference (ITNEC), pp. 1195–1202 (2019)

19. Zhang, L., Li, Q.: Research on consensus efficiency based on practical byzantine fault tolerance. In: 2018 10th International Conference on Modelling. Identification and Control (ICMIC), pp. 1–6. Guiyang, China (2018)

20. Wang, H., Guo, K.: Byzantine fault tolerant algorithm based on vote. In: 2019 International Conference on Cyber-Enabled Distributed Computing and Knowledge Discovery (CyberC), pp. 190–196 (2019)

21. Li, W., He, M.: EBFT: a hierarchical and group-based byzantine fault tolerant consensus algorithm. In: 2021 IEEE 12th International Conference on Software Engineering and Service Science (ICSESS), pp. 32–37 (2021)

22. Li, Y., Qiao, L., Lv, Z.: An optimized byzantine fault tolerance algorithm for consortium blockchain. Peer-to-Peer Netw. Appl. 14, 2826–2839 (2021)

Author Index

J. Chen et al. (Eds.): BlockSys 2023, CCIS 1897, pp. 353–355, 2024.
https://doi.org/10.1007/978-981-99-8104-5

Printed in the United States
by Baker & Taylor Publisher Services